Interpreting
Modern Philosophy

BY JAMES COLLINS

Princeton University Press, Princeton, N.J. 1972

Copyright © 1972 by Princeton University Press
ALL RIGHTS RESERVED
LCC 70-160259
ISBN 0-691-07179-9

This book has been composed in Linotype Times Roman
Printed in the United States of America
by Princeton University Press, Princeton, N.J.

Publication of this book has been aided by
the Whitney Darrow Publication Reserve Fund of
Princeton University Press.

Preface

"What is history?" asks the poet Robert Lowell in his *Notebook 1967–68*. And with the wisdom of his calling he replies: "What you cannot touch." Into the fabric of our existence we incorporate the markings, the records, the multifarious expressions of thought and action on the part of past men and social groups. All these signs put us in touch with our human history and yet they do not, through their sole power, enable us to touch that history alive. They arouse us to listen, and yet their sound alone cannot bring us fully within hearing presence of the word of history. Intangible and inaudible though it be, this historical reality is nevertheless formatively present in our lives and reflections. It is there in a manner that shapes us, without itself ever becoming fully manifest or obvious. Its meaning and intercommunication with us remain elusive, although we learn to catch more frequent glimpses of its shining presence. We even develop formal methods and disciplines for interpreting human history and rendering it more readily serviceable for our present needs and aims, throughout every phase of contemporary living. The poet's question remains to incite us, however, to strain after improving our understanding of the historical component in all its modes. And his answer also stands as a symbol of caution against any foolish persuasion that we have fully discovered the sense of what it is for us to include the historical quality in even our most intense efforts at present-minded talking and acting.

In my estimate, we have made a good start, but only a start, in the great task of fathoming the meaning of historical reality and knowing. More is required than a simple prolongation of the methods and argumentation which presently constitute the philosophy of history. Its high-level generalities could become so encompassing and settled that they would conceal or smother the distinctive initiatives coming from the more specific, limited forms of historical inquiry. Historians of science and philosophy, of social institutions and behavioral ways, of theology and art, are not destined to serve as the mere recipients and subordinate instruments of some general categorial schemes elaborated elsewhere for them. On the contrary, it is crucial that they take their own counter-initiative, make their independent reporting on the mode, intent, and human import of what they are doing. They have to spell out a twofold set of implications: not only those *within their special field* of historical research but also those *opening toward our general engagement* with the meaning of human history in all its aspects.

My aim in this book is to illuminate the methodology and epistemology of history of modern philosophy, by reflecting upon the concrete ways of historians in this field. Their methods and modes of knowing are adapted to the specific problems in the modern sources, and yet also have some broader implications for the knowledge achieved in history of philosophy as a whole. Looking at the actual practice of the community of researchers in modern philosophy, I propose a working hypothesis for understanding their procedures and the main components in their pattern of interpretation. This hypothesis involves a general schema which, of course, requires some careful testing and modification in its detailed development.

Throughout the course of this critical analysis and restatement, I have been guided by five leading questions. First, what is the active role of the source thinkers themselves in determining the historical meaning and structures of modern philosophy? The classical philosophers from Descartes and Locke down to Mill and Nietzsche are not sheerly passive and pliable subjects, but somehow manage to exert their own specifying influence upon the interpreting process—and this "somehow" has to be investigated in its own right. Next, what are the chief traits characterizing the work of twentieth-century historians of these sources? Out of the many research tries and published achievements, there has slowly emerged a broadly shared art of historical questioning which will repay close inspection. Thirdly, we may well ask: What difference does it make that the search after historical significance goes on today in our own philosophical climate? The twofold responsiveness of the historian both to the modern sources and to the contemporary issues in philosophy is a crucial point in establishing the present functional value of historical studies.

The fourth guiding question takes account of the fact that, whatever their official positions on the worth of history of modern philosophy, most philosophers today develop their own theories through seminar discussion of the basic modern sources. What contributions to historical methodology and knowledge derive from the engagement of the present community of philosophers in the teaching situation and the seminar experience? And finally, what are the purposive ideals of the working historian, the abiding aims which intimately shape his creative work of understanding, relating, and critically evaluating the modern philosophers? No account of how we gain historical access to modern philosophy can afford to neglect this teleological factor pervading the entire process. It is with these five primary questions constantly serving as guides and goads that my investigation has proceeded. The resultant theory of historical understanding of modern philosophy requires criticism, but the fivefold mode of questioning can itself serve as a valid instrument for developing new theories and judging their relative adequacy.

In the present study, there is a closer relationship than usual between the main text and the notes. Along with giving the necessary citations, the notes are designed to convey to the reader "the feel of things" in the research methods in history of modern philosophy today. Books and articles are gathered together in a note, not along purely bibliographical or citational lines but mainly as means of illustrating the particular phase of historical inquiry being discussed at that point in the text. This renders the general theory more concrete and suggests some resources for the reader to consult in his personal relationship with the great modern philosophers. A further use of the notes is to make us more definitely aware, through quoted statements, of the value of other interpretations of the historical approach to modern philosophy. Even to attain the limited and thoroughly revisable prospect of the approach given here requires the matrix and help of a community of investigators.

I owe a long-range debt of gratitude to colleagues and to students in my modern philosophy seminar, for holding me to a standard and helping me to understand better the nature of the work being done. The immediate impetus for this book came from a series of lectures which I delivered in 1968 at the University of Notre Dame. I have pleasant memories of the hospitable and scholarly climate provided by Father Ernan McMullin, Professor A. Robert Caponigri, and others in the philosophy department there. In the actual preparation of the manuscript, I have had the encouragement and financial support of Father Linus J. Thro, S.J., chairman of the Department of Philosophy in Saint Louis University. And Princeton University Press has made a generous allocation from the Whitney Darrow Publication Reserve Fund to aid in publication of the book. Finally, my wife Yvonne Collins has helped me cheerfully and skillfully throughout the final stages of preparing the typed copy.

James Collins

Saint Louis University
November 1971

Contents

PREFACE   vii

I. THE HISTORICAL TURN IN CONTEMPORARY
   PHILOSOPHY   3

   1. The Stimulus for Historical Study   7

   2. A Working Hypothesis   24

II. THE INSISTENCY OF MODERN SOURCES   35

   1. Journey toward the Sources   35

   2. Source Philosophizing as a Basal and
      Insistential Act   44

   3. The Demanding Text of Descartes   53

   4. The Communicational Spectrum   76

III. THE ART OF HISTORICAL QUESTIONING   97

   1. The Poles of Interrogation   99

   2. Exploring the Fundament: (i) Text,
      Translation, and Biography   102

   3. Exploring the Fundament: (ii) Genesis,
      System, and Conspectus   125

   4. The Modes of Interrelation   154

IV. THE INTERPRETING PRESENT   186

   1. Historical Understanding through Presential
      Act   188

   2. Ways of the Responsive Interpreter: (i)
      Reforming the From-To Perspectives   212

3. Ways of the Responsive Interpreter: (ii)
   Appreciating the Middle-Range Philosophers
   and the Paraphilosophers   231

4. Ways of the Responsive Interpreter: (iii)
   Serving Current Theoretical Aims   252

V. KANT OUR CONTEMPORARY   267

1. The Seminar Experience   268

2. Kant as Critic of Mathematical and
   Scientific Reason   272

3. Husserl and Heidegger: Lifelong Students
   of Kant   283

4. The Ongoing Analytic Conference on Kant   314

5. A Focus in Kantian Community   327

VI. TELEOLOGY OF HISTORICAL UNDERSTANDING   345

1. Our Philosophical Past: From Burden
   to Resource   347

2. The Historian of Philosophy and His
   Interpretants   359

3. The Mark of a Great Philosopher   377

4. The Intent to Do Historical Justice   390

5. Humanity and History of Philosophy   406

BIBLIOGRAPHY   419

INDEX   453

INTERPRETING MODERN PHILOSOPHY

I

The Historical Turn in Contemporary Philosophy

In every creative field, but perhaps especially in philosophy, we tend to use the term "contemporary" not only in a eulogistic way but also as expressing our relief at escaping the burden of the past. The term often conveys the sense of crossing a territorial border and cutting off a bridge behind ourselves, a bridge that would have permitted the great dead philosophers to count for too much in our present inquiries. We sometimes feel that their presence would be overbearing and would inhibit our own efforts at innovation and argument. Not a historical sense of perspective but a liberation from historical perspectives, a distancing of ourselves from the history of philosophy, seems to provide the proper conditions for doing good contemporary work in philosophy.

This view of the historical factor is an initial, yet essential, stage in the formation of any sense of contemporaneity in philosophy. Throughout the long development of philosophy, every age has had to struggle toward achieving its own identity and its own assurance of doing worthwhile new work. The sense of contemporaneity is never simply given to a group of philosophers but must be worked out and won by them through a painful process of discussion, which takes time and involves several stages.

It is particularly in the *opening* phase of such a process that creative philosophers find it necessary to regard the work of their predecessors as burdensome, as a weight to be sloughed off on peril of having one's own efforts dampened and underestimated. In this spirit, a Descartes and a Locke were impelled to treat their historical past as a crazy-quilt town which had to be reduced to rubble and cleared away, before they could arouse a sense of the contemporary for themselves and their age.[1] In the same spirit, Kant was obliged to declare a moratorium on the work of all previous metaphysicians and philosophers of man, so that he might breathe some clean contemporary air and think out the issues in a new fashion. Even the historically inclined Hegel had to break loose from previous conceptions of substance and spirit and renew the problem of the starting point in philosophy, so that the revolutionary aspect of his thought could find a present tense in which to actualize itself.

To appreciate the full nature of these notable efforts at achieving contemporaneity in philosophy, however, we must also notice that none of the thinkers just cited was content with maintaining forever the charge of burdensomeness against his own historical roots. That attitude toward the philosophical past did have a real function to perform. It helped to distinguish between the act of philosophizing and a mere repetition of earlier categories and formulas, as well as to shift the accent from timid respect for the past to a critical analysis of present issues. Yet once this office was performed, the freely developed stance of separating oneself from the past had served its purpose. It could not be allowed to harden into a conventional obstacle, in its own turn, against the further ripening of the contemporanizing process. The great minds

[1] Their attitude finds a contemporary counterpart in Ludwig Wittgenstein's self-interrogation. "Where does our investigation get its importance from, since it seems only to destroy everything interesting, that is, all that is great and important? (As it were all the buildings, leaving behind only bits of stone and rubble.) What we are destroying is nothing but houses of cards and we are clearing up the ground of language on which they stand" (*Philosophical Investigations*, tr. G.E.M. Anscombe, #118). Yet Wittgenstein himself saw the need for a genetic study of his own thought; and bioanalytic research is now examining his historical relationship with such thinkers as Augustine and Kierkegaard, Schopenhauer and Tolstoy, Schlick and William James. —[For complete bibliographical data on works cited in the notes, see the Bibliography, pp. 421-452.]

which constituted the Cartesian or Kantian or Hegelian modes of contemporaneity ultimately met their responsibility toward their own historical sources. A Descartes worked his way very carefully through the arguments of the schoolmen and the skeptics; a Kant acknowledged the dual challenge of the Leibnizian and Lockean notions of mind and its objects; and a Hegel incorporated into his philosophical present the endeavors of many great antecedents.

It is not unexpected, then, that our own meaning of contemporary philosophy should undergo a similar growth. We can all sympathize with, and enjoy, the remark which Frederick Woodbridge used to throw at his philosophy seminar in Columbia University: "Modern philosophy, thank God, is at last over."[2] What makes this an instructive observation is its twin-barbed purpose. For one thing, Woodbridge was calling attention to the unwarranted appropriation of the term "modern philosophy" by the nineteenth-century idealistic historians of philosophy, who sought to identify the historical study of the sources with their own interpretation and thus to reduce the history of modern philosophy to an arm of the idealistic argument itself. It is necessary to declare an end to this suffocating type of historical determinism, and indeed to any provincial use of history of philosophy which seeks to draw a single, exclusivist moral from the whole development. But, secondly, Woodbridge himself got over this historical monism in such a manner that he could still work as the most historically oriented of the American naturalists of his generation. Through his sympathetic efforts, American naturalism was led to make a new reading of Aristotle and Spinoza, Locke and the evolutionary sources. Thus he built into at least one strain of contemporary philosophizing a sense of the theoretical opportunities furnished by a study of past thinkers.

[2] Quoted by J. H. Randall, Jr., "Epilogue: The Nature of Naturalism," in *Naturalism and the Human Spirit*, ed. Y. H. Krikorian, p. 367. C. F. Delaney examines Woodbridge's own use of the historical roots of naturalism in *Mind and Nature: A Study of the Naturalistic Philosophies of Cohen, Woodbridge and Sellars*, chapter 4.

A similar broadening of the meaning of contemporary philosophy to include its historical dimension is going on in other philosophical movements. The initial phase is represented by the time-honored application of the terms "revolution" and "turn" to a new philosophical method. Thus we speak about the revolution in philosophy effected by Husserl's phenomenological method, by Carnap's positivism, or by the procedures of Wittgenstein and Ryle. The feeling of liberation from history of philosophy, regarded as burdensome, finds somewhat playful expression in the practice of dating contemporary philosophy from some favorite article or book. Perhaps contemporary philosophy begins with Husserl's *Logos* article of 1911, or with a John Wisdom article of 1938, or with some landmark of the 1950's. On this reckoning, everything done prior to the landmark belongs in a remote ancient history, for the serious study of which philosophers are no longer responsible.

Kant's word "turn" has the added advantage of suggesting that contemporary philosophers have rounded a bend which leaves the historical sources out of sight and out of mind. But now, in the latter third of our century, we are finding it increasingly difficult to translate this metaphor into any determinate meaning which the philosophical community finds acceptable, either as a theoretical statement or as a practical proposal. Whether we regard the decisive contemporary turning as being chiefly linguistic or analytical, phenomenological or existential, we are coming to realize that it does not signify any permanent rejection of philosophy's historical roots (however chronologically demarcated) or of the continuing responsibility to reconsider them with critical freshness. Our sense of contemporaneity matures in the degree that we recognize that history of philosophy has made the turn along with the new methods and in the function of being their still sustaining matrix.

Historically generated issues have rounded the bend with the other interests in contemporary philosophy. Now it is important to recover familiarity with *how* we study the historical sources and relate them to our other philosophical concerns. A certain amount of disuse of historical approaches has rendered this topic not only unhackneyed but also slightly strange and ready for new analyses. As an aid in reorientation, I will first of all take a closer look at some underlying reasons for this phenomenon of the historical turn, as constituting part of the meaning of contemporary philosophy. Working out from this situation, I will then suggest a working hypothesis concerning how we gain historical access to modern philosophy. The task of the later chapters will be to examine in detail the specific points contained in that hypothesis.

1. THE STIMULUS FOR HISTORICAL STUDY

For our own self-understanding, it is helpful to probe into the intellectual conditions which today are quickening the pace of interest in the historical aspect of philosophy. Certainly, the least significant influence is that exerted by purely cultural proponents of the historical approach in all phases of education. Their recommendations are too general, and too extrinsic to the actual work going on in philosophy, to exert any decisive influence. What counts for philosophers is not a cultural recommendation of history—which can always be kept at arm's length, as signifying an admirable adornment but not an essential need—but some internal developments in the course of philosophical inquiry itself.

Can the growing appreciation of the great philosophers in our past be attributed primarily to the efforts of the professional historians of philosophy? Surely, they have contributed something toward it simply by tending to their job, by continuing to improve their textual tools and interpretive studies of the major sources. The instruments for doing any level of historical work are today far richer and more serviceable to the philosophical community than they were a generation ago. One reason why the question of history and theory has to be reopened is that the historical pole in this comparison has not remained static. During the same years when our contemporary philosophies were under formation, the resources of history of philosophy were also making a steady growth. Thus the situation of a short generation ago has changed, not only in its theoretical components but also in its historical.

Nevertheless, I do not think that the historical advances are sufficient, of themselves, to accomplish the broad revision of thinking on the value of historical factors for the theoretical enterprise itself. To see the current relevance of the sources requires an act of recognition on the part of those minds engaged in original inquiries. The striking difference between the mid-century point and now is precisely that such recognition of the importance of history is forthcoming from a wide compass of creative thinkers, representing the main contemporary philosophies. This stronger appreciation is not peculiar to some one school, moreover, but can be observed operating within several quite different philosophical contexts. A revaluating of history develops in response to some definite problems and tendencies common to all the present ways of philosophizing. There are at least three features of the contemporary situation in philosophy which help to quicken an interest in the contributions of historical work. These centers of stimulus concern the dispersion technique, the purist split, and the pattern of university education.

One negative, yet significant, point is the failure of the *dispersion technique* for dealing with source materials. In many universities, there was a practice of consigning the ancient philosophers to the classics department or to a separate philological corps within the philosophy department, and then of regarding the medieval, Renaissance, and modern philosophers mainly as material for the history of ideas. If this practice had succeeded in the long run, it would have effected the dispersion of the tasks of history of philosophy and hence the destruction of its distinctive function within philosophy itself. But the experience of the past quarter century suggests that, while history of philosophy benefits tremendously from the services of philology and history of ideas, it never loses its identity and gets dissolved into these other disciplines. Their work is helpful to it in an instrumental fashion, without requiring either the reduction of these disciplines to a purely instrumental status or the reduction of history of philosophy itself to a shadowy repetition of their findings. Each is serviceable to the other, without either one losing sight of the tasks distinctively set for itself.

That there is more meaning in the ancient philosophical texts than can be delivered in purely philological terms is strikingly witnessed by the continuing effort of philosophers to understand and interpret Plato and Aristotle. It is not surprising that, when Husserl was trying to clear the ground for his later conception of phenomenology, he should feel obliged to proceed through a detailed comparison with Plato's dialectic. Husserl's lectures on *First Philosophy* take Plato in the ancient world and Descartes in the modern world as two steady landmarks in the philosophical search for foundations. It is primarily in reference to them that his own foundational method gets clarified. Similarly, at the crucial stage where he had to distinguish his own thought from Sartre's type of humanism, Martin Heidegger also had recourse to an interpretation of Plato. The thematic essay on *Plato's Doctrine of Truth* underlines the relationship between truth and the unconcealed or unhidden quality of philosophical thinking, while at the same time criticizing Plato and western metaphysics for binding truth too closely with ideas and the cultural needs of men. Yet Heidegger's own exegesis of the early Greeks and Plato offends many philosophers as being an outrageous reading of the texts. The significant point in such a reaction is that present philosophical purposes cannot justify just any use of the historical sources. Thus Heidegger's critics firmly imply that the wellbeing of present philosophizing is somehow bound up with a historically sound understanding of the enduring sources of thought.

The ideal of reading the Greek and Latin philosophers in order to gain nourishment for one's own speculations is reaffirmed by two contemporary philosophers, who hold otherwise quite diverse views: Karl Jaspers and Gilbert Ryle. The German existentialist prefaces his sympathetic analyses of

Plato, Plotinus, and Augustine with this statement of historical attitude:

> We hope to enter into the world of the great philosophers, to make ourselves at home in it, because it is in their company, the best there is, that we can attain to what we ourselves are capable of being. Admittance is open to all. The dwellers in that land are glad to answer provided that we know how to inquire. They show us what they were. They encourage us and make us humble. A great philosopher wants no disciples, but men who are themselves. With all our veneration, we can come closer to them only if we ourselves philosophize.[3]

Thus as Jaspers sees it, there is a creative reciprocity between studying the classical sources in philosophy and developing one's own capacities as a thinker.

For his part, Ryle is much more acerbic about venerating the great philosophers or becoming humble in their presence, since he fears that this can generate the wrong kind of respect and thus can unfit us for critical detection of conceptual confusions. Yet his own scrupulous examination of Plato's *Parmenides* (with the adjacent dialogues, the *Theaetetus* and the *Sophist*) shows that there is a proper sort of respect based on a critical investigation of the problems, as well as a dimension of comparative understanding which develops only from following the historical trail of a problem from its Greek origins into its modern and even quite contemporary reconsiderations.

[3] Karl Jaspers, *The Great Philosophers: The Foundations*, pp. ix-x. The problem of philosophical tradition is central also in Martin Heidegger's joint essays on Plato and historicity: "Plato's Doctrine of Truth" and "Letter on Humanism," in *Philosophy in the Twentieth Century*, ed. W. Barrett and H. D. Aiken, II, 251-302. There is need for a translation of Edmund Husserl's major analysis of philosophical sources, *Erste Philosophie (1923/24): Erster Teil, Kritische Ideengeschichte*, ed. R. Boehm. Husserl's theory of "critical history of ideas" is examined below in Chapter V, section 3.

We cannot even state what was a philosopher's puzzle, much less what was the direction or efficacy of his attempt to solve it, unless subsequent reflections have thrown a clearer light upon the matter than he was able to do. Whether a commentator has found such a light or only a will-of-the-wisp is always debatable and often very well worth debating. Thus I may be wrong in believing that there are affinities between Plato's enquiries in these dialogues and Hume's and Kant's account of assertions of existence, Kant's account of forms of judgement and categories, Russell's doctrine of propositional functions and theory of types, and, perhaps, more than any other, nearly the whole of Wittgenstein's *Tractatus Logico-Philosophicus*. I may be wrong in construing these dialogues as, so to speak, forecasting most of the logical embarrassments into which the infinitely courageous and pertinacious Meinong was to fall. But at least my error, if it is one, does not imply that Plato's puzzles were so factitious or ephemeral that no other serious philosopher has ever experienced any perplexity about them.[4]

The Rylean conception of puzzles encountered in Plato which turn out to be archetypal perplexities, recurring in the core thinkers in the modern analytic tradition, runs squarely counter to the policy of leaving the classical sources in the hands of the philologists alone. Our understanding of these sources is improved by working out the theoretical affinities which

---

[4] Gilbert Ryle, "Plato's *Parmenides*," in Gilbert Ryle, *Collected Papers*, I, 44 (this essay originally appeared in *Mind* in 1939). That a study of Plato fosters the historical aspect in the analytic turn is witnessed by Gilbert Ryle, *Plato's Progress*, and Kenneth M. Sayre, *Plato's Analytic Method*. Indeed, Jean H. Faurot, "What Is History of Philosophy?" *The Monist*, 53 (1969), 642-655, views Ryle as exhibiting both the professional historian's care for particularity and concreteness (in respect to Plato) and the philosopher-as-historical-layman's drive for present significance (in respect to Descartes as a protagonist in *The Concept of Mind*).

may hold between them and subsequent forms of philosophical inquiry. It may well turn out that some particular
hypothesis is faulty either in its formulation or in its historical
referents, but this cannot be actually known without making
some philosophical comparisons and establishing some historical bases of argumentation. In any case, the work of testing out a forecasting function for such complex variables as
Plato-Hume-Kant-Russell-Meinong-Wittgenstein helps to restore the classical sources to the full historical process, as well
as to endow the study of modern philosophers with a much
needed perspective of history.

The sequestration policy has failed just as decisively in its
attempt to identify the history of philosophy with the history
of ideas. The rich developments in the latter discipline during
the past half century have been invaluable for historians of
philosophy. To the student of Hegel, for instance, it makes
a very palpable difference that Arthur O. Lovejoy did not cut
off his study of the theme of the great chain of being with the
Enlightenment, but prolonged it into the Romantic thinkers
who transformed a static and uniformitarian view of reality
into a temporalized and diversitarian one. The Hegel scholar
cannot afford to dispense with Lovejoy's account of the literary, social, and scientific expressions of the Romantic appreciation of organic, developmental, and unique aspects of
existence; his presentation of the image of nature as found in
Jacobi, Schelling, and the Schlegels; and his consistently
plural and interdisciplinary conception of Romanticism. Such
research in the history of ideas alerts us to otherwise unde-
tected overtones and problems in those knotty sections of
Hegel's *Phenomenology* and *Encyclopedia* which seek to assimilate and overcome the diverse forms of Romantic
thought. To keep oneself ignorant of these findings, and thus
to come cold to the study of some difficult but important
texts, is not a virtue but a self-incurred handicap on the part
of a philosophical reader of Hegel.[5]

[5] For a more concrete understanding of Hegel's project of uniting
Enlightenment with Romanticism, the following researches by A. O.

Especially as developed by Lovejoy and George Boas, the history of ideas has attained to significant generalizations in its own sphere by focusing upon the major unit-ideas: the chain of being, primitivism, nature, natural right, and interior duration. The basic procedure is to trace out the life-histories and changing relationships between such complex centers of meaning. Nevertheless, the work of the historian of ideas never renders superfluous a distinctively philosophical reading of the same sources. For the historian of philosophy has questions of his own which are not already formulated and answered for him, in the course of a study of the growth of unit-ideas.

Thus in the instance we have cited from Lovejoy it is insufficient for the philosophical student to regard Hegel's work simply as a further stage in the life course of the seminal ideas found in the Romantic context. For Hegel's own thought and language are molded by a judgment about spirit and method which is not purely expressive of a cultural situation. His detailed treatment of the Romantic conceptions of reality criticizes their key unit-ideas, judges them in the light of his own theory of the developing whole, and thus demands a philo-

---

Lovejoy are still indispensable: *The Great Chain of Being, Essays in the History of Ideas,* and *The Reason, the Understanding, and Time.* Lovejoy's conception of the great unit-ideas is criticized for its latent atomism and inability to handle organically growing systems by J. H. Randall, Jr., *How Philosophy Uses Its Past,* pp. 54-55. In "The History of Ideas, Intellectual History, and the History of Philosophy," *History and Theory,* Beiheft 5, *The Historiography of the History of Philosophy,* ed. John Passmore, Maurice Mandelbaum remarks: "Philosophy depends both upon an impetus to philosophize and a tradition of philosophizing. Under these conditions it would be a mistake to attempt to understand a philosopher merely as a reflection of whatever intellectual or social factors impinged directly upon him because of the time and place at which he lived. It is only when we view philosophic thought both in terms of its own tradition, and in terms of influences focussed upon it because of the circumstances of the philosopher's life and his times, that we can see a particular philosopher's work in proper perspective: as a distinctive philosophic achievement which also belongs within the general intellectual history of the period" (p. 62).

sophical understanding and appraisal of the speculative principles at work. In order that the historian of philosophy may meet his prime responsibility, he must always keep the life-history of persistent ideas instrumental to his understanding and appraisal of the principles of inquiry which operate intrinsically to shape each philosopher's treatment.

A SECOND major impetus in favor of historical studies comes from our gradual recognition of the questionable consequences of making a *purist split* between doing philosophical analysis and criticism of the great sources and doing exegesis and historical explanation. A working distinction is indeed drawn helpfully between several sorts of questions which arise in regard to the great texts in history of philosophy. It is often useful to concentrate upon some mature expression of a philosopher's mind, without considering the stages required in his development before he could write this masterpiece. Or one can fruitfully focus upon the internal arguments supporting a theory—perhaps even analyze the main arguments drawn from different periods in a philosopher's work—while yet leaving to another time or to another researcher the task of tracing out the precise antecedents and comparative relationships with other sources. Such restrictions are imposed upon the individual investigator by his own background and interests, by his limitations, and by his sense of what is important and importunate *for him* to do.

Self-limitation on these grounds is part of the historical method itself and does not stand in opposition to it. For only by such strategies in the division of intellectual labor, can we develop new and diverse human energies for the interpretation of great texts in philosophy. However, any individual investigator conducts his restricted study within the context of the full community of research and in responsive openness to other findings, made from other limited approaches. Thus it is supposed that other investigators (or oneself under other circumstances) will, for their part, be concentrating upon the genetic study of a philosopher's system or will be focusing precisely upon the comparative issues raised by his problems, language, and principles.

Moreover, the relationship between *differently oriented members of the research community in history of philosophy* is not one of sheer juxtaposition, without any mutual influence. Membership in this community can be defined, in methodological terms, as a readiness to consult other workers in the field and to modify one's own account of some great philosophical text of the past, upon being shown the corrective relevance of findings being made along another route. Such openness for making revisions holds for all sectors of the horizon. The ideal of historical integrity and revisibility is strongly operative, whether it leads the close reader of a single argument or a masterwork to profit from the genetic and comparative aspects of new research or whether it leads the student of comparative problems to render his grasp of the theoretical issues analytically more precise.

What we are coming to realize more clearly, in the last third of our century, is that some limits must be placed upon the often helpful distinction between doing critical analysis and doing close commentary and comparison of the philosophical sources. The distinction can signify the normal distribution of tasks within the community of historical research or it can transform itself into a purist split, which would prevent that community from doing its full work and contributing its values to mankind. Perhaps what most encourages the doctrinaire separation and contrast of the two functions is a metaphorical way of regarding the philosopher's activity. One metaphor of questionable contemporary relevance is that which regards the philosopher as an alchemist. His work is to treat the philosophical texts of the past as so much dross, which must be melted down and removed in order to release an ounce of precious ore. Everything else except this philosopher's gold, extracted by one's special formula, constitutes a *caput mortuum*, a worthless residue destined only for being washed out of sight. Another anachronistic and uncritical variant is the metaphor of the philosopher as the village miller. Here, his function is imagined to be that of casting the philosophical texts on the threshing floor, infallibly separating good grain from quite useless husk, and eliminating the latter from attention.[6] Such metaphorical thinking leads to a rigid dualistic separation of theoretical and historical aspects, as though they were related in the ore-and-dross or the grain-and-husk fashion.

The purist split is sometimes expressed in more abstract terms. Thus in order to back his sharp dualism between descriptive metaphysics and revisionary metaphysics, P. F. Strawson correlates the former with a stylistic rendering of an invariant core of human categories and the latter with an effort to reach new conceptual schemes.

> There is a massive central core of human thinking which has no history—or none recorded in histories of thought; there are categories ànd concepts which, in their most fundamental character, change not at all. . . . If there are no new truths to be discovered, there are old truths to be rediscovered. For though the central subject-matter of descriptive metaphysics does not change, the critical and analytical idiom of philosophy changes constantly. Permanent relationships are described in an impermanent idiom,

[6] In his inaugural lecture as R. G. Collingwood's successor as Waynflete Professor in Oxford, Gilbert Ryle likened philosophical reasoning upon the great sources "to threshing, which separates the grain from the chaff, discards the chaff and collects the grain. Philosophical reasoning separates the genuine from the erroneously assumed logical powers of abstract ideas by using the *reductio ad absurdum* argument as its flail and winnowing fan, but knowledge by wont of the use of concreter ideas is also necessary as its floor" ("Philosophical Arguments," in Ryle, *Collected Papers*, II, 210). Ryle's search for "philosophically cardinal ideas," or key ideas constituting the intellectual geography of a philosophical region, recalls Collingwood's plan of balancing the historicity of philosophy (as inseparable from other modes of historical knowing) with the transhistorical categories, questions, and presuppositions that structure its map. See L. Rubinoff, "Collingwood's Theory of the Relation Between Philosophy and History: A New Interpretation," *Journal of the History of Philosophy*, 6 (1968), 363-380.

which reflects both the age's climate of thought and the individual philosopher's personal style of thinking. No philosopher understands his predecessors until he has rethought their thought in his own contemporary terms; and it is characteristic of the very greatest philosophers, like Kant and Aristotle, that they, more than any others, repay this effort of re-thinking.[7]

This is a highly ambiguous passage. From one angle, it is a vigorous plea for a more sympathetic and careful historical reading of the great sources, as exemplified by Strawson's own Kant book (to be studied below, in Chapter V).

But the rethinking process is justified by appeal to the same systematically misleading contrast which underlies the alchemist and miller metaphors. The descriptive metaphysician is asked to read the sources in a mainly dualistic spirit, separating the unchanging core of categories and concepts from the contingent historical clothing of an intellectual climate and a personal style. Thereby, he is granted some access to the past philosophers. Yet it is gained only at the twofold price of wafting the descriptive metaphysician into a sphere of invariant meanings which are only extrinsically affected by language and historical conditions, and of confining historical development in his discipline to a shift in styles and idioms. By definition, methodological and categorial innovations proposed by revisionary metaphysicians cannot radically af-

---

[7] P. F. Strawson, *Individuals: An Essay in Descriptive Metaphysics*, pp. xiv-xv. In actual practice, however, analytic historians liberate themselves from the doctrine of a timeless core and a transient idiom. Cf. G. E. M. Anscombe and P. T. Geach, *Three Philosophers*, on Aristotle, Aquinas, and Frege; Victor Preller, *Divine Science and the Science of God: A Reformulation of Thomas Aquinas*; and P. F. Strawson's own fine study, *The Bounds of Sense: An Essay on Kant's Critique of Pure Reason*. Such closer proportioning of analytic work to the historical texts helps to remove the arbitrary cleft between what was said historically and what was meant analytically by past thinkers, as shown by John Dunn, "The Identity of the History of Ideas," *Philosophy*, *43* (1968), 85-104, and more at length by Haskell Fain, *Between Philosophy and History*.

fect anything, since the central core remains changeless and the new principles count only as questions provoking a new idiom and climate for description.

This bifurcation cannot stabilize itself, however, since it rests upon a host of abstract stipulations which are constantly being subverted by historical realities. A philosopher develops the quality of greatness in the measure that he regards the massive structures of previous human thought and discourse as an opportunity for change, calling for his critical reform and creativity. His response may be to uncover the stages of genesis congealed in the recurrent patterns; or it may be to generalize the process whereby present forms are being transformed by the impact of scientific, artistic, and social innovations; or again it may consist in rescuing those spare and original features of human existence which consistently slip through our conceptual and linguistic grids. In any case, an influential philosopher does not seek an adjustment of an invariant core to a transient life style. His critique bites too deeply into the very intimate relationship of thought and language, tradition and contemporaneity, to be satisfied with such a dichotomous ideal. He aims at a radical reconstruction affecting both the old and the new methods of inquiry, the basic concepts, and the descriptive analyses. The practice of philosophical minds reveals that *all* these factors are concretely coadapted and deeply modified by any general reinterpretation. Thus the great creative efforts in philosophy belie the alchemist-miller metaphors and the description-revision dichotomy, upon which the purist split depended for credibility.

There is no sharp division between the exegetical, the comparative, and the analytical functions in our historical study of the philosophical sources. All these functions have been developed by mankind to improve our grasp upon difficult texts, and hence all of them contribute to the growth of history of philosophy itself. But sometimes we have to be brought to a limit situation, before acknowledging their mutual dependence and the bad effects of trying to isolate them. Some such experience of the unbalancing result of cultivating only one privileged manner of reading the sources has brought about a marked change of attitude toward the historical order of problems, on the part of such a leading logical empiricist as Rudolf Carnap.

The passage of time enabled Carnap (in his engagingly clear and honest autobiography and reply to critics) to set forth the presuppositions of logical empiricism concerning its own historical sources in philosophy. The original program of the Vienna Circle involved a very definite situating of the movement in respect to Hume and Kant, Mach and Brentano, some of whose theories were accorded a precursor status. Even on the negative side, Carnap's early attack upon metaphysics involved a position on history and not merely an abstract reference to metaphysical words and metaphysical pseudo-statements. For this schema was supported by sample statements taken from philosophers, as well as by a generalization about what characterizes the thought of most metaphysicians since antiquity. Thus, Carnap's central shift from the conflict between realistic, idealistic, and phenomenalistic systems of doctrine to his own principle of tolerance of the languages of realism, idealism (in some degree), and phenomenalism rested upon a general classification of historical kinds of philosophy. For many years, he remained unconcerned about the validity of these uses of historical materials, since he was not specifically interested in problems concerning the historical modes of intersubjectivity. But more recently these problems came to the fore for him, and along with them there also developed a new sensitivity to the history of philosophy.

This awareness has been growing ever since Carnap's move to America, where he has emphasized the humanistic component in his "scientific humanism." It has led him to make two historical kinds of comparison and, in turn, to search for a theoretical basis that can sustain the comparisons.

For one thing, the widespread American interest in Hume and the sense-data theory has forced him to analyze and criticize phenomenalism, so as to justify the position of placing limits on the use of phenomenalistic language. This has legitimated the question of historically different ways of limiting the scope of phenomenalistic analysis. In particular, Carnap now perceives the difference between his own nondialectical kind of limitation and the dialectical tradition of Hegel-Marx-Lenin. Carnap's American experience opens up a second type of historical comparison, due to the strong influence of pragmatism upon his thought and that of the other members of the Vienna Circle who came to America. The fact that logical empiricism has survived long enough to look critically at itself, and evolve under the pressure of American philosophical traditions, means that it is participating in the historical reality of philosophy at first hand. It cannot undergo historical growth and still remain aloof, as a pure metacritic of the systems and languages constituting the history of philosophy.

Out of his reflections on this situation, Carnap has come to emphasize the important role of conceptual frameworks and general categorial discussions in the historical transition from one philosophical context of interpretation to another.

Many problems concerning conceptual frameworks seem to me to belong to the most important problems of philosophy. I am thinking here both of theoretical investigations and of practical deliberations and decisions with respect to an acceptance or a change of frameworks, especially of the most general frameworks containing categorial concepts which are fundamental for the representation of all knowledge. [Charles] Morris thinks that the traditional metaphysical problems could be interpreted as problems of this kind. This may be the case for many metaphysical problems. But in the case of others, I doubt whether an interpretation of this kind would be historically correct, that is to say, whether the metaphysicians would have accepted such interpretations of their writings. In cases of this kind, I prefer, from a systematic point of view, not to take the framework problem as an interpretation of traditional metaphysics, but rather to abandon the latter and discuss the former. From a historical point of view, many metaphysical theses and discussions can certainly be regarded as more or less conscious preparatory stages on the way to a systematic logic and science, and as preliminary to framework analyses. I think this holds, in particular, for the metaphysical theories of Aristotle, Leibniz, Charles S. Peirce, and Whitehead.[8]

What is remarkable about this passage is not the usual rejection of an entity called "traditional metaphysics," but rather the discernment of the cognitive import of the level of fundamental problems and discussions in the great philosophers. Broad categorial questions and interpretive frameworks are significant objects of investigation from the historical standpoint as well as the systematic, since they involve an understanding of the continuities and revolutionary shifts which every humanistic philosophy must examine. Although Carnap himself has not developed the historical study of framework problems, he admits the need for doing so and is prepared, in principle, to temper his broader philosophical positions by its findings.

Michael Ayers voices a new sensitivity among analytic philosophers toward the contribution of modern sources and the need for historical probity in restating and criticizing them. The analytic thinker cannot dispense entirely with historical sources, and neither can he read them entirely apart from their specific context of meanings and with an eye only toward their reformulation in abstract counterpart terms.

It seems probable that more philosophers are now taking the history of philosophy seriously than has been the case for some time. But if there is one thing radically wrong with our approach to the past, it is the often unquestioned assumption that the first task of the commentator is to isolate from a philosopher's work what is consonant with currently respectable theories, as if the only way of bringing the

[8] Rudolf Carnap, "Replies and Systematic Expositions," in *The Philosophy of Rudolf Carnap*, ed. P. A. Schilpp, p. 862.

dead to life is to patch them up, by a kind of cosmetic surgery, as fit participants in some modern debate. . . . It is simply false that a training in analytical thought alone qualifies us to penetrate to the kernel of philosophical truth or interest within any historically conditioned husk. The less exhilarating fact is that it is often impossible to get more than a rough and distorted notion of the real meaning of a philosophical work, however deathless it may be, without a reasonable concern for historical context and scholarly comparisons.[9]

Although stringent, this judgment finds ample confirmation in Morris Lazerowitz's fragmentation of the thought of Spinoza and treatment of his texts as cosmic mood pieces; in J. O. Wisdom's divination about the unconscious origins of Berkeley's views on matter, the body, and the human spirit; and in Jonathan Bennett's industrious dedication to the search for muddles and howlers in the pages of Berkeley and Kant. The salutary effect of such performances is to show the disastrous result of making a purist split between the analytic and the historical approaches to the modern philosophical sources. Once we are brought up short by these extreme cases, we can see how necessary it is to encourage a use of all the human study methods, as they correct and enlarge each other's path into the basic writings.

THERE is a third, and increasingly effective, major stimulus for historical studies in philosophy today: *the aims and pat-*

[9] Michael R. Ayers, "Substance, Reality, and the Great, Dead Philosophers," *American Philosophical Quarterly*, 7 (1970), p. 38. The fruitfulness of using a comparative and genetic methodology in the history of American pragmatism is expressed by H. S. Thayer, *Meaning and Action: A Critical History of Pragmatism*, in this standard: "Instead of history *or* philosophy, the net product aimed for is history *and* philosophy" (p. vii). That policy would remedy the paucity of historical controls in: J. O. Wisdom, *The Unconscious Origins of Berkeley's Philosophy*; Morris Lazerowitz, *The Structure of Metaphysics* and *Studies in Metaphilosophy*; and Jonathan Bennett, *Kant's Analytic* and *Locke, Berkeley, Hume: Central Themes* (83-88, on Ayers).

terns of university education. Whatever a philosopher's official position may be on the history of philosophy, his teaching activity involves him ever more intimately in discussions
of the great sources. This close relationship leads the responsive teacher to seek something more than a handy method
(whether phenomenological or analytical) for making an introductory reformulation and evaluation of the arguments
embedded in the texts. The humanistic tradition itself inclines
him to dispel any illusion that a first acquaintance with the
major philosophers of the past is sufficient to master them.
He seeks to help his students become critical of the view that
it is enough to achieve a hasty in-through-and-beyond relationship with the historical bases. Together, the teaching philosopher and his students seek to develop a more sustained
and critical approach toward the philosophical sources.
Personal cultivation of one or another of the historical procedures is an effective way of arousing that sense of further
meanings and difficulties yet to be explored, toward which the
humane study of philosophy leads by design.

Philosophical classics are those writings which show a staying power, not only from one generation to the next but also
for the *same* generation. Such works contain an implicit invitation to be revisited and re-read at constantly new levels of
engagement by the inquiring student. The latter is usually left
unsatisfied by his initial acquaintance with great philosophers,
made with the aid of introductory outlines of their main doctrines. He may then discover for himself the value of the
various tools of historical study of the sources, so that eventually he can penetrate the latter more intimately through his
own research. The liberally educated student need not become a historian of philosophy in any narrowly professional
sense, but he can rightly expect to take personal hold upon
some historically fruitful way of reading the sources and thus
to share in the historical manner of understanding them.

Especially when teachers use the problem-centered method
of presenting the great philosophers of the past, it is helpful
to keep the student keenly aware of other approaches. It

would be a deadening illusion for him to think that all the resources of history are exhausted by tracing out some typical positions on knowing and the known, mind and body, freedom and determinism, the cosmological and ontological arguments for God, and the chief alternatives on moral duty and goals. A well constructed survey is balanced by deliberately arousing some further questions and curiosity about those aspects still left untouched in such broad schematizations.

A humane intelligence will want to vary the perspective on these problems, look at them from the central focus of some great philosopher, and discover how his method systematically treats and unifies them. What issues and levels of meaning may be escaping us, for instance, if we do not patiently follow Spinoza's own manner of conceiving the relation between freedom and necessity, his general principles for redefining these correlative concepts, and the systematic function and ordering of the topic within his broader ethical conception of human striving? To ask such a question is to open out one's appreciation for the historical study of philosophy along another route. University education should not blunt but incite this questioning, and yet to satisfy its aim we have to reflect more closely on the nature and methods of historical inquiry.

2. A Working Hypothesis

A study of the kind of understanding achieved in history of philosophy is facilitated by the fact that this discipline is at least the partial subject matter for several lines of investigation. It is one point of intersection for some otherwise different ways of reflecting upon the meaning of history and historical knowledge. Broadly speaking, there are two main avenues of study: the *indirect or instantial* approach and the *direct or internal* approach. The chief interest of the former is to develop some general theory of history, within which the history of philosophy can fit as a determinate instance. The advantage of this indirect procedure is that it furnishes some very general canons, applicable to the several modes of historical work and hence capable of correcting the biases found in the isolated viewpoint of history of philosophy. However, the history of philosophy does have its own source materials, problems, and goals of clarification, so that it cannot be understood adequately from a purely instantial perspective. To respect its own patterns and standards of inquiry, the kind of understanding gained in history of philosophy must fundamentally be examined through a directly proportioned method, one that is primarily responsive to its own internal operation. My analysis will follow this direct and, with some degree of emphasis, internally oriented path.

To see why it is insufficient to make a purely instantial reflection upon history of philosophy from a more general level, we must consider the very capacious range of the term "theory of history." In current usage, this term covers three related but distinct fields of philosophical endeavor. They are: the speculative, the analytic or epistemological, and the phenomenological or ontological approaches to history.[10]

---

[10] (a) There is emphasis on the speculative strain in: W. H. Walsh, *Philosophy of History*; Frank E. Manuel, *Shapes of Philosophical History*; and Bruce Mazlish, *The Riddle of History*. A sometimes overlooked idealistic argument for synthesizing history and philosophy in the university curriculum is presented by F. W. J. Schelling, *On University Studies*, especially lectures 8-10, on the religious and artistic reconstruction of the meaning of history (pp. 82-114). —(b) The passage from speculative to epistemological and analytic questions about history can be followed in: R. G. Collingwood, *The Idea of History*; P. Gardiner, ed., *Theories of History*; W. H. Dray, ed., *Philosophical Analysis and History*; and *Ideas of History*, ed. R. H. Nash. —(c) Two influential German sources for the theme of historicity and human reality are: Wilhelm Dilthey, *Pattern and Meaning in History*, ed. H. P. Rickman; and Martin Heidegger, *Being and Time*, especially pp. 425-455. Karl Jaspers' *The Origin and Goal of History* synthesizes a speculative ordering of historical periods with an existential search for historical unity of meaning. The problem of historicity and metaphysical truths is probed in Emil Fackenheim's *Metaphysics and Historicity*. The correlation between modern historical consciousness and the modern development of historical studies is examined by D. R. Kelly, *Foundations of Modern Historical Scholarship*.

First, there is philosophy of history in the sense of a speculative search after the governing laws, stages, and goal of historical process itself. A long tradition of philosophers, theologians, and historians have sought to determine the phases and ultimate meaning of history from the standpoint of their respective general positions on man, God, and society. The main varieties of speculative philosophy of history compose together what R. G. Collingwood called "the idea of history." It does not enjoy an autonomous existence but gains relevance by interpreting the actual movements of cultures and institutions, science and technology. This correlation is well expressed in Frank E. Manuel's theme of the "shapes of philosophical history." The most confident and influential of these modern philosophical shapings were proposed by Vico and Herder, Kant and Hegel, Comte and Marx. They also set the example of including the history of philosophy within their speculative generalizations, treating its growth as a specimen of the laws and phases found everywhere in historical developments.

Today, however, we are interested in re-examining more closely the philosophical presuppositions upon which the speculative readings of history depend for their validity. Hence a second meaning for "theory of history" is that of an epistemological and analytic study of statements made in the historical mode. Here, the focus shifts from discourse *within* the historical framework to discourse *about* the historical way of speaking and the kind of cognition it may yield. At this meta-level, there are some primary questions under consideration. What distinctive use of language is being made by the historian; what is the intent of his narration; and is some ideal of objectivity either desirable or attainable? Can we best understand historical explanation by using a model analogous to one which holds for physical explanation through nomological and predictive statements? Or is there a distinctive interplay between explanation and interpretation, in historical accounts, which requires us to look for our model rather in the use of intelligence and language in the social sciences?

Not much headway has been made as yet in applying these key questions specifically to the work of the historian of philosophy, but such application is bound to clarify what the latter is doing in ways parallel to those of other historians.

A third contemporary kind of theorizing on history centers upon the temporality and historicity of man's being and way of knowing. This is the ontological and anthropological road taken by the phenomenologists and existential philosophers. Not being content with Dilthey's correlation between the act of historical understanding and the various life expressions and cultural categories, they search for the roots of historical knowledge in the act whereby human reality constitutes itself and organizes its worlds. From this inclusive basis, the historical character of every kind of method, science, and institution is traced to the basic historicity of man's activities in each region. Philosophers employing this ontologico-anthropological view of history are as concerned with history of philosophy as were the earlier speculative philosophers of history. Heidegger, for instance, correlates the history of metaphysics with the history of western technological attitudes toward nature. He maintains that the contemporary social crisis over attaining human values in the world matches that, in philosophy, over the meaning of being and its call upon human freedom.

It is necessary that history of philosophy be inspected through *all* these registers of the general philosophical theory of history. Whether the general meaning of history and historical understanding be conceived speculatively, or in terms of logical analysis, or in those of the phenomenology and ontology of man, it has an application to history of philosophy and brings the latter within some broader conceptual frameworks. But it is not safe to make an exclusively one-way, applicational or instantial study of the materials and procedures in history of philosophy. There must be some direct inspection of this discipline, so that the proper adjustments of the general level of theorizing about history can be made. Such adaptations would be arbitrary and insensitive to the distinctive nature of historical work in philosophy, were there not some positive guidance provided by a study of the intrinsic uses of intelligence in history of philosophy. These uses are not simply a prolongation or exemplification of some broader meaning of historical process and understanding, but constitute a direct human response to the materials, problems, and intents involved in our philosophical past. Hence the aim of the present study is to respect this historical actuality, seeking whatever light can be shed on it by a direct consideration of how the historian of philosophy goes about his tasks.

The method used for this inquiry is *the method of functional reflection*. As developed in use here, it operates within three specifying limits. (1) Functional reflection always hugs as closely as possible to the actual procedures and conditions found in history of philosophy. It does not exclude any general considerations taken from the several kinds of theory of history and historical knowing. But its own responsibility lies squarely in making a critical reflection upon the working materials, tools, and operations which together constitute the standpoint of historians of philosophy. (2) For purposes of the present functional analysis, the source materials in question are those belonging in the three centuries of classical modern European philosophy, 1600-1900, with the usual overlaps at both terminals. This restriction raises the problem of whether the findings concerning this period also hold good for the historical study of other eras in philosophy. Although this question cannot be firmly answered without making an actual test, it will be kept in mind here as pointing toward the ideal of a general theory of historical knowledge in philosophy. (3) Also for present purposes, the historians of philosophy whose procedures come under examination are, for the most part, men of the twentieth century. There is no intent of underestimating the pioneer historical research done in the previous century. But this limitation recommends itself, both as setting a practical range of cases where our historical resources are in play and as conveying a sense of direct continuity between the immediately previous generation of interpreters and ourselves, with whom the present opportunities rest.

It may be asked whether there is any real need for specifying a method so closely, merely in order to improve our understanding of modern philosophy. Certainly, we do have to be cautious in developing methodologies, and guard against their needless proliferation. However, it is widely recognized now that severe difficulties face anyone attempting to gain a more precise and detailed acquaintance with the chief modern philosophers than the introductory analyses provide. The method of functional reflection examines the ways of improving our historical access to modern philosophy. And the term "access" has been deliberately chosen here. It serves to convey three facets of the problem of relating contemporary readers to the primary sources in modern philosophy.

For all their modernity and continuity with present modes of philosophizing, these sources do lie in somewhat alien country removed from us by a passage of time and thought. When we open the pages of the master works, we find that these pages remain in some degree unmanifest. We are not quickly flooded with an understanding of the author's intent and argument, but rather discover the texts to be unobvious and somewhat resistant. Thus a first meaning of the term "access" is to express our awareness of the elusive thought and the unobvious text in modern philosophy. This carries with it a sense of the corresponding effort required to improve our historical understanding.

Secondly, this term enables us to take a toolmaking view of the history of modern philosophy. The latter discipline responds to specific difficulties, by devising the historical procedures which do enable us to cope better with the sources. The instruments of research and analysis are designed to open up the modern territory more fully to our exploring minds. Quite literally, they are the tools rendering modern philosophy more accessible to our understanding and use. And a final significance is that the access routes are bound to be many and not confined to just one way. There is a persistent, confirmed pluralism in historical studies of modern philosophy, a pluralism generated both by the many tools of historical investigation and by the many philosophical standpoints which prove their helpfulness by actually furthering our mastery and interpretation of the sources. In this pluralistic spirit, there is always room for devising new tools and for discovering new ways to relate contemporary philosophizing to the modern roots.

Within the limits set by the method of functional reflection, we can now propose a working hypothesis concerning what is involved in the complex phenomenon of doing historical work in modern philosophy. This activity is constituted by the presence and interworking of at least *three co-factors of ingrediency*. They are: (1) the insistent modern sources themselves; (2) the art of historical questioning; and (3) the interpreting present as developed in its several modes. These components are basic enough to permit us to grasp this historical process in its distinctive traits and limitations. But their basic quality consists, not in an elementary simplicity on the part of each factor, but rather in the persistent need for the active contribution of each one taken in all its complexities and variations. Hence in testing out the adequacy of this hypothesis, we must try to do justice both to the complex structure of each factor and to the requirement of keeping them related precisely as co-ingredients in a common activity.

Even in a preliminary view, it is clear that these factors attain their precise character, as fellow constituents of the historical effort to understand modern philosophy, only through their active interrelation. Taken by themselves, the basic texts are not sources of meaning *to* anyone. They acquire this co-ingredient function only insofar as they become the subjects of historical interrogation and reference to our own concerns. Similarly, the art of historical questioning is not developed in a vacuum, but is a specific response to the difficulties furnished by the sources. Such questioning depends for its drive and relevance upon the interpreting act of a present generation of students, so that it can become an interrogation *of* the past and *from* the standpoint of contemporary inquirers into history. And finally, the interpretive act itself can acquire the historical quality only through its direction upon the philosophical sources, a direction which articulates itself in terms of appropriate modes of questioning. Thus the unification of all co-factors of ingrediency is an active achievement, the continuing consequence of an effort at gaining historical understanding through their mutual reference and aid.

Because of the need for bringing the related principles together and reshaping them for always new historical tasks, our working hypothesis must include more than the co-ingredient factors themselves. There must also be distinct and explicit recognition of the personal unifying activity of the philosopher engaged in the historical study of modern philosophy. His presence does not add yet another component, but rather the operational basis for achieving the historical perspective and meaning. Without him, the texts would not become sources, the questions would fail to get formulated and revised, and the interpreting work would wither for lack of an active center. Just as the historically oriented philosopher cannot produce sources, questions, and interpretations out of whole cloth, so these components gain their unifying relationships and operational reality only through his intent to engage in historical study.

The correlation involved in our working hypothesis can be illustrated by the following diagram.

Historical Understanding of Modern Philosophy

	Center of Unifying
Co-factors of Ingrediency	*Interpretation*
1. The insistent sources	The philosopher actively
2. The historical questions	engaged in a study of
3. The interpreting present	modern sources

In order to appreciate the depth and variety of our engagement today in the historical study of modern philosophy, it is essential to take a broader rather than a narrower view of the active center of unifying interpretation. It will include those who identify themselves as historians of philosophy, in a rather restricted and specialized way, but it will also embrace all those other members of the philosophical community who are studying modern sources with the help of one or another type of historical procedure and mode of interpretation. Our historical understanding of modern philosophy is presently being advanced along many new access routes, so that all those actually engaged in historical work constitute a wide and differentiated group. They need not all be interested in raising the same questions, using the same historical tools, or relating their findings to the same set of current methods and categories. I regard this widening of the signification of "historically concerned philosophers" as being crucial for making a functional reflection upon the actual range of historical activities today, and hence as crucial for understanding and verifying the hypothesis under proposal.

As far as potential workers in the history of modern philosophy are concerned, they are faced at the very threshold with an acute problem which sometimes discourages them from doing any actual research. This problem can be formulated in general terms as a question concerning economy and originality. Can one afford to spend any considerable amount of time and energy in the historical approaches to modern philosophy? Even if pursued very selectively, will not such studies sap one's own confidence and opportunity for innovation, thus weakening the sense of originality needed for doing vigorous philosophizing? Can the student do justice both to a radical pursuit of historical meaning and a radical pursuit of some present theoretical aims?

These pressing questions are not raised here in order to manage somehow for their easy dismissal. Rather, they help us to perceive the need of examining the complex relation between all the resources and tasks of historical study and the freedom of the philosopher himself. A useful consequence of the issues discussed in the present chapter is that the difficulty about impairing or strengthening our creativity through historical work need not remain a purely abstract question. We can bring to bear upon it some pertinent considerations drawn from our initial view of the historical turn in contemporary philosophy.

One notable point is that any appeal to economy belongs within the larger context of the principle of philosophical mendicancy. All of us are needy inquirers, who cannot afford to close off any instruments and sources of guidance in our investigations. Even from an introductory study of the great modern philosophers, we come to realize the magnitude of our dependence upon them for problems and procedures, language and modes of judgment. It would be a dangerous policy of self-despoilment were we to refrain from doing any sort of definite historical study in these sources as related to our own interests.

Supporting this consideration is a second observation that, in point of fact, the rigid dualism between history and theory is proving to be untenable. The highways between the central modern sources and the main lines of present inquiry are much too complex, broadly ranging, and heavily traveled to permit a neat dividing wall to be built at an imaginary frontier. There is no good reason for sealing off our current philosophizing from reflection on historical developments. Of course, there is a problem in finding the right proportions for one's own synthesis between these two aspects of philosophical investigation, but it concerns emphasis and not separation. That is why a distinct role is assigned to the interpreting present within the process of historical understanding itself.

And finally, personal creativity need not be dampened by the demands of historical studies, although some tension does and should exist between them. Within the terms of our hypothesis, the philosopher who concerns himself with the modern sources must develop his own appropriate historical relationship with them. He is invited to frame the sort of questions which not only illuminate some classical texts but do so in a manner that also bears upon such present day issues as he is engaged in examining. Thus the free development of philosophical intelligence contains a historical phase, closely affecting the quality of new theoretical contributions as well. This mutual enlivening of source questions and present theorizing is nowhere stated more lucidly than in Gilbert Ryle's procedural rule:

> My exegeses are exercises of a fairly definite theory about the nature of philosophy, one according to which it is always proper to look, whether in Plato or in Locke or in Mill, for dialectical moves of the same sort as those which we, in the same quandary, would be tempted or proud to make. It will be fairly objected that in expositions that are governed by this, or by any other, controlling theory of philosophy, the author must necessarily have an axe to grind. The risk is a real one. But the alternative policy of expounding a thinker's thoughts without reference to his puzzles and difficulties is what has given us our standard histories of philosophy, and that is calamity itself, and not the mere risk of it.[11]

We must now inquire *how* both textual and critical responsiveness join in historical work that is philosophically alive.

[11] Ryle, *Collected Papers*, I, x.

II

The Insistency of Modern Sources

In functional terms, the historian of philosophy is an inquirer who finds his way around in some region of sources and who tries to aid others to achieve a similar familiarity. Whatever theoretical and cultural comparisons he may draw from other disciplines, they can never constitute the heart of his peculiar task. Primarily, he is responsible for accepting the discipline of the sources constituting a definite era of philosophy. His effectiveness is judged, above all, by the relative skill with which he makes everything else subserve the main work of improving our understanding and use of these primary texts. The business of the present chapter is to look more closely at how the primary writings themselves help to specify the problems and achievements in historical research into the classical modern philosophers.

1. JOURNEY TOWARD THE SOURCES

In trying to grasp the procedures used by the historian of modern philosophy, we sometimes employ Wilhelm Dilthey's notion of *Verstehen*, or the kind of understanding which is proportioned to the reality studied in the human sciences.[1]

---

[1] In *Pattern and Meaning in History*, Wilhelm Dilthey describes the broad range of expressive forms upon which the act of *Verstehen* bases itself. "Insofar as man experiences human states, gives expression to his experience and understands the expressions, mankind becomes the subject of the human studies. The interrelation of life, expression and understanding, embraces gestures, facial expressions and words by which men communicate with each other, permanent mental creations revealing the profundity of the creator to the man who can grasp it, and permanent objectifications of the mind in social structures in which human nature is surely and for ever mani-

It is reasonable enough to consult Dilthey on this matter, since he speaks out of the rich experience of his own historical research and philosophizing. But in order to profit from his reflections, the present-day investigator finds it necessary to disentangle them from a host of elaborations made by other students of the methodology and epistemology of the social sciences. Their liabilities need not be assumed by us, when we seek to obtain a few clues from Dilthey about the act of historical comprehending of the sources in modern philosophy.

The discussion about *Verstehen* is instructive, insofar as it spells out the inadequacies in three recurring types of reductive analysis: separative, psychologizing, and computerizing. Our historical understanding of the modern sources eludes examination when it is reduced either to some quite special and separative power of the mind, or to a purely psychological attitude and mood, or else (in reaction against the two former treatments) to an operation objectively constituted and described in computer terms. By these methods, the complex process of bringing our intelligence to bear upon the texts of the great philosophers is made to shrink into the form of but one of its aspects or analogies. Not unexpectedly, the resultant account is a caricature of that process.

It is misleading to speak about "the" historical understanding, since this usage can be taken to designate a special *separate power* of mind. The historian of philosophy does not have access to some esoteric faculty, reserved from the use

---

fest" (p. 71). Dilthey regards his main task as "a critique of historical reason . . . how the real principle of comprehension in the human studies can be gradually drawn forth from experience. Understanding is the rediscovery of the I in the Thou" (p. 67). In history of philosophy, this comprehension of the-philosophizing-I-in-the-statemental-Thou is not achieved through fanciful surmise or sheer empathizing, but through a textually founded discernment of the human act in its expressions. The historian's self-transcending move toward the texts in their originative, connected, and yet open-ended quality is examined by W. B. Gallie, *Philosophy and the Historical Understanding*.

of others. In placing emphasis upon an ever renewed reading of the basic texts in modern philosophy, he does so in a manner that regards such reading as a common obligation among philosophers and that operates by methods at the disposal of all who see the point of using them. Coming to see the relevance of historical procedures and findings does not depend upon an appeal to a separate power of understanding, but rather upon a reflective grasp of the broader conditions involved in every sort of philosophical work.

A study of the historical sources does constitute a distinct operational enrichment of the philosophical use of intelligence, however, in which operational sense it is proper to refer to the developments we make in our historical understanding and comprehension of the master works. Thus one way of removing the ambiguity in talk about *Verstehen* is to correlate the reference always with the method of functional reflection being employed here. For this compels restriction to the active-verb sense of accepting the discipline of the texts and focusing all comparisons upon the task of elucidating the source materials.

In every sort of inquiry, the general framework of problems, concepts, and tools used by the investigator affects the outcome, even when that framework itself is undergoing criticism and transformation. This common condition is just as pervasive in historical research as it is in physics and the life sciences. Whatever the differences required by the subject matter of investigation, there is a common logic of inquiry strongly operative in all these areas. Considered precisely as an investigative use of human intelligence, history of philosophy realizes in its own fashion the guiding relationship between the inquirer's general conception of method and basic interpretive concepts and his specific treatment of a philosophical source. Because of the analogous presence here of a common pattern of inquiry, there is no need to invoke some special power of the mind as the basis for gaining historical understanding of the classical modern philosophers.

By the same token, it becomes unnecessary to reduce the

historical effort at understanding these thinkers to a purely *psychological relationship*. Whatever the dispositions and skills helpful in history of philosophy, they must all prove their worth in the task of elucidating the primary texts. Conceptual and emotive ingredients in the historian's attitude do shape his framework of research, but their importance is measured primarily by the degree in which they improve his comprehension of the original argumentation. Hence the sort of *Verstehen* for which he stands responsible is not chiefly constituted by an act of empathy with the great philosophers of the past.[2] Empathizing projects may or may not help his activity in history of philosophy, but they cannot serve as the ultimate criterion of his findings. Expressed in oral and written form, his work must be construed fundamentally as a proposal concerning how we are to read and use the classical modern sources.

In terms of such reference, however, historians find that certain psychological attitudes (whether deliberately or unthinkingly entertained) do raise obstacles against a more effective examination of the source philosophers. Some reorientation of mind is required, not precisely to constitute the act of historical understanding but to modify the working suppositions of readers sufficiently to permit such a developing acquaintance to occur. At least four steps can be taken in the transformation of attitudes, so that we will be making a journey toward the sources and not away from them.

(a) An initial move is to arouse critical dissatisfaction with the preconceived schemas under which the sources are already organized. Before a young inquirer gets to work, he finds the modern philosophers being presented to him in a framework of chronology, periodization, and doctrinal classification. Since this ordering distills the work of previous

[2] Peter Krausser, "Dilthey's Revolution in the Theory of the Structure of Scientific Inquiry and Rational Behavior," *Review of Metaphysics*, 22 (1968-69), 262-280, makes a nonpsychologizing analysis of *Verstehen* and views it as one form of a pattern of inquiry common to the several sciences, not as an esoteric or highly restricted procedure.

investigators, it cannot be simply junked without risking the loss of some historical values. One does not gaze upon the beauty of Spinoza's system, bare and bereft of all classificatory means of reference and interpretation, any more than one gazes upon the beauty of Euclid's geometry bare. But one can come to realize more pertinently the nature of the relationship between all such referents and the source writings themselves. Otherwise, these dates, periods, and schools quickly operate as an apparatus estranging the student from the sources. When the framework of presentation intervenes for its own sake, it arouses a dispiriting sense of distance from the sources and a conviction that every aspect of them has been thoroughly examined, definitively restated, and forever captured in the formulas. Nothing would then be possible except a rote relationship or a manipulation of the formal schema, at an illusory meta-level of domination over the master works.

As an educational countermeasure, the historian can point out the instrumental and pliable nature of his chronological designations. Upon what grounds does one regard the date 1600 as roughly helping to locate the close of the Renaissance era in philosophy and the beginning of the three centuries of classical modern philosophy? Many correlations can be drawn from the history of science, political institutions, and art for attaching some pivotal significance to the decades around 1600. But they become a decisive focus in history of philosophy primarily because of the character of the work done by the philosophers of that time. The treatment of ethical issues by Lipsius and Du Vair has the quality of being both a closure and an opening: Stoicism and Christian morality are coadapted, and yet the basic questions about the human source of obligation are left unanswered. Montaigne and Charron undermine any vaulting claims of humanism for man's knowledge and dignity, and yet they are unable to make significant progress beyond the position of the Greek skeptics concerning the mathematical and natural sciences. There is a similar transitional note in the metaphysical ethics of Bruno and the induction of forms celebrated by Bacon. A new groundswell of philosophical activity is detectable, however, in the original responses made by Descartes and Hobbes to both the skeptical challenge and the mechanical system of Galileo. Thus after mid-seventeenth century, philosophical reconstructions in a new vein are undeniable.

The historian's judgment is shaped mainly by the philosophical work done by these source men, taken in their several relationships. Thus the date 1600 functions as an indical sign of the historical judgments made on the basis of the actual work of these thinkers, considered in relation to each other domestically and in relation to the developments in other disciplines and modes of life. Fresh work of historical revision depends upon a return to these governing considerations about the sources, which are never dominated by our classifications and hence which always invite revision. The essential revisability of every schema is the historian's way of affirming the principle of fallibilism in his own domain.

(b) A second step in our historical self-education consists in becoming critical of the monistic usage we customarily employ in discussing the work of the individual philosopher. Thus we speak confidently about "the" philosophy of Leibniz and "his" position on this or that issue in later seventeenth-century philosophy. Such references are at best ambiguous, and at worst are a hindrance to engaging in historical study of a philosopher so mentioned.

Ambiguity arises from one's failure to specify whether the definite description depends upon accepting some historian's general survey which so characterizes Leibniz, or upon independent analysis of some selected work such as the *Monadology*, or upon thorough developmental investigation of the several phases of Leibniz's reflection and writing. Only by specifying the basis of his relationship with the source, can the speaker determine his statement sufficiently to indicate either that he is repeating a conventional generalization about Leibniz which demands critical review, or is basing himself upon one work whose relationship with the whole authorship remains to be considered, or else is stating the outcome of a full-blown genetic study of the unity in Leibniz's thought. Evaluation of assertions about "his" position must await some clarification of the sense in which they claim a backing in the Leibnizian texts.

Sometimes, such indeterminate monistic references do not merely delay historical judgment but actively prevent it from operating at all. This is the case when a flat characterization rests upon the supposition that a philosopher's meaning and argument can be adequately determined from an analysis of individual statements, taken separately and without regard for their setting in the sources. The method here is to cast the philosopher's statements one by one into a common bin. In this isolated form, the attempt is then made to analyze their structure and formulate some logical principles for relating the atomic nuggets in a system.

The value and the shortcomings of this procedure were well illustrated in Russell's reconstruction of Leibniz's philosophy.[3] He called attention to statements which could serve as basic principles; he suggested how the basic statements might be interrelated and how they might determine specific issues in Leibniz's thought; and he showed the contribution of this philosopher to the growth of modern logic. Yet this reconstruction eventually impeded the historical understanding of Leibniz, in the degree that it excluded the role of the actual context and developmental relation among the primary sources in specifying the precise meaning of the statements chosen for Russellian analysis. Until the contextual and developmental aspects of a body of philosophical work are taken into account, the ascription of a position to a philosopher cannot be safely accepted as historically intended and founded.

(c) There is a third mode of expression which comes easily

[3] Bertrand Russell's *A Critical Exposition of the Philosophy of Leibniz* is criticized on historical and analytic grounds by Gottfried Martin, *Leibniz: Logic and Metaphysics*, and by Nicholas Rescher, *The Philosophy of Leibniz*.

to our lips, but which must be critically reviewed as a prelude to doing historical work in modern philosophy. "Well, I have Nietzsche nailed down. Now that I have mastered him, who is next in line?" This is an instance of the unthinking use of the language of mastery in regard to the source philosophers. The language of mastery is inappropriate here, both because of the illusion upon which it rests and because of the debilitating effect its use has upon our capacity for growth in historical understanding.

The illusory supposition is that the philosophical sources are inert objects, laid out there for our immediate intuition and waiting to be totally dominated by the aggressive reader. We can disabuse ourselves of this notion only by making the actual effort to work historically into the texts. For we soon discover that we cannot barge in quickly upon a philosopher, and simply wrest his meaning from him easily and upon our own terms of domination. Our reading of him must be vigorous and critical, but we succeed in sharing his meaning only to the extent that we forego any approach couched in terms of conquering rule and exhaustive control. To persist in relying upon these imperialistic dreams in the study of Nietzsche, for instance, is to find that his mind constantly eludes our grasp and that our suzerainty ultimately embraces our own formalities alone. Almost by definition, the elusiveness of Nietzsche and other philosophical sources is in direct proportion to the use of categories of mastery to determine the research relationship.

This mode of study also weakens one's historical resources by inducing premature satisfaction with the results. When a source is treated as a territory to be invaded and subdued, then the achievement of historical understanding can be rigidly demarcated and measured. But in the process, a substitution has been made of one's own fenced-off conceptual system for the originating sources. For a distinguishing mark of the latter is that they always retain a latency of meaning, which surprises us and demands a fresh act of interpretation. This constant renewal of historical questioning does not depend primarily upon the historian's modesty as a private trait of temperament, but rather upon his very realistic appraisal of the nonconquering nature of his relationship with the written achievements of the great modern philosophers. Through continued historical investigation, he can share in their discourse; he can offer critical evaluations and alternative explanations; but he cannot reduce them to fully controlled pawns on his private chessboard.

(d) The positive side of the three previous points can now be stated in a final rule for historical re-education. We must learn to comport ourselves toward the source men and their works *as we would toward a company of critical inquirers*, with whom we are in personal relationship. This rule of historical comportment can be followed without reducing historical study of the texts to a psychologizing operation, a claim of special empathy, or an esoteric type of cognition. Interpersonal knowledge does not furnish the historian with a separate logic of inquiry, but it does urge him on toward an understanding of the integrity of thought and experience present in each of his philosophical sources.[4] Hence the analogy drawn from interpersonal relationships reinforces his criticism of the accepted classifications, the monistic descriptions, and the imperialist aims found in many studies of the modern philosophers. Just as one cannot always deal with other persons through intermediary reports, programs, and categorizations but must directly respond to their actuality, so there is a point at which the responsible historian must subordinate every schema to his own critical reading of the philosophical sources. In doing so, he exposes his judgment about them to a radical openness for revision and new perspectives which

[4] Within the experiential and linguistic continuum, the mode of knowing in history of philosophy rests upon a responsive engagement with the whole expressive experience of source thinkers in both its particularity and its general statement. The continuity between scientific and humanistic thought is argued by W. T. Jones, *The Sciences and the Humanities*, whereas the act of interpersonal comprehension in historical and philosophical knowing is central for G. W. Morgan, *The Human Predicament*, especially chapters 8, 10, and 14.

finds its most striking analogue in the attitude fostering interpersonal activities.

What makes this comparison specifically instructive for historians of philosophy, however, is the operative phrase "toward a company of critical inquirers." The kind of interpersonal relationship which historians find most illuminating is that realized within a community of researchers. For the creative modern philosophers conduct their inquiries within a field of relevance, that is, with some definite consideration of what others have done and are doing on the issue. In becoming attentive to an individual philosopher's thought, then, historians must remain alive to this social aspect of the original source and of their own investigation. Moreover, the social bond under study is not only that between an originative philosopher and humanity at large but also the more closely specified professional one between himself and fellow philosophers, whose work he may regard as specially challenging to his own endeavors. Hence the fully determinate interpersonal analogy concerns a methodology which will improve our historical understanding of a distinctive group of critical inquirers, namely, those constituting the modern philosophical tradition. That is why psychological and sociological studies of group relations can supply suggestions, but not imperatives, to historians of modern philosophy.

2. Source Philosophizing as a Basal and Insistential Act

The danger of psychologizing away the meaning of historical knowledge has to be faced not only on the side of the historian but also on the side of the texts themselves. The latter could be regarded as personal expressions of the philosopher's mind in so private and trivial a sense that study of them would degenerate into a divination of psychic images, one being just as intense and unfalsifiable as the next. Against this dissolution of historical judgment, various countermeasures have been devised and built into the historian's craft.

Any proposed interpretation must show its ability to survive the test provided by reading a given text always in its context, by examining parallel passages in the same thinker and counterparts in philosophers with whom he may be arguing, and by giving weight to any general statements of method and systematic connection. Appreciation of the essential role of language in a philosopher's activity, especially the mutual relation between the expressive and the communicative functions of language, helps to keep his work open to inspection and revisable interpretations. The resources of computer technology aid all these confirmatory operations considerably by setting up various indexes for the collected sources, bibliographies of current scholarship, and (with only marginal success so far) internal analyses of language usage. The history of modern philosophy is a major beneficiary of computer research in the humanities.[5]

Perhaps we could push the *computerization* of the sources one step further, by eliminating every historical consideration of the philosopher's mind or intention. This would seem to give an absolute safeguard against the psychologizing of history of philosophy from the side of the textual materials.

[5] For instance, *The Philosopher's Index* (1967 ff.) computerizes current periodical literature and also banks the cumulative information in the Philosophers Information Retrieval System. Kant's collected writings are being submitted to electronic data processing for the *Allgemeiner Kantindex*, under Gottfried Martin's general editorship. Thus the *Personenindex zu Kants gesammelten Schriften*, ed. K. Holger and others, facilitates the comparative historical study of Kant in respect to his own sources and contemporaries. A machine-readable version of Kierkegaard's collected works has been prepared, so that this champion of subjectivity will be well served by computer research. Alastair McKinnon is editing *The Kierkegaard Indices* in several volumes, and he offers a sampling of the interpretive results in his study of the vocabulary density of the several pseudonyms: A. McKinnon, "Kierkegaard's Pseudonyms: A New Hierarchy," *American Philosophical Quarterly*, 6 (1969), 116-126. The philosophical limits of computer intelligence are explored by H. L. Dreyfus, *A Critique of Artificial Reason*, who distinguishes between the calculative function of artificial reason and the intentional functions of human reason, operating within a horizon of giving patterned significance to the processed data or bits.

They could be treated as a self-contained entity, understood apart from any reference to an author's intention and purpose. There would then be no problem of bringing textual meaning into the public domain, and no conflicting interpretations based upon the different ways in which historians conceive the philosopher's mind or pervasive outlook.

Although this suggestion is alluring in some respects, it does not fit the actuality of trying to gain a historical understanding of the modern philosophical sources. It suffers from two serious defects. First, there are no absolute safeguards in our world against the entrance of a psychologizing and arbitrary factor into the human study of the great writings. The historian cannot simply renounce his function of trying to make further sense out of the texts, and hence he cannot entirely avoid the risks involved in mounting and testing a new interpretation. There is nothing quite so heavy and inert, in respect to definite and available meaning, as the printed results of a computer's scanning run over the complete works of a philosopher. It still remains the historian's task to see some significance in word-frequencies, to suggest a hypothesis for comparing several treatments of a problem, and to catch the significance of reference names for enlarging his comparisons and checking upon his interpretation. He cannot abnegate these responsibilities by refraining from questions about the source author's intention, but he can subject them to procedures of control and correction. Between the extremes of absolute fantasy and absolute depersonalization, he learns to follow a more humane course of using all the available means for criticizing and improving the textual footing for his account of the course of argument.

The second reason for rejecting the total evacuation of the component of intentionality is that something valuable in the meaning of the sources would be needlessly lost. The loss is avoidable, once we notice the indeterminate character of the terms "intention" and "mind" which are under criticism. One way of rendering them determinate is, of course, by invoking a severely claustral, walled-in conception of the human mind and thought, so that in principle no access can be gained to the philosopher's basic aims. This would prevent historians from devising any satisfactory methods for evaluating and improving their statements about such aims. But in fact, historians need not accept this manner of specifying their study of a philosopher's mind and intention. They can disengage entirely from the imagery of piercing the walls of privacy and hence from the particular epistemological presuppositions upon which that imagery feeds.

The intention with which the historian is concerned is that conveyed in the philosophical texts themselves. This is the intention actually achieving itself, with varying degrees of adequate expression, in the sources available for study. When the actuating intention is rendered determinate in function of the source writings, it constitutes an accessible foundation for historical inquiries from many directions and a decisive testing ground for statements about the mind of the philosopher or his fundamental intention. What the historian strives to render always more comprehensive and precise is an understanding of the philosopher's *central textual intent*. Thus as employed significantly in the present theory of interpreting modern philosophy, the phrase "the intent of the philosopher's work" incorporates both a methodological avoidance of claustral imagery and an ordination toward better understanding of the argument which is actually set forth in the texts.

The importance of this theme of the central textual intent lies in its regulative influence upon historical research. In effect, it asks the historian never to separate the philosopher's reflective activity from his expressed achievements, especially those in written form. To pursue the former apart from textual statements is to become lost in a mist of surmise and fantasy; to examine the latter apart from any reference to their reflective source is to disintegrate a pattern and lose the context and connotations. This would mean the loss of those values peculiarly sought by historians. The quality of work done in history of philosophy depends upon the inquirer's ability to bind together, rather than pull apart, the actuating intention and the shapes of language constituting the written achievement. Source statements are difficult to comprehend, and yet enormously rewarding in the attempt to do so, precisely because they furnish the anchorage in history for this complex reality of the philosopher's intent.

The regulative goal of seeking to understand this textually displayed intent gives emphatic meaning to the historian's primary obligation toward the modern sources. For these writings are sources in the doubly operative sense of marking the basic conjunction between the *sourcing* mind of the modern philosopher and the *investigating* mind of the historian. Here are the headwaters nourishing and measuring every advance in historical research. The master works are literally resourceful: they continually offer new aspects of the philosopher's originative work, and thus arouse fresh efforts at interpretation on the historian's part. To call them great classical fonts of philosophy is to certify, from the long experience of historians, that these works do indeed open up a relationship with a center of active reflection which challenges as it illuminates, and which resourcefully conveys a power to offer still more meaning than the community of research has yet grasped about it. The historian need never fear that his particular statement of the central intent of such a writing will exhaust its significance and rob it of further interest. For his interpretation never totally contains and categorizes the personal spring of thought.

There is one point upon which the modern philosophers strongly agree with their Greek and medieval ancestors. They share a common conviction that the philosopher's primary duty is not so much to build a house of specific doctrines as to engage wholeheartedly in the *act of philosophizing*. They all locate the lasting import and worth of their work in the act of sharing in philosophical reflection, to which they subordinate the set features of their philosophy.

Among the modern philosophers, the act of philosophizing is brought to the forefront and explicitly thematized. In his introductory lectures on philosophy delivered over a long span of years, for instance, Kant liked to challenge the student accustomed by his earlier studies to concentrate upon learning this content or that body of knowledge.

Now he thinks that he will *learn philosophy*. But this is impossible, since he must now *learn to philosophize*. . . . Not so much the knowledge itself, but the method of philosophizing, must be taught. For this, however, it is required that the teacher himself have philosophized.[6]

Behind these dry observations lie two important stresses in modern philosophy: its paramount concern with developing new methods and its responsiveness to the image of Socrates, the prototypal teacher of philosophizing. Methodology sharpens our appreciation of the active principle of reflection involved in every formulation and settlement of philosophical problems. And the personal figure of Socrates is there to urge the reopening of issues, precisely on the philosopher's own initiative and in line with the wise policy of constant revision of all teachings.

History of philosophy cannot remain unaffected by the philosophers' own accentuation of reflective agency in their writings. What they intend to convey is not only a doctrinal position or piece of knowledge but a sense of philosophizing in a certain methodic fashion. Hence to share historically in the fundamental intent of some modern source is to gain some

[6] Immanuel Kant, *Vorlesungen über philosophische Enzyklopädie*, ed. G. Lehmann, pp. 18, 32. Hence Kant does not stress methodology solely from the standpoint of formalization and architectonic, but also from that of insuring disciplined engagement in personal reflection. "No one can call himself a philosopher who cannot philosophize. Now it is only by practice and independent use of one's reason that one can learn to philosophize. . . . We must, therefore, for the sake of exercise in independent thought or philosophizing, look more to the *method* of employment of reason than to the propositions themselves, at which we have arrived by its means" (Kant, *Introduction to Logic*, pp. 16, 17). History of modern philosophy bears out the pre-eminence of questions of method and reflective activity since Descartes.

understanding of the originative act of philosophizing, which realizes itself in the texts. The historian must include the dimension of reading a major source work as an achievement of the act of philosophizing, as one actualization of the philosopher's life of reflection. Such a reference does not add any new textual finding, but it does operate as a regulative principle for always seeking to establish a reflective relationship *from* a sourcing mind and *for* our own philosophical acts. From his recognition of the source work as involving a methodic process of philosophizing, a historian draws encouragement that the texts can still speak to him and that they can sustain his general interpretation of their active and unifying intent.

Modern philosophers are among the great witnesses to the reality of *basal acts*.[7] There are some actions which we perform directly, not just in the course of doing something else, and hence which manifest the personal-agency basis of human life. But the reality of basic acts is grasped through analysis not only of our everyday actions and talk but also of many other modes of human achievement and discourse. Thus our present theme of source writings and the act of philosophizing is laden with significance for the theory of basal acts. It leads to historical recognition of the presence of acts which are basic for constituting the tradition of master works in modern philosophy. What is implied in the historian's move from the Cartesians to Descartes, or from the Hegelians of Left and Right to Hegel himself? This orienta-

[7] On the distinction between actions-caused-to-happen and basic acts of the human agent, see A. C. Danto, "Basic Actions," *American Philosophical Quarterly*, 2 (1965), 141-148. As Danto puts it in *What Philosophy Is*, p. 130: "If there are any actions at all, there have to be these *basic acts* (as I term them), acts we do without first doing something else." One aim of history of philosophy is to orient us toward its own central field of basal acts, namely, those constituting the fundament or authorship of the primary sources in modern philosophy. For recent theoretical discussion and bibliography on action, consult *The Nature of Human Action*, ed. Myles Brand.

tion of research is in response to the foundational role of certain writings and of the basal acts of philosophizing communicated through them.

There is no question here of actions which are held to be simply immediate, or basic in unconditionally every respect, or somehow uncontaminated by the development of thought. Basal acts of philosophizing come to be within the context and history of human actions of every sort. Within this complex setting, however, some men do take the initiative in engaging in the distinctive work of philosophizing. Acts of philosophical reflecting are basal in a definite functional sense, that is, they serve as the creative ground and guiding purpose for the philosopher's specific arguments.

It is the basal act of philosophizing, on the part of a great philosopher, which gives his writings their identifying quality and rank as primary sources. Its operative presence unifies and orients his many particular statements, just as it constitutes a school or a tradition out of those thinkers who work out his implications still further. The historian of philosophy does not seek some secret inlet to the basal act of philosophizing, but tries to discern its effective operation in the philosopher's writings in whatever style and degree of completion. By making explicit reference to this act, the historian bears witness, in his own manner, to the personal agent or reflective mind striving to communicate method, argument, and vision through the texts which serve as primary philosophical sources.

In this close mutual relationship between the historian and the texts, considered in their basal-act reference, there is a sound foundation for the intelligibility of history of philosophy and the hope of continuing to improve our understanding of the sources. There is something distinctive about the reality developed in the history of philosophy and the kind of intelligibility achieved through the historian's work. The reality involved here cannot be resolved into a simple and onesided principle: it does not spring from the primary sources alone or from the historian's mind alone. Rather, its basis is essentially complex, being constituted by two interweaving lines of activity. History of philosophy is developed in and through the union of the textual source and the historian's inquiry. The adequacy of understanding attained at any given stage will depend jointly upon the condition of the text and the interpretive skill of the historian, so that changes in either component are bound to generate a new form of historical meaning in this always developing discipline.

Through the theme of the act of philosophizing, we learn to correct an excessively passive view of the sources and an excessively activist view of the historian's work. They are not related as in the analogy of clay and potter, but in that of a marriage between two distinct but intertwining and mutually adapted partners. By remaining keenly aware of the basal act of philosophizing and the originative personal agency or center of reflection, the historian is enabled to respect and study the texts in their own insistential structure. His understanding of them is more properly described in terms of becoming ever more familiar and involved with them than in terms of molding them at will, or taking hold of them as a conquered possession. The relationship is not proprietal in nature, but is closer to that of a discerning friendship.

History of philosophy finds its significant genesis in a two-fold opening. There is *the research opening toward the sources* on the part of the historian, employing all his resources and levels of interpretation. This effort at understanding is encouraged and sustained by *the originative opening from the sources* themselves. Out of this meeting springs that historical meaning which is essentially confluential or chiasmal: the-philosophical-sources-being-interpreted or, reciprocally, the-interpretive-act-being-textually-grounded. The contribution of history of philosophy to human values consists in developing and criticizing specific interpretations of the sources, together with the methodic instruments for assuring new acts of research and improved presentations of the sources.

The insistential reality of history of philosophy

critical judgment upon the
confluence and active
intertwining of

1. the research opening toward
the sources: historian's
basal act of interpreting
the context, pattern,
and arguments

2. the originative opening
from the sources: texts
considered as conveying a
basal act of philosophizing
and its structure

Out of this "double helix," there grows the complex actuality
of historical meaning.[8] The vitality of work done in the history of modern philosophy depends upon the inquirer's ability to achieve a fresh correlation of these basal acts, with
special consideration given to the methods, arguments, and
general aims of the great sources. To appreciate the demands
which these sources place upon the interpreting mind, we will
now consider a concrete instance of the originative opening
and textual insistency of a major modern philosopher.

3. THE DEMANDING TEXT OF DESCARTES

It is sound teaching practice to introduce students to modern philosophy through a reading and discussion of Descartes.
He is not the "father" of modern philosophy, it will be
granted, in terms of some exclusive genealogical line. Poly-

[8] The interweaving of textual source and historical inquiry finds
an analogue in the genetic model described by James Watson, *The
Double Helix,* and in Maurice Merleau-Ponty's image of the reciprocal intertwining or chiasm of the two faces of every act of perception,
The Visible and the Invisible, chapter 4 and pp. 264-275. The latter's
remark that "every relation with being is simultaneously a taking
and a being taken, the hold is held" (p. 266), illuminates the historian's relationship of perceiving the modern sources. The historian's
interpretive taking is itself taken and tested by the primary writings.
His hold is held—aroused and sustained, specified and modified—by
the sourcing thinkers who exercise their own insistential initiative.

centrism is a good working hypothesis here as elsewhere, since it calls attention to the independent types of philosophizing done by Cusanus and Bruno, by Bacon and Hobbes. But there is a functional sense in which Descartes does father in his readers a lively appreciation of the problems, methods, and conceptual principles which animate most early modern philosophical developments until Kant. This representative quality extends to our present topic of the insistency of modern philosophical sources, since the chief insistential traits are strongly present in Descartes. As Hegel puts it in his lectures on history of philosophy, the journeying mind (including the historian of modern philosophy) will cry: "Land!" when he sights the writings of Descartes, and will at last feel at home.

Although the *Discourse on Method* is not solely an essay in personal reminiscence, it does communicate Descartes' methodology and doctrinal program within a vivid autobiographical context. It places a personal signature upon all his writings, obliging us to refer them quite definitely to his own life of reflection. Such personal reference is not meant in any trivial egoistic sense, as though it merely describes some private episodes having no general philosophical significance and validity. But it does serve Descartes' dual purpose of grounding arguments in his own perspective and act of judging the evidence, as well as of eliciting a similar personal use of intelligence on the part of his readers. They learn to interpret his references to "I," "me," and "myself," in a composite sense which always keeps his general theory of self and mind closely related with a testing basis in his personal pursuit of the truth.

One consequence of taking Descartes' writings in relation to the sourcing center of inquiry which authorizes them is to make us distinguish between at least three meanings of Cartesianism. The term "Cartesianism" can be taken in an originative sense, a continuative or school-tradition sense, and one that is recurrent-thematic-classificatory-polemical in use. A parallel to these distinctions can be found in the historical career of most of the modern thinkers.

Originative Cartesianism consists of the personally developed thought and course of argumentation of Descartes himself, as expressed in his own writings as a whole. *Continuative* or school-tradition Cartesianism is constituted by the work of those other philosophers whose main intention is to analyze and clarify, defend and develop, the teachings of Descartes within the framework of his own method and principles. Some type of historical continuity is thus realized, so that these followers comprise a distinctive school of thought having intellectual dependence upon Descartes.

The third sort of Cartesianism is *recurrent*, insofar as it involves fresh use of a position of Descartes, but without necessarily being in historical continuity with him or working within the frame of a Cartesian school. This or that view of Descartes can be thematized within a new intellectual context, quite apart from the systematic interconnections it once maintained within his own philosophy. In this sense, "the Cartesian position" will be meant as a classificatory note for one standard view on the object of knowledge, the nature of man, or some other philosophical issue. The actual linkage with Descartes' own philosophical argument may be very remote and abstract. Frequently, there is a polemical intent behind the pure position thus stylized: it furnishes a convenient peg for stating and criticizing what one characterizes as a reification of thought or an untenable dualism of mind and body. The mention of "Cartesian dualism" within this third setting is therefore more schematic than historical, more argumentatively dictated than based on an independent examination of Descartes' works.

We often find ourselves strangers to originative Cartesianism, because of the prismatic intervention of the Cartesian school or the stereotyping of Cartesian themes in someone's dialectical argumentation. In this predicament, it helps to become aware of one's distance and, by working patiently into Descartes' own writings, to permit the insistential reality of his own way of philosophizing to communicate itself. As we develop this source relationship more on its own terms, however, we also learn more concretely about the need to relinquish the language of mastery and monistic reduction fostered by the third meaning of Cartesianism. For we recognize the fundamental impropriety of these modes of talk, if seriously intended to characterize and evaluate the work of Descartes himself. When we accept Descartes' invitation "to meditate along with me"—*mecum meditari*—we are already underway in the passage from Cartesius (the second and third senses of Cartesianism) back into the philosophical method and reflective argument of René Descartes (the originative act of philosophizing as it achieves communicable form in the source writings themselves).[9]

There are two major considerations, intrinsic to the Cartesian way of philosophizing, which may well impel us to seek historical understanding of the sources for their own sake, that is, with primary concern for their insistential reality. One is the theory of the various kinds of order with which the philosopher is confronted, and among which he must make a choice affecting the development and presentation of his own views. And the other is found in the very structuring and diversity of several major writings of Descartes—who takes his own theory of order seriously and reflexively enough to have it make a difference in the organization and interpretation of his treatises.

[9] Precisely at that point where he accommodates his critics by restating his main arguments in a *non*meditative, geometrical form, Descartes also repeats his invitation to meditate attentively along with himself, so as to consider the matter in a more metaphysical way. For this *mecum meditari* or *mecum rem attente considerare ac meditari*, see *Replies to Objections II*, in *The Philosophical Works of Descartes*, tr. E. S. Haldane and G. R. Ross, II, 50, 51; and *Meditationes de Prima Philosophia*, in *Oeuvres de Descartes*, ed. C. Adam and P. Tannery, VII, 157, 159. In chapter 7 of *Descartes and the Modern Mind*, A. G. Balz contrasts Descartes (as the fallible man and historical thinker) with Cartesius (as the school authority and timeless voice of reason). Closer to my own usage here is the distinction drawn by Wilfrid Sellars, *Science and Metaphysics*, pp. 24-25, 140-143, between the historical René Descartes and an analytically postulated Renatus, similar to that between Charles Peirce himself and a Peirceish method of projection.

A. THE CARTESIAN THEORY OF ORDER

The Cartesian theory of order is unusually complex and subtle, because of its emphatically self-referential nature. The texts presenting this theory are themselves a reflective exemplification of the very theme being investigated. There are at least four key aspects of this theory which affect the exposition of Descartes' own views, and hence which have to be kept in mind by anyone reading him in a historical vein. That Descartes himself is fully aware of the import of these four points for the historical investigator is clear from the context in which they are treated, since he never fails to apply them to someone's effort to comprehend his philosophy. Although he is not much concerned about the fate of philosophical sources written prior to his own time, he takes great pains to incorporate a regulative factor of interpretation, for students of his own thought, into these points in his study of order.

1. The order of topics and the order of reasons. Toward the end of 1640, Descartes submitted the manuscript of his *Meditations concerning First Philosophy* to several people in order to get some pre-publication comments. None of these responses was more eagerly awaited than that from his friend, Marin Mersenne, who enjoyed a large circle of theological and philosophical acquaintants. But Mersenne's reply irked Descartes, partly because it promised to deliver a theologian's reply in eight days (whereas Descartes remarked dryly that it might take longer just to assimilate what he was doing), and partly because Mersenne's own objections indicated a failure of minds to meet on the metaphysical issues. He expressed doctrinal disappointment about the looseness of the *Meditations*, which scatters the topics of the conceptual distinction between mind and body and their real distinction in the existing order, and which fails to draw out the implication of either type of distinction for the soul's immortality. Mersenne felt that the work lacked sufficient tightness to deal with metaphysical problems in a well ordered and unified way. But Descartes' prompt response made it clear that there was a fundamental difference between them about what constitutes proper organization in a philosophical work, and hence also what constitutes an authentic basis for interpreting his own manuscript.

Descartes draws a pivotal distinction here between the order of topics or subject matters and the order of reasons (*l'ordre des matières* and *l'ordre des raisons*).

It is to be noted, in everything I write, that I do not follow the order of subject matters, but only that of reasons. That is to say, I do not undertake to say in one and the same place everything which belongs to a subject matter, because it would be impossible for me to prove it satisfactorily, there being some reasons which must be drawn from much remoter quarters than others. But in reasoning in orderly fashion from the easier to the more difficult, I deduce from thence what I can [at this point], sometimes for one subject matter, sometimes for another. In my estimate, this is the true path for satisfactorily finding and explaining the truth. And as for the order of subject matters, it is good only for those men, all of whose reasons are disjointed, and who can say as much about one difficulty as about another.[10]

[10] *Letter to Father Mersenne, December 24, 1640 (?)*, in Descartes, *Oeuvres philosophiques*, ed. F. Alquié, II, 301. Although here I make my own translation in order to sharpen the relationship between the Cartesian theory of order and my topic of the insistential source thinker, it is useful to consult Descartes, *Philosophical Letters*, tr. Anthony Kenny, p. 87, as well as the extensive use of this correspondence in A. Kenny's own *Descartes*. Descartes adds that, however receptive he is to Mersenne's suggested stylistic changes, he will not accept alterations that destroy the sense of his argument. The order of reasons is understood as a systematic entailment of arguments by Martial Guéroult, *Descartes selon l'ordre des raisons*; it is broadened to include a steady reference to Descartes' comprehensive and presystematic vision of the world by Henri Gouhier, *La Pensée métaphysique de Descartes*. My own present analysis of the Cartesian conception of order is intended to bring out its *auto*referential shaping of Descartes' own writings, along with its proportionate *allo*referential demand placed upon the conscientious historian of philosophy. For a detailed case study of this interplay between auto- and alloref-

The note of irony and reform in this last sentence should not be lost upon us. The Cartesian revolution shows itself more strikingly in the mode of reasoning on a topic than in the topics themselves, which seem traditional enough. But in stressing the kind of good reasons and the manner of reasoning as the chief principles for ordering his discourse, Descartes is unavoidably criticizing the mentality centered around the content topics.

He repudiates the ideal of trying to deal exhaustively with one subject matter before passing on to another. For this supposes that the supporting reasons for a position are all equally available, at some sole place where the topic is to be discussed. Arguments of this sort are available only because they are "disjointed," that is, because they are lacking in those systematic connections generated through the philosopher's long-range study of the evidence and its directional significance. The content-centered mind can say just as much about one difficulty as another, precisely because it says nothing based upon a personal inspection and gradual unification of the many reasons or evidential sources contributing to a warranted judgment, as it can be made at a particular stage of argument.

Descartes himself organizes his discussion around the good reasons which he can bring out at some specific phase of inquiry. From this perspective, he sees that not all the considerations bearing on a given subject matter are directly available for use. Some reasons enter here in the form of relatively remote inferences from basic principles; others must be newly perceived in the present state of inquiry; and still others must await some further questions before their relevance and evidence can be assured. Thus the Cartesian order of reasons or evidenced stages of inquiry seeks to reach as much of the truth on a number of issues as is warranted at this specific stage, rather than pretend to wring one issue

---

erences in shaping one area of Cartesian philosophy, see James Collins, *Descartes' Philosophy of Nature.*

completely dry before passing on to the next. It is only from the latter standpoint that Descartes' path of reasoning seems to be loose, repetitive, and arbitrary.

To show that he is actually criticizing the topic-centered ordering of a philosophical treatise and replacing it with a new metaphysical ordering, dictated by the inquirer's own growth in well evidenced principles and arguments, he adds a Synopsis or thread-of-reasoning overview of the *Meditations*. Its aim is to remove any confusion between the distinctive order of reasons opened up in that work and a norm of metaphysical sequence based upon the traditional linkage of subject matters. A further function of this Synopsis is to place a special demand upon historians of philosophy to notice and state explicitly the consequences of the Cartesian reordering of metaphysical reasoning.

2. *Order in things and in my perception of things.* Descartes gives his own stamp to the venerable distinction between the order of beings and the order of knowing. In the order among beings, it would be proper for a theistic philosopher to begin with God and then proceed to a study of the material world and man, considered (as they are in the medieval *Summae*) precisely as the outcome of divine creative activity. Yet an approach which would be proper enough in a faith-regulated context does not suit the situation where Descartes finds himself, namely, one in which that principle of faith is either contested or variously interpreted or else suspended within skeptical brackets, as far as concerns having any foundational role for settling the speculative issues in philosophy. Because he addresses himself to basic questions within the framework of his own age, Descartes is therefore compelled to explore and accentuate the order of philosophical knowing in much more radical fashion than was heretofore deemed necessary. He has to find grounds in his own experience for accepting the existence of God and even that of the material world. Hence he cannot avoid beginning with the method of doubt and the existential intuition of the

active self, with the aid of which he then treats of God and the physically described world.

The insistential quality of the Cartesian text comes out in many letters and critical discussions, which show the significance of determining the order of knowing by means of the methodology of doubt. The central role of that methodology in setting the course of inquiry indicates that Descartes is not just making a minor modification in the ordering of knowledge. Instead of cultivating an order of knowing which is already embedded in an assured and sacred order among beings, he develops an order of knowing which is responsive primarily to skeptical questioning and his own search for existential evidence, as the basis of assent and progress in philosophizing. Hence the Cartesian philosophy does not already concede a well established correlation between the two orders, but regulates the philosophical theory of ontological structures and causal relations by the warranted reach of whatever principles of knowing manage to survive the doubting process.

In the crucial move of calling into doubt our assent to the existing material world, for instance, Descartes also modifies the available starting points for theistic inference and the working meaning of God. The inference itself becomes more an exploration of implications of selfhood than an exercise in physical theology. And the meaning of God thus reached must always include a basic reference to the existing, reflective human self. There is a similar reshaping of the problem of man's unity, proportionate to the Cartesian conception of the order of inquiry. The human enigma is interpreted in terms of reconciling the metaphysical assurance of an existentially independent self or Cogito with the compelling experience of one's intimate union with his own body and emotive states. In every instance, the doctrinal meaning depends upon the principles and relationships worked out at some particular stage in the use of methodic doubt.

Descartes' point is that there is no standard meaning for "the order of knowing," and that his sense of the phrase can be gathered only from observing his expressed intent and practice. Hence instead of invoking the familiar contrast between the orders of being and knowing, he often prefers to distinguish between two ways of reading his own texts. They can be interpreted as organizing the inquiry either around *the order of the truth itself of the thing* or around *the order of my perception* (*in ordine ad ipsam rei veritatem* or *in ordine ad meam perceptionem*).[11] Descartes' way is the latter rather than the former. This does not mean that he is unconcerned to find the truth about the thing, but rather that he cannot disengage this truth from the process of searching and working it out. The reader of Descartes is thus being asked to become specially sensitive to this fundamental question: What warrants me to regard some particular statement about a thing as true? He is being advised to read every Cartesian text with a concern for maintaining an order of priority of the reliable perception of a thing's reality over every truth assertion made about that thing. In this way, the sourcing philosophical mind sets an imperative of the understanding for the historical investigator.

Descartes uses the personal possessive form deliberately in stating this exegetical principle of maintaining "an ordination toward *my* perception," since he is interested in evoking a personal act of apprehending the thing's reality. The danger is that the personal basis may be taken so privately and idiosyncratically that it affords no reasonable ground for a truth assertion about the thing. This objection is forcefully stated by Descartes' contemporary, Pierre Gassendi, who maintains

[11] *Meditations concerning First Philosophy*, Preface (Haldane-Ross, I, 137, 138; Adam-Tannery, VII, 8). In his earlier *Rules for the Direction of the Mind*, rules 8 and 12, Descartes had already made a careful methodological distinction between things themselves as they really exist (*res ipsae*, or *res singulares prout revera existunt*) and things as attained by the understanding or as ordered to our knowing act (*res prout ab intellectu attinguntur*, or *in ordine ad cognitionem nostram*), and had founded his judgments upon the latter respect. See the revised text of *Regulae ad directionem ingenii*, ed. G. Crapulli, pp. 31, 45.

that "my thought is not the rule for the truth of things." As a Christian skeptic and Epicurean, Gassendi is by no means scandalized by the Protagorean thesis about man being the measure, but he wants to restrict the measuring to the order within our own perceptions, and prevent it from counting as a determination of truth assertions about reality in any further sense.

Since a major principle for interpreting his own writings is at stake, Descartes is careful to treat this difficulty in detail. Gassendi's point seems weighty only because it trades in on a threefold ambiguity in the words "my perception" or "my thought" (*ma perception* or *ma pensée, perceptio mea* or *cogitatio mea*).

[1] If anyone wants to say that my thought ought not to be the rule for others, for obliging them to believe a thing because I think it true, I am entirely in agreement about it. But that is not at all to the point here. For I have never wished to force anyone to follow my authority; on the contrary, I have noted in several places that one should permit himself to be persuaded only by the evidence alone of the reasons. [2] Further, if one takes the word "thought" indifferently for every sort of operation of the soul, it is certain that one can have several thoughts from which one can infer nothing touching the truth of the things which are outside of us. But that also is not to the point in this case, where there is question only of the thoughts which are clear and distinct perceptions, and of the judgments which everyone must make on his own account in consequence of these perceptions. [3] That is why, in the sense in which these words should be understood here, I say that each person's thought, that is, the perception or knowledge which he has of a thing, must be for him the rule of the truth of that thing. That is to say, all the judgments which he makes about it must be conformed to that perception, in order to be sound. . . . Hence it is the most absurd and expensive error that a philosopher can commit, to want to

make judgments which are not related to the perceptions which he has of the things.[12]

Descartes does not remove all difficulties through this clarification, since he does not make explicit here the connection between a personal search for clear and distinct perceptions and a use of the method of existential doubt. But the quoted passage does show us an instance of a philosopher opening out to his readers and seeking to aid their effort to understand his thought. Thus the Cartesian interpretive principle of attending to the order set by my tested perception constitutes one of those visible, encouraging meeting grounds between the historian of philosophy and his insistential sources.

3. Weak and strong ordering. Descartes' carefulness to foster intelligent communication with his readers extends even to the form of his works and his style of writing. In casting his chief metaphysical treatise in the mold of "meditations on first philosophy," he deliberately employs an unusual form in order to alert readers to his unusual course of reflections. On several counts, the term "meditations" has an unsettling effect upon conventional expectations, whether among Descartes' contemporaries or among students historically related to his work. The expectation is that a treatment of metaphysics will be executed in the impersonal mode of either the Suarezian metaphysical disputations or in a new geometrical framework; that meditations belong in the family of spiritual exercises and not in that of philosophical argument; and that any mixing of these forms is bound to be disastrous for rigorous philosophy. But Descartes himself feels obliged to dissolve this expectation, as a first step toward providing readers with the requisite guidance for interpreting his distinctive path in metaphysics. Hence "meditations" serves as a cue word, signifying that Cartesian metaphysical investigation is not wholly impersonal but is regulated by a reference to my

[12] *Letter to Clerselier, January 12, 1646* (Haldane-Ross, II, 128-129; Alquié, II, 843-844). Here and throughout this book, I have revised existing translations wherever advisable.

own act of securing doubt-resisting evidence, or well tested perception, of the existential reality of myself and other actualities. The personal engagement of spiritual meditations is here joined with the methodological demands of existential claims put under fire.

But why do you not go one step further, asked one group of critics, and present your thought in the even more compelling form of a geometrical manner of writing? Descartes was not reluctant to furnish them with a sampling of his metaphysics as expressed in the geometrical style of definitions, axioms, and postulates, followed by theorems and lemmata. Having satisfied his critics thus far, however, he also felt bound to observe that much more was involved than a purely optional choice of styles and devices. It was not a question of choosing indifferently among modes of expression as one would among utensils made elsewhere and rated on a standard scale, but rather of doing one's philosophizing *in and through* that use of language which is most appropriate for the work being done, and most effective in communicating its sense to others. Sensitivity to the intimate union between philosophizing and communicating was not only a characteristic mark of Descartes' mind but also an indispensable condition, set by himself, for our achieving some valid historical understanding of his specific approach to problems.

Just how closely the question of Descartes' mode of writing —he refers to it as "that mode of writing I have chosen above others"—is bound up with theoretical considerations, can be seen from his distinction between *a weak* and *a strong meaning* of order.[13] In the weak sense, the order of reasoning refers simply to the rule of putting first things first, i.e., of beginning with those meanings and judgments which can be known independently of other points, subsequently to be demonstrated. In this weak meaning of order, Descartes always follows a geometrical manner of writing: his entire work is

---

[13] The supporting texts for this distinction, quoted here and in the fourth paragraph below, will be found in *Replies to Objections II* (Haldane-Ross, II, 48-51; Adam-Tannery, VII, 155-159).

organized around a project of first setting forth the principles of knowledge from which to move in the study of reality. The only difficulty comes in determining *which* statements can indeed serve as principles or evidential beginnings of inquiry. For its settlement, Descartes relies upon his internal philosophical theory of methodic doubt and meditational inference, rather than upon an already given extrinsic form of presentation. The Euclidean model is weak at this point, since it cannot specify the evidential grounds for treating a definitional statement as a first principle of metaphysical inference.

Hence to appreciate Descartes' thinking on how best to match inquiry with expression, we must turn to the stronger sense in which philosophical reasoning gets ordered. The decisive point concerns the relationship between the methods of analysis and synthesis. Whereas the classical geometers rightly gave the primacy in their science to synthesis, Descartes proposes a reversal in favor of analysis as the foundational method in philosophy. The synthetic way moves coercively from principles (the definitions, axioms, and postulates) to the proof of theorems, but it has the disadvantage of failing to show evidence for acceptance of the operative principles themselves. At least in philosophy, this is a fatal defect because it holds one captive in a skeptical suspension of assent to the truth of the principles and their inferred consequences.

Descartes refuses to adopt the geometrical manner of writing as his primary means of expression, because it reflects too closely the methodological primacy of the synthetic way of demonstrating. He remains unimpressed, for instance, by Hobbes' claim to be the pioneer geometer of the philosophy of man and society. Hobbes follows a synthetic mode of exposition which never reveals to his readers the analytically inspected grounds upon which they should accept his principles of motion, as applied to human nature. In the Cartesian philosophy, the way of synthesis and the geometrical style of writing must be kept firmly in an auxiliary position. They help to sharpen the intellectual habit of simultaneously scrutinizing the details of argument and surveying the entire course of reasoning, but they remain silent about primary metaphysical questions on truth, our perception of things, and the reality-basis of our principles.

Insofar as his mode of writing springs from a philosophical concern with such foundational questions and encourages others to share a similar orientation, Descartes prefers to use the distinctive form of a philosophical meditation. It is the mode of writing most suited for leading his readers into the analytic way of reasoning on metaphysical principles, and of finding an existential referent for every stage in a systematic reconstruction of philosophy. In the philosophical meditation, he finds a proportionate instrument for arousing a critical stance toward sensation, for discovering the existential reality of the human self, for clarifying and testing out the primary concepts and principles in their involvement with this existential basis, and for focusing attention upon the inferential relationships being developed from the Cogito situation to God and the physical world. Since all these operations comprise a functional description of the analytic way of demonstrating metaphysical propositions, there is a happy marriage between the manner of writing and the effective primacy of the analytic method. Descartes works in the meditation style to achieve maximum economy, both in his own effort to perform tasks previously left undone and in aid of historical investigators seeking a reliable lead into his kind of philosophizing.

In one passage where he discusses this deliberate proportioning of literary form to the demands of analytic and existential reasoning, Descartes expresses a concern not just for "my readers" but quite specifically for "the minds of those desiring to learn . . . in what way the thing was discovered." His writings are intended to arouse a sense of co-discovery in the minds of his readers, who are asked to remain critically dissatisfied until they fathom the originative grounds of his principles. This is precisely what the strong or analytic ordering of inquiry, expressing itself through the recollective meditation, is designed to do. "It shows the true way through which a thing has been discovered methodically and, as it were, from what is prior" in the realm of evidence and assent.

In the Cartesian shaping of texts, no split can be permanently tolerated between the path of discovery followed by the sourcing philosopher and the path of study followed by his historical interpreters. Hence Descartes recommends his own union of analytic reflection and meditative writing as *vera et optima via ad docendum*, as the true and best way of teaching others the Cartesian process of discovering and testing the evidential bases in philosophy. Whatever its comparative value, it does show an extraordinary sensitivity to the interpreting aims of others and an artful development of the means for improving their genetic understanding of the sources.

4. The retrospective and prospective aspects of order. Descartes' solicitude on this score is perfectly matched, however, by the equally stringent demands he places upon anyone seeking to enter sympathetically into the dynamism of his reflections. His type of analysis does not terminate in piecemeal results but serves the broader cause of philosophical vision and systematic reconstruction. Cartesian analysis is a methodic way of developing the continuity of philosophical reasoning, through testing it step by step and thus gradually building a more comprehensive human wisdom. Hence there is room and need for the synoptic use of intelligence, as long as the connectives are subjected to scrutiny and as long as some grounds are found for moving cautiously ahead. The values of synthesis are recovered at the heart of the analytic movement of reflection, rather than imposed from without on a postulatory basis. The meditation form of writing is perfectly adapted for breaking down the conventional antithesis between analytic carefulness and synoptic interest in the unity and direction of philosophic work.

The proportionate response which Descartes expects from his interpreters, in recognition of this kind of continuity, becomes evident in his distinction between *the retrospective* and *the prospective aspects of philosophical order.* Once the process of reflective inference begins, Cartesian analysis is responsible for exploring and unifying the various relationships which hold at some present phase of the inquiry. The goal is not to effect atomistic separation and bifurcation, but rather to discern the leading threads of meaning which bind a presently thematized reality with other subjects of cognition. Within the ongoing process, these relationships reach out retrospectively to modify the previously analyzed topics, and reach out prospectively to open a path toward the examination of new ones. Descartes formulates this twofold perspective succinctly in his own Synopsis of the *Meditations*, when he states that the consequence of every newly acquired truth must be both a strengthening of what has gone before and a coming to know what still remains to be considered (*ad praecedentia firmanda* and *ad reliqua intelligenda*).[14] Cartesian reflective analysis is thus empowered to carry a radiant and unitive quality into every particular problem, enriching our understanding of previous steps in the search for wisdom and directing us more intelligently along the remaining course.

In several instances, Descartes attributed his critics' misunderstandings to their failure to recognize the hermeneutic principle contained in his distinction between the retrospective and the prospective workings of philosophical order. The School theologians, whose opinions were solicited on the *Meditations*, seemed to be specially insensitive to the retrospective canon. They failed to see, for instance, that Descartes' analysis of the idea of God has a retroactive effect upon the earlier problem of human memory and the generalizing of the causal principle. Once the existence and nature of God are considered, Descartes is able to cast further light on the reliability of our powers of memory and general inference. Neglect of this same canon also rendered the university schoolmen insensitive to the contributions which sense

[14] *Meditations*, Synopsis (Haldane-Ross, I, 142; Adam-Tannery, VII, 15).

experience, opinion, and the emotions do make to his meaning of man, once they are rehabilitated. Retrospectively, such factors show that the pure thinking self is not the entire reality of man, and that the actual world of bodies is far richer than the definition of an extended thing.

On the other hand, Gassendi's peculiar blind spot was produced by leaving the prospective canon in disuse. His scattershot technique of objecting to a host of Cartesian positions, wrenched completely from their context and cumulative function in the sustained course of argument, thwarted any helpful discussion. Descartes could do little more than warn him to study the distinctive sort of synthesis or coherence produced by a retrospective-and-prospective ordering of the analytic reflections. "For I consider it [the coherence of what I have written] to be such that, to the proof of any one matter, all the stages which precede it contribute, as well as the greatest part of those which follow."[15] Along with making a diagnosis of the weakness in contemporary critical practice, Descartes was also supplying a reading guide for historians of philosophy. At least, their accounts of his thought could compensate for their distance in time with a more adequate conception of the reflective continuity in his writings.

Since a similar ideal of the constantly self-modifying character of philosophical inquiry faces readers of Spinoza and Kant, Hegel and Dewey, it may be useful to examine the precise Cartesian sense in which preceding positions get strengthened and subsequent knowledge gets anticipated during some particular argumentation. How can previously determined positions, especially principles, be affected at all by later investigations? The problem is not too acute in the specialized regions in philosophy of nature and ethics. There, the principles are often hypothetical in some respect, so that subsequent work is intended to test and verify the hypotheses through a process ordained to modify their original meaning. But even in the case of nonhypothetical metaphysical prin-

[15] *Replies to Objections V* (Haldane-Ross, II, 226; Adam-Tannery, VII, 379).

ciples, Descartes aims at producing a noticeable difference in their import through his further course of reflections. A metaphysical principle gets strengthened: (i) by being shown to be actually fruitful, when the mind bases further inferences upon its implicatory power; (ii) by becoming integrated within the process of systematic review, where its cumulative role in the whole enterprise is clearly fixed for attention; and (iii) by getting gradually adjusted to the play of later positions, so that their jointly constituted meaning can finally emerge into view. There is a certain delayed significance which cannot be rendered explicit at the first reading of a Cartesian text on principles, but which develops in the degree that the reader notices the retroactive influences at work in the remainder of the inquiry.

The other question concerns the prospective function of principles, or how they contribute to the better understanding of subsequent matters. This is bound up with Descartes' carefully selective reference to certain truths as being "basic," "important," and "so great" in import. These are not honorific titles, but are earned indexes of certain thematic meanings which decisively shape the direction of his philosophizing. Especially the existing, reflecting self and God earn the right to belong in the rank of such pivotal truths. (i) Meditating upon them, the philosopher is able to join expectation with memory, is able to look forward toward new prospects of knowledge as well as backward toward cognitive origins. (ii) With their aid, the philosopher can bring an orderly pattern and orientation into his scattered inquiries, marking out some lines of inquiry as more accessible and fruitful for a human philosophy. (iii) Thereby, they nurture our desire for wisdom and happiness together, thus keeping alive the central teleology of philosophy in every age and intellectual climate.

B. DIVERSE STRUCTURING

The four key distinctions on order, which I have singled out here, are Descartes' primary assurance that his writings will convey the authentic sense of his philosophizing, both in content and in manner of approach. These principles of interpretation are formulated explicitly in his effort to insure a proper understanding of his most original and fundamental book, the *Meditations*. But they are also operative throughout his other writings, serving as a port of entry and a reminder to respect the distinctive organization and flow of argumentation in each treatise. Thus the diverse structuring of his writings constitutes another index of Descartes' insistential opening toward us.

The historically instructed reader will not expect the topics of self and God to be pursued in the *Discourse on Method* with the same concentrated intensity and thoroughness as they are in the *Meditations*. But he will also be responsive to the peculiar intent and values communicated in the *Discourse*. There, Descartes employs "the artful I" in a superbly modulated range of uses. It has an autobiographical aspect, ringing true in its historical details and adding the note of personal engagement and attestation to the modern way of philosophizing. At the same time, the first personal usage is admirably suited to the programmatic character of the work. Descartes is sketching out what his rules of method are, what his safeguards are for practical living, and what hopes he entertains for systematically re-doing all the major problem areas in philosophy.

Here is an instance where the synoptic mode can be followed, just as long as the vision of a unified philosophy grows from some principles of methodic control and some exercise of personal intelligence, which must proceed painfully step by step toward the goal. What Descartes gives us is, more precisely, the prospect and program of a synthesis yet to be worked out. The ideal of a unified philosophy animates the reflections of the discourser himself, as he sets forth his as yet unactualized plans, and also adds a further dimension to our study of the analytic samples of his work. The *Discourse* confronts the reader with achievements in Cartesian geometry, optics, and meteorology, not merely as being impressive accomplishments in themselves but as harbingers of an even richer philosophical vintage.

Just how vigorous the insistency of modern sources becomes, can be experienced as one moves from the *Discourse* and the *Meditations* to the *Principles of Philosophy*. In the latter work, we find Descartes adapting himself to the university audience of his day: it is in some respects a primer and a lexicon for a scholasticized generation. Numbered paragraphs and compact definitions and distinctions abound here, as they do in the contemporary manuals of school philosophy. To this extent, the *Principles* marks the transition from the first to the second of the meanings of "Cartesianism" set forth above: it puts us on the road from the originative Descartes to the tradition of Cartesian Scholasticism, such as dominated continental universities during the second half of the seventeenth century.

But this book represents a school philosophy with some disturbing differences, since it is still a source work of Descartes himself. The problem of skepticism is taken very seriously, and along with it comes the method of doubt and an order of reasoning which still moves from the self to God to the world. Furthermore, the *Principles* is a textbook intended for students entering fully into the age of the new science, since it stresses the Cartesian laws of physical movement and the mechanistic description of perceptual qualities. And by emphasizing the limits as well as the positive scope of the mechanical principles, when they enter into scientific analyses of particular phenomena in our experience, Descartes maintains his epistemological honesty. He himself does not cross over the border into unrestrained dreams about a total mechanical explanation of reality and a univocal kind of certitude about physical and practical problems. Such restraint may have been cast aside by enthusiastic Cartesians of his own time, but now it cannot be ignored by historically prepared interpreters of the *Principles* as a demanding text.

Finally, we may notice how a distinct cluster of his writings

—namely, his Letters, Replies to Objections, and Conversation with Burman—prompts us to develop the theme of "the available Descartes." As a corrective for both the biographical talk about a masked or deceiving Descartes and the methodological talk about a solipsistic Cogito, there is the vast trove of the eight volumes of his *Correspondence*. Some letters serve the same function as journal articles do today, since they give reports on work in progress or deal with specific points of criticism. But they also retain their irreducibly epistolary character, showing that the act of philosophizing flourishes under highly contingent circumstances and as a response to particular occasions of challenge within the philosophical community. Descartes reveals himself in such contexts as adapting his argument and expression to the concrete requirements of different correspondents and their connotative use of terms. Under pressure from Mersenne and his circle, for example, he states his position very soon on the eternal truths and the divine freedom—doctrines which affect all of Descartes' subsequent inquiries and yet which are never enunciated as clearly elsewhere. Similarly, it is the socially available Descartes who meets the request of Princess Elizabeth of Bohemia for his ethical and religious views, which are fortunately outlined in his correspondence although never fully developed in a systematic treatise.

From the standpoint of textual insistency, Descartes' *Replies* to the objections systematically obtained from readers of his *Meditations* belongs in this same category of functional availability. Through the good offices of Mersenne, Descartes obtained the seventeenth-century equivalent of a Schilpp volume of critical essays on his philosophy representing the full horizon of his contemporaries: the School theologians and Arnauld, Hobbes and Gassendi. His detailed rejoinders showed that, while moving away from a disputational and refutational conception of philosophizing, he nevertheless accepted the discipline of critique and response.

The depth of Descartes' engagement in these discussions manifests him as being, not the ego-locked awareness of some caricatures, but a functioning member of the community of philosophical inquirers. The *Replies* gives the historical interpreter a heuristic lesson from an incisive teacher who elicits objections and treats them responsibly. Indeed, it is Descartes himself who determines the standard framework for three centuries of recurrent Cartesian criticism on circular reasoning, the mind-body split in man, and the assumptions about cause and substance. Here we catch the source philosopher in the act of putting his thought at the disposal of a long historical tradition of discussion, upon which each new generation of students of modern philosophy learns to feed.

Descartes made himself intellectually available, not only to men of settled reputation, but also to young people and their fresh difficulties. His *Conversation with Burman* contains the record of what today we would call a student reporter's interview with an important philosopher.[16] Two years before his death, Descartes conversed at length with Francis Burman, a 20-year-old Dutch university student. They ranged quite frankly over the whole field of originative and continuative Cartesian problems, both those aroused by his writings and those currently under discussion in the Leyden University classrooms.

This interview gave an opportunity for Descartes himself to place unusual stress on the experiential type of certitude, which is not wholly formalizable and reducible to clear and distinct ideas. He acknowledged the limitations in his theory of the mind-body distinction, but also set the record straight concerning the order among his convictions: first comes the fact of a composite union in man, and then comes a theory about substantial distinction and unity. His highlighting of the experienced union, rather than the argued otherness of mind and body, exactly reversed the classroom practice of the Cartesian professors. Burman elicited some afterthoughts,

[16] Charles Adam has edited the full Latin text, along with French translation and notes, in René Descartes, *Entretien avec Burman.* Here Descartes makes his own lively surrejoinder to the university and seminary critics of his *Meditations, Principles of Philosophy,* and *Discourse on Method.*

also, on what was already being called the Cartesian circle in our reasoning to God. Descartes even branched out into his interpretation of Genesis and his ideal of joining Biblical thought with the new mechanistic sciences, so as to realize the goal of a modern theistic humanism.

What he permitted to emerge from this interview was a set of important qualifications upon his claims for knowledge and wisdom. These interpretive qualifiers were already present in his main writings, but were now given a special emphasis and authorization for those readers who could henceforth be related to his philosophy only through a reliable historical understanding of the texts. Opening out his mind in this helpful yet insistent fashion, Descartes furnished a generous exemplar for the modern philosophers to come, as well as a beacon of hope for today's students of his books.

4. THE COMMUNICATIONAL SPECTRUM

Taken as a group, the classical modern philosophers make use of an extraordinarily rich and diversified spectrum of means of communication. They do not cast their thought into several literary forms indifferently and merely for variety's sake. The choice of form is carefully made; the variation serves often to clarify and improve the philosophical speculation itself; and in the act of communicating, new virtualities are found for the medium. Hence in reflecting upon a few of these communicational forms, we can appreciate the persistent effort of modern philosophers to employ a broad span of literary modes so that the insistency of their meaning will be, not esoteric, but accessible and functioning within the tradition of historical interpretation.

(a) *A master work in fitting form.* The musician Anton Webern has remarked that to live is to defend a form. This is as true for philosophical vitality as for artistic, provided that we take the defense of form broadly enough to include the creative innovation which brings forth the fitting form for developing and communicating the philosopher's argument and vision. Especially when engaged in bringing forth his master work, the philosopher seems to be aware that there is no standard pattern to follow, that he must modify and freely experiment with the previous modes of expression, and that his chosen presentation will be somehow unique and unfamiliar. Hence there is a wide variation among the chief landmarks in modern philosophy, corresponding to which is an equally diverse range of perceptions demanded of the responsive reader.

Coming upon Spinoza's *Ethics* as a monumental achievement, we are apt to think that doctrine and literary deployment are wedded here according to some foreordained ritual signified in the subtitled words: "demonstrated according to the geometrical order." But in historical fact, Spinoza had to search painfully over many years for his appropriate medium, whose sense of inevitability is an artful triumph reached through many tries and failures rather than a transcription of a given formula. He explored the capacities of commentary and analytic formalization, dialogue and essay, before finally reaching the precise form of writing which could best convey his own reform of the human understanding.

Whereas Descartes had regarded the synthetic mode of writing in geometrical fashion as a secondary tool, Spinoza erected it into the primary instrument for ordering human arguments in accord with the highest mode of definitional perception and with the idea of the primary cause and substance. Thus the style of the *Ethics* was intended to ratify and render unmistakable the Spinozistic correction of the theistic and creational approaches in metaphysics and ethics. Yet Spinoza never surrendered his intelligence to an automatic Euclidean schematism. Amid the impersonal flow of definitions and explanations, axioms and theorems, he found room for exploratory lemmata on the nature of bodies, for psychological detours on the problem of freedom and immortality, and for maxims helpful toward building an image of the virtuous life. These features of the *Ethics* are not departures from its plan but signatures of the shaping mind of its author, striving to reach all aspects of his reader's awareness.

Leibniz was an appreciative reader of Spinoza, yet felt no obligation to reduplicate his predecessor's approach. Indeed, it would be difficult to find philosophical masterpieces so contrasting in appearance as the *Ethics* and Leibniz's *Discourse on Metaphysics*. The latter does its job in only 37 propositions and scarcely twice that many pages. Each point is developed descriptively and with frequent use of the first personal pronoun. Yet Leibniz is justified in referring to this work as a basic statement of his system.

From this brief essay, we learn to appreciate a concentrated way of philosophizing. It displays the principles of contradiction, sufficient reason, and substantial perfection in concrete play; it subjects each issue to analysis from both the metaphysical and the moral standpoints; and it views every finite being as both an active expression of God and a harmonious correlate of all other agencies in the universe. Reading the *Discourse on Metaphysics*, one is skillfully introduced into a philosophy of plural substances (versus Spinoza's monism of substance), perduring and intrinsically active principles (beyond Cartesian inert extension and discrete physical entities), and complementary relationships between mechanical and teleological explanations (opposed to any split between the kingdoms of nature and grace). The very compactness of the presentation enables Leibniz to convey the importance of a personal perspective, an openness to new circumstances of thought and human policy, and thus a concern for adapting the systematic themes to the viewpoint of actual interpreters. His style not only instructs us about his meaning for freedom and contingency but also disposes us to expect a different rendering of his philosophy in the *Monadology* and other short treatises.

However dissimilar in tone and structure, Hegel's *Phenomenology of Spirit* and Nietzsche's *Thus Spoke Zarathustra* are alike in manifesting the philosopher's readiness to launch an unfamiliar form of composition, which nevertheless suits his distinctive reading of experience and furthers its ultimate communication to mankind. Seemingly without regard for literary niceties, Hegel plunges into a tangled jungle of investigations expressed in a technical and highly allusive language. Only a few trail markers enable us to follow his path of discoveries, as it moves from a study of direct consciousness of things to self-consciousness of the alienated mind and moral agent, and thence into the higher plateaus of culture and history, religion and philosophical knowledge. Yet the thought at every stage is vibrant with an effort to reflect upon the modes of human experience, thus inviting the reader to make another try at grasping the total movement of spirit at work in the pages of the *Phenomenology*. Persistent students of this book eventually come to share in Hegel's project of living through and reflectively criticizing the pluriform shapes of life—which means that he successfully introduces them to the theme and method constituting his entire philosophy. In retrospect, then, readers of the *Phenomenology* are able to transform it from the ponderous monolith of first appearance into the very economical and well structured instrument of philosophizing that it is for the patient historical interpreter.

From quite another direction, Nietzsche scandalizes the conventional expectation about a philosophical masterpiece. Whereas such a work is supposed to be weighty, prosaic, and unemotive, *Zarathustra* presents itself as a diaphanous, highly poetic, and emotionally charged piece of writing. It is filled with parables and songs, exhortations and hymns (whose musical potentialities can be perceived in Richard Strauss's related symphonic poem, *Hence Spoke Zarathustra*, 1896). Metaphor is the explicit medium, so that both the progression of thought and the unification of the themes are achieved through the development of master images of the prophet and the crowd, the ultimate conforming man and the radically transforming superman. Here, the reader's difficulty is to discover anything except the fiats of a Zarathustra, the pleasing garlands of imagination, and the shock phrases hammering against current idols. Nietzsche requires one to work toward the presence of philosophical intelligence and to acknowledge that truth is often blocked by psychological habits and social rules of conformity.

Thus the very form and style of his book enable him to continue the tradition of the philosopher as critical moralist and as proposer of a new pattern of values. "The most cautious people ask today: 'How may man still be preserved?' Zarathustra, however, asks as the sole and first one to do so: 'How shall man be *overcome*?' "[17] With steely insistence, Nietzsche keeps proposing this central question of human revaluation and self-transcendence, and keeps refusing to reduce it comfortably either to accepted moral and religious ideals or to an evolutionary modification of human genes which would evade the critique of values and goals. His use of story and poem is perhaps the most direct way of bringing men to face the issues as formulated by his philosophy. Thus *Zarathustra* represents his solution for obtaining the most economical adaptation of philosophical argument and general intent to the communicative and persuasive power of language.

(b) *The strategic introduction.* It is a safe rule of thumb that we should never ignore or glide over a philosopher's "front matter": the dedicatory letter, preface, or introduction to which he devotes so much care. Not only does the modern philosopher want to state the circumstance and concrete context of composition, the general tone and intent of his work, but he often wants to present in a preliminary form some of the essential problems and principles of the entire inquiry. Just how much importance he attaches to the introductory materials can be seen, when we consider some of the services which they perform for their author and for ourselves as interpreters.

One function of such materials is to furnish the dispositional imagery which conveys the spirit and approach of a

[17] Friedrich Nietzsche, *Thus Spoke Zarathustra*, tr. R. J. Hollingdale, p. 297.

philosophy, in memorable form. Thus Descartes takes the occasion of a prefatory letter to the translator of the French version of his *Principles of Philosophy* to depict his philosophy as a great tree, having metaphysics as its roots, theory of nature as its trunk, and the practical disciplines as its fruitful branches. Not only does this metaphor give us general orientation about his aims, but it also has a context for answering Heidegger's question about the kind of soil into which the metaphysical roots are plunged, namely, the dynamic relationship between man's basically sound mind and his search for humane wisdom. Indeed, it is to this letter and Descartes' accompanying dedication of the *Principles* that we must turn for the main texts of his conception of philosophy as a growth in wisdom.

Another influential metaphor for the nature and ordering of philosophical inquiry is presented in the introduction to Hume's *Treatise of Human Nature*. To bring home the centrality of the study of man in respect to all other philosophical and scientific topics, he advises us, "instead of taking now and then a castle or village on the frontier, to march up directly to the capital or center of these sciences, to human nature itself; which being once masters of, we may every where else hope for an easy victory."[18] In the same place, Hume makes his basic recommendation of using the method of experience and observation in moral or humane subjects, together with his phenomenalist postulate about the limits of experiential knowledge. Certain conditions are thus laid down at the very threshold, so that a careful study of this entrance soon repays itself with an understanding of Hume's central goal of becoming the Newton of the moral world organized by human nature.

Locke and Berkeley are also past masters in the art of

[18] David Hume, *A Treatise of Human Nature*, Introduction, ed. E. C. Mossner, p. 43. The famous Appendix to the *Treatise*, pp. 671-678, where Hume frankly discusses the inadequacies in his theory of belief and of self, is his essential counterpoise to the program of anthropological phenomenalism so confidently announced in the Introduction.

packing a great deal of argumentation, implicit as well as explicit, into their opening pages. Locke does not permit us to move very far into the *Essay concerning Human Understanding* without calling attention to some crucial points. His epistle to the reader proposes that the operations of the understanding are a pleasurable sort of hawking and hunting, and that everyone should verify Locke's assertions by his own experience rather than by abstract given definitions. We learn that a balance must be struck between the diversity of minds and the philosopher's drive toward generalization, and that the aim is to obtain some modest working certainties and probabilities rather than a rigidly demonstrated totality. Whatever his nostalgia for the grand linkage of propositions in the school manuals and the continental systems, Locke is involving readers at once in the passage toward a new scene of thought. Hence it is in the introduction to Book I of the *Essay* that he alerts us to "this historical, plain method," to his very pliant meanings for "idea," and to the ensuing importance attached to an analysis of the grounds and degrees of belief and opinion.

As for Berkeley's introduction to the *Treatise concerning the Principles of Human Knowledge*, it carries the full freight of formal argument. For it is here, at the very outset, that he traces speculative and moral skepticism back to a false theory of abstraction and a misconception of the purpose of language. Without ceremony, the Irish philosopher raises important questions about whether there are any abstract ideas fitting Locke's description, how words can have general meaning and use without supporting the myth of abstract ideas, and whether the emotive and dispositional uses of language are not as important to consider as its use for theoretical communication. Berkeley develops his critique of abstraction so much in depth that the introductory sections themselves constitute a major part of the *Principles*, a precondition for grasping the sense and the consequence of his positive development of empirical immaterialism. An entire philosophy is being introduced here, just as Spinoza's *On the Healing of the Understanding* is a methodic introduction to another philosophical universe.

Using the negative criterion, we may ask what loss would result from omitting the prefaces and introductions composed by Kant and Hegel. Such omission would deeply impair our comprehension of their works. In the case of Kant's first *Critique*, it would mean loss of his image of the Copernican turn or the revolution in thinking wrought by one mind, as well as his guiding emphasis upon the problem and kinds of metaphysics. He would not be riveting our attention at once with his provocative statement that "I have therefore found it necessary to deny *knowledge*, in order to make room for *faith*," that is, for the practical data concerning God-freedom-immortality.[19] We would also lack the orientation furnished by his division of judgments, his stated search for those of an a priori synthetic type, and his reversed conception of truth (a conformity of objects to the questioning mind) in accord with the model of a Newtonian researcher into nature.

Without the prolusory materials of Kant's moral *Critique*, we might not appreciate the full strength of the difficulty of making a transition from the theoretical order to that of practical reason. It is here that he also brings home the altogether pivotal nature of the concept of freedom for his moral philosophy as an interpretive balance to his later stress upon universal duty. We are forewarned about the severe limits of a moral critique which is concerned about resolving general practical antinomies and reaching general foundations of duty, but which is not equipped as such to determine specific types of duties. And the several versions of the introduction to the *Critique of Judgment* serve as a clear signal, by their length and comprehensive scope, of how essential they are for understanding Kant's synoptic view of the nature of philosophy, considered both as critique, as architectonic, and

[19] Immanuel Kant, *Critique of Pure Reason*, Preface to Second Edition, B xxx, tr. N. K. Smith, p. 29.

as doctrinal reconstruction. Readers are ill advised to plunge directly into the specific problems of esthetic and purposive judgment, without first gaining their bearing on the general theory of judgment and on how this study of nature and freedom integrates the entire critical enterprise.

Hegel's prefaces and introductions comprise a literature of their own, a world within the world of his philosophy, so much so that they are sometimes printed as a separate unit and made the subject of entire seminars and commentaries. It is to this part of the *Phenomenology*, for instance, that we must go for firm clarification of the Hegelian absolute as joining the traits of substantiality and subjectivity, for the developmental and social meaning of experience, and for the ultimate equating of philosophy with a scientific knowing of truth in its evolving course. To slight the preliminary paragraphs of the *Science of Logic* would be to miss Hegel's exalted conception of his logic as reaching a perfect union of form and content. For there he prepares readers to catch the ontological import of his treatment of specific issues, by proposing the radical identification between speculative logic itself and metaphysics.

All these fundamental topics are reworked in the several prefaces and introduction to the *Encyclopedia of the Philosophical Sciences*. Here is one of the best places for following Hegel's evaluation of his empiricist, Kantian, and romantic predecessors. He distinguishes his inclusive position of dialectical and speculative reason carefully from the partial approaches of other scientific, religious, and philosophical methods. Furthermore, no one who examines the text of his introduction to the *Philosophy of Right* can fail to notice the prominence given to the will and the struggle for freedom, and hence to include these aspects explicitly in the Hegelian meaning of social rationality and the state. It is to the preface of this same work that we owe those two enigmatic statements over which the commentators linger and disagree: "what is rational is actual and what is actual is rational," and "the owl of Minerva spreads its wings only with the falling of the

dusk."[20] A unique function of the well wrought preface is to
arouse our interest and critical study through just such pithy
dictums, which can puzzle and provoke us until we are prepared to make a careful historical study of the whole work
into which they lead.

(c) *The philosophic dialogue.* Plato's shining example has
always challenged thinkers to express the tensions and movement of their argument in dialogue form. Even when they
cannot hope to rival his artistry, many modern philosophers
nevertheless take the risks attendant upon this medium in
order to explore its communicational possibilities. At the very
point of passage from Renaissance into classical modern philosophy, the dialogue is used as a primary mode of writing by
Giordano Bruno. It enables him to convey the dramatic quality of his thought just as naturally as the play form conveys
that of Machiavelli and the Elizabethans.

What is specially remarkable about Bruno's dialogues is
their broad philosophical range. Highly metaphysical issues
concerning the unicity, infinity, and divine nature of substance are worked out in *On the Cause, Principle, and One.*
But the dialogue presentation leads us to better appreciate the
resistance of many people to this revolutionary view of
reality. The dialogal form of *On the Infinite Universe and
Worlds* enables Bruno to mount a detailed critique of the
Aristotelian cosmology and theory of natural place, so that
his own protagonist for an infinite universe "will have at once

[20] G. W. F. Hegel, *Philosophy of Right*, Preface, tr. T. M. Knox,
pp. 10, 13. The German text of this Preface, as well as those accompanying Hegel's *Phenomenology of Spirit, Science of Logic,* and *Encyclopedia of the Philosophical Sciences*, has been separately published, along with a commentary, by Erwin Metzke: *Hegels Vorreden,
mit Kommentar zur Einführung in seine Philosophie.* Translations of
Hegel's introductory lectures *On Art, Religion, Philosophy* are edited
together by J. Glenn Gray. Walter Kaufmann's translation of, and
commentary on, the Preface to the *Phenomenology*, in his *Hegel*, pp.
363-459, is a good example in English of how much can be gained
from a careful study of the "front matter" of a great philosopher.
Basic sketches of positivism are drawn in Auguste Comte's *Introduction to Positive Philosophy*, ed. F. Ferré.

cut the roots of one philosophy and implanted those of another."[21] But Bruno also seeks to show the moral consequences of his epistemology, metaphysics, and cosmology.
The moral teleology of his speculative investigations is reinforced by the use of the same literary form in his ethical
writings: *The Heroic Frenzies* and *The Expulsion of the
Triumphant Beast*. These dialogues suggest that there is a
dramatic continuity between the obstacles encountered and
the reforms achieved in all areas of philosophy and social
living.

British philosophy is far richer for the dialogue countribu-
tions made by Berkeley and Hume. Students find *Three Dialogues between Hylas and Philonous* a skillful introduction
both to the philosophical way of conducting an argument and
to the specific positions of Berkeley himself. He displays the
care and artistry which effectively enhance for us the insistency of modern philosophical sources. His interlocutors em-
body in personal depth the difficulties raised by the Lockean
way of ideas, the skeptical implications of every philosophical
conception of matter, and the value of an empirico-religious
interpretation of knowledge and the universe. Like Bruno,
Berkeley achieves a carry-over effect by also casting his moral
thoughts in dialogue form, in *Alciphron, or the Minute
Philosopher*.

Even more effective for showing how a philosophical tool
can also be a work of art is Hume's *Dialogues concerning
Natural Religion*. It serves as a basic sourcebook both for the
empiricist critique of arguments for God's existence and for
the emerging discipline of philosophy of religion. This book

[21] Giordano Bruno, *On the Infinite Universe and Worlds*, annotated
translation included in D. W. Singer's *Giordano Bruno: His Life and
Thought*, p. 362. In A. M. Paterson, *The Infinite Worlds of Giordano
Bruno*, pp. 173-92, there is an axial exchange of letters (written in
1709-10) between Leibniz and John Toland on the incipient impact
of Bruno's dialogues upon continental and British Enlightenment. In
one of the earliest uses of the term, Toland refers to "the Pantheistick
opinion of those who believe no other eternal Being but the Universe"
(p. 184). This moot opinion stirs the German philosophers from
Herder and Jacobi to Hegel and Schelling, with unifying expression
in F. W. J. Schelling's 1802 dialogue *Bruno*.

truly develops a complex position in and through the interchange of the three main participants. They remain sufficiently elusive and personally charged to sustain the beginner's interest, and yet still furnish interpretive challenges to veteran students of Hume. The Scottish philosopher opens himself outward toward us through careful description and critique of opposing views in natural theology, through his own sallies of imagination and satire, and through the manifest courage of his mind in rethinking the human meanings of God, religion, and moral responsibility. There is also a much defter use of language and the natural rhythm of discussion here than in the ponderous and lengthy *Dialogues on Metaphysics and on Religion* of Malebranche.

Perhaps the dialogue is specially favored during the French and German Enlightenment as a provocative, yet socially safe, way in which to explore new paths in moral and religious matters. Voltaire's *Philosophical Dialogues and Anecdotes* is not just a dodge against the censor but a remarkably lively instrument for criticizing accepted ideas on passions and virtues, forms of government and articles of the creed. Diderot manifests the opening-out tendency of the philosophical sources even more strikingly in *Rameau's Nephew* and *D'Alembert's Dream*, interior dialogues which Hegel rightly hailed as an intense expression of the divided modern consciousness and social alienation. The interplay of dialogue and dream gives Diderot sufficient imaginative room to test a wide range of hypotheses on the nature of God, the presence of life throughout the universe, and the diversity of moralities. As he remarked in a letter to his mistress, "I much prefer to have people say, 'All the same, it isn't so crazy as you might think,' than 'Pay attention to these words of wisdom I am about to utter.' "[22] Dialogues provide sufficient give-and-take and an atmosphere of tentative thinking to save

[22] Denis Diderot, *Letter to Sophie Volland, September 11, 1769;* quoted in Denis Diderot, *Rameau's Nephew and Other Works,* tr. Jacques Barzun and R. H. Bowen, p. xi. That nothing prevents an imaginative historian of the Enlightenment from himself using the dialogue form, is shown by Peter Gay's *The Bridge of Criticism,* with Lucian, Erasmus, and Voltaire as interlocutors.

philosophers from their occupational temptation of always pontificating, in heavy-going prose, about their favorite ideas.

J. G. Herder takes full advantage of the dialogue situation created in his *God, Some Conversations* to criticize the prevailing intuitional, fideistic, and moral approaches to God from the standpoint of a revised Spinozism. Thus he can avoid embroilment in the bitterest phase of the controversy on Spinoza and atheism, while nevertheless exercising his full freedom to propose a more immanent and vitalistic theory of God's relation with nature and man. And we seem to have come full circle in the modern cultivation of the dialogue, in Schelling's work entitled *Bruno, or On the Divine and Natural Principle of Things*, where a similar conception of God is formulated for its synthesizing power. Bruno himself is made to speak with the accent of German Romanticism, advocating a philosophy of ultimate identity between the visible living cosmos and the world of knowledge. The conversation closes with Schelling's suggestion for uniting in polarized relationship the four persistent directions taken by modern philosophies: materialism and intellectualism, realism and idealism. He regards dialogue as the most suitable instrument for bringing these tendencies into a speaking relationship and thus within focus for a new synthesis.

(d) *Essays and discourses.* Montaigne and Bacon are recognized within their national literatures as supreme practitioners of the art of essay writing. This form is very effective for furthering the former's philosophical plan of exposing the speculative pretensions and encouraging the chastened moral ideal of men of all ages. It also helps Bacon to deal informally, and yet reflectively, with humane problems even within a philosophy centered in the study of physical reality. More significant for our task of instantiating the modes of textual insistency, however, are those cases where a philosopher already adept at the more elaborate sort of treatise nonetheless makes the effort of presenting his position in the concise and accessible essay.

British philosophy is definitely enriched by the essay

achievements of Hume and Mill. One way of regarding the relationship between Hume's *Treatise of Human Nature* and his two *Inquiries* concerning human understanding and the principles of morals is to view the latter writings as a reformulation of selected topics from the *Treatise*, but done in more pointed and readable essay style. This intent is clearly indicated in the original title which the first *Inquiry* bears: *Philosophical Essays concerning Human Understanding.* By comparing this *Inquiry* with Book I ("Of the Understanding") of the *Treatise*, we can supply ourselves with a laboratory specimen of how the transformation occurs and what philosophical changes it induces. Hume was moved to make this adaptation, not only on the grounds of satisfying his ruling passion for literary fame but also on those of restating his argument in a different perspective and emphasis. In the age of Addison and Steele, his own *Essays, Moral and Political* (together with his somewhat more elaborate *Four Dissertations*) allowed him to range still more widely over the esthetic and social aspects of human nature, and to do so in an informal yet precise style which was comprehended and discussed by literate men everywhere. His hope of becoming the Newton of the moral world through the application of experimental philosophy to moral subjects—that is, to man considered in his passional, political, and religious acts and beliefs—found an instrument for its partial realization in the essay mode of treating such areas.

What Mill calls the logic of the moral sciences receives its actual fleshing-out chiefly in his numerous essays.[23] In his hands, the philosophical essay does not merely rephrase doctrines established elsewhere but assumes creative responsibilities of its own. We turn quite properly to his essays on *Nature* and *Utilitarianism* for his authoritative statements on

[23] John Stuart Mill's main essays are well selected and introduced in two collections edited by J. B. Schneewind: *Mill's Essays on Literature and Society* and *Mill's Ethical Writings*. Another attractive selection illustrating the essay form is Arthur Schopenhauer's *Essays and Aphorisms*, tr. R. J. Hollingdale.

moral law and the utilitarian argument; to *On Liberty* for the spirit of his social and political humanism; and to *Theism* and *Utility of Religion* for his mature critique of natural theology and his own religious position. And it is becoming increasingly evident that Mill's study of literature is not just a transient, therapeutic moment in his private development. His literary essays on the nature of poetry, on conservative and liberal poets, and on the specific writings of Coleridge and Browning, compel us to attend to his esthetic thought. They also underline his general remarks on the connection between probability, imagination, and hope which would otherwise go unnoticed or unstressed in his moral logic.

No other philosopher has enjoyed the freedom of the essay more than did Schopenhauer. It had multiple, important uses in the growth and presentation of his philosophy. To prevent his masterpiece *The World as Will and Presentation* from dying on the vine, he equipped its later editions not only with lively introductions but especially with an entire panoply of supplementary essays, which soon outgrew the size of the original text. They enabled him to serve as his own commentator, to make fresh statements of his key concepts and historical filiations, and to meet the objections of critics. This growing matrix of essays incorporated both Schopenhauer's early wrestling with Kant and his later esthetic-moral reflections, thus giving a uniquely organic character to his book as a lifetime's achievement. Like Kant and other predecessors in the German line, he submitted prize-essays (*On the Freedom of the Will* and *On the Basis of Morality*—the latter *not* being awarded the prize, as he pointedly noted), which combined the advantages of formal organized argument with brevity and readiness to quote proverbs and poems. Schopenhauer's literary sensibility and responsiveness to human situations, great and small, were best manifested in his several series of essays constituting *Parerga and Paralipomena*. Readers extending far beyond philosophical circles have continued to appreciate his reflections on authors and literary forms, his distinctive attitude toward suicide and women, his dialogue on religion, and his concrete observations on genius and moral virtue. For they have discovered, to their delight and benefit, that philosophical sources remain insistentially alive and concerned for reaching men of every condition through the resources of the essay.

The philosophical address or discourse is another means of building a bridge of understanding from the philosopher to later generations of students. It takes several forms, all of which have the common trait of bringing a resonant and directly persuasive quality to the argument, and thus of evoking something analogous to the response of an attentive listener. Sometimes it comes in a classical rhetorical form, such as the *Oration on the Dignity of Man*, which Giovanni Pico della Mirandola planned to deliver in Renaissance Rome as the announcement of disputations concerning the study of philosophy and man's freedom and moral role in the cosmos. Giambattista Vico actually did deliver his inaugural address *On the Study Methods of Our Times* at the University of Naples in 1708. Thus we can still catch the rhythms of his defense of humanistic education, his criticism of the Cartesians, and his search for a basis of uniting scientific analysis with the historical meaning of man.

The term "discourse" appears in the titles of some cardinal works in French philosophy and culture, primarily with the connotation of a forcefully stated written program of a method designed for humanity's betterment. Descartes' *Discourse on Method* sets this genre on a distinctive course, with its fusion of inventive logic and epistemology, mechanistic physiology and morality, all aimed at enhancing human values in the natural world. Both the promise and the problems of scientific humanism are set before the mid-eighteenth century in the still arresting prose of D'Alembert's *Preliminary Discourse* to the *Encyclopedia* and Rousseau's *First and Second Discourses*.[24] D'Alembert seizes us with the energy

---

[24] The two phrases quoted in these paragraphs come from Jean Le Rond D'Alembert, *Preliminary Discourse to the Encyclopedia of Diderot*, tr. R. N. Schwab and W. E. Rex, p. 96; and from Jean-

and hopefulness of his plan for setting forth the resources of the physical and social sciences for the improvement of human society. Yet his plea does not exclude the admission that "men abuse the best things," and that the analytic spirit in philosophy and culture can deprive life of its warmth and direction toward value goals.

The critical moralist comes through even more vividly in Rousseau's *Discourse on the Sciences and Arts* and *Discourse on the Origin and Foundations of Inequality*, which are actually essays submitted for prize contests. They retain the particular flavor of their century and circumstances of composition, from the general declaration that "the most useful and least advanced of all human knowledge seems to me to be that of man" down to the specific criticisms of customs and opinions, conceptions of moral law and forms of government. Yet it is a personal thinker who discourses with us, urges the paradoxes of his society and learning upon us, and thereby clears out a road of recognition leading from his problems to ours.

That the discourse form merges readily with the lecture course is clear from the context of Comte's *Discourse on the Positive Spirit* (the philosophical preamble to his popular lectures on astronomy) and *Discourse on Positivism as a Whole* (later annexed to his *System of Positive Polity*). Taken together with the two opening lectures in his *Course of Positive Philosophy*, these programs seek to provoke a general positivistic transformation in our way of seeing things and conducting our lives. In bringing within manageable focus an entire framework for reorienting our objective and subjective interests, Comte's discourses are comparable to the introductory lectures in Hegel's great courses on right and religion, art and world history. Both philosophers use their

---

Jacques Rousseau, *The First and Second Discourses*, tr. R. D. Masters, p. 91 (the opening sentence of the Preface of the *Discourse on the Origin and Foundations of Inequality* which Rousseau supports with a footnote quotation from Buffon's *Natural History: On the Nature of Man*).

introductory talks to enliven their students' appreciation of a general philosophical method and principles, underlying their treatment of the specific topics in their course.

Hegel and Comte set a significant example by incorporating the values of the essay and the discourse into the written record of their lecture work. This literary ideal continues to influence the philosophical community, especially as thinkers gradually return to the university environment in the nineteenth century, after the withdrawal made during the early modern period. When Bergson lectures and writes in careful style on metaphysical, cultural, and moral topics, he is ratifying by his practice the aim of many philosophers to join rigorous argument with a more effective language for reaching thoughtful men outside their professional circle. The Gifford Lectures of William James (*The Varieties of Religious Experience*) and of Josiah Royce (*The World and the Individual*) manifest this same power of source communicativeness, upon which the entire search for historical knowledge depends.

Our four selected bases for observing the modern philosophers in their insistential activity by no means exhaust their constant reworking of the linguistic possibilities. For instance, the pregnant aphorism and the cutting *pensée* are regularly used to puncture systematic pretensions and to advance the reform of social experience. This weapon is finely honed by such social critics as Pascal and Hamann, Schopenhauer and Nietzsche. Furthermore, when it will somehow improve the course of their *philosophizing-with-others*, modern philosophers are not reluctant to widen still further their stylistic scope. We find them: composing or commenting on poetry (Hobbes and Hegel, Whitehead and Heidegger); moving from the very formal dissertation to the very informal mode of table talk (as Kant does); speaking in the tongue of sermon and lay catechism (Berkeley and Butler, Fichte and Comte); and using such forms as the philosophical letter and the gallery of pseudonyms (Leibniz and Montesquieu,

Schelling and Kierkegaard).[25] Embodying their thought in all these modes of textual insistency, the modern philosophers show themselves to be surprisingly inventive and resilient. They are truly bent upon communicating diversely with us and furnishing us with a rich choice of routes for our historical interpretations.

Is there any likelihood of reconciling the different methods and perspectives proposed in these many philosophical sources? This is a question of futurity and, from Bacon and Descartes onward, the modern philosophers have dealt with this modality through the interpretation of myth, dream, and utopian thinking. To the values of systematic argument and analysis, such interpretation adds the dimension of vision and hope for humanity. It is fitting to conclude

[25] We must distinguish between the stylistic device of *imaginary Philosophical Letters* (a literary form employed by such philosophers as Wolff, Voltaire, and Schelling to convey their doctrines) and *the actual letters written by philosophers* on philosophical topics. For English-reading students, there is a rich lode of such actual correspondence which furnishes a splendid path into the problems, aims, and human conditions constituting the matrix of modern philosophizing. Our historical comprehension of the following nine philosophers is deepened by this approach. (a) Descartes, *Philosophical Letters* (see above, n. 10). (b) Spinoza, *The Correspondence of Spinoza*, ed. A. Wolf. (c) Leibniz, *Philosophical Papers and Letters*, ed. L. E. Loemker, as well as the Leibniz-Arnauld and Leibniz-Clarke exchanges cited below, Chapter III, n. 25. (d) Until the critical edition of Locke's correspondence is issued, we must use *The Works of John Locke* (tenth ed., 10 vols.; London, 1801), vol. 4 (correspondence with Edward Stillingfleet, Bishop of Worcester), and vols. 9-10: *Familiar Letters*; and *The Correspondence of John Locke and Edward Clarke*, ed. B. Rand. (e) Berkeley, *The Works of George Berkeley, Bishop of Cloyne*, ed. A. A. Luce and T. E. Jessop, vol. 8: *Letters*, and vol. 9: *Notes to Berkeley's Letters*. (f) Hume, *The Letters of David Hume*, ed. J. Y. T. Greig; and *New Letters of David Hume*, ed. R. Klibansky and E. C. Mossner. (g) Kant, *Philosophical Correspondence, 1759-99*, ed. A. Zweig. (h) Mill, *The Letters of John Stuart Mill*, ed. H. S. R. Elliot; *The Earlier Letters of John Stuart Mill, 1812-1848*, ed. F. E. Mineka (vols. 12 and 13 of the University of Toronto edition of Mill's *Collected Works*); and *John Stuart Mill and Harriet Taylor*, ed. F. A. Hayek. (i) Nietzsche, *Selected Letters of Friedrich Nietzsche*, ed. C. Middleton; and *Nietzsche: A Self-Portrait from His Letters*, ed. P. Fuss and H. Shapiro.

our study of the insistency of the source men, therefore, with Wilhelm Dilthey's account of a dream, intended as his response to the above question.

He once described a summer evening spent in an old castle, where an engraving of Raphael's "School of Athens" faced his bed. In a state of reverie, he seemed to see the leading modern thinkers joining with the classical figures of ancient philosophy shown in that painting. D'Alembert and Comte strengthened the group of naturalistic philosophers down the ages; Descartes and Kant added themselves to those stressing the idealism of freedom and moral personality; and the presence of Spinoza and Leibniz, Schelling and Hegel, deepened that philosophical tradition centering around a perception of the esthetic harmony and divine unifying power in the universe. Anxiety over our question of achieving an ultimate synthesis between these recurrent philosophical views of life led Dilthey to wake up and (in much the same condition, between dreaming and waking, described by the young Descartes) to make this interpretation.

> These types of world views exist along side each other through the centuries. The liberating element here is that the world views are grounded in the nature of the universe and in the relationship between the finite perceptive mind and the universe. Thus each world view expresses within its limitations one aspect of the universe. In this respect each is true. Each, however, is one-sided. To contemplate all the aspects in their totality is denied to us. We see the pure light of truth only in various broken rays. . . . If the course of our life brings us closer to a particular aspect of the incomprehensible harmony, if the truth of the world view which this particular aspect expresses fills us with creativity, then we may quietly surrender. For truth is present in them all.[26]

[26] Wilhelm Dilthey, *The Dream*; translated as an Appendix to William Kluback, *Wilhelm Dilthey's Philosophy of History*, pp. 106-108.

This aspectual approach, together with its assumption of an underlying but unattainable unity, must be submitted to meta-philosophical criticism. Yet it can stand here as a symbol of the insistential openness of modern philosophers to their mutual differences and their community relationships alike. Dilthey's dream also expresses the historian's lively hope of saving all the values in modern philosophical sources, despite the theoretical and practical obstacles against any actual consolidation of their reflective paths.

III

The Art of Historical Questioning

Anyone working in a historical discipline experiences within himself, at certain times, a sympathetic reverberation of Stephen Dedalus's cry that history is a nightmare from which he must awake. This feeling of suffocation steals over the philosopher when he attends to the long tradition of texts and studies in his field. Then, the history of philosophy seems to be an externally imposed and pressing structure, controlled entirely by lines of investigation laid out in the far distant past and extending into one's present activity only in order to cramp and discourage the creative mind. This is indeed a nightmarish view of the historical factors in philosophy, one from which every philosopher must break himself loose at the price of losing his own integrity and fresh initiative.

The only question concerns the manner and quality of our awakening. The liberation cannot be reasonably sought in a denial or systematic ignoring of the influence of past philosophers upon the present course of discussion. To dehistoricize philosophy entirely has the same consequence as to dehistoricize human reality as a whole: it only exchanges one nightmare for another, and still keeps us in a dream condition. What can be done, however, is to criticize the preconception that the historical influence is bound to be oppressive and alienational for present-day philosophical minds.

There are two highly general ways of attacking this preconceived notion: through a study of the nature of historicity and through a study of man's questioning activity.[1] The for-

[1] Theories of historicity are analyzed in Gerhard Bauer's *"Geschichtlichkeit": Wege und Irrwege eines Begriffs*; the general relation between nature, man, and the historic is the philosophical theme of Paul

mer route has the advantage of showing that human life in all its modes is thoroughly and permanently historical, yet in a developing and open fashion which gives encouragement to the uses of freedom. And the general analysis of man as a questioning animal enables us to see that history is no rigid encasement, defying modification. Our historical reality constitutes and prolongs itself in the very process of raising new questions and putting every existing framework to a radical test. Such considerations are sufficient to weaken the general arguments supporting a nightmarish or juggernaut image of history. Yet they cannot dispel entirely the notion that, at least for the free and creative philosopher, the systems of past thinkers and the canons of historians are impediments to exploratory work today.

Our general method of functional reflection suggests, however, that some further headway can be made by making a more specific examination of the actual ways in which twentieth-century historians of philosophy develop the art of historical questioning. Hence our focus will not be directed upon a general theory of historicity and human questioning, but rather upon the specific interrogator-functions devised for the study of modern sources in philosophy. Within the framework of our working hypothesis on the three chief factors involved in gaining historical access, we are now shifting the emphasis from the structuring of the sources themselves to the questioning process directed toward them. Neither component can remain in splendid isolation, but their complex relationship must now be inspected from the standpoint of the historian's acts of interrogation. For these acts are not only illuminative of the great modern texts but also liberative of contemporary philosophical energies, so as to dispel the preconception about the imparing effect of historical considerations upon present creativity.

Weiss's *History: Written and Lived.* The roots of philosophizing are traced back to man as wonderer, questioner, and critic, by B. J. Boelen, *Existential Thinking*, and by R. C. Kwant, *Critique: Its Nature and Function.*

1. THE POLES OF INTERROGATION

Reflective analysis of the historian's craft must reckon with the fact that every investigator takes his start within an ongoing tradition of ways of inquiry. If fruitful, his work will open out a new path of its own, but this path will find its originality within the context of procedures already operative for maintaining the continuity within history of philosophy itself. As a human activity, this discipline confirms a perceptive maxim of St. Augustine which also provided guidance for Ludwig Wittgenstein: *Plus loquitur inquisitio quam inventio.*[2] Searching speaks more powerfully than does finding —an observation that holds good in history of philosophy as elsewhere. Just as the great modern philosophers are those who raise powerful questions about human experience and who keep up the search persistently in the face of efforts to render everything in our existence obvious and settled, so also the great historians of philosophy are those who remain forever queryful in the presence of the source works.

The persistent searching on the historian's part is his proportionate response to that characteristic of the philosophical sources which may be called *the open yet unovert page*. In seeking to communicate his argument, the source thinker must work through a specific linguistic and literary structure, must respect the control of his own conception of method and orderly investigation, and must develop his own context for the meaning of problems and the weight of the supporting evidence. His text conveys a communicative intent only under these restrictive conditions, so that the historical import of what he says is no more obvious and settled than is his own relationship to life. The philosophical page opens out toward the historian for his scrutiny, but does so without ever becoming fully overt and comprehended by him. It retains a power to say more, and to say something other, to men of different times, interests, and research means. Thus it is a source of

[2] Augustine, *Confessions*, 12.1.1; quoted by Ludwig Wittgenstein, *Zettel*, 457, p. 82. The Augustine quotations in Wittgenstein are analyzed by Herbert Spiegelberg in a forthcoming article.

constant provocation to the historian, who must learn to struggle with the unovert aspect by means of newly framed questions. The historical interrogation of the modern sources never ceases, since fresh lines of query continually redefine the bonds of relevance between these sources and a new generation of philosophers.

Since contemporary philosophers may belong to widely different schools, it is not immediately clear how the history of philosophy—itself involving many types of questioning—can function as a common tongue for the different groups.[3] At least one part of this complex problem can be dealt with pertinently here, since it concerns the process of continually formulating new questions about the modern sources. For in the very course of examining the peculiar features of this or that source and its relationship to changing current concerns in philosophy, historians build up a pattern of unity amid their quite diverse acts of interrogation. There are recurrent and widely useful kinds of questioning which can be shared by all the historical investigators and which, indeed, must be used in order to test and improve any particular set of findings. These shared modes of interrogation provide a common pattern for historical research and a meeting ground for philosophers of every speculative persuasion.

[3] This problem is raised by Wilfrid Sellars' remark that "the history of philosophy is the *lingua franca* which makes communication between philosophers, at least of different points of view, possible. Philosophy without history of philosophy, if not empty or blind, is at least dumb." *Science and Metaphysics*, p. 1. From our present standpoint, three qualifications must be placed upon this perceptive observation. (a) Although the communication function of history of philosophy is important, it is related to other aims of this discipline and hence cannot serve as the sole basis of establishing the meaning and value of history of philosophy. (b) Not only philosophers of differing points of view but also those sharing a general viewpoint (or belonging to the same school) have communication and argumentation difficulties, which call for the common tongue of historical studies. And (c) communication between all the parties depends upon their recognition and acceptance, at least in some degree, of the common discipline of questioning whose structure and modalities are examined in this chapter.

It is the effective presence of this *interrogatio franca*, in the realm of historical methods, which enables the history of philosophy to serve as a common tongue for the different theoretical standpoints today. Our functional reflection upon the questioning process will concentrate, therefore, upon the procedures most broadly shared by working historians today.

In identifying the primary modes of historical questioning, we do not look for any ranking based upon some prior logic of historical inquiry. In this sense, there is no intrinsically privileged method of interrogation which can appeal to a conceptual definition of its primacy or a guarantee of its perpetual success. The predominance for which we are looking is one that is determined functionally by the actual contribution, made by each line of questioning, to the growth of historical understanding of the modern philosophers. Each one must be proven out pragmatically and modified through the long-run tests furnished by the work of successive historians, as they seek to enhance our reflective grasp of the argumentation in great philosophical sources and the comparisons among them.

What an examination of the praxis of historians of philosophy reveals is a grouping of the specific types of questions around two basic poles.

Poles of historical interrogation

1. The Fundament: creative center founded in the work of the individual philosopher himself.

2. The Interrelations: thematic context of problems, and comparisons sought among several source philosophers.

(Through their polar interplay, there develops the basic art of historical questioning and the reliable use of modern philosophy.)

There is no strict segregation of the different modes of questioning which help to constitute the one pole or the other, but every research project does acquire a distinctive sense and orientation insofar as it is serving chiefly the one interrogative intent or the other. When our primary purpose is to improve our understanding of a particular philosopher as the center of research, then there is a marked convergence of the cultural and biographical data, the textual analyses and synoptic views, upon this fundament-directed intent of investigation. These same instruments of inquiry are differently used and ordered, when our main aim is to follow the development of a problem or to compare several systematic positions. Yet there is never a total split between these two forms of organization for historical work, since they aid and modify each other in the long run. Indeed, the historian's art consists precisely in discovering fruitful ways of correlating the two poles of interrogation, so as to achieve a new unification of the full field of interpretation.

It will now be our task to examine more closely those modes of questioning which group themselves around the fundament and the interrelations. In terms of our general working hypothesis, we are moving from the first to the second co-factor of historical ingrediency, that is, from the insistential sources themselves to the equally but differently insistential activity of the inquiring researchers. This involves a shift of attention from the communicative opening outward of the source thinkers to the interrogational opening inward toward the texts, through the activity of historians of modern philosophy. This interrogational opening is concretely achieved through studies directed toward the fundament and the interrelations. This is where the life and art of historical research find their roots.

2. EXPLORING THE FUNDAMENT:
(1) TEXT, TRANSLATION, AND BIOGRAPHY

There is a difference between studying the fundamentals and studying the fundament. It is the difference, for instance, between seeking the basic method and principles *of* Spinoza and seeking them in a perspective centered *upon and within* Spinoza. The former is the question of the fundamental positions of his philosophy; the latter is the question of taking his philosophy as the fundament or integrating context of our studies. It is not sufficient to ask about the fundamentals of Spinoza's philosophy, since this still leaves undetermined whether we are treating these principles mainly in a framework of comparison with other philosophies or mainly as the internal organizers of his own thought. To accept the latter standpoint, which is that of the fundament, is to incorporate Spinozan fundamentals within the historical intent of unifying all phases of research around the elucidation of Spinoza's philosophy as a whole. The spirit of the fundament is to make his philosophy the central reference for all our inquiries. They come together in the primary aim of deepening our grasp of Spinoza's mind from within its own integrally expressed shape and tenor.

Correlated with the historian's recognition of the altogether crucial nature of the individual philosopher's creativity is a cluster of methods for listening to, and interrogating, that creative fundament. In this section and the next one, we will selectively consider four of these methodic responses. They are: the editing and translating of source texts, the biographical approach, the tension between genetic and systematic accounts, and the effort at synoptic presentation.

At the particular moment when a student makes his first acquaintance with history of philosophy, he is confronted with a long tradition of work along these four lines. Hence he is apt to regard them solely as tool-things, as pre-given channels into which his research work must be fitted and submitted. But one purpose of our functional reflection upon historical access is to enliven for ourselves a sense of *the human grounding for every instrument of research*. They all proceed from, and forever receive their sustenance from, the historian's questioning activity. In the case of the four methods under consideration, they are specific modes of articulating and pursuing questions directed chiefly toward the fundament factor in history of philosophy. In principle and in fact, they are freely open to variation and development, in accord with our own changing estimate of how to perceive more satisfactorily the source philosopher's unique Gestalt.

Editing and translating of source texts. The work of textual editing and translating is a special beneficiary from the rule of referring standard forms of research back to the interrogational situation. Viewed in that light, the activity of establishing accurate texts and rendering them skillfully into other languages is not an exercise in pedantic erudition, but an indispensable and always controlling element in history of philosophy. Interpretations of a philosopher's thought must prove themselves against the established text, and are essentially open to revision and even radical alteration in the wake of textual modifications of any consequence. There is nothing which can undercut an account of a philosophy so quietly and yet so radically as a major change in the original text or a newly definitive edition of the writings. Correlated with the textual improvements are fresh translations, which can be construed from our present perspective as a re-questioning process, necessitated both by newly established or presented sources and by philosophical changes in the language area into which the sources are to be rendered. The function of a source philosopher within our contemporary discussion depends in part upon the translation tradition, a transformation which is bound to have a proportionate repercussion upon how we view this philosopher and make use of his argumentation.

Some specific examples will bring out these somewhat subdued yet important correlations. The English language is blessed with a long and healthy tradition of Descartes translations. The nineteenth-century version done by Veitch was adequate enough for its day, but its day had passed with the coming of the splendid edition of the original text of Descartes' writings prepared by Adam and Tannery. The appearance of this edition made it both possible and necessary for English eyes to read Descartes more carefully, reliably, and comprehensively than ever before. The visible expression of this fresh scrutiny is found in the translation by Haldane and Ross, whose undertaking is in some respects still unsurpassed. The great majority of English-language studies, whether in article or book form, are shaped by the Haldane-Ross reading of the Adam-Tannery text. The prominence presently given to the Cartesian theory of intuition, experience, and simple natures derives in some measure from the circumstance that these translators were able to work from a good text of the early *Rules for the Direction of the Mind*. For English readers, the latter treatise is now firmly established alongside of the *Discourse on Method* as a major statement of methodology and theory of knowledge.

Why have translators nevertheless persisted in preparing new English versions of Descartes?[4] In the preface to his translation, N. K. Smith reminds us that the great commentaries on Descartes by Gilson, Gouhier, and others have appeared in the decades since the Haldane-Ross version, and have forced upon us a greater precision in rendering terms and passages elucidated at length in these historical studies. This reciprocity between historical research and translation is further illustrated by Smith's own *New Studies in the Philosophy of Descartes*. His interpretations required him to retranslate many passages in order to render with more precision the Cartesian thinking on physics, on the mind-body problem, and on the bearing of his optical model of perception upon his entire theory of man.

The growing demands in the history of science have also exerted an influence on Cartesian translators, leading Olscamp to replace the *Discourse on Method* in its original setting along with a full translation of the treatises on optics, geometry, and meteorology. By restoring the *Discourse* to its scientific context, this version corrects the tendency to give

[4] References to the Adam-Tannery, Alquié, and Crapulli editions of Descartes, as well as the Haldane-Ross translation, are given in the notes of Chapter II. Newer translations include: Descartes, *Philosophical Writings*, tr. N. K. Smith; Descartes, *Discourse on Method, Optics, Geometry, and Meteorology*, tr. P. J. Olscamp; and Descartes, *Philosophical Essays*, tr. L. J. Lafleur. Each offers a value of its own for making Descartes speak to us in contemporary English. J. R. Vrooman's *René Descartes, A Biography* situates these writings within a life web and a personal growth of mind.

stress only to the metaphysical and anthropological implications of the Cartesian method. However, as a challenge to the comfortable assumption that now we do have an adequate rendition of the metaphysical and methodological writings, the Lafleur translation meticulously indicates the variations between the Latin and the French editions for which Descartes himself is responsible or approbative. Lafleur is spurred into making this more complex version both by the textual and printing advances made by G. Rodis-Lewis and other Cartesian scholars and by the increasing interest shown by analytic philosophers. The latter want to have at their command the precise wording used in the different formulations of the Cogito, the problem of dreaming and waking, and the mind-body relationship.

In an interrogational perspective, the likely course of future translating will respond to the opportunities opened up by more recent textual work in Descartes. Since Crapulli has established a better text for the *Rules*, based upon Latin manuscripts and a contemporary Dutch translation, discontent is being generated about all existing English versions. They raise some delicate doctrinal questions which will have to remain suspended, for those who cannot consult the Crapulli text, until a completely new translation of the *Rules* is forthcoming. Even more far reaching is the probable impact of the achievement of Alquié, in organizing the French and Latin texts and translations in his three-volume *Oeuvres philosophiques de Descartes*. Not only has he placed an often better text than Adam-Tannery at our disposal and made superior French translations, but he has shown us what it is really like to read Descartes chronologically and (as far as is practically feasible) in full intellectual context. He gives us the great works in their own life world of Descartes' correspondence, criticism, and annotations for that year, along with the editor's well informed background information. This contextual presentation increases our facilities so noticeably, for grasping Descartes as a fundament, that a similar approach to him in English is bound to be demanded by the questioning process.

To appreciate the calculable ratio between the quality of source translations and the use of the same source in current philosophizing, we can next consider a negative instance. Whatever other reasons drawn from the metaphysical and systematic character of Spinoza's thought may be operative in reducing close discussion of his arguments within the English-speaking world, the status of translations of his writings is a strongly inhibitive factor. Philosophers are uneasily aware that the existing English versions of his methodological and ethico-metaphysical masterpieces—*On the Healing of the Understanding* and the *Ethics*—were made long before their critical text was established by Gebhardt. French and German scholars have already met the need in their language areas for a completely new, one-volume translation of the entire Gebhardt edition of Spinoza, but a similar project in English is only now getting launched.[5]

Meanwhile, Spinozistic studies have been raising the requirements for a viable translation. Dutch as well as Latin manuscript readings must be consulted to reach the exact sense of Spinoza; such key couplets as *wezentheid-zelfstandigheid*, *essentia objectiva et formalis*, and *esse actuale et formale*, must be rendered more accurately and consistently; and generally speaking, the transition from paraphrase to close equivalent is long overdue. Even Wolf's pioneer version of Spinoza's *Correspondence* and *Short Treatise* needs overhauling, in order to keep pace with historical research being done respectively in seventeenth-century history of science and in the manuals used for philosophy instruction in the Dutch universities. Under such

---

[5] The older generation of Spinoza translations (by Elwes, White and Stirling, Britan, and Wolf) is being replaced piecemeal by: Spinoza, *Earlier Philosophical Writings*, tr. F. A. Hayes; and Spinoza, *The Political Works*, tr. A. G. Wernham. But Edwin M. Curley is preparing a one-volume translation of Spinoza's complete works (to be published by Princeton University Press), based upon the C. Gebhardt edition of Spinoza's *Opera* (4 vols.), which hopefully will do for English readers what the Caillois-Francès-Misrahi translation of Spinoza, *Oeuvres complètes*, has done for French readers. Edwin M. Curley's experience in writing *Spinoza's Metaphysics* convinced him of the need to make a fresh translation of the critically edited sources.

conditions, it is only prudent that analytic treatment of Spinoza (on the part of those who must rely on existing English renditions) should confine itself to the gross features, without really coming to grips with his specific argumentation in a manner paralleling our reading of Descartes.

Finally, the case of Hegel is there to caution us about the delicate symbiotic relations holding between text, translation, and historical interpretation.[6] Only through the heroic efforts of a succession of twentieth-century editors have the various editions and manuscripts of his writings been collated, so that since 1968 a genuinely critical edition of his collected works could start to be issued. Although the translations made from the early editions were able for their day, they no longer meet our standard of distinguishing between Hegel's own text and the conflations made by his students. T. M. Knox has set a good example, in his careful translation of the *Philosophy of Right*, by maintaining a clear separation between Hegel's basic text and the variant lecture note additions. This is also done by A. V. Miller and M. J. Petry in renditions of *Philosophy of Nature* (Part Two of Hegel's *Encyclopedia of the Philosophical Sciences*). Indeed, the precisions made possible by their textually well grounded translations of Part Two of the *Encyclopedia* have generated, by comparison, an urgent need for a new version of the first and third Parts (so that Part One on *Logic* will give the complete text of Hegel's Prefaces, and Part Three on *Philosophy of Spirit* will give the relevant *Zusätze*, or editorial conflations of Hegel's lecture notes and written materials of his students).

Hegel's own influence on later continental philosophies has so far outrun our retranslating projects in English that there is still a dangerous discrepancy between his thought, in its

---

[6] The gnarled story of the editions and English translations of Hegel is told by Walter Kaufmann, *Hegel*, pp. 470-478. The critical text of the sources will be Hegel, *Gesammelte Werke*, now under the general editorship of Otto Pöggeler, and planned to include 40 volumes. Pöggeler describes the problems of present Hegel scholarship: "Hegel Editing and Hegel Research" (forthcoming essay in *The Legacy of Hegel*, ed. Lee C. Rice).

own textual statements, and the very free paraphrases of Hegelian phenomenology, metaphysics, and dialectic which have depended on the older translations too completely. Yet it is precisely this disproportion between Hegel's contemporary importance and our ability to control statements about his own method and argumentation which makes us aware of the fundament-role of text and translation. Out of this demand for a more reliable access to his authentic speculations have come the fresh versions of *Phenomenology of Spirit* and *Science of Logic* made respectively by K. R. Dove and A. V. Miller. They help to bring more historical accuracy and caution into discussions of Hegelian philosophy in our language world and especially in university seminars.

The most serious crisis in Hegelian studies, however, concerns the famous series of lectures he delivered in Berlin on world history and esthetics, on history of philosophy and the meaning of religion. The confusion about these oft-quoted "philosophy-of" writings stems from the practice of Hegel's original editors to weave together various auditors' reports, to smooth out the language in accord with their own views on style, and to bring the course of thought into line with what they conceived to be the orthodox Hegelian position on the topics. Not only are all the existing English translations of these lecture courses based upon such conflations, but a good many of the expositions of Hegel in various languages are dependent upon the same versions. Tracking down a colorful phrase or a memorable example can be a disillusioning process, since it often leads back to the surmise of early editors rather than to the manuscript of Hegel. By carefully disciplining our inclination to use such attractive but questionably authentic passages, however, we can now adhere to Hegel's own text on the philosophy of religion and the proofs of God's existence. Hopefully, the critical edition under Pöggeler's superintendence will sort out the several layers of writing and thus lay the basis for responsible translation of all the lecture courses, which do give us a precious glimpse of Hegel in his ultimate searchings.

The biographical approach. The fundament approach to modern philosophy depends considerably upon biographical materials, which are more plentiful for this age than for ancient and medieval philosophy. One index of a student's maturing readiness to move beyond predigested outlines of modern periods and isms lies in his willingness to learn what he can about the life and setting of the individual philosopher. To recognize the worth of a biographical study and its contribution to philosophical understanding is to grasp the role of fundament-oriented questioning.

The skilled biographer, in his concern for the total concrete context of thought, helps to direct us toward the personal center of philosophizing. There is wide variation in the degree of engagement which a biographer will choose to make with the formally theoretical issues treated by his philosopher and, in fact, it is helpful to be able to consult both the more factual and the more intellectual type of biography. But wherever situated in the scale of philosophical concerns, the well-executed biography makes us thereafter dissatisfied with purely abstract and timeless presentations of a man's philosophy. For its purpose is to make us permanently aware of the individual thinker and the concrete matrix within which his problems arose, and in reference to which his methods and principles received their determinate sense and limitations.

Many of the fundament-values contributed by the biographical approach can be observed in John Locke's case. Here, we are in the midst of a biographical explosion or, more accurately speaking, a biodoctrinal explosion in which new findings about the man are triggering new insights into his philosophy. Until the last quarter-century, the philosophical and the biographical sides of Locke had been rather woodenly segregated, the former resting upon a purely analytic reading of the *Essay concerning Human Understanding* and the political treatises, and the latter confining itself to a historical description of his everyday life and duties, along with a quite unscholarly transcription of some manuscript remains. What brought analysis and history together was the release,

for scholarly inspection, of the vast trove of Lockean manuscripts known as the Lovelace Collection. There are now
properly edited texts of his Oxford lectures on the moral law
of nature, his journals of travels in France, the several early
drafts of his *Essay*, a relatively conservative early political
essay, his own final version of the *Two Treatises of Government*, an improved text and translation of his letter on toleration, his educational writings, and correspondence with many
people—all of which will hopefully be incorporated into a
truly critical collected edition of his writings.[7] Keeping pace
with these textual resources is a steady stream of studies
which relate the new materials to the scientific and philosophical, cultural and political, history of the latter half of the
seventeenth century. Maurice Cranston's 1957 biography of
Locke made an excellent provisional synthesis of the then
available comparative data, but more detailed intellectual
portraits of Locke will have to be drawn in the nineteen-
seventies.

What significant differences in our philosophical understanding of Locke are traceable to these biodoctrinal investigations?[8] The first and subtlest modification affects our view

[7] The textual breakthrough affects every period and every field of
Locke's writings: *Essays on the Law of Nature*, ed. W. von Leyden;
Locke's Travels in France 1675-1679, ed. John Lough; *An Early
Draft of Locke's Essay*, ed. R. I. Aaron and J. Gibb; *Two Tracts on
Government*, ed. P. Abrams; *Two Treatises of Government*, ed. P.
Laslett; *Epistola de Tolerantia: A Letter on Toleration*, ed. R. Kliban-
sky and J. W. Gough; *The Educational Writings of John Locke*, ed.
J. L. Axtell. Oxford University Press is sponsoring the critical edi-
tion of Locke, which will begin with his correspondence.

[8] All the source works cited in the previous note contain informative and revisionary introductions by their respective editors. Other
biodoctrinal studies conveying current research are: Maurice Cranston, *John Locke*; C. A. Viano, *John Locke: Dal razionalismo all'illuminismo*, the last chapter of which (rather than the first) treats of
"L'esperienza e i limiti del sapere," pp. 545-609; Kenneth Dewhurst,
*John Locke 1632-1704, Physician and Philosopher: A Medical Biog-
raphy*; J. W. Yolton, editor, *John Locke: Problems and Perspectives*;
and John Dunn, *The Political Thought of John Locke*. Information
about Locke's library is obtainable from G. Bonno, *Les Relations
intellectuelles de Locke avec la France*, and from J. Harrison and P.
Laslett, *The Library of John Locke*.

of the general relationship between his theory of knowledge and his other positions. Pedagogically, it is so convenient to discuss Locke's historical plain method and analysis of ideas at the outset, that we often fail to notice how deeply rooted these teachings are in his own experience and social relationships. In probing into the man's life, however, we come to realize that he was no pure epistemologist imposing an abstract schema of method and ideation upon the human understanding and its more specific fields of interest. Instead, the biographical turn opens up an existence which is always plurally and thoughtfully engaged in teaching students and advising parents, in medicine and other current scientific pursuits, and in the wider political, economic, and theological issues of his century and country.

Locke does his philosophizing in conjunction with, and on the experiential basis supplied by, each of these lifelong relationships. Although he himself refers ironically to his *Essay* as patched together out of many tries, parcels, and strands never wholly rendered coherent, this description is modified by biographical findings into a reminder that Locke's epistemology grows out of a vivid life context and retains the jagged concreteness of its sources. Perhaps as a symbol of this transformed perspective, Viano's 600-page study of his philosophy terminates, rather than begins, with a chapter on "experience and the limits of knowing." The biographically educated mind learns to regard the Lockean theory of experience as an outgrowth of a manysided reflectivity, instead of as a rigid prior enactment.

A second service rendered by biodoctrinal studies is to remove the note of philistine national insularity from the term "British empiricism," as applied to Locke. This English philosopher is also a thoroughly international person, as evidenced by his travels and educational recommendations, his friendships and correspondence, his readings and range of problems. The Latin manuals which he studied and used in his own Oxford tutorials were authored by men from every European country, religious persuasion, and modulation of

School metaphysics and ethics. His early notebooks were filled with bibliographies of Descartes and the Cartesians, with practical plans for studying Descartes himself and supplementing him in ethics and physics from other Cartesian sources, and with close argumentation against all these writers.

The leisurely years which Locke spent traveling around France educated him to other customs, placed him in first-hand contact with the friends of Gassendi and Pascal, and kept him abreast of scientific currents abroad. Many passages from his notebooks and letters of this period provide us with exemplary instances of the historical plain method in actual operation, as he built up the sensuous, intellectual, and moral qualities of the personages, intellectual encounters, and social situations filling his reports. The broadening process continued during his time of exile in Holland, where he was able to feel the impact of Bayle's skepticism at closer range and appreciate the need for tolerance as both a political necessity and an intellectual reality. During this stay, he also increased his respect for the resources of the theological tradition, as represented by his friends among the moderate or Remonstrant theologians, Philip van Limborch and Simon Episcopius, as well as the philosopher and publicist Jean Le Clerc. They helped to shape his own moderate position, not only on toleration and the ends of government but also on theoretical issues connected with the realm of belief and freedom.

Just how open and responsive to all the currents in continental learning and philosophy was this British empiricist, can also be gathered from his working library. Although biographers cannot draw many strict inferences from the list of Locke's books, they can point out some illuminating facts. The library is multilingual, with English, Latin, and French as the dominant languages used by Locke. In these language areas, there is a common pattern of his intellectual interests. Apart from ancient classics and modern dictionaries, there is a very broad selection of current books on geography and voyages (which supply the grist for many of Locke's remarks on savage mentality, on the functions of language, and on the variant forms of society). Books on money, economics, and pedagogy are fairly well represented, but those in medicine and pharmacy are more plentiful, reflecting his continued professional interest in these latter fields and their type of cognition. He makes a determined effort to obtain almost all the outstanding scientific publications of his century: Cartesian and non-Cartesian physics and theory of light, Boyle's experiments and chemistry, biology and especially microscope research.

Locke's holdings in religion and theology are broad and plentiful enough to box the compass: classical Catholic and Calvinist theologies, Protestant-Catholic controversies, Anglican-Freethinking pamphleteering, the drama being played at Port-Royal, and even the revolutionary suggestions of Richard Simon on interpreting the Bible. Hence when Locke does permit himself to be drawn into theological controversy, he has the background information for determining how to relate himself philosophically to the issues and how far it is profitable for him to go. His library is similarly well stocked for orienting him in the philosophical developments on the continent. The French humanist and skeptical tradition is strongly represented by Montaigne and Charron, Naudé and La Mothe le Vayer, Huet and Bayle. Locke has several editions of Descartes at his fingertips, along with Rohault, Malebranche, and Cordemoy. Spinoza figures in his reading both as a Cartesian expositor and in his own systematic right, as well as in the secondary account given by Lamy. Arnauld, Nicole, and Pascal furnish the heavy artillery of intellectual Jansenism, while Bernier expounds the middle way of Gassendi in corpuscular physics, probability attitudes, and Christian Epicureanism.

Locke is also a reader of his own countrymen: Bacon and Newton, Cudworth and (much more discreetly than the others) Hobbes. In addition, he can keep up with Leibniz and the first steps toward international research and the Enlightenment. For Locke subscribes to the three great journals of the day: *Acta Eruditorum, Journal des Savants,* and the first volume of the Jesuit *Mémoires de Trévoux*. When the owner of such a working library strikes out on a new path in philosophy, he does so neither in a state of ignorance of other efforts nor without manifesting many traits which are shared in common with the best minds of his age.

A third aim of the biographical approach in history of philosophy is to insure the saving presence of a strain of *historical contingency* in every systematic analysis of a philosophy. Two sorts of contingency are brought into play through the intellectual biography: the extrinsic contrast and the intrinsic qualifying consideration. Less important is the *extrinsic* contrast between the philosopher's sometimes sorry personal life and his shining tower of ideas—a contrast often sardonically developed by Kierkegaard in his polemic against the builders of idealistic systems. But this personal discrepancy is never intellectually decisive. For once such a comparison is made, there still remains the problem of determining the manner and degree of impact of a life history upon a specific philosophy. This is the task of formulating and controlling some considerations which contingently yet *intrinsically* qualify the method, argument, and vision incorporated into a philosophy. In what fashion and to what intellectual depth is a theoretical explanation responsive to its being developed by this personal existent, working within the horizon and resources of his own age in human history rather than in some other situation? Biographical work sharpens our appreciation of those contingent intellectual conditions which do in fact affect the shape of a philosophical achievement quite intimately and determinately, thus installing an element of contingency and historicity at the heart of even the tightest and most universal system.

Such an intrinsic qualifying consideration begins to affect our interpretation of Locke, the more closely we inquire into his relationships with his own generation of scientists, theologians, and politicians. It becomes clear that his intent is not to propose a timeless theory of the understanding in its acts and limitations, but rather a theory that will account for the human understanding's operations as actually manifested in the peak achievements and social forms of his own day. His famous reference to Boyle and Sydenham, Huyghens and the incomparable Mr. Newton, is not just a warm rhetorical flourish but a very salutary reminder that he is undertaking a philosophical analysis of human intelligence at the precise historical phase of its development constituted and signified by the work of these men. This operational and developmental approach finds expression in Locke's remark that the understanding's "searches after truth are a sort of hawking and hunting, wherein the very pursuit makes a great part of the pleasure. Every step the mind takes in its progress towards knowledge makes some discovery, which is not only new, but the best too, for the time at least."[9] Hence it matters a good deal to the historian to study the intellectual features of the time in which Locke lived, and the great men in whom he discerned the hawking and hunting of the mind at its living best.

Biodoctrinal research of this sort is aided by the rapid growth in the history of seventeenth-century science, which catches the exact register of Locke's appeal to the generation of Boyle-Sydenham-Huyghens-Newton. These men characterize the scientific experience of the last third of the seventeenth century, the phase that is moving beyond Galileo and Descartes and that has not yet reached the time of consolidation of doctrinaire Newtonism. It makes a noticeable difference in our consideration of Locke's *Essay* that it is proportioned to this generation of thinkers, for we can expect that the book will display some signs of the transition.

[9] Locke, *An Essay concerning Human Understanding*, Epistle to the Reader, ed. J. W. Yolton, i, xxxi. The facts about Locke's involvement in seventeenth-century scientific thinking are presented in two essays by J. L. Axtell: "Locke and Scientific Education," in *The Educational Writings of John Locke*, pp. 69-87, and "Locke, Newton and the Two Cultures," in *John Locke: Problems and Perspectives*, ed. Yolton, pp. 165-182; in J. W. Yolton's commentary, *Locke and the Compass of Human Understanding*, pp. 44-75; and in M. J. Osler's "John Locke and the Changing Ideal of Scientific Knowledge," *Journal of the History of Ideas, 31* (1970), 3-16. Locke's epistemological use of his medical sources is weighed by F. Duschesneau, *Les Sources de l'empirisme de Locke* (unpub. diss.).

Predictably in these intellectual circumstances, the Lockean theory of the understanding will show a high regard for pure mathematical demonstration and pure ethical definition; it will accept the corpuscular view of the material universe, shy away from abstract Cartesian hypotheses, and look for those physical hypotheses which can relate a mathematical system to the corpuscularian universe and the phenomenal look of things; and it will find room for that middle range of experimentation and likely inference cultivated by Boyle and Hooke, Leeuwenhoek and Swammerdam. Yet the concrete human understanding in which Locke is interested does not find its sole exemplar in the physical and biological modes of thought. Some of its characteristic operations find their primary model, instead, in the medical work of a Sydenham or a Mapletoft, for whom the probable diagnosis and the tentative explanation are the normal goal to strive after. Still other types of probable judgment and belief are exemplified in the work of those religious thinkers and political leaders, judges and educators, with whom Locke was on familiar footing.

Under pressure from these biographical considerations, we then begin to read the *Essay* more closely and take some of its distinctions more seriously. It is indeed an attempt to reflect upon *all* sides of our human understanding, not just upon some one mode of understanding which, in its privileged separation, would be unreal and inhumane. Locke invites us to interweave our general knowledge (in the strong sense of certitudinal intuition and demonstration) with the many degrees of opinion and belief needed for practical living. To know, in the strict certitudinal sense, does not exhaust our responsible uses of the understanding, which also judges and assents to probabilities in many scientific areas as well as in everyday life. In the Lockean perspective, then, the human condition can be described as a combining of "knowledge" and "judgment," strict certitudes and well-grounded probabilities.

Only through this modest and practically ordered synthesis

can Locke expose the inhumanity of the skeptical demand, as well as of the purely rationalistic view of the human mind.

> We shall not have much reason to complain of the narrowness of our minds, if we will but employ them about what may be of use to us; for of that they are very capable. And it will be an unpardonable as well as childish peevishness, if we undervalue the advantages of our knowledge and neglect to improve it to the ends for which it was given us, because there are some things that are set out of the reach of it. It will be no excuse to an idle and untoward servant, who would not attend his business by candle light, to plead that he had not broad sunshine. The candle that is set up in us shines bright enough for all our purposes. The discoveries we can make with this ought to satisfy us; and we shall then use our understandings right, when we entertain all objects in that way and proportion that they are suited to our faculties, and upon those grounds they are capable of being proposed to us; and not peremptorily or intemperately require demonstration and demand certainty, where probability only is to be had, and which is sufficient to govern all our concernments. If we will disbelieve everything, because we cannot certainly know all things, we shall do much what as wisely as he who would not use his legs, but sit still and perish because he had no wings to fly.[10]

However homely the metaphors in this passage, it is noteworthy also for the precision with which it distinguishes the

---

[10] Locke, *An Essay concerning Human Understanding*, I, i, 5 (Yolton ed., I, 7-8). Locke's moderate position is fitted historically into the efforts of two generations of English scientists, theologians, and philosophers to defend probability against the rationalist and skeptical extremes, by H. G. Van Leeuwen, *The Problem of Certainty in English Thought 1630-1690*, chapter five. Whereas most of the men studied by Van Leeuwen employ a theory of degrees of certainty in order to associate probability and belief with at least a moral certainty, Locke pairs off certainty with demonstrative knowledge and links probability, instead, with the assent of judging and believing. The overtones of Cambridge Platonism in his reference to the candle within us make it useful to consult Ernst Cassirer's *The Platonic Renaissance in England*.

order of certitudinal demonstrative knowledge and that of probability, belief, and practical concern (where we judge and assent, rather than suspend these acts for lack of being able to demonstrate). The biographical study of Locke is helpful here for illumining his confidence in a middle ground of judgment and belief, which will not submit to the artificial antithesis of rationalism versus skepticism. For he finds this middle ground and its useful candle light—the metaphor is popular with his favorite preacher, Whichcote—being developed by his friends among the chemists and physicians, the preachers and parliamentarians of this world.

There is one further value to obtain from biographical considerations, but it is difficult to formalize. A philosopher never fully conveys his spirit through his formal treatises. That is why we like to attend his lectures and question periods during his lifetime, and thereafter like to have some historical record of a pungent remark or a revealing story which continues to communicate the informal side of his mind. The conscientious biographer has to excise the apocryphal tales, but he also has to present the authentic materials for gaining this informal view of the philosopher in everyday relationships.

Locke provides many such extracurricular avenues of access to his philosophical temper. His wry and critical mind stands forth in this brief notation about a final examination which he attended at the medical faculty of the University of Montpellier: "*Much* French, *hard* Latin, *little* Logic *and little* Reason."[11] Again, it is reassuring to find him able to make a similarly witty and detached appraisal of a situation affecting the fortunes of his own philosophy. During the last winter of his life (1703-04), he suffered the common fate of innovative philosophers. A proposal was made by several nervous masters of Oxford colleges that their tutors and students be forbidden to read Locke's *Essay* and a similar book by his friend Le Clerc, on the usual ground of their contributing to

[11] *Locke's Travels in France*, ed. Lough, p. 50. His remarks about Oxford leaders are quoted in Cranston, *John Locke*, pp. 466, 469.

the decay of logical thinking and the corruption of young minds. Locke's composed reaction was to comment that the worthy heads of colleges at his alma mater were "not yet grown up to perfect infallibility." And to his young friend Anthony Collins, he dryly added: "To be rational is so glorious a thing that two-legged creatures generally content themselves with the title."

The purpose of such biographical sideglances is not to reduce a philosopher to his anecdotes but to help us discern his life pattern and his ideals, as conveyed in overtones and indirections. In these remarks, Locke shows himself engaged in reformulating the meaning of man and rationality. The many-modal human understanding cannot be reduced to formal exercises or to an overblown set of claims for evidential reason. Rather, a humanly proportionate rationality functions as a modest ideal sought by men along many routes, rather than as a definitional property of which they need not strive to become worthy.

A correlation can now be shown between biography and one of the bands on the communicational spectrum of sources not expressly mentioned in the previous chapter. If the intellectual biography is regarded as an effective way for the historian to pose the fundament question, then the *autobiography* of a philosopher can also be regarded as a corresponding insistential opening from the source pole. Not all modern philosophers can or will compose autobiographies, but those who do employ this medium provide us with a rare avenue to their minds. Perhaps we do not gain very much from deciphering the Latin verses of Hobbes' account of his own life, except for a valuable report of his resolve to take a phenomenalistic attitude toward all the qualities and motions in the physical and social worlds. It is quite otherwise with Vico's autobiography, however, since readers need all the background he can provide about his upbringing and professorial life at the Neapolitan segment on the rim of Europe.[12] His

[12] Acquaintance with *The Autobiography of Giambattista Vico*, tr. M. H. Fisch and T. G. Bergin, is an essential aid for better ap-

sober, third-person account of his wrestling with Gassendi and Descartes, his disappointment with Boyle and Pascal, and his avid readings in Bacon and Hobbes and Grotius as students of the mythic mind and the nonformal modes of thinking, supplies some landmarks whereby to chart one's course into the *New Science* itself. Especially with the aid of the helpful English translators, Bergin and Fisch, Vico's story of his life introduces us to an unfamiliar set of problems and guiding concepts on human history and imagery.

Philosophical autobiographies can be as brief and witty as David Hume's *My Own Life* or as detailed and weighty as John Stuart Mill's *Autobiography*. In either case, it is well to read the originative account along with a good biographical study, such as Mossner's massive work on Hume or Packe's life of Mill. The intermeshing of autobiography and biography renders concrete the reciprocal opening between an insistential source and a questioning historian, and it gives special point to the interrogation of the fundament. The historian's duties shift with the nature of the autobiographical statement itself, as the above two examples indicate.

---

preciating *The New Science of Giambattista Vico*, also tr. T. G. Bergin and M. H. Fisch. The passages quoted below from David Hume's *My Own Life* can be found conveniently in the N. K. Smith edition of Hume, *Dialogues concerning Natural Religion*, pp. 234, 236. Until the Toronto edition text is ready, John Stuart Mill's *Autobiography* can be read in the J. J. Coss edition with an introduction by C. V. Shields, and in *The Early Draft of John Stuart Mill's Autobiography*, ed. Jack Stillinger. In the case of Hume and Mill, their correspondence serves almost as a second autobiography. Indeed, Mill establishes a circular relationship by making the problems, aims, and values of his *Autobiography* a major theme in letters exchanged with his wife, Harriet. "I find there is a great deal of good matter written down in the Life which we [J. S. Mill, aided by Harriet] have not written anywhere else, and which will make it as valuable in that respect (apart from its main object) as the best things we have published" (*Letter of February 10, 1854, to Harriet Mill*, in *John Stuart Mill and Harriet Taylor*, ed. F. A. Hayek, p. 194). See A. W. Levi, "The Writing of Mill's Autobiography," *Ethics, 61* (1951), 284-296, and the unusually extensive use made of the *Autobiography* and *Letters* by contributors to *Mill: A Collection of Critical Essays*, ed. J. B. Schneewind.

Hume achieves an extremely deft compression of facts and judgments into a few pages. To obtain maximum instruction, the historian must engage in an unpacking operation, by relating Hume's concentrated remarks to a context of relevant biographical information. His thematically repeated phrases about having "laid that plan of life, which I have steadily and successfully pursued" and being "ever more disposed to see the favorable than unfavorable side of things," can have a double effect upon the historically alerted reader. They open out a prospect of specific events in Hume's young manhood and, simultaneously, they illuminate the motivations of his writings and the hopeful view of man underlying his moderate skepticism. Thus a thoughtful, biodoctrinal explication of *My Own Life* constitutes one of the most effective introductions to his philosophy.

As for Mill's symphonic *Autobiography*, its potential for enlarging our historical understanding is presently appreciated perhaps more by students of nineteenth-century literature and history than by philosophers. But it is the linchpin binding together his many essays, giving them a center of reference and intercommunication. Just as his *System of Logic* provides the methodological basis of his arguments in many fields, so does his autobiographical account provide a basis in the personal fundament for interpreting all his work. Without the orientation which it gives concerning his crisis over relating the intellectual and the emotive, the social and the imaginative factors in man, we would be unable to detect the humanistic themes underlying and unifying all his specific analyses. What it means concretely to pass from Bentham's calculatory utilitarianism and Comte's fantasizing cult of humanity to Mill's powerful synthesis of libertarian and social humanism comes across most authoritatively in the latter's *Autobiography*—studied in conjunction with the biodoctrinal correctives and supplements now available.

Along with the positive contributions of the biographical and autobiographical works, however, we have to face the real question of whether this approach may be pushed to the extreme condition of swallowing up the entire enterprise of history of philosophy. There is a constant threat of such ingestion, which would psychologize and trivialize the work of philosophical analysis and criticism. This danger is strongly felt by historians of modern philosophy, where the materials are sufficiently detailed and fascinating to invite the biographical reduction. By the personal intensity of their thinking and writing, such philosophers as Rousseau, Kierkegaard, and Nietzsche lead some of their readers to substitute psychiatric for philosophic appraisal. Since the results are often arbitrary and divert attention away from the philosophical questions raised by these sources, many students interested in the theoretical issues become generally disaffected with the biographical aspects and thus deprive themselves of some useful interpretive leads.

We can learn a lesson in disciplined balance from the historians of philosophy who have concentrated upon Rousseau, Kierkegaard, and Nietzsche.[13] Without denying that there are psychiatrically significant problems in these thinkers, the historians nevertheless refuse to make any psychiatric reduction but keep the biographical analysis firmly ordered toward a philosophical appreciation of the life and theories. This ordering is not a matter of easy decree but one of persistent schol-

[13] There is a similar pattern of historical methodology in these six biodoctrinal studies: F. C. Green, *Jean-Jacques Rousseau*; Jean Guéhenno, *Jean-Jacques Rousseau*; Walter Lowrie, *Kierkegaard*; Johannes Hohlenberg, *Søren Kierkegaard*; Walter Kaufmann, *Nietzsche*; and R. J. Hollingdale, *Nietzsche*. (a) Loose psychologizing is avoided, not by thinning out a philosopher's life but by examining it more intently and accurately than before. (b) The central aim is to achieve a biodoctrinal synthesis of "the man and his philosophy," always considered in mutual reference and from a standpoint that is at once textually founded and critically concerned for the truth of the matter. (c) In the end, the reader is left advantageously placed, but free to make his own evaluation of the philosopher's methods and theories. (d) These historians show by their careful example the importance of using only the best established textual sources, and—in the case of Lowrie, Kaufmann, and Hollingdale—they themselves also serve as leading translators of their philosopher into English.

arly investigation, joined with a twofold rule of fundament methodology. As proposed within the history of modern philosophy, fundament questions are both *addressed to* a personal center of creativity and *centered upon* those leads which will help us make better theoretical sense out of the philosopher's writings, taken as a whole.

The close interdependence among our fundament questions about text-translation-biography is evident in the story of English-language presentations of Nietzsche. The older translations of him were triply flawed. There were distortions and forgeries introduced into the canon of the original texts; ideological and cultural preconceptions foreign to Nietzsche himself regulated the translation policy; and numerous outright misreadings blunted the precision of thought and the play of style. The Nietzsche who emerged from these translations, and from the studies built around them, was sometimes a mad and dreamy poet lacking in all intellectual discipline, sometimes the athletic carrier of the life force against bourgeois society, and later on the patristic source for the racist and military fantasies of Nazism.

This situation required a radical cure, not that of abandoning intellectual biography but rather of founding it upon critically established texts and competent translations, and of orienting it toward Nietzsche's complex critique of culture and transformation of moral and cosmological values. Using the resources of international research, this philosophical recovery of Nietzsche's thought is being advanced by such historically grounded philosophers as Kaufmann and Hollingdale. They make a contribution to history of philosophy by improving the translations and scholarly bases which determine the fundament questions concerning Nietzsche as man and thinker, instead of splitting these aspects apart. Their patient work paves the way for our making a reliable analysis of the Nietzschean themes of dual moralities, the coming of the superman, the innocence and eternality of cosmic becoming, and the constant redefining of life values.

A similar self-corrective power within the method of fundament questioning has liberated the study of Rousseau and Kierkegaard from distorting imagery. History of philosophy develops its own instruments for overcoming the distractions of triviality, pathos, and psycho-diagnosis in their regard. Thereby, we educate ourselves to recognize that Rousseau and Kierkegaard are distinctive contributors to the modern theme of subjectivity and freedom, within the context of nature and society. Our philosophical judgment about them could not be accurately and sympathetically formed, were we to make an antiseptic separation between biographical information and philosophical analysis. In order to keep these two approaches in mutually helpful communication, however, we do have to bring into full play another cluster of fundament questions designed to inquire formally into the philosophical issues uncovered by our textual, translational, and biographical activities. Only with the help of this further reach of questioning can we hope that our historical synthesis of findings will be genuinely bio-*doctrinal* in nature.

3. Exploring the Fundament:
(ii) Genesis, System, and Conspectus

There is a straightforward and, within its limitations, a practically effective procedure for keeping the personal factors within the gravitational field determined by a modern philosopher's methods and doctrinal arguments. This is the practice of beginning a presentation with a brief look at "the life and writings," and then moving directly into an outline of his major ideas and a schematic analysis of his representative positions. We employ this proportioning of materials regularly to set forth the main problems of philosophy or an introductory history of modern philosophy. It is useful and not misleading, as long as everyone involved realizes that a first acquaintance with the philosopher does not uncover all the problems and, indeed, that the problems yet to be encountered concern not only the details of his thought but its general pattern and historical interpretation as a whole. One can reasonably expect that advanced study of *any* element, contained in the initial look, will uncover considerations rich enough in meaning to disturb and eventually transform the entire introductory viewpoint.

One aim of twentieth-century research is precisely to induce such creative unsettlement of the conventional proportions. One way to unravel the introductory formula is simply to examine in depth the biographical and autobiographical resources furnished by any major modern philosopher. The opportunities for developing the fundament question in the biographical terms just considered are so varied and rewarding, that there is real danger of reducing our entire study of a body of thought to these terms. Hence in the present theory of historical understanding, I argue that this fundament question is irreducibly complex. Every biographical consideration *must* be integrated with methodological and doctrinal analyses, in order to constitute a contribution precisely to the history of modern philosophy. And on the side of method and doctrine, the historian *must* move beyond schematic statements to a fullblown inquiry into the genetic-systemic-synoptic aspects of the philosopher's meaning.

Genetic and systematic accounts. The chief and most characteristic drive of research in our century has been to subject the source works to a thoroughly developmental investigation. They cannot be taken statically and in isolation, but must be understood genetically as phases in the philosopher's continuous development. Thus even when the fundament question is reformulated in terms of method and argumentation, it centers around the creative thinker's growth of mind. The effect of historical research thus oriented toward the internal personal evolution of thought is not to weaken philosophical judgment, but to render it more intimately and concretely founded upon the actual life history of the philosophy itself. Systematic analysis loses its illusory autonomy only in order to take possession of its real strength and permanence, within the historical genesis of the philosophy.

What effectively integrates biographical findings with theoretical analyses is recognition that both these types of inquiry are approaches to a philosopher's development of reflectivity, and hence that both of them are modes of pursuing the same fundament question. The story of a mind's growth discloses the bond between the man and his argued positions.

Our method of functional reflection suggests, therefore, that the most illuminating focus will be to observe the themes of *genesis and system in their mutual transaction* rather than in separation. The genetic trail cannot be followed very far without deeply modifying the systematic account of a philosopher's method, principles, and interconnections. Conversely, as the doctrinal view receives its historical dimensions, it does not shrivel up but becomes a more adequate interpretation and thus a more effective center of unification for genetic studies themselves. As genesis and system interpenetrate and serve each other's purposes, they comprise the living circulation of history of philosophy in its fundament phase of activity.

The genetic motif in historical research is sounded in the very titles of some outstanding monographs.[14] Henri Gou-

---

[14] Some general points are noteworthy about the studies treated in the next three paragraphs of the main text. (a) We see the genetic approach employed helpfully for all the modern centuries and the main philosophical traditions, with historical contributions being made in the major scholarly languages. (b) The "origins" in question include both the internal genesis of a philosopher's thought and his intellectual dependencies upon other thinkers. (c) In almost every instance, the historian accepts the twin tasks of both widening the crucial role of a philosopher's early speculations and also allowing him sufficient room for freedom and genuine development in his mature reflections. These representative studies of the young philosopher are: H. Gouhier, *Les Premières Pensées de Descartes*; W. Kabitz, *Die Philosophie des jungen Leibniz*; P. Wiedeburg, *Der junge Leibniz*; J. E. Hofmann, *Die Entwicklungsgeschichte der leibnizschen Mathematik während des Aufenthaltes in Paris (1672-1676)*; A. E. Baldini, *Il pensiero giovanile di John Locke*; A. A. Luce, *Berkeley and Malebranche*; L. G. Crocker, *Jean-Jacques Rousseau: The Quest (1712-1758)*; M. Campo, *La genesi del criticismo kantiano*; G. Tonelli, *Elementi metodologici e metafisici in Kant dal 1745 al 1768*; I. Görland, *Die Kantkritik des jungen Hegel*; G. Lukács, *Der junge Hegel*

hier's *The First Thoughts of Descartes* introduces us to the two decades of intellectual ferment which prepared Descartes to compose his methodology and metaphysics. Kabitz's pioneer study of *The Philosophy of the Young Leibniz* opened up so fertile and complex a field that its lineaments are still being determined. Present investigations of Leibniz's early views extend in range from the very broad cultural formation described in Wiedeburg's *The Young Leibniz* to the specialized account of *The Developmental History of Leibnizian Mathematics during the Stay in Paris (1672-1676)*, done by Hofmann. In British philosophy, Baldini's *The Early Thought of John Locke* finds in Locke's initial concerns with moral law and civil peace a persistent framework for interpreting his mature epistemology and political philosophy. And A. A. Luce has combined genetic, comparative, and systematic considerations in his two treatments of Berkeley: *Berkeley and Malebranche* and *Berkeley's Immaterialism*. And because Rousseau himself intertwines personal and theoretical questions so closely right from the start, his early years are subjected to specially close inspection. Einaudi's *The Early Rousseau* follows circumstantially the formation of a subjectivity which will communicate itself and not merely insist upon itself, while Crocker's *Jean-Jacques Rousseau: The Quest (1712-1758)* presents the questioning years as essential for understanding the later responses.

Genetic inquiry into the post-Enlightenment German philosophers is broadly footed and indispensable for entering into their intellectual worlds. The general topography of the young Kant's mind is well drawn in Campo's *The Genesis of Kantian Criticism*, while the problems streaming in from Leibniz and Newton receive careful comparative analysis from Tonelli, *Methodological and Metaphysical Elements in*

---

und die Probleme der kapitalistischen Gesellschaft; P. Asveld, *La Pensée religieuse du jeune Hegel*; A. T. Peperzak, *Le Jeune Hegel et la vision morale du monde*; H. P. Adams, *Karl Marx in His Earlier Writings*; G. M. Cottier, *L'Athéisme du jeune Marx*; A. Cornu, *The Origins of Marxian Thought*.

Kant from 1745 to 1768. There is an unusual blending of genetic phases and perspectives when Görland follows the transition from the mature years of Kant to the early reflections of Hegel, in *The Young Hegel's Critique of Kant.* Indeed, there is now almost a canonical requirement that Hegelian scholars will issue studies under the rubric of "the young Hegel," even though the individual approaches remain quite different and critical of each other. Thus the socioeconomic perspective predominates in Lukács' *The Young Hegel and the Problems of Capitalistic Society;* Asveld's *The Religious Thought of the Young Hegel* makes a theological reading of his first manuscripts and articles; and the strong moral strain in these writings receives proper emphasis in Peperzak's *The Young Hegel and the Moral Vision of the World.*

A similar concentration upon the first stages in Marx's development gets reflected in such studies as: *Karl Marx in His Earlier Writings* (H. P. Adams), *The Atheism of the Young Marx* (G. M. Cottier), and *The Origins of Marxian Thought* (A. Cornu). There is also a genetic impetus behind the flood of English-language translations and studies of Marx's "economic-philosophic manuscripts of 1844" and the other writings in what Marxian scholars sometimes call "the pre-March-1848 period" in the growth of his ideas. This way of denominating the first phase of Marx's thought is similar to the kind of reference that historians make to "the Berkeley of the philosophical commentaries" or to "the two lives of Comte," as marked by the dividing line of Comte's 1844 meeting with Clotilde de Vaux and his subsequent passage from the objective to the subjective synthesis of positivism. Genetic considerations leave a deep mark upon the historian's vocabulary and descriptive ways of referring to modern philosophers.

There is a natural alliance and continuity between the biographical aspect of the fundament question and studies of a philosopher's early thought, in order to broaden out our comprehension of his theoretical achievement as a whole. What methodological and doctrinal modifications are introduced into our historical understanding of a modern philosopher, through the convergences of so many genetically oriented studies? This question can be answered only by examining the functional meanings which historians of philosophy give to such terms as "young" and "early," to "origins" and "pre-this-or-that," in the fundament investigations conducted along genetic lines. Since these cue words have several significations, it will be helpful for us to distinguish between three primary usages of them: the textual, the analytic, and the revisionary.

(i) One indispensable function of this family of words is simply to convey *the textual imperative*, namely, that historical interest and research facilities ought to be focused directly upon the discovery, editing, or critical re-editing of a philosopher's early writings. Their value has not always been evident to guardians of manuscript remains, to enthusiasts who think that their favorite philosopher's reputation may suffer from the evidence of his fledgling starts and misstarts, or even to the philosophical community itself. Thus Descartes' early essays and "private thoughts" were treated cavalierly by his own age, coming down to us only in the morcellated form of the excerpts fortunately made by Leibniz and by Descartes' first biographer, Baillet. Even Foucher de Careil, the nineteenth-century editor of the Leibniz transcriptions from Descartes, allowed the manuscript notes to disappear so that we cannot check the accuracy of his printed version. Cartesian experts are still groping to correlate the precious fragments with the outline and citations of the early Descartes made by Baillet, in the hope of reconstructing the original order of these speculations.

Just how important the proper ordering of early materials is for making an informed estimate, can be seen in the checkered history of Berkeley's first efforts at philosophizing. The manuscript was not even brought to light until 1871, and the first editor (Fraser) issued the fragments in so confused a manner that he regarded them as a mere commonplace book, a scrapbook of quotations on metaphysical topics. Not until 1930 were Berkeley's apprentice thoughts published in approximately their original order by Johnston, but even then the numbering of the entries was regulated by the editor's peculiar thesis about the development of Berkeley's philosophy. Only with Luce's diplomatic edition of 1944 and his text in the 1948 critical edition of the first volume of Berkeley's works, was the *Philosophical Commentaries* finally placed at our disposal in a textually reliable edition. The even more agonizingly slow progression toward accurate texts of Locke's early manuscripts and drafts of his theory of the understanding manifests the same need for continuing the textual imperative as a basic signification.

(ii) In accenting the early stages of a philosopher's thought, we also intend to open up a new region of *historical analysis*. In this usage, the genetic imperative is addressed, not to the condition of the text, but to the condition of our historical understanding of the young philosopher. His first years of reflection are often a rich yet unknown territory, one that has until now been charted only with the aid of a fanciful intellectual topography in the *mappa mundi* style. Hence our talk about his early years serves as an invitation to engage in historical research of this period, considered in its own texture as well as in its preparatory function for his later achievements.

But the historical explorer must adapt himself to a wide range of problems, set partly by the nature of the surviving early materials and partly by the current state of research into them. There is a significant contrast, for example, between the brief and fragmentary Cartesian records, the persistent centering of the Berkeleyan commentaries around some well marked targets for attack and principles for expansion, and the profusion and multidirectional spread of topics in the early Leibniz papers. Different historical skills are called forth to meet these three different textual situations. The judgment which the historian makes about the textual and interpretive problems is his concrete way of framing the fundament question in its genetic modality.

In trying to discern the mind of the young Descartes, it is necessary to combine a close reading of the actual sentences with a controlled sense of their likely connotations and linkage. The process of expanding his stenographic notes, tracing down their concrete referents, and discerning a general pattern of thought, has been carried through most successfully in the case of his accounts of the famous set of dreams of 1619-20. With the help of such historical reconstructions, Descartes is seen as a thinker endowed with a vivid imagination as well as analytical power, with a religious sense of mission as well as an intellectual appreciation of the power of method to unify the sciences and transform man's practical relationships with nature.

The research of Gilson, Sirven, and Gouhier in this field enable us to perceive a mind of very complex aims and proportions, as expressed in such an observation as this:

> It might seem strange that opinions of weight are found in the works of poets rather than philosophers. The reason is that poets wrote through enthusiasm and imagination. There are in us seeds of knowledge, as [of fire] in a flint. Philosophers extract them by way of reason, but poets strike them out by imagination, and then they shine more bright.[15]

This is a Descartes manifesting himself at the moment of shaking loose from a conception of reason which admits no affinities with either scientific intelligence or poetic imagination, and which has devitalized itself in the memory routines

[15] Descartes, *Private Thoughts*, in the E. Anscombe and P. T. Geach translation of Descartes, *Philosophical Writings*, p. 4. The most thorough and judicious analysis of these *cogitationes privatae* and other early fragments is made in H. Gouhier's above-mentioned *Les Premières Pensées de Descartes*.

and schematic divisions of Renaissance pedagogy. We learn
from the young Descartes to look forward toward a philosophy which will find room for symbolic imagery alongside of
mathematical explicitness, and for self-limitation in physical
and moral inquiries alongside of securely footed general
foundations.

Quite a different situation confronts the reader approach-
ing Berkeley along the genetic slope. For one thing, there are
not as many reliable historical monographs to aid in the preliminary survey. Indeed, the young Berkeley has been usually
examined from the comparative standpoint of his later writings, but without the support of historical analyses concentrating integrally upon the early work. The analytic
imperative is urgent here, so that there can be a well informed
footing taken inherently in these first thoughts. Otherwise,
there is no way of estimating the historical soundness of those
genetic hypotheses which do get advanced, in the course of
systematic discussions of his mature immaterialism.

Another peculiarity is that Berkeley's early period must be
defined somewhat unsubtly as the years prior to publication
of his *Treatise concerning the Principles of Human Knowledge* (1710). The difficulty is twofold: he was only twenty-
five years old in 1710; and the extant writings prior to that
date were crowded into the immediately previous three-year
span (*Philosophical Commentaries* of 1707-08, and the
Essay Towards a New Theory of Vision published in 1709).
Berkeley is a philosopher growing up in a hurry. He does not
permit us to give a very leisurely sense to "the early writings"
which breathe hard upon the composition of his *Principles*,
or to maintain any great distance between "the young Berkeley" and the fully panoplied philosopher. Conversely, there
is nothing superfluous about the task of submitting his first
thoughts to full scale historical investigation in their own
right.

The young Berkeley does not yield his treasure easily but
compels us to develop the art of historical questioning at

three specific levels.[16] First, he engages in ceaseless conversation with the older generation of modern philosophers represented by Descartes and Malebranche, Hobbes and Locke, Newton and Bayle. Many of his entries are empathetic restatements of their positions; other entries contain an interior dialogue between himself and these predecessors; and still other passages mount a specific criticism from which Berkeley's own new position emerges. In order to appreciate what is going on in the *Commentaries*, then, the historically alert reader must first sort out these different kinds of relationship with the past. In the process of so doing, he will learn experientially how to conduct comparative questioning and thus how to discern the continuity in modern philosophy. Berkeley's notebooks provide an excellent case-study in the collaborative work which must go on incessantly between the originating sources and the historians, if the textual basis of historical comparison and continuity is to be illuminated and made functional.

To help us follow the internal development of his major doctrines, Berkeley supplies a second set of trail markers. Nearly every one of his entries is accompanied by a marginal sign or combination of signs. Their dual function is to indicate conveniently to Berkeley himself (and ultimately to the historical researcher): (1) the intellectual standing and role of a particular statement within his ongoing speculations, and (2) the major topic to which the entry contributes something.

Thus one system of symbols consists of the mathematical signs for addition and multiplication, often accompanied by

[16] These three aids to interpretation stand out clearly in the *Philosophical Commentaries* as printed in *The Works of George Berkeley, Bishop of Cloyne*, ed. A. A. Luce and T. E. Jessop, I, 1-139, including the introduction and notes of the editor Luce. The historical strength of A. A. Luce's *The Dialectic of Immaterialism* and of A.-L. Leroy's *George Berkeley* lies in the use which these authors make of the *Commentaries* throughout their expositions of Berkeley's theoretical philosophy, showing in practice that these early reflections are not a mere dispensable backdrop. Similarly, John Henry Newman's *The Philosophical Notebook*, ed. E. J. Sillem and A. J. Boekraad is the workbook for appreciating *A Grammar of Assent*.

numerical superscripts. They show whether an entry is primarily a notation about ideas found in other philosophers or a record of Berkeley's own past growth (the plus sign); or whether it is a problem on mathematical knowledge and the language of vision which still needs rethinking (the multiply sign); or, in any case, where to fit an idea into his proposed *New Theory of Vision*, in some one of its main divisions (the superscript number). Berkeley's other basic system of signs uses capital letters to designate the following persistent topics: Introduction (the nature of philosophy, the uses of language, and the problems of abstraction, abstract ideas, and general meanings), Matter, Primary and Secondary Qualities, Existence, Time, Soul:Spirit, God, Moral Philosophy, and Natural Philosophy. Any reader of Berkeley's *Principles of Human Knowledge* will recognize here the makings for that book's chief divisions and problems.

But in the anticipated form of the notebooks, these symbols (both singly and in the various combinations given in the margin of the manuscripts) enable the historical interrogator to follow the actual genesis of the method and doctrines. He can track down several tentative stages and discarded alternatives, a full accounting of which helps to make Berkeley's final position more understandable and more sharply related to his intellectual milieu. And by attending to the several ways in which Berkeley blends the symbols from these two main systems, the historian can improve the range of his comparisons and connections internal to this philosopher's outlook. Thus the genetic interpretation is seen to concern itself not only with the growth of separate themes but also with their systematic interrelations and synthesis.

To avoid spoonfeeding us, however, Berkeley educates our historical intelligence in a third manner by including in his notebooks some unovert clusters of theoretical issues. He leaves it up to our initiative to recognize the recurrence of some important topics and to trace out their ramifications in his thought. This is the case with such persistent topics as the universal language of nature, the meaning of person, the sense in which something can and cannot be said to be "in the mind," the role of will in spiritual beings, and the general problem of predication concerning the powers of finite and infinite minds. The historian's inquiring mind must discern and name these themes, must follow their provisional formulations and permutations in relation to each other, and then must incorporate the genesis of the problems into his conception of their ultimate statement in Berkeley's main works.

The *Commentaries* raises, in acute form, the question of how to achieve a historically satisfactory connection between genetic and system-centered studies of a modern philosopher. If the case of Berkeley is at all decisive, there are various legitimate ways of making the genesis-system integration, in accord with the *multiform* relationships afforded by the sources and by our historical views of the early development. Historians of philosophy have good textual reasons for remaining skeptical about rigidly monistic accounts. Some saving leeway, some freedom to vary the perspectives on a philosopher's growth, is an essential safeguard for responsible historical work.

It is not surprising, then, that there should be such wide variations in twentieth-century studies of the young Leibniz. He poses a research situation which differs in notable respects from that of our two other examples. For unlike Descartes, he confronts us with a profusion of early writings, so that our problem is not to fill in the gaps among a few fragments but to attain some unification amid a rich welter of notations and sketches, commentaries and essays. And unlike Berkeley, Leibniz does not point us steadily toward one underlying premise—such as Berkeley's immaterialist hypothesis and his New Principle on being, perceiving, and being perceived— but uses many principles and offers several ways of viewing the foundation of his philosophy. There is no unique formula for consolidating and gradating his seminal ideas.

We cannot expect the genetic approach to provide an automatic means of tracing back the various principles and perspectives to some single root in Leibniz's early reflections.

For from youth to old age, Leibniz presents us with a remarkably consistent report of his speculations as being nourished constantly upon a *foundational pluralism.*[17] Especially those historians who concentrate upon his initial work learn rapidly to forego any reductive talisman. What they are able to do is to exhibit the generalizing and unifying power now of his mathematical-logical-metaphysical principle of order and continuity, now of his theistic basis in the divine creative action and the cosmic harmony, now of his epistemological theme of mutual representation and his metaphysical theme of substantial activity, and now of his moral and practical concerns for justice and unity. At least in the present stage of historical research, the cautious and fruitful thing is to explore these several avenues into the mind of the young Leibniz. Whether further investigation will uncover a textually grounded and historically satisfactory convergence of the genetic studies is an open and exciting prospect, but one that will not be realized simply by invoking the metaphor of a single taproot of his philosophic growth.

(iii) Thirdly, the large role assigned to historical examination of a modern philosopher's earlier work carries with it a *revisionary implication.* There is a definite expectation that such research will notably modify, and perhaps even radically transform, our understanding and judgment about his philosophy as a whole. This consequence can be brought about

[17] A veteran Leibniz scholar gave this wise procedural counsel: "One can penetrate a work as varied as that of Leibniz, but with parts so compacted, only by alternating analysis and synthesis. The master thought of harmony, that is unity-from-a-multiplicity, does not permit itself to reduce to a single curious fact or to one sole formula. Moreover, it is not contented to juxtapose different investigations but puts them ceaselessly into relationship, in varied orders, underlining now the one and now the other. Since monographs dissect a living thing, we must replace them in a perspective of the whole." Gaston Grua, *Jurisprudence universelle et théodicée selon Leibniz*, p. 7. Openness to several principles of perspectival synthesis marks these four Leibnizian studies: W. Janke, *Leibniz: Die Emendation der Metaphysik*; A. T. Tymieniecka, *Leibniz's Cosmological Synthesis*; Nicholas Rescher, *The Philosophy of Leibniz*; and C. A. van Peursen, *Leibniz*.

only by altering the standard interpretation of, and emphasis upon, the chief works of his maturity. Hence it is here that we experience most strongly the great tension, in historical studies, between the claims of genesis and those of system. Since both sets of claims are being vigorously backed up by current research tendencies, their polarity is not a passing phenomenon destined to subside but is, rather, an essential condition for the development of history of modern philosophy in our time. To explore the fundament in the sources, we have to use to their utmost the joint resources of genetic and systemic questioning. Thus it is necessary to understand, rather than suppress, the differences and the creative strain between these two modes of historical inquiry.

Clear thinking on their methodic interrelation is inhibited by two extreme positions. One is *the great-works syndrome*: it not only regards the chief works of a philosopher's maturity as the main subject of study, but it treats them as static structures without a history. From this standpoint, a study of the earlier writings is an exercise in triviality and irrelevance, since such materials are preliminary tries which have no permanent significance in themselves and no appreciable effect upon the internally sufficient, systematic totalities which are the philosopher's great works. Opposed to this one-sided evaluation is the other extreme: *the mystique of the young thinker*. It nourishes itself upon a set of prejudicial antitheses between fresh and codified thought, between the creative springs of early speculation and the ossified doctrines set forth in the subsequent standard treatises of the philosopher. Each of these positions would discourage basic research in the other area, and hence an uncritical acceptance of either one would prevent the process of interaction and mutual illumination which constitutes the very life of historical interpretation of the modern philosophers.

It is important to notice, however, that the two extremes are not upon a perfect par in their argumentative force and their impact upon the course of historical work. The great-works syndrome actively *prevents* one from studying either the developmental problems internal to the composition of the major writings or the continuity problems leading from the first effort to the mature achievements. Hence it is doubly inhibitory of historical interpretation. It depends on a nominalistic and definitional approach to the philosopher's major writings. Furthermore, it takes them in an excluding sense, which deprives his other efforts of value and which tends to identify the meaning of even the major writings with some conventional account of them.

The remedy for this position is to be found, therefore, not in some equally abstract counterdefinition but in reflective weighing of the lesson taught by historical treatments of the philosopher in question. Such investigations show the actual developments within his central treatises, as well as the relationship of continuity which such developments retain with earlier phases in the genesis of his thought. This is the procedure followed in the study of the Kantian *Critiques*. They are acknowledged to be the central achievements of Kant, without entailing any blindness to their internal growth or any depreciation of the crucial contribution of the so-called precritical writings to their genesis and ultimate significance.

In the case of the young-thinker mystique, however, it is often generated by manuscript discoveries and is directed toward encouraging their historical investigation. Temporarily, there may be a strategic need to lessen our concentration upon the better known works, in order to bring the necessary resources to bear upon their genetic background and in order to give due hearing to the whole developmental story. Historical work is *partially redirected*, rather than wholly arrested, by this accenting of the young philosopher. For a while, the depreciation of his mature treatises can safely be endured, since the interrogational dynamism aroused by a study of his first steps is bound to point ahead toward a new appreciation of these treatises from an enriched historical base. Usually, it will be found that what comes under attack is some conventional reading of the great texts entirely apart from the light afforded by genetic studies. Our historical understanding of the main works is eventually improved by detaching ourselves from the "official doctrine" account of them. Thus the most fruitful response to an enthusiasm for the philosopher as a young man is to translate it into so thorough a historical examination of his early writings that, as a deliberate and long range consequence, it will incite an equally thorough revision of the standing interpretation of his mature teachings.

A moderate approach is well expressed in this remark by Schelling:

> If you want to honor a philosopher, then you must apprehend him at that point where he has not yet proceeded to the consequences, [apprehend him] in his basic thought. . . . The *true* thought of a philosopher is precisely his basic thought, that from which he sets forth.[18]

The intent of doing honor or historical justice to a philosopher must include a careful study of his basic or foundational thought, *sein Grundgedanke*, taken as the genetic source for his subsequent inquiries and not just as a logical basis of reduction. Such a research intent need not specify beforehand whether the foundational thought consists in one or several principles, any more than it need stipulate the precise sort of cognition involved. There is no precommitment to one privileged logical model, or to a Bergsonian primary and central intuition (in some closely determinate sense), or to a monistic image of how everything else flows from this root. What does count is the methodic resolve to respect the integral development of the philosopher's thought and thus to examine its living basis in his early reflections, adapting one's historical analysis to the actual shape and course of the extant genetic sources. Just what sort and degree of revision

---

[18] F. W. J. Schelling, *Philosophie der Offenbarung*, in M. Schröter's new ordering of Schelling's *Werke*, Ergänzungsband 6, p. 60. This rule pervades the developmental study of the link between Schelling's early essays and later masterworks by A. Bausola: *Lo svolgimento del pensiero di Schelling*.

in the established version of the main treatises are demanded by taking this genetic perspective, will also be determined uniquely in accord with the particular philosopher's growth of mind and argument.

The research community in modern philosophy is presently involved in two related instances of systematic revision which is being induced in the wake of concentrated research into the early writings. The philosophers in point are Hegel and Marx, who can be taken together for our present purpose of observing how the historical study of each one's early writings raises similar issues bearing upon the genesis-system relation in him (postponing until the next section the further question of the relationship between the two men themselves). All the factors involved in our analysis of that tension come into play here in their concrete form.

At the outset of the present century, historians of philosophy were generally content to begin their serious examination of these thinkers with a well marked event or publication. In Hegel's case, it was the publication of the *Phenomenology of Spirit* in 1807, at the time when Napoleon's invasion broke up his work at the University of Jena and sent him off as a newspaper editor and director of the Nüremberg secondary school. Marx came upon the scene with the issuance of the *Communist Manifesto* and his peripheral involvements in the revolutions of 1848. Given the intellectual and social importance of these writers, however, the genetic question could not help getting formulated: What led up to 1807 and 1848, enabling these men to come forth with so mature and powerful expressions of thought and so distinctive methods for analyzing human experience?

No real progress could be made in answering this question, until the extant materials of the preparatory years were edited in reliable and convenient form and eventually translated into the main working languages for philosophical research. This involved two kinds of textual work: the collecting and reprinting of the first printed writings of Hegel and Marx in unified volumes, where their continuity and genetic significance could become visible; and the transcription and editing of their unpublished manuscripts. A start was made on these projects by the Hegelian scholars Nohl and Lasson, and by the Marxian scholars Riazanov and Adoratsky. But this basic editing process was long and painful in execution; the preliminary genetic studies which it did generate only fueled the demand for more critically edited texts; and the work of editing and translating the early writings is only now being successfully concluded.

As students of Hegel and Marx began to realize the import of these fresh sources and the ensuing modifications likely to be needed in the official portraits, they also began to engage in moves indicative of a clash between the great-works syndrome and the young-thinker mystique. There was an initial reluctance to grant that early sketches and youthful articles could substantially affect our understanding of the *Phenomenology* or the *Science of Logic*, the *Critique of Political Economy* or *Capital*. But it soon became clear that what were being protected from any disturbing influx of genetic insights were not precisely these classical books, but rather a standard version of what they signified. Not an appreciation of the great works as such, but an established and nonhistorically oriented account about them, constituted the real obstacle to reinterpretation in the light of genetic research. The latter had to be carried on, however, rather than proclaimed. Thus for a while, a somewhat romantic image of the young Hegel and the young Marx was stimulating and perhaps even necessary for doing developmental studies.

There was no need to fabricate either attractive intellectual features or problems of interpretation, however, since both were found in authentic abundance in the sources. It was no accident that, out of research into the early writings, came a vivid picture of the young Hegel as humanist and the young Marx as humanist.[19] Among other significations, the term

---

[19] This humanistic interpretation is all the more striking for being proposed by scholars working in both the principal philosophers. From the Marxist viewpoint, Alexander Kojève's *Introduction to the*

"humanist" carried, in this context, at least five notes of guidance bearing on the methodology of historians of philosophy.

(1) It means a rediscovery of the philosopher himself within his philosophy, and of the everyday man in the philosopher. Although in principle this biodoctrinal relationship can be perceived at any stage in the philosopher's life and writings, it becomes strikingly manifest when a Hegel and Marx are studied in their early years and then in their unbroken development.

(2) The early writings permit us to go behind the scenes and enter the philosopher's workshop more easily. Instead of being simply overwhelmed by the imposing mature figure of the philosopher of spirit or the diagnostician of capitalist economy, we are introduced to him at the trial-and-error stage. Seeing that so many tentative proposals, blind alleys, and great leaps of insight go into the making of the philosophies of Hegel and Marx, we are reassured about their human genesis and their permanent accessibility to our own inquiries and critiques.

(3) Although not at all lacking in the works of full maturity, the plural themes and motivations of these two bodies of thought stand out more strikingly for us in their first

---

Reading of Hegel opened up the humanistic side of the Hegelian theory of spirit and experience. The Hegelian scholar Jean Hyppolite brought out the humanization of Hegel's logic in *Logique et existence,* and showed in his *Studies on Marx and Hegel* that both sources share a preoccupation with the human meaning of existence, life, and history. The young Marx's humanism was rapidly sketched by Luc Somerhausen, *L'Humanisme agissant de Karl Marx*; magisterially developed in Auguste Cornu's *Karl Marx et Friedrich Engels*; and shown to permeate and dominate his mature economic positions by Pierre Bigo, *Marxisme et humanisme.* These researches are phenomenologically reformulated by H. J. Koren, *Marx and the Authentic Man*; given a social-psychiatric twist by Erich Fromm, *Marx's Concept of Man*; and related to the New Left by Leszek Kolakowski, *Toward a Marxist Humanism.* The textual bases for these humanistic portraits can be found in *Writings of the Young Marx on Philosophy and Society*, ed. L. D. Easton and K. H. Guddat, who see a severe conflict between Marx's existential humanism and his immanent dialectic of history (pp. 26-32).

phases. That is why historians of the young Hegel must grapple with the full circle of his human interests: in history of philosophy and his immediate German antecedents, in the religious spirit of ancient Greece and Israel, in the medieval cultural forms and the upheavals in modern consciousness and society, in the destiny of the Holy Roman Empire and the political proceedings in his native Wurtemberg, and in the whole band of convictions which the Enlightenment and Romanticism brought along for reconciling the scientific, emotive, and institutional values of mankind. Similarly, historians of the young Marx find him to be moralist, poet, and student of Greek philosophy; informed critic of Hegel and Feuerbach, as well as of true socialism and true humanism so-called; working political journalist and analyst of Rhineland political and economic conflicts; satirist of university life, the higher Biblical criticism, and Parisian novels about the proletariat; and a searcher after the better union between social theory, the vast factual materials of the British and French economists, and revolutionary practice. The humanistic challenge to historians consists in finding a conception of Hegel and Marx capacious enough to do justice to their youthful burgeoning interests, without blotting out the humane horizons from their systematic achievements of maturity.

(4) More specifically, a study of their early writings makes us recognize the centrality of the problem of man for both thinkers. This overriding concern with human reality in all its complexity accounts for the wide scope of their inquiries, the intensity with which they pursue clues and make their criticism, and the difficulty of finding a unifying basis that will not rub out the many levels of value and significance. When a Hegel does finally develop his master theme of self-developing spirit, and Marx his master theme of social man laboring in nature and history, they are both ready to move beyond the years of apprenticeship. But they do not make the passage to intellectual maturity by cancelling out their basic fidelity to the problems of human experience, activity, and

goals. The persistence of their humane orientation is the primary conviction we derive from a genetic approach, and thereafter we cannot read their great masterpieces without doing so in this same light.

(5) Finally, to call the young Hegel and the young Marx "humanists" is often a means for relating their groping efforts to our present searchings. We see in their formative years something similar to the humanistic problems occupying ourselves. Hence in those concerns where they resemble us, we draw closer and profit more from their reflections. This last connotation of humanism as an affinity with ourselves manifests the active role of the interpreting present in all historical investigations, genetic and otherwise, and hence it deserves further consideration in the following chapter.

Eventually, the research situation in history of philosophy catches up with itself. That is, the gross imbalance between genetic and systemic studies is corrected with the publication of successively improved editions of the early texts, monographs on highly specialized points, and general interpretations of the young philosopher. At some point in historical work, the primary need ceases to be that of giving strategic overemphasis to the early years and becomes, instead, that of making a balanced assessment of the contribution of the work of these years to the analytic and systematic exposition of the philosopher. The historical aim now is *to correlate all the phases* in his development, determining as definitely as possible how they work together to achieve the continuity of a living philosophy. Within this more comprehensive end of inquiry, the genetic studies of the young philosopher can be made to yield some further systemic significance which would remain stifled, were the historian to persist in overcultivating the isolative mystique.

This new vein of historical meaning crops out when the genetically well informed reader revisits the philosopher's classical works. There can be no sheer repetition of previous interpretations which lacked the genetic perspective, and therefore the new reading must have a dissolving effect. But the historian clearly realizes that what is being displaced is not the great treatise itself but a conventional interpretation shown to be historically inadequate, that is, unable to assimilate and interrelate all phases in the philosopher's lifelong inquiry. We can now make more historical sense out of the master work, both in its main thrust and in specific arguments. For with the aid of the genetic context, we can view the mature texts as prolonging, correcting, and transcending the methods and problems of the early years. With the philosopher's *Grundgedanke* permitted to operate, we can perceive new purposive relationships between the earlier and the later writings. The former can no longer be dismissed as inconsequential sketches, and the latter cannot be denied their dimension of advancement.

Once the historian is able to take a developmental-and-systemic look at the philosopher's achievement, he can bring out the meaning of a mutual adaptation among its stages. There is the *foreshadowing* aspect of the early writings, their powerful latency of principles and problems shaping the course of future development. And there is also the *fulfillment* aspect of the central classics, as their detailed arguments respond to the early challenge and redeem the promise of the initial strivings of thought. In his prime, the philosopher deepens his hold upon the basic issues and insights of his youth, so that even his most mature statements are laden with an incorporated genetic meaning to which the historian of philosophy cannot remain insensitive.

To make one more analysis of the situation in Hegelian and Marxian studies, they are now entering the most productive phase of historical interpretation where this mutual adaptation is becoming apparent. Jean Hyppolite has shown that, although Hegel's *Phenomenology of Spirit* is the immediate place to reap the fruits of a genetic-systemic comparison, this same approach must be gradually extended to the other major books. The *Science of Logic* and the *Encyclopedia of the Philosophical Sciences* have much more significance to yield, once they are studied historically in terms of how Hegel's humanistic range of experience pervades and shapes his metaphysical logic of spirit. Wilhelm Seeberger, John Findlay, and other Hegelian scholars are revisiting the systematic treatises and lecture courses to show how they contribute toward such overarching themes as "the development of spirit toward freedom."[20] We are bound to gain a juster estimate of Hegel's philosophical genius, as we follow his unceasing attempts to apprehend human reality in its many relationships to the drive of spirit and the search for freedom in its earthly shapes.

In the study of Marx, there has been a greater danger of establishing a deep rift between his earlier and later phases, with the former receiving unrestrained admiration and the latter equally undisciplined depreciation. Faced with such an antithesis, Marxian scholars have recognized the need for adopting the ordinary canons of historical methodology, especially those concerning the fundament. The task of interrogating the fundament in its own textual completeness and integrity cannot be faithfully pursued, if an uncritical and extraneous evaluation is permitted to tear apart the actual body of texts.

[20] The effort to make a balanced appraisal of Hegel's mature thought, as being the fulfillment of early promise and not its betrayal, marks W. Seeberger's *Hegel, oder die Entwicklung des Geistes zur Freiheit* and J. N. Findlay's *Hegel: A Re-Examination* as models for historical synthesis. A similar direction for Marxian research is set by Jean Calvez, *La Pensée de Karl Marx*, and Shlomo Avineri, *The Social and Political Thought of Karl Marx*. The special interest of Robert Tucker's two books, *Philosophy and Myth in Karl Marx* and *The Marxian Revolutionary Idea*, lies in their self-corrective relating of the genetic stress with the systematic analysis of Marx's main writings and impact on later revolutionary thought. In *Die Marxsche Theorie*, Klaus Hartmann makes a comprehensive analysis of Marx the young humanist and the scientific economist. Hartmann establishes: (a) the strong continuity and interdependence of these aspects; (b) the operative influence of Hegel-Feuerbach as specifying Marx's thought-problems-language; (c) the presence of theory in a *sui generis* sense (whether called "philosophy," "antiphilosophy," or "a-philosophy") in Marx; and (d) the use of argument to justify and clarify this doctrine. Karl Marx establishes his own historical continuity of theory and argument in his *Critique of Hegel's 'Philosophy of Right,'* ed. J. O'Malley.

Fortunately for the health of Marxian studies, methodological considerations are beginning to prevail sufficiently so that balanced historical judgment can be formed on the basis of a full and continuous reading of the sources. The continuity and steady growth in Marx's thought are being underscored by Calvez and Avineri, Tucker and Klaus Hartmann. They are bringing to clearer notice both the humanistic strains in his mature analyses of capitalist economy and also the directedness of his pre-1848 investigations toward a closer, more concrete engagement with economic history and revolutionary practice. The historical conception of Marx's mind which is emerging from these more comprehensive interpretations shows him to be more persistently committed to a philosophy of social man than the established view of his *Capital* could recognize, and at the same time more centrally ordered toward the historical economic analyses and revolutionary politics of his later life than the first partizans of his early manuscripts would concede.

The mature conspectus. Just as I began this section with a reference to the sketchy "life and writings" accounts which historical research respects but also criticizes and moves beyond, so I would like to round it off with an acknowledgment of the distinctive function of the mature conspectus or full-length study of a philosopher and his thought. At its best, such a synthesis comes after a particularly intensive period of specialized research into the biographical, genetic, and systemic aspects of the thinker. The function of a conspectus is to draw together these particular lines of investigation, to develop from them a unifying pattern of the philosophy in its development and general significance, and thereby to refine our judgment about it and suggest the most fruitful directions for further inquiry. In the synthetic mode, we can gain a fresh comprehension of the whole authorship— taken in the generous sense of a lifetime devoted to bringing philosophical reflections forth into the expressed word, so that they can be shared by the community of men. Renewing our grasp upon a great philosopher's whole authorship serves as a beacon for many historians engaged in the specialized investigations, as well as a needed bridge between history of philosophy and the life of human culture.

A synoptic presentation of a modern philosopher does not merely sew together the patchwork investigations of the specialists, but is the medium for realizing at least three distinctive historical values. For one thing, the overview brings into prominence that quality of *steady originality* which marks the lifework of a great philosopher. It enables us to see that, together with the plans of his early years, the philosopher also has the power to work out his argumentation and make originative moves at every subsequent phase in his philosophizing. The tide of surprising methodological and conceptual innovations continues to rise during his maturity. The continuity of his thought does not mean any rigid genetic precoding, any philosophical DNA predetermination, such as would rule out his ability to summon new instruments of analysis or to redirect the search along some unmarked terrain of experience.

Closely connected with this constant reserve of creativity is a second lesson often learned from the conspectus approach: the unique contribution of the philosopher's *later years* of reflection and writing. The likelihood of doing valuable and even basic work during the later span is higher among philosophers than among many other intellectual workers, and so an important function of the comprehensive study is to encourage us to stay around long enough to appreciate these ultimate accomplishments of the whole authorship. For a Hobbes or Kant, a Schelling or Bergson, it is true that ripeness is all, that the work of their later years joins wisdom with innovation. Their later philosophy often manifests an unexpected degree of self-criticism and courageous exploration. Here, we can often best discern the reflective linking between the generations, in a time of philosophical transition.

A third fruit of the well wrought conspectus is that it

enables the historian, using the whole armory of available tools of study, to satisfy what Whitehead calls the three stages in *the rhythm of education*: romance, precision, and generalization.

> In relation to intellectual progress I would term them, the stage of romance, the stage of precision, and the stage of generalization. The stage of romance is the stage of first apprehension. The subject-matter has the vividness of novelty; it holds within itself unexplored connections with possibilities half-disclosed by glimpses and half-concealed by the wealth of material. In this stage knowledge is not dominated by systematic procedure. . . . The stage of precision also represents an addition to knowledge. In this stage, width of relationship is subordinated to exactness of formulation. It is the stage of grammar, the grammar of language and the grammar of science. It proceeds by forcing on the students' acceptance a given way of analyzing the facts, bit by bit. New facts are added, but they are the facts which fit into the analysis. . . . The final stage of generalization is Hegel's synthesis. It is a return to romanticism with added advantage of classified ideas and relevant technique. It is the fruition which has been the goal of the precise training. It is the final success.[21]

History of philosophy listens in its own way to the requirements of human education and tries to meet them with its own modes of rhythm.

These philosophical modes of romance-precision-generalization are displayed in superior works of historical conspectus. Such works have an introductory function, arousing a romantic or pre-analytic first interest in the philosopher as man and thinker. But the initial disposition is not left to flounder complacently and inarticulately. It is then directed toward the demanding task of penetrating the philosopher's methodology, precise argumentation, and systematic proportions. Along with the genetic interest and the analytic preci-

---

[21] A. N. Whitehead, *The Aims of Education*, pp. 29-31.

sion, the historian also aims at their purposive unification. He leads us toward a synoptic and generalizing grasp of the philosophy as a developing, articulated whole of reflective meaning. Thus a successful historical synthesis is one that communicates a sense of the source thinker's mind, using all the rhythmic approaches which will educate us into his thought.

Yet there is no pre-programed schedule for developing and ordering the conspectual components. Just how to do so is decided by *the art* of historical questioning, where each solution is unique and cannot be read off from a universal formula. There is a remarkably wide variation of helpful forms of conspectus in the history of modern philosophy. Even confining ourselves to a few instances available in English, we can take heart from the freedom and originality displayed by historians working in the synoptic style.

At first glance, we might be inclined to regard as methodologically routine the life-and-works studies prepared by Richard Peters on Hobbes, by N. K. Smith on Hume, and by Philip Hallie on Maine de Biran.[22] Yet each of these synoptic books holds a surprise of its own, a separate worth for appreciating the possibilities opened up by the conspectus approach.

Peters finds a way of overcoming the separatism which plagues Hobbesian studies, where the social analyst and the historian of science and the narrow philosopher never seem to consult each other's interpretation or make the appropriate adjustments. He gives us a complex Hobbes, who is simultaneously worried about seventeenth-century social upheavals, excited by the revolution in mechanical sciences, and sustained by a strong belief in the efficacy of method. Hobbes resembles his philosophical contemporaries by taking as the

[22] Richard Peters, *Hobbes*; Norman Kemp Smith, *The Philosophy of David Hume*; Philip Hallie, *Maine de Biran, Reformer of Empiricism 1766-1823*. These three books can also be thematically interrelated, since they pursue the problem of human experience as it gets interpreted mechanistically by Hobbes, morally by Hume, and in terms of interior spiritual effort by Biran.

first article of his credo "Method maketh man." But he is also a disturbing intellectual force in his age because of his specific proposal to achieve systematic continuity of reasoning through prolonging the mechanical synthesis of nature into the realms of perception and moral judgment, social relationships, and church politics. Thus from the example of Peters' conspectus, we can learn the art of bringing different specialized interpretations within hailing distance of each other, and of adjusting them to the source philosopher's own peculiar thrust.

Smith provides us with an exemplary case where the historian can achieve a quiet revolution in perspectives, by organizing a synopsis around a new ordering of the flow of a philosopher's thought. Whereas Hume is conventionally treated as a pure epistemologist who also applies his analysis of perception to moral and political fields, Smith challenges the assumption of the isolated purity and priority of the epistemology. Instead, he takes seriously Hume's underlying moral concerns, shared with his countrymen Francis Hutcheson and Adam Smith. Viewed in the light of this radical moral teleology, the Humean principles of understanding are already adapted to a moral estimate of human nature. And conversely, Hume's work in esthetic, social, and historical areas makes a distinctive contribution to his conception of man, and does not merely function as a set of corollaries or an afterthought. By reordering his conspectus around the moral nature of man, N. K. Smith gives a new look to the familiar writings of Hume and evokes some new meanings for specific texts. His reinterpretation has not gone unchallenged, but it has broadened our search for that philosopher's primary intent and provided a model for the moral accentuation of other modern sources.

Hallie's brief monograph on Maine de Biran represents another sort of historical unsettlement, one achieved by championing what is ordinarily classified as a minor figure. Directing us toward Biran's acute criticism of the empiricist positions on self-identity and will effort, as well as his anticipatory contributions to later French philosophy of spirit, Hallie prevents us from taking "a lesser philosopher" to mean one that can be safely ignored. Not only does Biran loom larger in the French tradition than in the English, but he also provides one of those oblique channel crossings which keep the provinces of modern European philosophy together.

How is a synthesizing unification of a complex philosophy to be reached, within the economy of a single volume?[23] One suggested way is worked out with skill and concision in Vleeschauwer's *The Development of Kantian Thought*. Instead of hurrying through a digest of the main works and then concentrating on a systematic analysis, this historian follows Kant's writings decade by decade, working contextually in the main problems facing Kant at different periods. Our perspectives get enlarged when we can view together the preparatory writings leading up to the conception of the critical problem, the main themes of the first *Critique*, the completional function of the other two *Critiques* in facing the further issues, and even the workings of Kant as an older man defending himself against the Kantians and groping toward new horizons. Here is a concrete expression of a whole authorship, as found in Kant's treatment of the categories of experience.

Another method of synopsis serves as the organizing prin-

---

[23] The broad range of stylistic and perspectival freedom permitted within the conspectus form of history of philosophy is plain in comparing these three examples: H.-J. de Vleeschauwer, *The Development of Kantian Thought*; J. A. Passmore, *Hume's Intentions*; T. H. Croxall, *Kierkegaard Commentary*. Vleeschauwer's chapters are modeled upon the descriptive monograph on each period in Kant's life; Passmore cultivates the art of the brief essay in each chapter; and Croxall gives a modern equivalent of the venerable commentary approach, with attention centered on the actual wording of the Danish text. Vleeschauwer achieves unification by following Kant's master problem of the categories through several stages; Passmore interconnects the plural intentions of Hume through the theme that skepticism keeps invading every effort to establish a science of human nature; and Croxall organizes the voluminous writings of Kierkegaard around his self-appraisal as midwife of the personal reality of men before God. Other styles and guiding principles will yield another conspectus for each thinker.

ciple of Passmore's introduction to Hume. Under the title of *Hume's Intentions*, the author identifies some seven methodic aims of the Scottish philosopher to be: defender of the moral sciences (Kemp Smith's perspective), critic of formal logic, methodologist, positivist, phenomenologist, associationist, and skeptic. Passmore teaches us not to be confused in the presence of several philosophic and humane intentions, and not to ask that "the real David Hume" stand forth in terms of only one of these functions. In history of philosophy, the rhythmic demand of the educational process is precisely to acknowledge a great philosopher's many aims, to detect and appreciate each one in its season of predominance in his writings, and to struggle toward some comprehensive interpretation that incorporates them all in a relationship.

Finally, the forbidding title of Croxall's *Kierkegaard Commentary* should not prevent us from recognizing here still another elegant methodological solution for the problem of conspectus. His table of contents reads like a special lexicon: existence, pleasure, imagination, suffering, border conflicts, living "before God," works of love, and authority. The individual chapters do attempt to define these concepts and trace their turnings in Kierkegaard's mind; but in the process of analysis, the interlacings among the main themes also become clearly visible. In the end, readers find that they have traversed the main stages in Kierkegaard's own way of life and the main writings in his authorship, and have done so through following the thematic analysis rather than the other way around. Croxall's procedure suggests that conceptual analysis and interest in the historical development of a philosopher need not be incompatible approaches and, indeed, are profitably interwoven by the practised historian of philosophy.

4. THE MODES OF INTERRELATION

We must now shift our central attention from the fundament to that other pole of historical interrogation: the interrelations among the originating philosophers. This move is dictated by the requirement of distinct moments of analysis in our method of functional reflection, rather than by any ontological theory of history and human relationships. Hence it does not support the implication that the fundament sources are isolated monadic minds in search of a community. Quite to the contrary, one striking feature of our first acquaintance with the great modern philosophers is that we find them already in an intellectual company, already related to each other by the effective bonds of language and persistent problems, mutual study and discussion, influences acknowledged and departures made significantly from one another within a common historical context. Correlatively, the historians try to develop some general procedures for doing justice to these interconnections in the modern philosophical community. They are procedures designed for discerning, inspecting, and evaluating the operative historical bonds, not for trying to fuse together some initially unrelated atoms of intelligence.

In order to show the continuing collaboration between the insistential sources and the interrogating historians, we will select three modes of interrelational questioning which bring out different forms of the collaboration. These three modes are respectively concerned with: the originative philosopher as radial center, the "from-to" span of development, and the persistence of common themes and problems. The first mode stresses the awareness of interworkings on the part of the source thinkers themselves; the second one typifies the interrogative initiative which historians of modern philosophy must take; and the third form of questioning gives fitting prominence to the dedication of sources and historians alike to the central problems binding together all members of a philosophical community. Although these are not the sole modes of historical comparison, they do belong among the essential acts which enable us to work out the interrelations among the modern philosophers.

(a) The originative philosopher as radial center. Historical continuity is not a categorial mold imposed externally upon the textual materials in modern philosophy but is,

rather, a relational dimension within the philosophizing activity and its interpretation. As our previous treatment of strategic prefaces and introductions to the master works indicated, the sourcing philosophers themselves recognize the factor of continuity and build it into their own formulation of the problems and new solutions. The fact that their self-interpretation of the philosophical connectives is usually adapted to their own project of reconstruction does not detract from the reality of these connectives. But it leaves plenty of room for alternative interpretations of the continuity on the part of other philosophers and historians. Thus the acts of comparison made by the company of modern philosophers constitute one powerful source for the questioning which revolves around the interrelational pole.

Judging in terms of the performance achieved in both the primary texts and recent historical studies, Leibniz provides the most instructive angle of vision for this phase of the inquiry. He is the exemplar of the originative philosopher who deliberately acts as a radial center for many lines of communication with other thinkers. Fittingly, in his philosophy every finite mind is regarded as a *stella hians et radians*, a living star which opens forth and radiates light from others and for others.

Especially a philosophic life, concerned with the problem of referential centers, develops its own reality through the three referential operations of concentration-expression-origination. A Leibnizian mind must remain receptively open to the methods and concepts of others, so as to bring the many philosophical efforts of the past into focused *concentration* in his own reflectivity. His philosophy also springs from recognizing his own capacity to express reality anew, in a unique vision of both its divine source and its unifying order in the universe. In accord with this range of *expressiveness*, the philosopher can develop a distinctive perspective of his own, with methods and principles of judgment for moving beyond his predecessors in tackling the theoretical and practical problems of mankind. Hence a thinker in the Leibnizian spirit must also exhibit the power of *origination*: he is a source of new departures and a provocation for other men to make their own sightings and soundings. Such a radial center is no inert, timeless, and vacuous point, but rather a living historical agency engaged in receiving, reworking, and suggesting within the context of an open philosophical tradition.

Leibniz lives his own ideal of how a philosopher should stand related to others in this tradition. There is scarcely a page of his writings, from early youth to old age, which does not bear the record of his conscientious and thorough reading of other sources in philosophy and theology, mathematical and physical sciences, political and social theories. In Leibniz's *Unedited Texts* published by Grua from the Hanover manuscript collection, we can begin to appreciate the breadth and depth of his comparative studies, as well as the background preparation for what may seem to be only casual references to other positions as stated in his polished essays. This thousand-page selection of reading notes, commentaries, sketches, and letters on work in progress, can serve as an experimental field station for observing how a philosopher consults, criticizes, and assimilates the preceding tradition into his own universe of meaning.

The Leibniz field station permits us to observe the process of historical continuity in the making. For example, under the heading of "Twofold Infinity in Pascal and Monad" in his own philosophy, Leibniz makes this cool appraisal:

> What M. Pascal says about the twofold infinity which environs us in respect to increase and decrease, when he speaks in his *Pensées* about our general knowledge of man, is only one entry in my system. . . . [My monad or primitive subject of life and action is] a micro-divinity, a universe of matter eminently contained; God in ectype and this same universe in prototype; imitating God and imitated by the universe in respect to its distinct thoughts;

like God through its distinct thoughts, like matter through its confused ones.[24]

Pascal's view of man, as standing midway between the infinities of God and matter, becomes here a subordinate paragraph within Leibniz's own more general theory of active substances. In the same section of critical papers on various theories about the relation between man's soul and the world, Leibniz enables us to follow his interpretation and transformation of the positions of his favorite Plato and Aristotle, Augustine and Malebranche, Spinoza and Henry More. Thus his own practice serves as a school in the interrelational modes of interrogation, insofar as these modes are activated by the source philosophers themselves.

Leibniz's two longest works are also two of the most richly sustained essays in comparative philosophizing. The *Theodicy* and the *New Essays concerning Human Understanding* are similar in some important respects. They both succeed in avoiding the archaicizing fallacy, which pretends that all other philosophies are safely reposing in the past and hence constitute no living challenge to the philosopher engaged in interrelational studies. Instead, the *Theodicy* springs

[24] Leibniz, *Double Infinité chez Pascal et monade*, in his *Textes inédits*, ed. G. Grua, II, 553-555. Leibniz is meditating upon Pascal's question: "For after all, what is man in nature? A void in comparison with the infinite, a whole in comparison with the void, a middle term between nothing and all. Infinitely far from grasping the extremes, the end of things and their origin are completely hidden from him in impenetrable mystery; he is equally incapable of seeing the void whence he comes, and the infinite in which he is engulfed. . . . I am convinced that it is impossible to know the parts without knowing the whole, any more than we can know the whole without a detailed knowledge of the parts" (*Pascal's Pensées*, tr. M. Turnell, pp. 216, 220; Lafuma number 390, Brunschvicg number 72). But Leibniz counters the conclusion of skeptical fideism by using mathematico-philosophical ways of gaining some reliable knowledge (but not comprehension) of the whole-parts correlate. See Michel Serres, *Le Système de Leibniz et ses modèles mathématiques*, II, 648-810, for the Pascal-Leibniz comparison in respect to their differing mathematical models and conceptions of man (Pascalian man as a point, and Leibnizian man as an active representational center of reference or *stella hians*).

out of the present weight of Bayle's skeptical argumentation
on God and the presence of suffering and evil in our world,
just as the *New Essays* responds to the contemporary impact
of Locke's account of the genesis, nature, and limits of human cognition. To understand what is going on in these complex treatises, we have to cultivate the comparative mode of
reflecting upon the relationships between Leibniz and these
two contemporaries. But more, we must also notice how
Leibniz makes his private historical and critical studies become functional parts of his public discussions of evil and the
human understanding. He puts his preparatory readings and
reflections to work on these issues. Not only the reinterpreted
views of other philosophers in the European tradition but also
relevant concepts drawn from scientists, theologians, and
jurists—all are made to converge upon the question at hand.
History broadens the alternatives to Bayle and Locke on any
issue, thus enabling Leibniz to define his own doctrine at
many levels of comparative reference and criticism.

Books have their separate destinies, of course, so that
Leibniz's essays in theodicy seem more oriented toward the
past, recapitulating many previous methods, distinctions, and
lines of justification, and bringing them to a classic termina-
tion. But his essays on human knowing are laden with consequences for the future history of modern philosophy. Leibniz's manuscript of the *New Essays* is a good instance of the
delayed intellectual time bomb. Not published until 1765, it
was then able to implode quietly in the mind of the maturing
Kant. Thereafter, Kant never failed to take an interrelational
approach to the problem of the human understanding, which
involved a twofold reference to Locke's conception of empirical reality and Leibniz's suggestion of transcendental
ideality. In turn, historians of philosophy have the responsibility of developing their interconnective inquiries with sufficient skill to interpret still further the relations among the
fundamental modern philosophers.

Leibniz serves as our instructor in interrelational questioning also by means of his many series of correspondences. He

firmly believed in the power of reasonable discussion and disciplined polemic to articulate and improve his own philosophy, as well as advance the general state of a question in the philosophical community. Hence he devoted much care and thought to exchanges of letters with thinkers of great and small stature, discussing basic issues with them over many years and sometimes with the aid of intermediaries. His most fruitful interchanges were made with Arnauld and De Volder, Malebranche and Clarke.[25] These documents give us a concrete image of Leibniz, the truly radial and radiating mind, conscientiously bent upon developing his own thought and assuring the historical continuity in one strain and one phase of human philosophizing.

Leibniz gladly submitted to the acute interrogation of the Jansenist theologian and logician, Antoine Arnauld. For in the process, he was able to work out more carefully the link between his theory of truth and his conception of the individual active substance. Hence if we want to appreciate the cutting edge of criticism in Leibniz's *Discourse on Metaphysics*, we have to read it together with his letters to Arnauld. The latter supply the requisite commentary on the meanings of form and matter, the union of soul and body, the degrees of expression and perception, and the intricate relation between the principle of the best and the identity of indiscernibles. In his letters, Leibniz affords us a somewhat informal, indirect, and comparative look at these key doctrines.

As for De Volder, he furnished Leibniz with a good occa-

---

[25] We are fortunate to have excellently edited separate translations of *The Leibniz-Arnauld Correspondence*, tr. H. T. Mason and G. H. Parkinson, and *The Leibniz-Clarke Correspondence*, ed. H. G. Alexander. Full sources for the Leibniz-Malebranche exchange are edited by André Robinet, *Malebranche et Leibniz: Relations personelles*; see Leibniz, *Philosophical Papers and Letters*, tr. L. E. Loemker, Index s.v. "Malebranche," for much of the Leibniz comment, and pp. 515-541 for the correspondence with De Volder. Together, these letters offer a distinctive access to the radial mind of Leibniz. The pitfalls of simply interpreting Clarke as spokesman for Newton are pointed out by M. R. Perl, "Physics and Metaphysics in Newton, Leibniz, and Clarke," *Journal of the History of Ideas, 30* (1969), 507-526.

sion for describing his own philosophy as a middle way between Descartes and Spinoza, between regarding inert extension as substantial and reducing all substantial centers to the one divine reality. In effect, Leibniz laid down in this correspondence *the hermeneutic canon of co-consideration* for the study of his philosophy. Anyone who wants to grasp Leibniz's distinctive meaning and role for substance can do so only by considering his direct textual statements in relation with the doctrines of Descartes and Spinoza, as detailed and criticized in his treatises and letters.

The most sustained, subtle, and difficult-to-unravel relationship is the Leibniz-Malebranche one, the complete texts of which fill 500 closely packed pages in Robinet's superb critical edition. Beginning with an exchange of letters in 1675 (following Leibniz's visit with Malebranche in Paris and his reading of the Oratorian's *Search after the Truth*), the direct interchange continued until 1711-12, while the enveloping correspondence with the Malebranche circle persisted right up until Leibniz's death in 1716. All the major topics in their philosophies were covered, with no holds barred but with remarkable courtesy, keenness, and pertinacity being displayed by both of these searchers after the truth. They helped each other to reach greater clarity and fuller awareness of the difficulties and consequences in their respective positions on mathematical knowledge and physical motion, the nature and modes of causality, God's presence in the world and in the human soul, and vexed points in theodicy and the controversy on grace and nature. On all these basic issues, historians of philosophy find it necessary (again, in accord with the canon of co-consideration) to keep Malebranche in mind when examining the arguments of Leibniz.

Although the Leibniz correspondence with Newton's champion, Samuel Clarke, is well known and thoroughly analyzed in several editions, its yield of fresh insights into Leibniz's philosophy is somewhat disappointing. The atmosphere in which the papers were exchanged was too charged with recrimination to permit a genial presentation or the unfolding of new views. And yet the very bluntness of the clash over the nature of space and time made this correspondence required reading for Boscovich, Euler, and above all Kant. Just as Kant found it profitable to retain reference to the Leibniz-Locke disagreement on the human understanding, so did he develop his positions on space and time with constant reference to the Leibniz-Newton-Clarke controversy. Kantian space and time combine Newton's objective pervasiveness with Leibniz's basis in human perception. This comparative mode of genesis of the Kantian theory of space and time, as forms of sensibility in the 1770 *Dissertation* and the first *Critique*, actually incorporates into that doctrine an interrelational complexity of meaning. This has to be matched by the historian's willingness to develop the comparative viewpoint and render the relationships more explicit, in his own analysis of what Kant opposes and defends.

No matter how instructive the source thinker may be in his radial capacity, he does not spell out all his intellectual links and hence does not render superfluous the interrogational research of the historian. What further interrelational understanding can be expected from history of philosophy, is suggested by the actual accomplishments of three Leibnizian scholars investigating the most basic and complex areas of comparison.[26] Gottfried Martin has read Leibniz in the light of the long medieval and school-manual tradition of metaphysics; Yvon Belaval's perspective is determined by the axis running between Leibniz and Descartes; and the Leibniz-Spinoza relationship is the center for historical probing by Georges Friedmann. Moreover, Belaval and Martin are also working (in the same vein as Heinz Heimsoeth) on Leibniz's metaphysico-epistemological impact upon Wolff and especially upon Kant himself. Out of these researches comes a sense of the multi-form relationships and transformations

[26] G. Martin, *Leibniz: Logic and Metaphysics*; Y. Belaval, *Leibniz, critique de Descartes*; G. Friedmann, *Leibniz et Spinoza*. Comparisons between Kant and Leibniz are made in essays by Belaval and Martin, in *Kritik und Metaphysik*, ed. F. Kaulbach and J. Ritter, pp. 1-9, 99-105 (Kantian essays in honor of Heinz Heimsoeth).

whereby modern philosophy constitutes itself as a continuing tradition, and wherein the historian of philosophy finds his tasks defined and his judgments grounded.

One task is to furnish a *groundlevel description* of the types of connection and the textual materials involved in some specific comparison. Sometimes, there is a personal contact to be described, such as Leibniz's visits with Malebranche and Spinoza. The historian has to present such meetings from the standpoints of all the parties involved, using their own notes and letters and the observations of others. Personal relationships often are mediated and altered by those with other members of a school or a circle: Leibniz knows and reacts to Schoolmen and Cartesians, Spinozists and Malebranchians. In addition to the biographical factors, the historian must acquaint us with the whole range of writings which state his philosopher's engagement with the doctrines and methods of another thinker. In every period of Leibniz's intense study and criticism of Descartes, for example, there are dozens of notes and working papers, portions of treatises and passages in articles and correspondence, where this relationship continues to grow and get expressed. Just to attain descriptive adequacy, an interpreter must enter sympathetically into this full trove of materials, must respect the chronological factor and aspects of development, and then must attempt to give an orderly account of Leibniz's understanding, criticism, and use of Descartes and the Cartesians.

To achieve such unification, the historical investigator accepts as a second responsibility the determination of some *organizing themes of comparison.* Since he is not making a mirror report but a responsible interpretation, he must bring his own judgment to bear upon the textual materials in order to recognize, reformulate, and mutually order the leading principles governing the interrelation of the philosophers in question. Thus Belaval finds a key in the difference between Descartes' kinship with geometry and Leibniz's primary cultivation of arithmetic and the calculus. This leads Leibniz to dissociate certitude from Cartesian intuition of evidence and to connect it, rather, with a grasp of the formal relationships among functions in a system which yields knowledge in terms of probability, continuity, and harmony. This befits the new conception of the human condition and the new center of gravity for Leibniz: "At the center of this philosophy is not *Cogito*, but *Deus cogitat mundum*," not the thinking self but the correlation of God-thinking-the-world.[27] It is in terms of these basic shifts that Belaval is able to establish a synthe-sizing perspective upon the topic of Leibniz as a critic of Descartes.

Still a third requirement of historical comparative ap-proaches is to permit some *counter-initiatives* to develop against the central philosopher. A sheer monologue, spoken from a single standpoint only, would make not only dull reading but also misleading history. For it suggests that philosophical criticism is a one-way process, in which a subse-quent thinker always has the last word and scorches away the potencies for response on the part of his predecessors. But in fact, the source thinkers enjoy a remarkable resilience vis-à-vis each other, a capacity to return with further meanings and more pertinent arguments. Part of the historian's art consists in devising means to enliven these potencies and keep the dis-cussion among philosophers at a peak.

This can be done literally and with relative ease in the analysis of an interchange among contemporaries, as in the case of Leibniz's relations with Arnauld and Malebranche. But since Spinoza did not live long enough to engage in sig-nificant discussion with Leibniz, it is incumbent upon Fried-mann to make his own statement of the kind of rejoinder that Spinoza might have made in terms of his actual positions. This he does by showing the independence of the two philos-ophers. The myth of the young Leibniz as an ardent Spinozist is untenable, since from the outset each thinker draws upon a radically different conception of the nature of philosophy. In the eyes of Spinoza, Leibniz is too much the religious

[27] Belaval, *Leibniz, critique de Descartes*, p. 532. See M. A. Haley, *Mathematics and Method in Leibniz's Metaphysics* (unpub. diss.).

apologist, too much saddled with an extra-philosophical vocation to still our doubts about a personal God and to assuage human miseries in a world of free creation and sin. By sympathetically drawing us into Spinoza's outlook and likely countercriticism of Leibniz, Friedmann satisfies one of the chief aims of interrelational questioning. He keeps the philosophical alternatives alive and strong, within the bounds set by the textual sources and their temporal distancing.

One last desideratum of comparative studies is that they open up the opportunity for *further research* on the terms of comparison. The wise historian refuses to create the illusion of exhaustive analysis and sealed-off finality in his interpretation, but instead points out other perspectives that could be taken and other readings that ought to be tested out. Hence Martin rightly assesses his role as that of an advance scout on the question of how Leibniz's logic and metaphysics are affected by his vast readings in the Greeks, medievals, and Schoolmen. The Leibnizian text offers historical *continuant indices* pointing to Plato and Aristotle, Scotus and Ockham, Suarez and Jacob Thomasius. Since Leibniz listened to these earlier voices on questions about predication and the categories, transcendentals and the nature of metaphysics, this side of his intellectual ancestry cannot be safely ignored.

Yet Martin also reminds us that this direction of comparative questioning has barely started with his few steps, and that even the preliminary description of Leibniz's readings and critical analyses of these sources remains incomplete. Such investigation is hardly trivial, since upon it hinges our understanding of how Leibniz serves as a continuant agency for several later medieval and Renaissance philosophies. And this question in turn controls, to some extent, the historical legacy which Leibniz passed on to Wolff and Kant. But this is already verging upon our next kind of interrelational inquiry.

(b) The "from-to" span. Historical studies organized on a from-to basis meet several irreducible needs in history of philosophy. They are not constructed merely by stitching to-

gether a series of analyses of individual philosophers, although they do receive support and revision from the more specialized monographs. But there are some other questions to ask, other ways of interrelating the philosophers, other developmental meanings to uncover than those obtained by concentrating upon only one mind, however radial. The from-to approach is distinctively founded upon these other modes of interrelational querying. Hence it makes quite manifest the active intent of the historian in proposing new goals of research and new perspectives for illuminating the sources.

Although practical needs enter into the division of materials in the multivolume histories of philosophy, the arrangement in the better histories also involves some theoretical considerations.[28] Thus Frederick Copleston's ordering of his exposition in volumes five (Hobbes to Hume) and eight (Bentham to Russell) of his *History of Philosophy* is made upon a basis of language and national culture, but not exclusively thereon. For he also finds sufficient unity and persistence of problems, along with a return to the same core sources, to make it philosophically rewarding to view the British philosophers together. They are never isolated from continental influxes, but neither are they ever unaware of some special obligation to face the questions central to their own educational and philosophical tradition.

Albert Rivaud's *History of Philosophy* implies a similar recognition of the impact of a shared language, culture, and national milieu, by giving separate treatment to German philosophy from 1700 to 1850. In this case, the division into two volumes (going from the Enlightenment to Schelling, and then from Hegel to Schopenhauer) has the added significance of recognizing the usefulness of such a cultural referent

[28] Frederick Copleston, *A History of Philosophy*, vol. 5: *Hobbes to Hume*, and vol. 8: *Bentham to Russell*; Albert Rivaud, *Histoire de la philosophie*, vol. 5: *La Philosophie allemande de 1700 à 1850* (part one: *De l'Aufklärung à Schelling*; part two: *De Hegel à Schopenhauer*). See Lewis W. Beck, *Early German Philosophy: Kant and His Predecessors*, chapter 1: "A National History of Philosophy?" (pp. 1-15).

as the Enlightenment, as well as the pre-eminence of Kant and Hegel in their ages. Thus the practice of Copleston and Rivaud suggests that, although a Hume and a Hegel do enter into many other philosophical relationships, they are also intimately bound up with the philosophers in their respective national traditions. Historical research seeks to determine the precise issues which have unifying power among British and German philosophers, and to do so on philosophic rather than nationalistic grounds.

Another function of a from-to span is to thematize, by this designation, the development of a philosophical movement or *school*. Something is gained in historical understanding, when a philosopher is viewed from the standpoint of the school of thought which he fathers. The philosophical school has three important functions in working out the implications of a system. (i) It tests the original theory for coherence; (ii) it spells out the residual problems in more detail and force; and (iii) it shows the vitality and limitations of the basic source by applying its principles to new questions and deliverances of our experience.

The *Cartesian Studies* of Balz and of Watson help us to observe these school-functions in concrete operation.[29] Their research enlarges our access to the meaning and the diffi-

---

[29] A. G. Balz, *Cartesian Studies* (1951), and R. A. Watson, *Cartesian Studies* (1968), represent two successive generations of historical research upon the same group of school-sources, and permit us to see how the general trends in investigation compel historians to make new interpretations. The new factors here are skepticism and the history of science. Watson reads the Cartesians, not so much with reference to their medieval sources (as did Gilson and Balz), but with an eye to the skeptical criticism whose import is established in the following from-to studies: R. H. Popkin, *The History of Scepticism from Erasmus to Descartes*; Henri Busson, *La Pensée religieuse française de Charron à Pascal*; R. A. Watson, *The Downfall of Cartesianism 1673-1712*; and J. S. Spink, *French Free-Thought from Gassendi to Voltaire*. Descartes and the Cartesians are also now better situated within the broader scientific movement by A. Koyré, *From the Closed World to the Infinite Universe*, and by G. Buchdahl, *Metaphysics and the Philosophy of Science: The Classic Origins, Descartes to Kant*.

culties inherent in Descartes' philosophy, precisely by following out its school relationships. We realize more sharply the
tensions, ambiguities, and silences in the primary thinker,
when he is seen in the light of the quandaries unearthed by
such acute Cartesian Schoolmen as Régis, Rohault, and Le
Grand, as well as by the occasionalist authors Cordemoy and
de La Forge. Precisely because they do not merely repeat
their master, they spell out the problems which might otherwise go unnoticed in Descartes' own teaching on certitude,
the substance-qualities schema, the mind-body relationship,
and the whole project of achieving a unified science and philosophy of nature.

Furthermore, we can make more unified sense out of the
entire story of the rise of Descartes and the breakdown of
school Cartesianism by relating this rise-and-fall to its historical countermovement and destiny: the growth of classical
modern skepticism. The latter furnishes a more ample context
within which to understand the needs that Descartes himself
fulfilled, as well as the shoals upon which his school became
shipwrecked. The complicated relations between these two
lines of philosophizing are the subject of some effective inter-
rogations in the from-to modality: *The History of Scepticism
from Erasmus to Descartes* (Popkin); *French Religious
Thought from Charron to Pascal* (Busson); *The Downfall
of Cartesianism 1673-1712* (Watson), that is, from Foucher's first skeptical counter-blast against Descartes to Malebranche's last surrejoinder; and *French Free-Thought from
Gassendi to Voltaire* (Spink). These comparative studies not
only enable us to appreciate the tremendous incitive role of
skepticism in modern philosophy generally, but also pinpoint
the exposure of Descartes and his school to different phases
in the skeptical critique.

To exhibit the traits of continuity and interdependence in
modern philosophy, historians must find ways of intermeshing
such long-span studies as those dealing with Cartesianism and
skepticism. Here, the art of historical inquiry resembles the
development of a symphony out of several master themes,

even more than it does the interlaying of topographical-economic-political features in a complex map. For the historian's ear always remains open and searching for other motifs, which help to organize the fuller meaning of an age of philosophizing. In seeking to characterize the seventeenth-century and Enlightenment situation, for instance, he will thematize the strong scientific component along with the skeptical and religious considerations affecting philosophical work. The interrelations of scientific and metaphysical thinking furnish the orientation for such from-to spannings as Koyré's *From the Closed World to the Infinite Universe* and Buchdahl's *Metaphysics and the Philosophy of Science: The Classic Origins, Descartes to Kant*. These comparisons show that, in some important respects, the historical continuity and interdependence among philosophers stem from their common engagement with a scientific methodology and outlook. Thus history of philosophy is involved constantly in reworking the weave, so as to incorporate the scientific contexts and other conceptual sources which research keeps uncovering for the better understanding of the philosophical master works.

There is no purism or a priori law restricting the historian's choice of intellectual correlate, perspective, or time span for his from-to interpretation. His only justifying consideration is whether the comparison in question helps, in some fashion, to improve our grasp upon the problems, methods, and argumentations found in modern philosophy. Sometimes, the overriding aim is simply to illuminate the intellectual matrix within which a major philosophical treatise has arisen. The first half of Kant's third *Critique*, treating of esthetic judgment in the modes of the beautiful and the sublime, is a notoriously slippery text to master. One can outline all of its analytic moments in purely abstract fashion, without ever developing a historical sense of the actual problems, inductive materials, and philosophical alternatives facing Kant and intimately affecting the significance of his esthetic principles. In order to bring such information to bear upon the reading of the *Critique of Judgment* in its actual context, we can use Nivelle's research on *The Esthetic Theories in Germany from Baumgarten to Kant*.[30] This instrument enables us to follow the pre-history (from a Kantian viewpoint) of the Latin and German terms, the analytic divisions of the beautiful and the sublime, and the preparatory contribution not only of the Wolffian philosophers but also of great literary critics: Winckelmann, Lessing, and Herder. These connective points in the matrix help us to gain a firmer historical grasp upon Kant's esthetic theory.

Historical investigators are also free to inquire: What differences of a philosophically significant sort are noticeable, over the long run, in philosophies maintaining a common religious reference? Although this question is customarily asked in regard to a Christian referent, it must also be raised in regard to Judaism in order to learn how modern philosophy is affected by this specific comparison. Rotenstreich's *Jewish Philosophy in Modern Times: From Mendelssohn to Rosenzweig* and the parallel chapters in Guttmann's *Philosophies of Judaism* employ the from-to procedure with good effect. They show that the problem of revelation and philosophy receives a distinctively Jewish, as well as a Christian, form in post-Enlightenment times.

The philosophers linked in this from-to perspective are important for gauging the impact of Kant's criticism of metaphysics, as well as the historical reasons why philosophy of God and philosophy of religion have flourished even when the Kantian critique remains in force. For although some Jewish thinkers have reworked Hegel's philosophy of spirit into a

[30] Armand Nivelle, *Les Théories esthétiques en Allemagne de Baumgarten à Kant*. Kant is the pivot of comparison with modern Jewish philosophers in Nathan Rotenstreich's history of *Jewish Philosophy in Modern Times: From Mendelssohn to Rosenzweig*, as well as in Julius Guttmann's *Philosophies of Judaism*, part three: "Jewish Philosophy of Religion in the Modern Era," pp. 289-398. Thus at least part of Kant's significance in ethics and philosophy of religion is captured only when we view him within some modern Jewish, from-to perspectives.

reaffirmation of speculative theism, the mainstream has explored the nonmetaphysical but ethical approach to God. The dividing question is whether to achieve philosophical rigor through an ethical religion of humanity or to obtain an existential footing in the unique religious relation of persons to the holy God, heard amid historical realities. In terms of the from-to standpoint, it is advisable to study Mendelssohn and Lazarus, Hermann Cohen and Rosenzweig, not only in relation to Kant and Hegel but also (and perhaps primarily) as a distinctive plane of modern philosophical argumentation on the respective claims of reason, duty, and the ideal of holiness.

Doubtless, the most intensively cultivated historical span is that reaching from Kant to Nietzsche. Here, the from-to thematization signifies both some grounds of comparison and some genetic interdependence among the philosophers thus interrelated. Indeed, one of the fascinating features of this research field is that the comparative mode of thinking is already authoritatively exercised by the primary philosophers themselves. They clarify their principles and make their distinctive systematic moves in full view of each other, and with the explicit intent of moving the entire discussion up to a new level of reflective criticism and reconstruction.

Thus Kant writes a prize essay on the progress of metaphysics since the time of Leibniz and Wolff, and also sets down some essays and notations sharply critical of the idealism of Fichte looming on the horizon. In turn, Fichte's own versions of the *Wissenschaftslehre* seek to incorporate and move beyond Kant. Both early and late in his own career, Schelling takes great pains to establish his originality in respect to Kant's critical position and Fichte's transcendental idealism. And Hegel never fails to regard his own speculative logic and ontology as the surmounting culmination of all past efforts in German philosophizing. Under changing intellectual and social conditions, however, Hegel's totality of spirit and freedom becomes a deliberate point of departure for Feuerbach, Marx, and the Hegelians of the Left. Nor does the philosophical ferment stop here. For just as Schopenhauer protests against Hegel in the name of life and unappreciated Oriental values earlier in the nineteenth century, so there is an explosive yet incorporative criticism of all the prior developments in philosophy, religion, and society voiced by Nietzsche as the century closes. Thus the chief German philosophical sources are themselves comparison-minded and help to compose their own genealogies.

Since these genealogies are partly argument and partly myth, however, they raise difficulties of interpretation and hence call forth the distinctive work of historians working in the from-to vein. The sources are not just echoed but critically reconsidered in such classic historical studies as Kroner's *From Kant to Hegel*, Hook's *From Hegel to Marx*, Löwith's *From Hegel to Nietzsche*, and Lukács' *The Destruction of Reason: The Beginnings of Modern Irrationalism from Schelling to Nietzsche*.[31] All these historians are con-

---

[31] Richard Kroner, *Von Kant bis Hegel*; Sidney Hook, *From Hegel to Marx*; Karl Löwith, *From Hegel to Nietzsche*; Georg Lukács, *La Destruction de la raison*, vol. 1: *Les Débuts de l'irrationalisme moderne de Schelling à Nietzsche*, and vol. 2: *L'Irrationalisme de Dilthey à Toynbee*. Although these historians are treating the same source philosophers, they bring to their own from-to analysis some quite different principles of interpretation and evaluation. Kroner here treats epistemological and ontological idealism as the norm; Hook brings along his background in Dewey and social pragmatism; Löwith retains a religious perspective and an interest in existential and cultural issues; and Lukács judges the post-Hegelians by the same standard of functional Marxism which guided his study of the young Hegel. In *The Young Hegelians*, W. J. Brazill reminds us that the Germanic world of 1835-50 had moved beyond Hegel to an activist humanism, which was neither dominated by Marx nor ordered toward his specific patterns. Hence it is historically unsatisfactory to make a purely transitional, from-Hegel-to-Marx interpretation of Strauss and Bauer, Ruge and Stirner, Feuerbach and Vischer. "If the Young Hegelians are to be considered apart from a continuum of thought from Hegel to Marx, if their unique historical experience made of them something more significant than mere shadows of Hegel or forerunners of Marx, then it is essential that historians recognize their intrinsic historical meaning" (p. 21). Brazill orients the Young Hegelians more toward the experience of the death of God, or the temporalizing of eternal values, but without Nietzsche's anguish over this experience.

fronted with the same predicament, which we can observe most strikingly in the case of Hegel's treatment of his German philosophical milieu.

Hegel wields the from-to type of relatedness among philosophers as a weapon, a tool used primarily for making judgments of philosophical evaluation. He *makes* Kant-Jacobi-Fichte-Schelling *to be* his antecedents, in the emphatic argumentative sense of being forerunners and stages in a single line of development, leading toward Hegel's own philosophy as their total actualization of method and meaning. These other thinkers become supervened and surmounted predecessors, by being assimilated to Hegel's *interpretive logic of filiation and surpassing*. This perspective is one of filiation and genetic dependence, since Hegel acknowledges his debt to each antecedent for supplying some valuable gleam of the truth. But the dominant note is that of ultimate surpassing, as Hegel subordinates all previous methods to his speculative logic of positive reason. This permits him also to assign a partial role to every other principle and concept, within the concrete totality of his philosophy of spirit.

Nevertheless, his composite judgment of filiation and surpassing is not entirely arbitrary, but rests upon a careful reading of these German sources and a powerful argument with them. Hegel's version of the from-to relationship still remains a challenging interpretation for historians to ponder. For it fits many of the texts, rests upon evaluative principles showing their coherence and comprehensive range, and furnishes one conceptual framework within which to interrelate the philosophers concerned. Something similar can be said about Marx's account of his filiational surpassing of Hegel and the Hegelians, as well as about the Nietzschean version of the from-to movement in modern philosophy leading toward his nihilation and reaffirmation of the world.

Nonetheless, historians of philosophy are not there simply to ratify these autointerpretations. Their continuing work upon the Kant-to-Hegel span involves a critical sifting and reworking of the relationships. The basic aim is to open up, through more careful and inclusive textual studies, the grounds for formulating the problems otherwise, for taking new points of emphasis, and thus for *recasting* the interconnections in other forms.

As a case in point, Kantian researchers note that Hegel surmounts Kant only by underplaying the first *Critique* and the epistemological qualifications it sets upon other cognitive claims. This means that Hegel surpasses Kant only by overcoming Newtonian science and biological procedures much too rapidly and easily through the distinction between scientific understanding and philosophical reason, along with supposing that man and nature are already overreached by dialectical logic and the workings of absolute spirit. Kantian scholars seek to recover the proportions and orientations found in Kant himself, thereby also freeing him from the lockstep role of serving only as a stage in the resolute and exclusive march of modern philosophy toward Hegel.

Along two research fronts, a similar historical liberation is being accomplished for Fichte.[32] His work can be regarded as foundational, rather than transitional, in respect to two main currents of nineteenth-century philosophy: the theme of *Wissenschaftslehre* and the question of man. In both areas, his closeness to Kant signifies a distinctive stand and not a

[32] There is a fresh understanding of the Kant-Fichte approach to objectivity, intersubjectivity, and human freedom in: Didier Julia, *La Question de l'homme et le fondement de la philosophie (Réflexion sur la philosophie pratique de Kant et la philosophie spéculative de Fichte)*; and the two studies by Alexis Philonenko, *La Liberté humaine dans la philosophie de Fichte* and *Théorie et praxis dans la pensée morale et politique de Kant et de Fichte en 1793*. In conjunction with the new Heath-Lachs translation of Fichte's *Science of Knowledge (Wissenschaftslehre)*, one should consult the research of K. Schuhmann, *Die Grundlage der Wissenschaftslehre in ihrem Umrisse: Zu Fichtes "Wissenschaftslehren" von 1794 und 1810*, and W. Janke, *Fichte: Sein und Reflexion*, on several versions of the theory of science. On recent Schelling studies, see below, Chapter IV, note 9. This resurgence of Fichtean and Schellingian research rests upon basic historical procedures: mutual comparison and internal genesis, more scrupulous analysis of classic texts and more capacious interpretation of the theme of man.

half-hearted move in the direction of Hegel. For Fichte seeks to develop a theory of science and a moral ontology within the limitations of human nature, that is, of a striving reality which never permits itself to become absolutized or to attain the unconditioned totality. In terms of this self-limitation, Hegel no longer represents a surpassing *resolution* of Kant and Fichte but remains an *alternative* to their conceptions of man.

There is a similar loosening of the frame of reference within which Schelling is ordinarily viewed. As a direct consequence of specific historical studies of the early, middle, and later phases of his philosophy, it is no longer bound down to measurements calibrated on the Hegelian scale. Schelling's thought cannot be contracted and frozen into the initial search after a principle of identification between nature and spirit. Nor in historical fairness, can it be dismissed with the often cited remark of the *Phenomenology* that here is the chaotic night wherein all cows are black. For Schelling's contributions to the problems of divine freedom and history, human existence and mythopoeic imagination, are sufficiently distinctive in themselves and consequential for later discussions to prevent their historical miniaturization as steps leading only toward Hegel. Certain methodological features of recent Schelling research will occupy us in section two of the following chapter.

The concentration of historical analysis upon Feuerbach and Stirner, Marx and Nietzsche, also generates new terms of comparison. The Hegel who figures within such studies is not the climax of Western thought, but is either a point of departure or a waystation toward some new center of convergence. This is not a fate reserved peculiarly for Hegel, however, but follows from historical reinterpretation of any from-to relationship. Some designated culminating point is usefully taken, since it does mark the attainment of reflective comprehension in a long discussion. But this is a recuperative pause and reordering of philosophical energies rather than their ultimate completion, and hence every climactic philosophy must submit eventually to a new interpretation made in terms of some other historical evolution.

On the basis of his own conception of self-evolving spirit, Hegel himself acknowledges the incessant development required both in the act of philosophizing and in its historical interpretation. History of philosophy

> is a history of all the internal developments of spirit, an exposition of these moments and stages, as they follow upon one another in time. . . . We have to investigate the series of these gestations, this millennial work of thought to bring itself forth, this journey of exploration upon which thought embarks in order to discover itself.[33]

Even apart from Hegel's special theory of spirit, it is clear that any particular span of philosophical growth (specified either by the participating philosophers or by reflective historians) is subject to a *reopening* of its closure and a *reorienting* of its components. For every terminal "-to" contains some further implications, which transform it eventually into a new "from-" or starting point for further paths of historical comparison and ordering.

Exploratory historical study of the philosophies involved in one line of development is bound to suggest other paths, leading in a different from-to direction. The responsive historian perceives that innovations of method and argument are bound to remove the definitive note from any specified terminal. The alternative modes of interrelation and the new reaches in a historical span prevent any absolutization of a particular from-to comparison among modern philosophers.

[33] Hegel, *System und Geschichte der Philosophie*, ed. J. Hoffmeister, pp. 81, 118-119. Hegel's own presupposition that the "system" and the "history" of philosophy are ultimately identical is itself subject to critical reconsideration, and hence cannot serve as a unique theoretical substitute for our method of functional reflection on the praxis of philosophizing and of historical interpreting. The contrast between Kant and Hegel, on whether there is ultimate unification of essential system and epochal history in philosophy, is studied by N. Rotenstreich, "The Essential and the Epochal Aspects of Philosophy," *Review of Metaphysics*, 23 (1969-70), 699-716.

However brusque and unsettling the intervention of another reading may prove to be, this revisionary process expresses both the pluriform continuities binding philosophies together and the research ferment in improving our historical understanding of modern sources.

(c) The continuative problem. One of the most potent of interrelational instruments is the problem-centered study. Here, the problem itself is the organizing principle of historical interpretation. Individual philosophers are treated and emphasized only in the degree that they make some notable contribution to continuing discussion of this one chosen issue.

To follow a problem through its treatment by many thinkers—who may belong to quite different philosophical traditions and schools, national climates and time periods—is a way to see relationships and threads of meaning which would otherwise escape our notice. It also gives a functional basis, in the practice of historians of philosophy, for coming to recognize that modern philosophy is neither solipsistic nor loosely episodic in its foundations, but rather that it enjoys a real persistence and community of meanings. The great modern philosophers are not engulfed in temporal and intellectual insularity but belong in a community of reflection and discussion, whose interrelations are constituted by the abiding problems shared among them. Historical studies of these continuative problems help to show both the force of tradition and the thematic openness among modern philosophers. Even where there is no strict *interdependence* based on genetic descent, there are determinate likenesses and differences available for *comparison*.

One functional way to settle upon the meaning of philosophical modernity is to make a reflective survey of the chief themes which have nourished the problem-oriented studies. A first finding is that modern philosophical awareness is not closeted off from its Greek and medieval past. This broad receptiveness of modern philosophers to earlier thought is attested by the comparative studies done on such perennial problems as: substance and matter, nature and history, will and freedom, evil and error, the great chain of being, the possibility of metaphysics, and the great tension between speculative thought and revelation.[34] In each instance, there is a significant carry-over from the Greek and medieval philosophers, whose heritage constitutes a genuine operating fund upon which their modern successors make generous drafts.

[34] In a representative dozen of such books, we can find resources bearing upon many historical and theoretical problems: F. Billicsich, *Das Problem des Übels in der Philosophie des Abendlandes*; V. J. Bourke, *Will in Western Thought*; H. Cairns, *Legal Philosophy from Plato to Hegel*; R. G. Collingwood, *The Idea of History*, and *The Idea of Nature*; A. L. Hammond, *Ideas about Substance*; L. W. Keeler, *The Problem of Error from Plato to Kant*; R. Kroner, *Speculation and Revelation in the History of Philosophy*; R. Lenoble, *Esquisse d'une histoire de l'idée de nature*; Joseph Maréchal, *A Maréchal Reader*, selections by J. Donceel from Maréchal's five-volume *The Starting Point of Metaphysics*; E. McMullin, ed., *The Concept of Matter*; A. G. Van Melsen, *From Atomos to Atom*. The problem of the overlapping relationship, yet interpretive difference, between history of philosophy and history of ideas (as illustrated by the above books) is treated by P. O. Kristeller, "History of Philosophy and History of Ideas," *Journal of the History of Philosophy*, 2 (1964), 1-14. "That part of the history of philosophy which consists of the history of problems, concepts or terms as used by different philosophers at different times evidently belongs to the territory of the history of ideas. However, there is a large and important area which belongs to the history of philosophy—above all, the monographic treatment of the entire thought of a given philosopher, as well as the comprehensive account of the development of philosophy as a professional discipline during a shorter or longer period or through the course of its history. . . . The historian of philosophy will stress the relation of a given idea to the entire context of the thought of the philosopher who expresses it, and to that of his contemporaries, predecessors, and successors in the history of professional philosophy. . . . A historian of ideas unconcerned with technical philosophy will be inclined to treat the ideas of past philosophers like those of other writers, as incidental opinions unrelated to the basic and continuing philosophical quest for truth, and as merely decorative elements of a historical pageant that can be enjoyed and described without being seriously or precisely understood" (p. 13). The philosophical resources furnished by history of ideas are exemplified by *Dictionary of the History of Ideas*, ed. P. P. Wiener; and the relationship is separately treated by George Boas, *The History of Ideas*.

Yet such long-range comparisons also underline the radical transformations and departures brought about by the modern ways of conceiving the problem of substance and the rest. Historical judgment about the modern treatments is thus sharpened by those problem studies which take a broad measure in Western philosophy as a whole.

But the complexity and divergence among modern philosophies also require a specialized concentration of historical analysis upon the issues within the Renaissance and modern eras. Our historical thinking has been indelibly marked, for instance, by the combination of a specialized theme and the broad range of its development in Ernst Cassirer's classical four-volume study of *The Problem of Knowledge in the Philosophy and Science of the Modern Age*.[35] He enables us to follow the problem of knowledge from the Renaissance to our own time, to notice the permutations and ramifications of this question, and thus to acquire the historical basis for affirming the centrality of epistemology in modern philosophy.

Cassirer suggests that the specific quality of the modern

[35] E. Cassirer, *Das Erkenntnisproblem in der Philosophie und Wissenschaft der neueren Zeit* (vols. 1-3; Berlin: B. Cassirer, 1906-1920), and vol. 4, *The Problem of Knowledge: Philosophy, Science, and History since Hegel*. For the period since Hegel, Cassirer describes his historical method of immanent analysis and unification of the several sciences and philosophy of science. "From the richness as well as the divergence and conflict of individual tendencies and efforts a unified and comprehensive tendency begins to disclose itself. But of course all this requires a persistent, patient steeping of oneself in the work of the separate sciences, which must not only be investigated in respect to principles but explained correctly, that is, in the way they conceive and handle their primary and fundamental problems. . . . The era of the great constructive programs, in which philosophy might hope to systematize and organize all knowledge, is past and gone. But the demand for synthesis and synopsis, for survey and comprehensive view, continues as before, and only by this sort of systematic review can a true historical understanding of the individual developments of knowledge be obtained" (*The Problem of Knowledge*, pp. 18, 19). Marjorie Grene's *The Knower and the Known* offers a recent epistemological synopsis of modern philosophy. From the standpoint of God and religion, a modern problem-conspectus is made by James Collins, *God in Modern Philosophy*, and by Cornelio Fabro, *God in Exile: Modern Atheism*.

preoccupation with the problem of knowledge derives from
the continuing interrelations between philosophical analysis
and the new scientific methods and concepts. In testing out
this impact of modern science, subsequent historians of philosophy have had to probe even more deeply than did Cassirer into the cosmological theories of Cusanus and Bruno,
as well as into the philosophical relevance of Galileo, Newton, and Darwin. Their findings reinforce the theme of interdependence between the dominant epistemology and the corresponding scientific outlook of every phase in modern
thought. Problem-oriented studies have this capacity of
knitting together the history of philosophy and topics in the
history of science on the nature of scientific revolutions, different meanings of scientific objectivity, and evolution.

The very inclusiveness of a historical synopsis, made in
terms of some recurring problem, may tempt us to absolutize
this theme as constituting the unconditional center of modern
philosophizing. In testing this suggestion, historians are led
eventually to a definite breaking point in the explanatory net.
They find themselves unable to do full justice to a significant
portion of the modern sources, unless they shift the perspective and treat some other problem as pivotal. Historical work
done on the theory of knowledge, as a case in point, cannot
be permitted to overcloud the concern of modern philosophers for issues which take their rise in metaphysics or psychology or social ethics, and which leave their original and
distinctive mark upon the ordering of epistemological inquiries. Hence there must be a contrapuntal emphasis placed
upon these other organizing principles and their dominant
historical relationships.

Among the central modern problems, there is no purely
one-way determination but rather *a reciprocity of initiative
and orientation*. This can be seen when the historical focus
moves from the problem of knowledge to that of God, as hap-
pens in Cornelio Fabro's *God in Exile: Modern Atheism*.
Here, we can see that a modern philosopher's approach to
God and atheism is not dictated sheerly by his other positions,

but enjoys its own primacy and infuses its own coloration into his conception of knowledge, reality, and ethical freedom. Similarly, the problem of God and religion has a continuative influence upon the kinds of relationships between philosophers, so that this constitutes one major way of synthesizing the problems discussed among them. In order to avoid an impoverishing concentration upon but one master problem, historians must take account of this reciprocity among the great staying issues and hence must vary the bases of historical synopsis. Comparative inquiries flourish better on the supposition of a polycentrism among master-problems-in-the-plural and among the paths of interrelationship radiating from them.

Finally, at the most restricted level of specialized problems, there is a remarkable flexibility of research in regard to the particular topic, time span, and interconnecting sources. Often, these points get specified in response to a nest of difficulties unearthed by historians during their more broad-gauged forms of from-to investigation.[36] Thus as a result of the work done on continental types of rationalism and skepticism, some parallel movements are being noticed in Britain during the seventeenth century. This lead is followed out in Van Leeuwen's *The Problem of Certainty in English Thought 1630-1690*, which shows that the question of the power and limitations of human knowledge was truly a common concern of the British intellectual community during these years. The philosophical responses of Bacon and Locke are situated within a field of discussion agitating the scientists of the Royal Society, the literary minds, and the theologians. The problem approach compels us to recognize the sharp diversity and spread of positions among these reflective minds, not all of whom were content with the wholesale solutions offered by skepticism and dogmatism.

[36] Van Leeuwen is cited above in note 10. The philosophical ideal of unified science is examined by Robert McRae, *The Problem of the Unity of the Sciences: Bacon to Kant*. The main problem-paths through Kant himself are mapped by L. W. Beck, *Studies in the Philosophy of Kant*.

One middle path between these epistemological extremes is found in the modern ideal of synthesizing all our forms of knowledge in a mutually supportive unity. McRae's *Problem of the Unity of the Sciences: Bacon to Kant* concentrates upon this problematic unification of philosophers from different centuries and national traditions and theoretical contexts. It is worth noticing that Kant functions here as the terminus of a long tradition of French, British, and Enlightenment philosophizing, rather than as the overture to the later German systems. One of the purposes of problem-oriented research is precisely to marshal sufficient momentum of evidence to liberate the history of modern philosophy from calcification, such as that caused by viewing Kant or some other great thinker always within but one line of comparison.

Until the historian actually exercises his freedom to vary the theme and the scope of his problem analyses, however, he cannot really ascertain the increase of understanding which may accrue from his experiment. What will the historical findings yield, if he defines his scope in terms of some one modern century, and then searches out the contributions of the philosophers of that age to a basic issue? This is the guiding question behind three otherwise quite different examinations, centered around problems in each of the three modern centuries.[37]

W. von Leyden's *Seventeenth-Century Metaphysics* achieves some unusual advantages from its specification of time and subject. Taking heed of recent research, it admits skepticism to full membership on a par with rationalism and empiricism. Then it breaks down the artificial school divisions, by examining the concern of all three philosophical tendencies (in England as well as on the continent) with a common set of problems in metaphysics. The central metaphysical issues are identified as: certainty and doubt, self and material substance, essences and individuals, mind-body and

---

[37] W. von Leyden, *Seventeenth-Century Metaphysics*; Émile Callot, *La Philosophie de la vie au XVIIIᵉ siècle*; and Maurice Mandelbaum, *History, Man, and Reason: A Study in Nineteenth-Century Thought.*

causality, and the tension between absolute and relative conceptions of space and time. This is a functional way of determining the nature of metaphysics in the seventeenth century, by watching the philosophers of that age in their reciprocal criticisms.

With Émile Callot's study of *The Philosophy of Life in the Eighteenth Century*, some other historical values emerge. The Enlightenment preoccupation with the problem of life is historically unique: it is a move beyond the mechanism of the previous century, and yet it contains only the prefigurements of evolutionary conceptions. In the division of biological philosophies into the more naturalistic (La Mettrie, Holbach, Diderot, Maupertuis) and the more theistic (Fontenelle, Montesquieu, Linnaeus) types, we encounter not only the sharp diversity in Enlightenment theories of life but also the problem which this diversity posed for Kant. The latter's firm determination (in the latter part of the *Critique of Judgment* dealing with purposive judgment in biology) to take account of the best contemporary scientific and philosophic thinking on life can be better appreciated, with this range of alternatives in mind. Callot's problematic analysis helps us to understand why Kant remains critically uncomfortable with either position, taken as the exclusively valid interpretation of life. We can see that the Kantian synthesis of mechanistic and purposive factors in the study of organisms is intended to meet this division of eighteenth-century opinion.

How can a unified interpretation be made of the divergent nineteenth-century English, French, and German philosophies, without positing some overriding "spirit of the age"? A powerful methodology for resolving this question is developed in Maurice Mandelbaum's *History, Man, and Reason: A Study in Nineteenth-Century Thought*. Its three thematic strands of historicism, man's malleability, and the limits of reason trace the interworkings of Hegel with positivism and materialism, evolutionism and religion. The history-progress-reason coordinates also support a historical judgment on our loss of belief in progress, as well as our need

to balance any tragic reading of man with the actual achievements of analytic understanding to date.

Thus *the art* of historical questioning finds reality in the
historian's judgment. Formulating a problem of his own, he
considers how best to bring to bear upon it the many modes
of interrogation. In some degree, he has to develop those
forms of questioning which look primarily to the fundament,
to the creative agency and work of the individual philosopher. Some responsible use must be made of the biographical data, the stages of genesis, and the systematic analysis of
the major treatises. The selection of materials, the ordering
of the philosophical arguments, and the achieving of peaks
of emphasis and unity—these are acts of historical interpretation which cannot be either preordained or bypassed. They
must arise out of one's prolonged and many-forked engagement with the fundament. Furthermore, the historian has to
cultivate the interrelational pole of inquiry, lest he violate the
continuities of thought in order to perform a neat dissection.
His comparative aim may eventually become paramount, as
he follows out the hints of a radial philosopher, or focuses
upon a from-to span, or thematizes a dominant problem over
a specific passage of time.

If he can artfully proportion these many factors for a
unifying purpose, however, the result will be satisfying as an
act of historical knowing. It will enlarge our understanding
of either a broader or a more specialized aspect of the modern philosophical sources, and will do so in such fashion that
we can never view them again in quite the same light as we
did before this investigation was undertaken. A fresh contribution to history of philosophy is like an art work, in that it
engenders some delight on the part of both the historian and
those who share his fruits. For it enables them all to perceive
the difference this work makes in what modern philosophers
can say henceforth to the community of reflective men.

Looking in retrospective wonder at all the complications
uncovered by his analysis of legislation and morals, Jeremy

Bentham appealed to the analogous reaction of the famous dancing-master, M. Marcel:

> Leaning on his elbow, in an attitude of profound and solemn meditation, "*What a multitude of things there are,*" exclaimed the dancing-master Marcel, "*in a minuet!*"— May we now add?—*and in a law!*[38]

Our present analysis of the components involved in historical questioning may perhaps permit us to add still a further exclamation: *and in a well turned historical study!* However, I would like to use the Penderecki analogue for a contemporary comparison.

Krzysztof Penderecki's *Passion according to St. Luke* brings many elements into harmonious and functional relationship. It develops out of a selective use of sacred texts from the Psalms and Gospels, great hymns and sequences from the Roman Missal and Breviary which translate the sacred history into religious responses, and a whole range of musical resources ranging from Gregorian and Baroque down to twelve-tone psalmody and voice intonation. Insofar as a study in history of philosophy fuses the component factors of fundament and interrelational questioning into a unique interpretation, it approximates in a very halting way to the complex unity of a work of art. And just as a Penderecki keeps us aware of the contemporary context in which the St. Luke Passion bears upon the sufferings of Hiroshima, so does a historian of philosophy execute his work within our present world of philosophizing. We must now examine this contemporary bearing of historical inquiry and its essential contribution to our understanding of modern philosophy.

---

[38] Bentham makes this comparison in the concluding note to *An Introduction to the Principles of Morals and Legislation*, in *A Bentham Reader*, ed. M. P. Mack, p. 144. Krzysztof Penderecki's *Passion according to St. Luke* is RCA recording VICS-6015 (Library of Congress card number R67-3744).

IV

The Interpreting Present

We sometimes imagine the history of philosophy as being a Janus-faced colossus.[1] One of its legs is firmly planted in times past and the other in the present, just as one face is pointed resolutely toward the sources and the other toward contemporary discussion. This metaphor serves a good purpose in suggesting the wide diversity of materials and comparative questions which fall within the historian's responsibility. But it blurs over the ground of their "interface" or communicative union, and hence it cannot ward off the tendency to introduce a neat split, down the middle, between man's historical interests looking to the past and his present theoretical concerns in philosophy. The image soon outlives its usefulness by breeding the separatist conviction that historical research has nothing to say to the point of current philosophical issues, and conversely that creative philosophers today can neither contribute toward historical studies

[1] "The study of any concept or theory of an earlier period, in order to be relevant, is bound to have a peculiar Janus-faced character: it must look towards the present as well as to the past" (W. von Leyden, *Seventeenth-Century Metaphysics*, p. xiii). "History has one foot in the present and one in the past" (George W. Morgan, *The Human Predicament*, p. 176). Looking beyond the metaphors and toward the nature of historical cognition, however, I agree with Morgan that history seeks a twofold validity of being veracious and valuable, of being in accord with past intents and acts and effectively related to present questions. And I agree with von Leyden, here and in his "Philosophy and Its History," *Proceedings of the Aristotelian Society*, n.s. *54* (1954), 187-208, that the historian of philosophy seeks to steer a course between ineffectual antiquarianism and a sheer instrumentalism to current theorizing which remains insensitive to source insistencies.

nor make significant use of them in new areas. No metaphor can substitute for a reflective theory of historical understanding, especially at that point where the bearing of historical research upon our contemporary theorizing needs to be clarified in detail.

This is not a problem peculiar to philosophy but one which confronts men working in any discipline where the tension between past accomplishments and present innovations is severe. Much can be learned from the manner in which poets and novelists, musicians and painters, grapple with the tendency to divide their own working community into an antiquarian camp and one infected by extreme presentmindedness. A loss is felt when either group renders its position absolute and closed off to the values and resonances of the other. To open up the pathways of creative influence once again, an artistic mind will often have resort to paradox and the unexpected association.

Thus when the Argentine writer Jorge Luis Borges was somewhat routinely queried about the strongest contemporary influences upon his work, he took the opportunity *not* to mention either the older generation of Croce and Shaw, Kafka and Valéry, or the new generation of Berryman and Beckett, Robbe-Grillet and Sarraute.[2] Instead, he replied that the present thinkers most strongly affecting his own creativity are Plato and Spinoza and Schopenhauer. The purpose of this response was not to indulge in facile shock technique, but rather to fasten upon the hard reality of the stimulation continuing to be exerted so perceptibly by these past philosophers upon the imagination of Borges himself. He was signaling that their reflections upon life and death, appearance and ideality, are not really immured in some distant past but

[2] See P. Marx and J. Simon, "Jorge Luis Borges: An Interview," *Commonweal*, *89* (1968), 107-110; Richard Burgin, *Conversations with Jorge Luis Borges*; and J. L. Borges, *Other Inquisitions*, on Spinoza and Schopenhauer. Borges makes a playful, fabular use of literary and philosophical sources, but with a discriminating sense of responsibility for both the historical reality and the imaginative attractiveness of Schopenhauer and the rest.

keep coursing in upon his own vision of the human character. Although it was not Borges's responsibility to make a theoretical analysis of his active use of such past thinkers in his own writing, he did give concrete witness to the difference between their intimate historical presence and any dichotomous metaphor of a two-faced and slewfooted relation with a Spinoza or a Schopenhauer.

It is our obligation in trying to develop a general theory of the historical act of interpreting modern philosophy, however, to reflect formally upon this problem. That is why the theme of the interpreting present must be distinctively treated as constituting an essential co-ingredient in the historical understanding and use of the sources. To do some justice to this knotty issue, I find it helpful to begin the present chapter with a more general analysis of the interpreting present and its role in achieving the historical relationship with modern philosophers. It will then be necessary to test and modify this general hypothesis by looking at some of the specific tasks performed by responsive historical interpreters. The reality of the interpreting present can be seen concretely in the changes introduced into a familiar from-to span, in the effort at selective appreciation of philosophers operating at something less than the highest peak, and in certain forms of historical analysis deliberately cultivated for their service to our contemporary needs in philosophy.

1. HISTORICAL UNDERSTANDING THROUGH PRESENTIAL ACT

The use of a fitting metaphor in one context involves the longterm responsibility of pointing out where it eventually fails to convey the proper meaning, and thus unfits itself. In Chapter II, I used the metaphor of the double helix (taken from geometry and genetics) to guide our thinking about two basic elements in our historical understanding of philosophy. It helped to suggest a relationship of close proportioning between the textual sources themselves and the historian's modes of research. As long as the correlation between the source opening and the research reopening was being considered apart from the peculiar emphases and pressures of one's own day, this metaphor aided our investigation of the ingredient factors in historical understanding. But its illuminating power begins to fade precisely at that point where questions arise concerning the adjustment of history of philosophy to the constant shifting of contemporary intellectual contexts. The danger of the uncorrected metaphor of the helix lies in the misleading inference that the intertwining of source and interrogation is a timeless, unchanging process, not very radically affected by the always altering network of current problems in philosophy.

The painful historical fact is, however, that the classical texts do not speak to us simply by themselves and through immutable patterns of communication, but must always be rendered fluent anew in the tongue of our present philosophical concerns. Similarly, the kinds of interpretive questioning do not constitute a separate standard apparatus, for they stand in fundamental need of being reminted and newly equipped with the specific means for bringing the sources to bear upon the problems we are facing. The confluent principles of source and interpretation cannot join together automatically, immediately, and under their own impetus alone. There is always need for fresh acts of judging just how best to relate the modes of textual insistency with ever more pertinent and serviceable modes of interrogation. The helix figure fails us here, because it does not convey the urgent experimentation of the historian's craft, seeking to devise the enabling means whereby the sources can keep on sourcing away for us today.

To render proper account of this exploratory aspect of historical understanding, we must underline the *threefold* character of our basic working hypothesis and direct the burden of analysis now squarely upon the third factor itself: *the interpreting present.* For the distinctive task of the latter is to serve as the intrinsic mediating principle between the insistent sources and the historical questions. These two poles might soon drift apart and become merely disparate items in the inventory of human resources, were they not constantly being reintegrated with each other through the unifying activity of the present interpreting mind. Only in this mediating operation does the history of philosophy escape the fate of getting sundered into the mere echoes of earlier interpretations on the one hand and, on the other, into source materials which never quite become reformulated in terms of current forms of philosophizing. As a factor of co-ingrediency, the interpreting present signifies that steady purpose of historical inquirers to realize a more adequate, present-tense proportioning between the great modern philosophers and ourselves.

We can determine more closely the methodological and epistemological meaning of the interpreting present by analyzing those cognate aspects of historical understanding which together constitute its activity and display its role. When cultivated soundly and creatively, the history of modern philosophy engenders a mode of understanding marked by four distinctive traits. It remains essentially critical and revisionary about its own achievements to date; it sifts and evaluates the several senses in which its sources are classical and past; it incorporates a futural reference into all historical inquiries; and amid all other tasks, it quietly builds up a teleology toward historical presence as an act of philosophical knowing. In order to identify, accent, and unify these four basic features in the historical study of modern philosophy, we will use here the functional expression "the interpreting present."

(a) *The revisionary process.* The interpreting mind is always being prodded to revise and re-present the basic positions of the great philosophers, in a way that will take account of new methods and issues in the philosophical community. This reference to present resources and problems serves as a built-in principle of dissatisfaction with all previous historical accounts. To be responsive to the interpreting present means that the historian methodically commits himself to the working rule that the great modern minds always have something more to say to us, and that he himself must press forward to find some more effective means for releasing their further significance.

One vantage point from which to observe the workings of the revisionary process is furnished by historical studies which are generally acknowledged to be definitive in their kind and day. This acknowledgment is always accompanied in principle by a certain qualifying note, which looks forward at least indeterminately toward another situation requiring a thorough revisualization of the philosophy in question. Thus Harry Wolfson's *The Philosophy of Spinoza* was welcomed as a triumph of historical intelligence, especially for its thematic treatment of problems which had a long development before coming into Spinoza's range. At the same time, Wolfson achieved his perspective into the Greek-Jewish-medieval roots only by taking a jigsaw-puzzle approach to the separate elements in Spinoza's thought. The community of historians has not regarded his presentation as being so definitive that it places a moratorium upon Spinoza research, either at the level of restricted questions or at that of general reinterpretation of the entire philosophy. Whatever the difficulties raised by the condition of Spinoza translations (as discussed in the previous chapter), the search has gone on for contemporary modes of reformulating his specific patterns of argument and especially for re-envisioning the unity of his thought as a whole.

The search for a new Spinoza clearly reveals the gadfly influence of the interpreting present upon the historical researchers.[3] In a deliberate effort to replace Wolfson's mosaic-laying method, they are stressing the internal ribs of coher-

[3] Fresh winds of Spinozistic research are felt in these five French studies: S. Zac, *L'Idée de vie dans la philosophie de Spinoza*; J. Préposiet, *Spinoza et la liberté des hommes*; B. Rousset, *La Perspective finale de "L'Éthique" et le problème de la cohérence du spinozisme*; A. Matheron, *Individu et communauté chez Spinoza*; and M. Guéroult, *Spinoza*.

ence and immanent teleology in this philosophy. They take a more componential and systemic view of the relationship between Spinozistic theory of knowledge and metaphysics, philosophical anthropology and political theory. The synthetic power and co-implication of the leading themes of life, freedom, and immanent actuation are being explored in a manner that corresponds with tendencies in other research fields. Spinoza's concept of life is being examined, not only with the aid of Biblical and medieval research on the theme of the living God but also in the light of twentieth-century evolutionary theory and process philosophy. And his unique project of correlating his political theory with a reflective and reality-based humanism becomes more comprehensible today, both in view of the ideal of social humanization and because our historical studies are yielding a better understanding of the political actualities in seventeenth-century Holland and Britain.

In their readiness to bring these additional resources of intellectual work and the present life situation to bear upon their reinterpretation of the *Ethics* and other familiar sources, historians of philosophy are well on the way toward realizing a more pertinent and appreciative synthesis of Spinoza's thought. In the operational terms of our theory of historical understanding, they are giving heed to the revisionary spirit of the interpreting present.

(b) The classical and the past. A second major function for the interpreting present is to institute some critical controls over two key terms, frequently used to designate the modern philosophical sources: "classical" and "the past." There is one entire register of meanings of the classical which is clearly incompatible with the revisionary aspect of the interpreting present. For it is contrary to this latter principle's actual role in historical cognition to regard the great works in modern philosophy as being classical, in a sense that would entomb them in stiff and remote splendor, totally settled in their own accomplishments and wrung dry of any further his-

torical significance. Classical treatises, thus reduced to the condition of objectified monuments, could never serve as sources for some new modes of philosophizing. They could never continue sourcing away for us, showing us in surprising ways that they have *not* been reduced to altogether overt possessions whose reflective implications for mankind are entirely spelled out and laid to rest.

The living nature of a modern masterwork is respected only in the very act whereby the historian accepts the principle of the interpreting present. Such a source is classical for him in the provocative sense that its arguments and vision are never fully rounded off and rendered totally explicit. Skilled historians never escape the burden of specifying some new mode of a source thinker's involvement with the present range of problems. The source thinker is constantly becoming problematic once more to ourselves. He offers us some historical access only in the sense of provoking us to share in his self-awareness and thus of aiding us to transform our own critical self-awareness, in the light of his arguments. It is solely within the life of this mutual transformation process that a modern source philosopher establishes his right to be regarded as a classic thinker and author.

In conformity with this meaning of the classical sources, history of modern philosophy does not concern itself with some formalized entity called abstractly "the past." It is the latter which is often defined as that which is done-and-gone beyond retrieve, as that whose life has ceased to be and cannot be brought within our comprehension again. This is that preteritized past, the cutoff or passed past, whose relationships are entirely immobilized and sealed back upon itself.

One can indeed appeal to an entity thus defined to maintain that philosophers can gain no historically grounded and unitive knowledge of the past and hence must engage in sheer constructionism, when they attempt to restate the modern developments in their discipline. This skeptical opinion is a strong, salutary reminder of the ultimate consequences of taking an archaicizing approach to the modern philosophical classics. For there is a relation of mutual adaptation and support between the archaicizing and the skeptical conceptions of the past sources of philosophy. Together, these two conceptions form a closed circle which would alienate us from our modern wellsprings and would discourage the effort to gain historical access to them. But all that this alliance of the antiquarian and the skeptical approaches tells us about historical understanding is that it remains irreducible either to an exhumation process or to an arbitrary form of freehand sketching. And here is the basic reason why the image of the historian as Janus-faced colossus collapses at a touch of criticism. For this image furnishes us with no theoretical criterion for distinguishing between the purely *formal* oppositions contained in the abstract contrast between "the past" and "the present" and the living *historical* relationships between modern sources and the interpreting present.

The difference is that which holds between a procedure which distances the past from us and then seeks to immure us within its remote fastness, and one which engages in rethinking the sources in order to liberate their capacity to speak to us and nourish our philosophical inquiries today. The former conception finds a concrete image in Thomas Mann's portrait of Professor Dr. Cornelius, who directed a history seminar during the troubled days of the Weimar Republic.

> History professors do not love history because it is something that comes to pass, but only because it is something that *has* come to pass. . . . The past is immortalized; that is to say, it is dead; and death is the root of all godliness and all abiding significance.[4]

[4] Thomas Mann, "Disorder and Early Sorrow," in his *Death in Venice and Seven Other Stories*, pp. 189, 190. In his poem-in-prose "Anywhere Out of the World," Charles Baudelaire expresses an analogous attitude of flight to a frozen immortality in this proposal to one's restless soul: "Let us set up house at the Pole. There the sun only grazes the earth obliquely, and the slow alternations of light and night abolish variety and enhance monotony, that half of nothingness. We can take long baths of darkness there, while for our

Mann's Professor Cornelius regards the past as a marmoreal refuge. It is an already enacted and changeless region, into which the historian escapes and where he finds security from the uncertainties and surprises of current living. But in history of philosophy as elsewhere, this view of past developments is a doomed illusion. For the importunate present has a way of seeping into every historical turret, just as the insistential power of the historical sources keeps on manifesting its active bearing upon contemporary thinking. The working historians of modern philosophy would be rasping against the grain of their own best practice, were they to consign the writings of a Leibniz or a Mill to some frozen pantheon of philosophies that have come to pass and can no longer convey further forms of significance to us. Such a forever fixed immortality of meaning is an ideal for embalmers rather than for historians of philosophy.

That is why neither nostalgia for some past era in philosophy nor the sentiment of escape from present theoretical urgencies belongs among the basic affective equipment for doing good historical work. These attitudes can only thwart the historian's responsibility for developing his historical

---

amusement the Aurora Borealis will from time to time send us its rosy sheaves, like reflections of a fireworks-display in Hell!" (Baudelaire, *Selected Verse*, tr. Francis Scarfe, p. 192). For a dialectical development of the skeptical consequences of either taking the past as fully enacted in itself (R. G. Collingwood) or separating historical fact from practical valuation (Michael Oakeshott), see J. W. Meiland, *Scepticism and Historical Knowledge*. A much more realistic appraisal of the reciprocal openings between history and present philosophizing is given by Stanley Cavell: "Innovation in philosophy has characteristically gone together with a repudiation— a specifically cast repudiation—of most of the history of the subject. But in the later Wittgenstein (and, I would now add, in Heidegger's *Being and Time*) the repudiation of the past has a transformed significance, as though containing the consciousness that history will not go away, except through our perfect acknowledgment of it (in particular, our acknowledgment that it is not past), and that one's own practice and ambition can be identified only against the continuous experience of the past" (*Must We Mean What We Say?*, p. xix). The passage quoted below from Maurice Merleau-Ponty is taken from his *Signs*, pp. 10-11, 127.

judgment as an effective mediation between the sources and some present discussions. Feelings of nostalgia and escape do an injustice to the vitality of the always incompletely disclosed sources, as well as to the interpretive judgment which relates them freshly to the central topics of our day.

Maurice Merleau-Ponty has stated well the corrective sense in which the writings and doctrines of modern philosophers prove to be classical in their constant reachievement of historical presence among us.

These do not endure because there is some miraculous adequation or correspondence between them and an invariable "reality"—such an exact and fleshless truth is neither sufficient nor necessary for the greatness of a doctrine—but because, as obligatory steps for those who want to go further, they retain an expressive power which exceeds their statements and propositions. These doctrines are the *classics*. They are recognizable by the fact that no one takes them literally, and yet new facts are never absolutely outside their province but call forth new echoes from them and reveal new lustres in them. . . . The past transgresses upon and grows through the present.

Hence it is an explicit rule of historical methodology that the terms "classical" and "past" must include rather than exclude this ingressive relationship with an open present, whenever they are used to characterize the primary sources in modern philosophy. For this usage is a manner of affirming the continuing intellectual life enjoyed—not indeed by an abstractly defined past entity in tensal discourse, but—precisely by the historically understood, concrete past of modern philosophizing.

(c) The intention toward futurity. A third assignment for the interpreting present, working as a component in historical understanding, is to recognize the intention toward futurity operative in the modern sources and to clarify the conditions under which this intention is able to renew itself in and

through our historical studies. The historical function in question is not being encountered here for the first time in our theory, but only now are we in a position to recognize its proper reality and analyze it upon its own terms. In our previous examination of the insistential nature of the sources, especially as manifesting itself in the diversified communicational spectrum, we noticed the persistent efforts of modern philosophers to open up their argument and outlook to independent readers and interpreters. Now, however, we must observe explicitly that the interpreters in view include not only the strict contemporaries of these source thinkers but also philosophers and historical investigators coming along in the future.

Moreover, the future minds toward which the modern philosophers also addressed their theorizing could be only partly envisaged through the philosophical tendencies already at work. In some degree, the source writings were being launched out into the unknown, that is, into a future intellectual situation whose shape was admittedly unforeseeable. The great philosophers hoped that their methods and leading principles would prove sound enough and powerful enough to affect the course of later speculation, but this was a hope concerning new settings and problems lying beyond their determinate vision. Thus the great modern source works were faced by their authors toward a partly uninterpreted future, where they might influence (even though never sheerly dominate) the original acts of philosophizing born in a different age. This places a special, correlative responsibility upon the historical inquirer to perceive such futural meanings and to aid in their becoming more determinately accessible within his own philosophical context. Such a task is fittingly included under the operations of the interpreting present.

We cannot enter sympathetically into the philosophical worlds of Descartes and Leibniz, without noticing how strongly suffused these worlds are with the reach toward futurity. Methodological and doctrinal reforms are proposed not only to the living colleagues of these philosophers but also, and perhaps principally, to generations of reflective men yet to come. A comprehensive method and system of reasoning may be proposed, but they never lose the quality of being a first vintage or sampling of work still to be done and redone. Descartes and Leibniz never cease to present methodic and conceptual proposals concerning positions which they themselves can only sketch, and hence which are laden with the destiny of being reworked and reorganized by subsequent philosophers reflecting within as yet unenvisaged frameworks. The notation sometimes added by their early editors—*the rest is missing*—applies not only to the incomplete condition of some of their manuscripts but also, and more fundamentally, to that acknowledged philosophic incompletion which solicits the critical reconsideration and collaboration of later readers of Descartes and Leibniz.

Nor is this futural orientation confined to the philosophers of the exploratory seventeenth-century and the progress-minded Enlightenment, since its presence helps to characterize the great system building enterprises of the nineteenth century as well. Correlative to the sense of past historical development in Hegel and Comte is an equally lively awareness of the future intellectual and social growths of mankind, which cannot be entirely foreseen and encompassed within their own explicit levels of reflective analysis. Hence their methods and principles contain an *implicit* aspect which is left for later thinkers to actuate, criticize, and render concretely determinate in ways that cannot be prophetically predetermined. In making allowance for new modes of consequential interpreting and reorganizing of their meanings, Hegel and Comte show themselves to be contributors toward what Feuerbach terms "the principles of the philosophy of the future." There is an open-ended reference to future acts of philosophizing, an allowance which genuinely modifies the claims to systematic completeness and closure sometimes advanced by these philosophers, in moments of enthusiasm for their actual accomplishments.

An interesting difficulty arises, however, in trying to coordinate the futural intent of the modern source thinkers with the historical operation of the interpreting present. What distinguishes historical reassessment from sheer playback of a cassette is precisely the active use of those modes of interrogation and those shapes of experience which are predominant in the interpreter's own day. The futural intention of the modern sources becomes actuated, therefore, only through a specification of meaning made in terms of this concrete contemporary base of interpretation. But there is great latitude in the choice of present perspectives, as well as constant revaluation of the present significance of the modern sources, a point which will be elaborated in the remaining sections of this chapter. What enables the source writings to exert their influence in some continuous and definite fashion, while still affording the opportunity for innovative readings which do not degenerate into fanciful constructions, lacking any historical referent?

The ground of union between source openings toward the reflective future and diverse contemporary acts of interpreting lies in *the binding, yet creative, power of language*. Both the great philosophers and the outstanding historians recognize and count upon the capacity of language to achieve historical continuity and newness of understanding simultaneously.

On this theme, Hegel is a good representative of the community of practising philosophers and historians alike.[5] Every time he analyzes a phenomenological attitude as pervading the particular shapes of human experience, or traces the development of a concept and suggests its future course, or marks out some barrier reefs to be avoided by would-be architects of new social forms, or simply teases and recomposes the existing vocabulary in many philosophical areas, he is also co-affirming the ability of language to unite reflective minds of every age in communication. Although extraordi-

[5] Theodor Bodammer, *Hegels Deutung der Sprache*, gives a concise yet comprehensive study of the main texts on language in its various usages; J. Simon, *Das Problem der Sprache bei Hegel*, is more diffuse and comparative.

narily developed, Hegel's sensitivity to the potencies of language expresses an insight shared, in some manner and degree, by other workers in philosophy and its continuing historical analysis. There is agreement, based upon our common linguistic experience, that the originative thought of every modern philosopher can learn to speak in new tongues, not only through translation but also through historical reinterpretation. The linguistic actuality of a philosophical work has the additional resource of presenting itself through other modes of philosophical judgment and historical questioning, thus enriching those subsequent inquirers who take the trouble to rethink the methods and resentence the texts themselves.

When a philosopher sets forth his arguments and reflections in written form, all is completed and yet all is prolegomenal. There is completion in the order of explicit expression and abiding textual reference. But there is also the announcement of at least the possibility of a new life form for his philosophy, as it begins its career of interworking with other centers of reflection and linguistic formation.

But the language context within which a philosophical treatise finds its second life span is broader than the boundaries of technical philosophical usage. In order that the philosopher's futural intent may become genuinely operative, his expressiveness must be related and assimilated in some fashion to the general continuity and growth of *human language*, integrally considered. Without this larger participation of the philosopher's text in the historical resources of human language as a whole, the convergence sought between the futural source and the present interpretive act might never be realized. Hence historical understanding in philosophy is integral with the broader human quest for self-understanding, because it uses the common resources of language (even though modalized in special ways) to keep the wellsprings perpetually flowing and convivial for new minds. It is only within this human community of language and reflection that historians are able to perform their specific acts of renewal: resentencing, newly envisioning, and deliberately implicating the great modern philosophers in our going inquiries.

This dependence of historical knowledge and development upon the binding power of language was dramatically affirmed toward the end of the remarkable month-long seminar conducted jointly by Martin Heidegger and Ernst Cassirer in Davos, Switzerland, in 1929 (shortly after the former had published his *Being and Time* and his study of Kant, and shortly before the latter issued the third volume of *The Philosophy of Symbolic Forms*).[6] The two philosophers attempted patiently to clarify their divergent conceptions of the Greek and Kantian traditions in metaphysics, as well as their own meanings for being, freedom, and transcendence. At the concluding meeting, each man made a reflective generalization about the seminar experience itself. Heidegger observed: "What you have seen here, writ small, namely, the differences between philosophers within the one-ness of a problem, sug-

---

[6] Carl H. Hamburg, "A Cassirer-Heidegger Seminar," *Philosophy and Phenomenological Research*, 25 (1964-65), 208-222; the passages quoted here are from pp. 220-222. Cassirer devotes chapter 5 of *The Logic of the Humanities* to "the tragedy of culture," i.e., the life-giving tension between tradition and creativity, inheritance and transformation, in which the binding and creating power of language consists. History of philosophy develops through receiving the source works in a linguistic-cultural act, which remains textually faithful and also moves beyond the limits of previous judgments concerning them. In his commentary on the Introduction to Hegel's *Phenomenology of Spirit*, Heidegger analyzes an instance in which our human language prepares and sustains the emergence of new philosophic significations for words in the developing modern sources. When Hegel uses the word "experience," Heidegger responds by taking it to signify anticipatively his own theme of "the Being of beings," thus developing the linguistic power of modern philosophical texts. "The strange word 'experience' enters into our reflection as the name of the Being of beings for this reason: It has come due. True, this use of it falls totally outside of ordinary usage, and of philosophical usage as well. But it falls to us as the result of the very thing to which Hegel's thought remains attached. The justification of this usage, which is essentially different from a mere manner of speaking, lies in what Hegel, with the preceding paragraphs [in his Introduction to *Phenomenology of Spirit*], has brought to light concerning the nature of consciousness" (Heidegger, *Hegel's Concept of Experience*, p. 114).

gests, however modestly, what is so essential and writ large in the controversies in the history of philosophy: the realization that the discerning of its different standpoints goes to the very root of all philosophical work." To do radical innovative work in one's own philosophical present, one must rethink the basic positions achieved in history of philosophy and grasp them together in their differences-within-unity of the continuing human questions.

For his part, Cassirer wondered how it could be that Aristotle and Kant were still made to count in present inquiries, and that even his own sharp differences from Heidegger on both historical and theoretical issues did not prevent a useful discussion from taking place.

> My position is essentially different from Heidegger's. I remain within Kant's basic methodological version of the transcendental. What is important about the transcendental method is that it takes its departure from what is actual fact. Thus, I ask how the fact of language is possible. How can it be made intelligible that we can communicate through this medium from one individual existence to another? . . . And so I ask: where, after all, is that area of agreement in our disagreement? There is no need to search for it, because we have it exactly because there is a common objective and a common human world in which individual differences are not so much eliminated as (symbolically) bridged from one individual to another. This is always brought out for me by the (primal) phenomenon of language. We all speak our own language, and yet we understand each other through the medium of language. There is such a thing as "Language," something like the unity of the infinite variety of languages. This is decisive for me. It is for this reason that I start with the objectivity of symbolic forms because, with them, we possess in *fact*, what, in *thought*, seems impossible.

Cassirer's intention was not to hypostasize human language, as though it exists apart as a thing-entity, but rather to stress the functional intercommunication of meanings achieved through the mutual activity of speakers from many diverse regions, ages, and intellectual contexts.

As might be expected, the eminent seminar leaders were unable to agree more closely on a way of understanding the communicative actuality of language, as it sustains the historical and speculative pathways among philosophers. Cassirer remained more methodological by treating the interconnective quality of language within the general framework of his theory of symbolizing acts and forms, whereas Heidegger became increasingly attracted toward the difficult problem of the ontological relationship between man, language, and our thinking of being. But their fortunate meeting did lead them to enunciate one jointly held conviction: that human language, as an ever continuing and ever self-transforming reality, constitutes not only a common world for men but, more specifically, the base of communication and creativity which permits history of philosophy to flourish as a living agency.

(d) Teleology toward historical presence. The fourth general trait which the interpreting present assures for historical understanding in philosophy is its persistent teleology toward presential act or historical presence. This teleology can be perceived, only if we pursue our examination of the crucial term "interpreting" beyond the three traits already established, in order to reach their converging focus. We have seen that the aim of historical understanding is always self-critical and revisionary; that historical sources have the greatness to refuse to be consigned to a done-and-finished past; and that the bridgemaking operations of human language are required to join philosophers of different times in a relation that is both historically faithful and speculatively helpful. But to terminate our analysis of the interpreting present at this point would be misleading, and would block our main task of developing and verifying the hypothesis about historical grasp of modern philosophy. For the reference of all these elements toward a present act of understanding might be construed as

a methodological collapse of everything historical into the contemporary moment. This would only mean exchanging the solipsism of a classical past for the solipsism of a current present. In such an exchange of solipsistic abstract tenses, the primary victim is that act of historical understanding which we are seeking to comprehend, not to obliterate.

Consequently, the co-ingredient function of the interpreting present is not only to secure the *presential* character of every historical judgment but also to qualify the latter as always being an *interpretive* kind of judging. The historian's proper concern is neither with an archaicized past nor with a detemporalized present but with seeking the significance of past philosophizing, as being brought in relation to the present existence and problems of men. Such a relationship supposes that we are not in possession of complete lucidity about either pole: whether ourselves or the great philosophers of the modern centuries. Indeed, by bringing both components into the reflective proportioning required in history of philosophy, we render both ourselves and the great sources problematic together. Inquiry gets turned upon our own philosophical achievements and sureties, which have to be further questioned in the light of alternate proposals streaming in from the sources. And the latter are recognized, in terms of present fact and method, not to have said the last word on their own themes and not even to have fully predetermined their own resonance for contemporary intelligence. Thus each component in the interpreting process is made to feel the bite and initiative of the other, as we strive to achieve a new comprehension that is both truthful to the sources and valuable to our own explorations.

The act of historical interpretation will tolerate no smoothing over of this mutual probing between sources and interpreters. There can be no pretence that *the now* of a past act of philosophizing—its self-referential presence—has been transported into our own present, since this is hard to reconcile with the methodological inventiveness and interpretive variations required in order to improve our understanding of a major writing, even in a slight degree. In any case, historians of philosophy are not engaged in the transportation business. Their task is not to seek to reduce to insignificance the difference between the concrete present belonging to a source philosopher and their own actual present. Instead, their historical understanding rests upon a twofold recognition: both of the irreducible distinction between these presential centers and of the constantly improvable relationships which can get established between them.

The source's *self-referential presence* remains its own, and yet we achieve the *historical presence* of that source to ourselves through interpretive judgment. Our historical inquiry seeks to re-enliven the meaning of an insistential source in its bearing upon our own questioning, without wiping out their mutual differences by reducing the one to the other. The mediating function of the interpreting principle consists negatively in a critical refusal to seek the illusory immediacy and intuitionism of such a reduction, and affirmatively in respecting the integrity of open relatedness of the modern sources to the interpretive mind.

In order to signify this complex and method-regulated relationship governing the theory of historical interpreting, I will specify compoundly that historical understanding is *a presential-act-for-achieving-historical-presence*. Presential act springs from the historian's presentifying effort. He tries to render freshly pertinent the meaning, argumentation, and vision of some modern philosopher, through an act of reconstruing the method and structure of the original textual expression. The two centers of reflectivity are brought into a new judgmental situation, not through some form of immediacy and cancellation of their difference but through the historian's search after other modes of releasing the textual intention and the latent power of language. The source thinker is enabled to speak anew within our range of hearing and judging.

The presence thus incessantly being reconstituted in reference to our developing problems is precisely historical in nature. It is not a fantastic mode of contemporaneity, wafting the interpreter into a *past-present* not his own, or wafting the source philosopher into a *present-present* not belonging to him. Historical presence is an active grounding in one's own present, but in one's present precisely as qualified by the interpretive work of relational analysis and critique of a past philosopher's statements.

With these four general characteristics of the interpreting present thus set forth, we can now make certain further precisions concerning our use of this principle in the general theory. It is worth specifying that we are making a *componential* study of the interpreting present, rather than a completely unqualified analysis of it. That is, our examination of the interpreting present is confined to its functional contribution to the general task of improving our historical understanding of modern philosophy. In most instances of historical research, however, this philosophical aspect of the interpreting present is blended with other intentions and made to serve some broader purposes than that defined by history of philosophy.

For instance, a historical study of Charles Darwin's impact upon philosophy since 1859 belongs properly (but not exclusively) within the scope of history of philosophy.[7] The philosopher's intention in the interpreting present makes such research a component in illuminating our historical understanding of evolutionary theories in philosophy, as well as in furnishing a frame of reference for current discussions of the meaning of life. Yet such a study also belongs within a wider range of inquiries into Darwin's impact upon all facets of contemporary life and thinking, and the reflective theory of historical interpreting of modern philosophy must take this broader context into account. For the fact that the Darwinian theme functions as a component both within the

---

[7] See M. T. Ghiselin, *The Triumph of the Darwinian Method*, and James Collins, *Crossroads in Philosophy*, chapter 7: "Darwin's Impact on Philosophy," pp. 136-188, 404-409.

history of modern philosophy and also in other disciplines, such as the history of biology, intimately affects the receptive relationship which the historian of philosophy must maintain with these other disciplines. Hence our theory of the interpreting present focuses upon the philosophical intention, but not to the exclusion of those other concrete intellectual aims which modify the import of the philosophical interpretation in relation to the broader development of humanity.

Even within the componential context, the historian of philosophy has to guard against treating the interpreting present as though it were a subsisting entity. For it figures in the general theory precisely as a *methodological and pluriform* requirement for understanding modern philosophy. Thus in speaking about "the" interpreting present, we are referring to an ingredient or constitutive factor in the method of gaining historical access to modern philosophy, not to an independent reality or process. Moreover, in its actual constitution every specific project of historical inquiry demands its own manner of meeting the general constitutive requirements. Concrete acts of historical understanding always incorporate "this or that" particular mode of the interpreting present, since historical meaning depends upon relating the source work to some unique blending of research intents, procedures, and perspectives.

The reality of historical presence is found, not in a reference to some uniform abstraction, but in the pluriform functions of "these and still other" modes of the interpreting present. In order to respect the concrete actuation of this and that interpreting present, we will be testing our basic hypothesis by specific reference to the rich variety of work done by twentieth-century historians of philosophy. The subsequent sections in this chapter will therefore serve to right the balance in our conception of the interpreting present, by showing its foundation in historical praxis to be emphatically many-visioned.

Within that company of investigations, however, does the

theme of the interpreting present impose any further restrictions or gradations? This is asking whether there is a *means test* for inclusion or exclusion of any proposed way of treating the modern sources. No such test known to me can be proposed beforehand and in a universal manner, without courting the risk of impoverishing our historical knowledge.

It would be unwise and theoretically unjustifiable to specify that, in principle, one or another current method or doctrinal position is incapable of being put to good historical use in the continual retempering of the source works. The interpreting present is not an excluding club but an open, hospitable basis for relating these writings always to this and that center, to these and still other centers of contemporary study. Methods and systems which in their day yielded splendid historical results may now be diminishing in their interpretive power; other contemporary standpoints which have not yet adapted themselves to historical inquiries may yet find unexpected developments in this quarter. All that the co-ingrediency of the interpreting present requires is that the approach prove itself fruitful through actual performance, by improving our familiarity with the sources and our sense of their bearing on philosophical issues which challenge us.

Once an effort is actually made to treat a source work in terms of some current questions and methods, then a determinate evaluation can be made of this interpreting center. A negative judgment about its interpretive capabilities will follow, if the effect of the procedure is to inhibit our appreciation of many aspects of the source or to substitute some other schema of arguments entirely for a close reading of the source argumentation. Such narrowing or deflecting of historical vision runs counter to the functional purpose of an interpreting present.

Historical frustration often stems from taking a monistic model for determining the significance of a past philosopher. If he does not become directly related to one's dominant concern with self-alienation or a formal logic of science, for instance, one may be tempted to treat the philosopher as a straw man who has no brains.[8] Or else, one may attribute blunders and dilemmas to him which have no textual warrant, thus preventing other students from perceiving the structure of his own reflections and his value for some phases in their philosophic gropings. Thus it is not through any a priori inference from the theory of the interpreting present, but through making a critical and pragmatic scrutiny of the actual outcome as measured against the increase of historical comprehension sought by this co-ingredient, that the effectiveness of any contemporary base of treatment is judged.

Even in an instance where such narrowing or deflecting is observed, however, there may not be sufficient grounds for concluding that the underlying philosophy is absolutely incompatible with historical studies. The following four considerations suggest that modern historians must remain cautiously reluctant to rule out the possibility of valuable contributions coming from *any* present philosophical method.

First, the unpromising consequences of its actual application to a modern source may be due to the historical inexperience of the individual inquirer, who may subsequently grow in historical skill or in the wisdom to steer clear of such questions. Second, since a contemporary philosophy is not totally fixed and immobilized, restrained criticism of its present inadequacies of historical interpretation may well spur it toward a new level of development, which can indeed increase our understanding of the modern philosophers. A third point is that the difficulty often lies in an unnecessarily constricted and conventional image of the historical approach in philosophy, leading to a flat dichotomy between doing historical studies and making an original, theoretically signifi-

---

[8] For a critique of polemical attacks against source philosophers, undertaken by hasty arguers who disregard the actual proof-structures and historical connotations involved in the texts, see John Passmore, "The Idea of a History of Philosophy," *The Historiography of the History of Philosophy*, pp. 1-32.

cant use of the sources. To relieve a pioneer inquirer's uneasiness about whether his departure from standard treatment disqualifies his work from having any historical value, the theory of co-ingredient factors of historical understanding emphasizes the open spectrum of methods found to be useful in historical studies.

Finally, what keeps history of philosophy a living discipline is precisely its assimilation of new ways of reading, interrogating, and redeploying the basic writings. The initial narrowing effect of a correlation between these writings and a contemporary methodology is to be expected. It provides the inciting spur toward improving a new path in historical interpretation, one which quite properly unsettles the traditional view and generates novel relationships among all the components of historical meaning. Once the exclusive and absolute note is removed from this perspective, its enrichment of our entire appreciation of the modern sources will become apparent. One function of the interpreting present is to discipline the historian's judgment by these long-range expectations concerning contemporary innovation. Therefore, it is a good working rule that the historical spirit be encouraged to take many surprising forms, all of which are to be provisionally welcomed and tested by their actual interpretive fruits.

In concluding this general phase in our analysis of the interpreting present, we must call attention to a somewhat paradoxical *reversal of critical norms* which this factor entails. Usually, philosophers like to make their own paraphrase of Hölderlin's famous question: "Of what use are poets in a time of need?" and ask in turn: "Of what use are philosophical sources in a time of need?" From the standpoint of urgent theoretical issues today, we challenge the practice of studying the past thinkers and demand that their philosophical relevance be clearly shown. The interpreting present does not soften this demand, but it does furnish the intellectual conditions for coupling it with an opposite line of questioning. The presential act relates modern sources to the contemporary interpreting judgment in such fashion that the great philosophers are given an added lease of energy and initiative. This is seen clearly enough when critical comparisons are made between philosophers who belong together in the modern past. The interpreting historian enables a Spinoza to adduce further evidence against the strictures of Leibniz, or enables a Hume to have another word telling against the German thinkers who transcended his standpoint so readily. But historical presentiality also releases the capacity of a modern source to confront our contemporary philosophies, compelling *them* in turn to submit to scrutiny and justification of their philosophic status.

It is not entirely idle or impertinent, then, to ask whether a current methodology is able to make sense out of the classic modern texts. In this reversal of perspective, the interpreting mind tests a contemporary philosophy by the measure of *its* relevance for illuminating the abiding themes developed in the modern tradition. The direction of challenge is thus shifted from the questionable study of past theories to the questionable sufficiency of present ones, instancing once more the process of their becoming simultaneously problematic for the historically educated mind.

Certainly, it is not a definitive test of a contemporary philosophy to determine how closely it can relate itself to the main modern sources and how meaningfully it can deal with their problems, even when they are labeled pseudo-problems and linguistic bewitchments. But this is at least one way of securing an independent check upon the claims of philosophical adequacy which we advance for our favorite procedures and theories. Such adequacy should include a proven capacity to understand and treat the major issues raised by modern philosophers. It is well for any going philosophy to submit to the reverse evaluation which the interpreting present spurs us to make in the relationship between past philosophizing and those modes which fill our own horizon so impressively and yet often so oppressively.

2. WAYS OF THE RESPONSIVE INTERPRETER:
(1) REFORMING THE FROM-TO PERSPECTIVES

That every historian brings along the peculiar philosophical interests, problems, and limitations of his own day to his interpretation of the modern sources, is not an embarrassing fact to conceal but an essential requirement of good historical work to recognize. Our initial recognition of this factor comes in making a general analysis of the componential role of the interpreting present, when we see that this role is to give a contemporary context and accenting to every well conducted historical inquiry. But it is not enough to state minimally that the historian's contemporary coloration can enhance, rather than disqualify, his effort at reaching a reliable understanding of historical developments. What we must also do is to perceive, through an examination of some particular patterns of investigation, that the interpreting present is always constructively reshaping and enlarging our comprehension of modern philosophy.

Under the common rubric of "ways of the responsive interpreter," then, we will now study three basic features in historical research which manifest this internal operation of the principle of the interpreting present. It can be seen concretely in: research that reforms our conventional from-to relationships; fresh evaluations of philosophers in the middle range and of paraphilosophers; and adaptive use of historical themes to serve present-day theoretical needs. Along all these paths, the historian develops his grasp upon modern philosophy in the same degree in which he responds to the co-insistential requirements of the interpreting present, taken in disciplined interplay with the source structures and the general modes of questioning.

Regardless of how inevitable and imposing it may appear as the result of comparative studies, no historical from-to lineage sustains itself exclusively from cross-references in the sources and from the general pattern of from-to inquiry. Both for originating the initial comparison and for keeping it alive as a major guide in the reading of modern sources, there must also be some determining sense of relevance which relates the classical thinkers *to* ourselves, as well as *among* themselves in that specific way. Otherwise, there will be no preliminary judgment that one particular ordering of comparative study looks more promising, and consequently no major allocation of research energies toward exploring this from-to perspective. Or if some work has already been done in the past upon that comparison, it is likely to fade away rapidly and become inconsequential for our current historical interests.

There is one piece of unfinished business, left over from the previous chapter, which can now be concluded because it illustrates the nourishing power of the interpreting present in continuing a from-to investigation, rather than in abandoning it as a spent vein. Along with all the internal source considerations for probing still further into the German developments from Hegel to Marx, there is also our awareness that every new finding here helps to enlarge our understanding of the cultural, social, and political realities of our own time. This correlation surely does not constitute a ground for disqualifying such comparative work as being historically suspect, even though it does lead prudent historians of German philosophy to be specially careful in testing the research by all the canons of source interrogation. The point to be stressed here is that our vigorous historical study of the Hegel-to-Marx development incorporates a response to the lines of relationship which this comparison has with our own social and philosophical situation. That the critical and corrective functions of the historian must be unusually alert here is an indication of the co-insistential relationship between the interpreting present and the other principles of historical meaning, not a confession that contemporary bearing is essentially corruptive of historical integrity.

More particularly, our analysis of the genetic approach to Hegel and Marx within this from-to framework has uncovered one powerful contemporary motivation for the research. That is the special interest which historians take in the humanistic quality of the thought of the young Hegel and the young Marx. Sometimes even at the expense of a balanced account of the mature systematic achievements of these two thinkers, their early writings are minutely analyzed for humanistic implications. The impetus for such concentration comes largely from *our* concern with humanism in its many varieties and our eagerness to be tutored by great predecessors in some major expressions of its meaning.

Granted that our concern and eagerness have led to inflated claims for the early speculation of Hegel and Marx, still these manifestations of the interpreting present have also focused attention upon one valuable aspect of their development and have insured the incorporation of the humanistic motif into all subsequent restatements of systematic Hegelianism and Marxism. It is precisely by such strategic accentuations that the responsive interpreter insures a humanistic facet, not only in the genetic study of Hegel or Marx taken separately, but also in every living conspectus of the movement of German philosophy from Hegel to Marx and Nietzsche. Historians of modern philosophy show their conscientiousness through many forms of methodic rigor, not the least of which is that of shaping their research directions partly by the leading questions and values of their own times.

Usually, such responsiveness results in a historical revision of the *individual philosophers* involved in a from-to span, and not only of the doctrinal threads constituting its pattern as a whole. In treating of the British span from Bacon to Mill and the German span from Kant to Nietzsche, we have already noticed that the joint insistency of source writings and modes of interrogation secures for a philosopher a historical meaning which is irreducible to his transitional role within a from-to development. A Berkeley or a Fichte stands forth in his own contoured act of reflection, marking him as his own man in the history of philosophy and not merely as a comparative term, always instrumental for understanding a transition to someone else. This critical taming and reorienting of our historical from-to thinking would not be carried out so vigorously, however, if considerations of general methodology were not reinforced by the connective relationships, independently maintained by the philosopher under revision, with some pressing philosophical issues of our day. In a word, the third factor of the interpreting present must be brought fully into play, if historical reform is to center quite particularly and emphatically upon this rather than that from-to purview and, within the same, upon this rather than that philosopher.

To instantiate this selective reforming function of the interpreting present, we will consider the extraordinary outpouring of historical studies on Schelling published since the centenary of his death in 1954.[9] Except rather indirectly, this intensive cultivation is not prompted by such broad social motivations as those which quicken the Hegel-Marx-Nietzsche field. It is true that, in an already mentioned instance of the from-to method, Lukács takes his point of departure in Schelling as a means of answering the question of how Germany came to be the homeland of marxistically defined irrationalism and inhumanism. In response to this guiding question, Lukács dwells upon the theme of im-

---

[9] Volume 1 of Georg Lukács's *La Destruction de la raison* bears as its subtitle *The Beginnings of Modern Irrationalism from Schelling to Nietzsche* (see above, Chapter III, note 31). The Schelling studies used here to show the concrete operation of the interpreting present in determining the revisability ratio in history of modern philosophy are: Walter Schulz, *Die Vollendung des deutschen Idealismus in der Spätphilosophie Schellings*; Adriano Bausola, *Metafisica e rivelazione nella filosofia positiva di Schelling*; K.-H. Volkmann-Schluck, *Mythos und Logos: Interpretationen zu Schellings Philosophie der Mythologie*; Horst Fuhrmans, *Schellings Philosophie der Weltalter*; Christoph Wild, *Reflexion und Erfahrung: Eine Interpretation der Früh- und Spätphilosophie Schellings*; Judith Schlanger, *Schelling et la realité finie*; and Dieter Jähnig, *Schelling: Die Kunst in der Philosophie*. The main lines of research are concisely sketched in Claude Bruaire's *Schelling, ou la quête du secret de l'être*, and are more fully synthesized in Xavier Tilliette's *Schelling, une philosophie en devenir*. Schelling is chosen for analysis here, rather than some other modern philosopher whose historical investigation is more burgeoning at present in the English-speaking world, in order to sharpen our awareness of still other incitive influences of the interpreting present than those most widely recognized ones prompting the study of (for example) Locke, Hegel, and Nietzsche.

mediacy of intuition, its primacy over reason, and the leap of freedom required in Schelling's theory of creation and the origins of history. But in line with our methodological caution concerning "the" interpreting present, we find that the actual pluralism of interpreting presents is a mode of self-criticism practiced by historians of modern philosophy. Thus the proposed Lukács judgment on Schelling has to be tested and modified by other insistencies of the sources and research methods. No contemporary bearing, marxist or otherwise, is uncritically accepted by investigators but furnishes the impetus for several new trial runs, which still have to be compared with each other and integrated with the other historical access routes.

The very act of periodizing Schelling's thought into its early, mature, and later phases has moved far beyond the schematizing predilections of the older idealist historians of German philosophy. Today, this periodization corresponds to some pertinent relationships between Schelling and a range of our current interests. Especially the concentration of studies on his *later* philosophy indicates a sensitivity toward the demand to learn more about this period than can be gathered from the offhand impressions of Kierkegaard or from the gracious acknowledgments of such theologians as Tillich.

Walter Schulz's *The Completion of German Idealism in Schelling's Later Philosophy*, Adriano Bausola's *Metaphysics and Revelation in Schelling's Positive Philosophy*, and Karl-Heinz Volkmann-Schluck's *Mythos and Logos: Interpretations of Schelling's Philosophy of Mythology* are excellent examples of historical inquiries which accept a nudge from contemporary theological and religious needs, but which execute their tasks in accord with the intrinsic standards of philosophical interpretation. These works analyze Schelling's ultimate conception of existence and history, myth and rational reflection, within the philosophical context of the source itself and the history of philosophy. But they leave it to researchers in religion and theology to make their own use of the findings, in accord with the methods and aims of religious and theological understanding.

In the analysis of the interpreting present, it is a working rule that we must distinguish between the *inciting cultural origin* of some contemporary stress in historical research and the *functional philosophical significance* of that stress, once it becomes incorporated into the history of philosophy. In respect to the former element, the interpreting present keeps the historical study of modern philosophy alive to all the new interests and problems of men in our age. And yet the historian must exert his own methodic judgment to assure that the inciting suggestion will serve the elucidating purpose of his own discipline. Schulz, Bausola, and Volkmann-Schluck meet their prime responsibility as historians of philosophy by analyzing Schelling's later conceptions, weighing the various interpretations, and offering their own orientation therein.

Still other features of the interpreting present stand out in Horst Fuhrmans' study of *Schelling's Philosophy of the Ages of the World*. This work bears a twofold subtitle: "Schelling's Philosophy in the years 1806-1821," and "Toward the Problem of Schellingian Theism." The years under investigation are precisely the *middle* span, the time of maturity when Schelling composed his accounts of human freedom and of world development. Fuhrmans leads a tendency to rehabilitate the philosophical values of this middle period, so that Schelling's philosophy will not be torn apart by the allure of the young thinker and the religious and literary veneration of the older sage. Our intense contemporary concern with the meaning of freedom and the modes of cosmic process is here mediated by an equally strong regard for the methods of historical interrogation. The research is not only pertinent but historically discerning of the philosophical continuity underlying Schelling's diverse themes and phases.

With his second subtitle, however, Fuhrmans indicates that his shift of the periodizing perspective is itself encouraged by broader discussions among contemporary philosophers of religion and theologians on alternate ways of breaking out of the rigid dichotomy between pantheism and a purely transcendent theism. Schelling's middle years of work hold special interest for anyone wrestling with this basic topic. His explicative theism unfolds the central thought that all worldly reality is best denominated as the *explicatio Dei*: It is the process for actualizing God throughout all the modes of our experience and history. Schelling gives a more modern form to Nicholas Cusanus's conception of the correlation between God (as involving worldly reality in its condition of implication) and experienced being (as involving God in the condition of explication). This relationship has the negative impact of breaking loose from the traditional theism of finite participation in unchanging pure act, as well as the positive purpose of insuring that modern evolutionary thinking will recognize the religious character of every developmental process. By thematizing this doctrine of explicative theism, Fuhrmans gives historical recognition to Schelling's contribution to the modern rethinking of the living presence of God in the world.

Why are we surprised, then, when Karl Jaspers (in his subtle conspectus of Schelling's greatness and philosophical import) remarks that "Schelling is perhaps the first modern thinker, in the sense of a spiritual rupture inherent in our world"?[10] We do not ordinarily include Schelling among the prototypal modern thinkers, let alone among the forerunners of a sense of tragedy and alienation in human life. For this reason, we are predisposed to regard historical research into his thought as a peripheral activity, a dispensable luxury that cannot be justified by any saving judgment of its relevance for the interpreting present.

Upon closer scrutiny, however, this assumption is seen to rest upon our appeal to but one criterion of contemporary philosophical significance: the chordal subtending of a phi-

[10] Karl Jaspers, *Schelling: Grösse und Verhängnis*, p. 7; the next quotation is also from p. 7. Fritz Marti's "Schelling on God and Man," *Studies in Romanticism*, 3 (1964-65), 65-76, is a useful conspectus which relates the problems and principles of Schelling to those of Kant and Jaspers, thus strengthening the comparative grounds for studying the former.

losophy within the arc formed by the joint interests of the analytic and the phenomenological methods. This criterion is indeed a powerful indicator of the attractiveness of a philosophical source to our interpreting present, but it is not the sole and sufficient basis for determining such relevance. A case in point is furnished by the convergence of historical studies around Schelling's writings. To appreciate the grounds for this convergence, we have to look beyond the analytic-phenomenological agreement to some other criteria specifying the significance of modern philosophers for ourselves.

In this sense, the theme of the interpreting present has an educative function to perform. It teaches us to weave patiently together many different strands of relatedness between the modern sources and ourselves. We discover something about both poles of the relation, when we try to apprehend the mode of responsiveness that instigates and sustains research into a philosopher such as Schelling, who stands neither at the start nor at the climax of the usual from-to comparisons.

There are at least three instructive comparisons between the new directions being taken in Schellingian studies and other, perhaps more familiar, paths in contemporary philosophizing. First, the developmental theism stressed by Fuhrmans is akin to some conceptions of the divine nature being worked out by process philosophers. The theme of divine relatedness, struggle, and growth provides a connective line between Schelling and the finitistic theories of God advanced by Whitehead and Weiss, Hartshorne and Cobb. Second, the existentialist exegesis made by Jaspers suggests that Schelling's theory of human destiny and his own mode of speculation are illuminating guides into the split awareness of modern man and the absurd aspects of life. In Jaspers' own words, "to study him [Schelling] means to understand ourselves better, because he shows us abiding possibilities of our age: the transition from grandeur to gesticulation, from truth to absurdity, from clear communication to magic."

And, thirdly, there is an emerging group of young his-

THE INTERPRETING PRESENT   220

torians who are intent upon broadening still more the bases of comparison and affinity between this relatively obscure philosopher and ourselves, thus enriching the interpreting present through their investigations of Schelling. A common pattern of argument for his new relevance is discernible in Christoph Wild's *Reflection and Experience: An Interpretation of Schelling's Early and Later Philosophy*, Judith Schlanger's *Schelling and Finite Reality*, and in Dieter Jähnig's *Schelling: Art in Philosophy*.

These Schellingian scholars complete the reverse movement of periodization by revisiting the *early* writings, and then face the problem of genesis and system by working out the unity of thought throughout Schelling's entire development. Next, they specify his unifying principles both epistemologically and ontologically, so that the theoretical grounds for our taking an interest in his philosophy can be broadened. When Schelling seeks to move beyond both idealism and realism into what he calls *ideal-realism*, we can catch the resonance of his impatience with theories which isolate formal reason from empirical life. His philosophy grows out of a lifelong search for the unification of reflection and human experience. Furthermore, these historians refuse to be scared off by the excesses of his romantic view of nature. For they find in Schelling's persistent correlation between nature and the human self a sane path between reductive naturalism and undisciplined interiorism.

Perhaps the most elusive and difficult theme to match with a contemporary orientation is the unifying role assigned to art by Schelling. He broadens the purposive task of art to include the philosophical and existential integration of nature and selfhood, science and history. Yet this integrative view of art serves not only to bring Schelling beyond the idealism-realism dichotomy but also to guide his vision of university studies, as a humanistic venture in specialization-and-interconnection together. In this German philosopher as well as in Dewey and many Oriental thinkers, art functions to integrate and consummate our experience. Thus the historical thematizing of art and esthetic value has the twofold creative effect of reawakening a basic strain in Schelling's philosophy and also expanding our own historical awareness of instructive analogues in intercultural theories of art.

In addition to what we learn about the revisionary workings of the interpreting present from studies in the Schelling field, there are two other vantage points where we can observe this same reforming activity. When the historian of philosophy is pressed about two aspects of his from-to methodology, he displays a very marked sensitivity to the common destiny shared by historical investigations and contemporary philosophical discussions. Why is it that some from-to developments *assert their open-ended character* more vigorously than do others, refusing to be nicely rounded off at some set terminals? And what prompts the historian to break through certain older patterns of comparative association among the modern philosophers, in order to *interrelate them in new modes* of from-to ordering? Such research moves lie at the heart of living developments in the history of modern philosophy. They also bear witness to the insistent operation of the interpreting present, as it helps to improve our historical understanding through taking advantage of correlations with some new emphases in contemporary philosophizing.

(a) Open-endedness and the realignment of perspectives. Certain spans of philosophical development can be demarcated quite satisfactorily on the basis of a definite time period, or a particular philosophical school, or a transit from one thinker to another. Thus the historian may neatly restrict himself to the seventeenth-century philosophers of science or to the ethicians and political philosophers of the Enlightenment age. Similarly, he can confine his attention comfortably to the fortunes of the Cartesian school or of the Scottish realists, or else define his research in terms of the passage from Malebranche to Berkeley. Nevertheless, he must also be prepared to have these limits rudely set aside, in cases where his own findings or those of other investigators uncover

some unsuspected complications and implications which overflow his original boundaries and lead in new directions.

There is always a drive, stemming from both the source situation and that of current philosophical discussion, to assert the open-ended and provisional nature of any designated from-to relationship. The historian of philosophy finds that his working restrictions, although validly taken for a particular comparison, tend to unravel at their outer limits and thus invite a reformulation of the entire historical perspective in question. This transformation of perspectives is deepened and hastened, whenever it is perceived to be somehow correlated with contemporary issues in philosophy and life.

We can observe this revisionary process operating in research on the history of skepticism and on the growth of German philosophy. Richard Popkin was following good research practice in delimiting his initial study of the growth of modern skepticism to the period from Erasmus to Descartes. Not only was this a manageable scope for the examination of source materials, many of them previously unexplored by historians of modern philosophy, but it also took due account of the notable peaking of the Pyrrhonian crisis in Descartes and his circle. Yet it also makes good historical sense for Popkin and associated researchers now to regard the Erasmus-to-Descartes development as being only the first phase in the modern life of skeptical method and themes.[11] In the revisionary judgment of these historians, there cannot be any definitive

---

[11] The following half-dozen articles by Richard H. Popkin describe a fruitful trajectory for the historical study of post-1650 skepticism: "Pierre Bayle's Place in 17th-Century Scepticism," in *Pierre Bayle, Le Philosophe de Rotterdam*, ed. P. Dibon, pp. 1-19; "Scepticism in the Enlightenment," *Studies on Voltaire and the Eighteenth Century*, 26 (1963), 1321-1345; "Berkeley and Pyrrhonism," *Review of Metaphysics*, 5 (1951-52), 223-246; "The Sceptical Precursors of David Hume," *Philosophy and Phenomenological Research*, 16 (1955-56), 61-71; "David Hume: His Pyrrhonism and His Critique of Pyrrhonism," *Philosophical Quarterly*, 1 (1950-51), 385-407; "Kierkegaard and Scepticism," *Algemeen Nederlands Tijdschrift voor Wijsbegeerte en Psychologie*, 51 (1959), 123-141. The skeptical fallout from Pierre Bayle can be measured from his *Historical and Critical Dictionary*, annotated translation by R. H. Popkin.

closure of that from-to span. One major reason is simply that the Cartesian school continued to be dogged by fresh skeptical criticism during the latter half of the seventeenth century. And Pierre Bayle functioned as a conduit channeling skeptical argumentation into subsequent centuries, so that there would be new forms of the Pyrrhonian crisis throughout the Enlightenment age and well into the time of the idealistic system-builders.

The broadening of our historical horizons on modern skepticism receives further encouragement from the contemporary impact of such research. We are presently engaged in a close and many-faceted analysis of the classical texts of the British empiricists. But our understanding of the problematic background and full connotation of these supposedly familiar writings is hampered, as long as we fail to give due weight to the migration of skeptical sources from the continent to Britain. Locke and Berkeley, Hume and the Scottish school, are centrally and persistently affected by skeptical views on human knowledge and belief. And unless we are content to remain careless of the historical adequacy of our analytic restatements of the British philosophers, we will find it intellectually helpful to encourage those historical studies of modern skepticism which move into this further region of from-to comparison.

There are comparable grounds in contemporary theorizing for extending skepticism research into its nineteenth-century modalities. Otherwise, the preoccupation of Hegel and Schopenhauer, Kierkegaard and Nietzsche, with skeptical problems will remain a puzzling quirk in these individual thinkers. And we will not have prepared the historical context for understanding why such diverse minds in our age as Husserl, Russell, and Wittgenstein have also felt obliged to grapple so radically with skepticism. With all these contemporary demands hinging upon a better historical understanding of the skeptical motif in modern philosophy, the interpreting present can only respond by adding its imperative to the widening scope of from-to studies of skepticism.

Similar methodological inducements are operative, in the study of German philosophy, to keep the historical comparisons open and growing in all directions. The transformations undergone by Richard Kroner's working framework of a Kant-to-Hegel basis do not confirm the brickmason's theory of historical methodology, which would view them as a series of merely external stretchings and accretions. Instead, the development in our comparative understanding of German philosophy is guided by the joint insistency of the source writings and the interpreting present. In the case of the research tendencies leading from Hegel to the Young Hegelians and Marx, we have already seen that this broadened context improves our comprehension of the problems occupying Kant and Fichte, Hegel and Schelling. It also constitutes a historically framed response to our own theoretical and practical interest in the modes of humanism, especially Marxist humanism and its social expressions.

But even a Kant-to-Marx purview is insufficient to satisfy our contemporary uses for German philosophy, so that this from-to framework has been redrawn by Karl Löwith and Walter Kaufmann to accommodate Nietzsche as a new culmination. Löwith stresses the interplay between the bourgeois spirit and Nietzsche's critique thereof. Kaufmann expressly recognizes that such a research growth involves recognition of Nietzsche's variating connectiveness with the interpreting present. It is on this basis that he makes the strong claim that "no other philosopher since Plato and Aristotle, with the exception of Kant and Hegel, has influenced so many widely different thinkers and writers so profoundly. . . . What gradually becomes more and more obvious is the unexampled richness of Nietzsche's thought," considered in its manysided relations with the creative minds and core issues of our century.[12]

[12] Walter Kaufmann, Introduction to his edition of *Basic Writings of Nietzsche*, p. xii. In addition to Karl Löwith's *From Hegel to Nietzsche*, see L. Gleiman, "The Challenge of Nietzsche," *Thought*, 42 (1967), 52-68, for some theistic correlations.

The more we discover the intellectual ties binding Freud and Joyce, Buber and Tillich, Jaspers and Heidegger, with the philosophy of Nietzsche, the more pointed becomes the revisionary influence of the interpreting present. It re-educates our historical sense of the continuity in German philosophy to include its cultural and moral reassessment by Nietzsche. The resulting realignment of perspectives serves not only to improve our understanding of the contemporary crisis in values and the image of man but also to develop a new quality in our historical judgments. For we discover that Hegel and Marx reveal a different profile when they are approached, not as terminals in a from-to line of comparison, but rather as important stations along a pathway leading toward an explosive critique in Nietzsche.

It is worth noting that, in the process of historical revision of from-to relationships, new openings are sought at the "from" pole as well as at the "to" pole of the comparison. In the instance of German philosophy, a good portion of the research is being concentrated upon the long-neglected pre-Kantian thinkers.[18] Heimsoeth, Tonelli, and Beck have been sensitive to the threat against historical credibility contained in the reigning impression that "it all started with Kant, anyway," that the interspace between Leibniz and Kant in German philosophy was therefore insignificant except for antiquarian diversions, and that the main thrust of European philosophizing simply moved from Hume to Kant without any important preparations being made on the German side of the hop. These assumptions run counter to Kant's own lively feel for his Germanic setting, his inheritance of language-problems-and-methods from his German predecessors, and his very careful reflective study of the developments in metaphysics from the time of Leibniz to his own day.

[18] This historical tendency becomes visible in: H. Heimsoeth, *Studien zur Philosophie Immanuel Kants*; H. Heimsoeth, ed., *Studien zu Kants philosophischer Entwicklung*, including G. Tonelli's essay, "Kant und die antiken Skeptiker," pp. 93-123, which advances the research cited above in note 11; and Lewis W. Beck, *Early German Philosophy: Kant and His Predecessors*.

Furthermore, ignorance concerning these developments cannot be justified, except at the expense of those other interrogative modes of historical study in terms of continuity, genesis, and evolving context which together comprise the second co-ingredient principle of historical understanding. The interpreting present works to strengthen these modes of historical questioning, not to weaken them. Thus in the test case of pre-Kantian German philosophy, we can see the interdependence of history of philosophy and the histories of science and society. Recent research into the reception of Newtonian thought in the Prussian Academy of Sciences and into the *Aufklärung* views on peace-progress-civil-society is bound up reciprocally with research into the growth of German philosophy prior to the 1781 edition of the *Critique of Pure Reason*. To press home such intellectual solidarity among the historical disciplines which enrich our understanding and social options so considerably, is a primary avenue used by the interpreting present to reconsider the conventional "from" pole in the Kant-to-Nietzsche comparative account of German philosophers.

(b) New historical comparisons. Sometimes, the from-to ordering of philosophers is all too successful, that is, it becomes an exclusive way of taking these philosophers and stifles their other historical relationships. We have already noted that in order to overcome this narrowing effect of the genetic and school approach, historians will return to the primary works for evidence of the other philosophical influences and lines of argumentation which break out of some habitual from-to pattern. Our present purpose is to observe that new historical comparisons also receive impetus from contemporary modes of philosophizing which, taken by themselves, may seem uninvolved in any such historical problems.

One major sphere where the historical repercussions are beginning to be felt is the theory of perception. In the introductory part of his *Phenomenology of Perception*, Merleau-Ponty formulates his philosophical program in these terms:

The first philosophical act would appear to be to return to the world of actual experience which is prior to the objective world, since it is in it that we shall be able to grasp the theoretical basis no less than the limits of that objective world, restore to things their concrete physiognomy, to organisms their individual ways of dealing with the world, and to subjectivity its inherence in history. Our task will be, moreover, to rediscover phenomena, the layer of living experience through which other people and things are first given to us, the system "Self-others-things" as it comes into being; to reawaken perception and foil its trick of allowing us to forget it as a fact and as perception in the interest of the object which it presents to us and of the rational tradition to which it gives rise.[14]

The rational tradition mentioned here is not only the ideal of scientific objectivity but also the modern philosophical theories built around the accepted system of reference to self-others-things. These theories include both the empirical self and the transcendental self, both the sense experience of qualities and the rational determination of forms—in a word, the interpretive schemata developed by all the major traditions in modern philosophy. By measuring them against our basic perception of the world and an awareness of the embodied, societal cogito, Merleau-Ponty does more than criticize the separate lines of rationalism and empiricism, transcendental and naturalistic philosophies. He also suggests that these historical lines share many more common presuppositions than we might infer from treating them always in separate from-to lineages. His comprehensive view of our perception of the living world and social reality encourages historians to cast

[14] Maurice Merleau-Ponty, *Phenomenology of Perception*, p. 57. This program is strongly influential for D. W. Hamlyn, *Sensation and Perception: A History of the Philosophy of Perception*, and for Fraser Cowley, *A Critique of British Empiricism*, especially chapters 1-11, on Hume. Similarly, the phenomenology of fictions binds together Hume-Kant-Husserl, in R. Sokolowski, "Fiction and Illusion in David Hume's Philosophy," *The Modern Schoolman*, 45 (1967-68), 189-225.

a more critical eye upon the separatisms proposed for modern philosophy.

This thrust of the interpreting present is just beginning to show its impact upon historical studies. Working from an analytical background, D. W. Hamlyn centers his history of the philosophy of perception around the persistent, unifying theme of the relationship between perception and sensation. Along with Merleau-Ponty, he finds it useful to distinguish the reality of perception from the opposing orthodoxies which treat it either as something passive (as sensation is abstractly supposed to be) or as a pure activity of organizing judgment itself. What is significant for history of modern philosophy is that, in trying to avoid these extreme reductions of perception, we can recognize that there is no absolute segregation between a Descartes and a Locke, a Kant and a Mill. All these modern philosophers share a strong sense of the human irreducibility of our perceptual relation with the world, as well as an ultimate intention of differentiating this relationship from the condition of either total passivity or pure creativity on man's part. Thus Hamlyn finds some good reasons for giving a more sustained and exacting historical interpretation of the *crossover relationships* between the seminal modern philosophers. Rigid segregation of rationalists from empiricists is becoming increasingly difficult to maintain, at least with any strong claim of historical justification.

Another example of this long-range move toward new interrelationships in the from-to sphere is afforded by Fraser Cowley's critique of British empiricism. The first half of his study is, in fact, a reading of Hume's *Treatise of Human Nature* in the light of some suggestions made about this classic work by Husserl and Merleau-Ponty. They view the Humean theory of belief, imagination, and fiction as standing in a crucially midway position between a dogmatic postulation of the reality of Newtonian nature and a more reflective acknowledgment of man's founding acts of meaning for the components in experience. This point is being made by historians working from both the phenomenological and the analytic backgrounds in contemporary thought. It is becoming increasingly untenable to seal up Hume's philosophy completely within a Locke-to-Mill frame of reference, since there are so many themes which he shares in common with continental philosophers of the active self and its founding of human meanings.

Historians of modern philosophy who are attentive to the interpreting present come to regard every from-to perspective as being *porous in principle*. It brings to meaningful unity some themes and arguments in a grouping of philosophers. But the grouping is never intended to be so fixed and isolated that it blocks the development of still other historical relationships, still other modes of synopsis for understanding the company of modern philosophers.

A modest first vintage of historical possibilities, opened up by analytically generated inquiries, is offered in J. P. Day's study of hope. Having noticed the involvement of hope in current discussion of emotion and belief, right and duty, he looks for some cues on this almost forgotten problem in four philosophers who are often kept doctrinairely apart: Aquinas and Hume, Kant and Mill.

> Aquinas regards Hope as the second Theological Virtue. Hume finds Hope and its opposite, Fear, to be the most important of what he calls "the direct passions." Kant tells us that "What may I hope if I do my duty?" is one of the fundamental questions of philosophy. Similarly to Kant, Mill maintains that the fundamental question in religion is not "What is it legitimate to believe?", but "What is it legitimate to hope?"[15]

[15] J. P. Day, "Hope," *American Philosophical Quarterly, 6* (1969), 89. See Ernst Bloch, *The Principle of Hope*; Jürgen Moltmann, *Theology of Hope*; Josef Pieper, *Hope and History*; and symposium on "Hope," *Cross Currents, 18* (1968), 257-335. This is an instance of the permeability of philosophy and its history to other research and cultural interests, which must nevertheless be judged capable of being reoriented in accord with some philosophical and historical methodologies. Alan Ryan's *John Stuart Mill* specifies the chief analytic themes in Mill, as do the previously cited essays in J. B.

This comparative study shows both that contemporary philosophers should not give up on hope as a rewarding theme and also, from the historical standpoint, that *historical regroupings* made in the light of current questions help to develop our understanding of modern philosophy.

The Aquinas-Hume couplet does much more than remind us of the fundamental openness of modern thinkers to elucidation from the Greek and medieval past. It serves notice to historians that, for all their repudiation of the monkish attitudes, such thinkers as Spinoza and Hume nevertheless bring to their analysis of human nature many insights analogous to the older treatises on the passions of the soul and the virtues of man. The long stretches in Descartes, Spinoza, and Hume on the passions and virtues lose their aridity for those historians who are prepared to recognize there the continuation of a long tradition in philosophical anthropology, as well as a valuable source of conceptual usages bearing on analytic issues today.

Further reinforcement comes (for those historians of philosophy who remain responsive to all forms of intellectual concern) from developments being made in the theology of hope. The discussion between Moltmann and Bloch on utopian, humane, and evangelical modes of hoping raises many questions which affect our historical manner of relating the modern philosophers.

A conspectus of Hume-Kant-Mill around the topic of hope has internal implications for historical research. It is another reminder that the movement from Hume to Mill cannot be kept insular, cannot be kept from including Hume's impact upon Kant and, in turn, the latter's challenge for Mill. For the hope question indicates how impoverished the relationship between Hume and Kant would be, were it confined to the epistemology of causal necessity and the moral comparison

Schneewind's *Mill* (see above, Chapter III, note 12). But a thorough historical treatment of his philosophy, viewed in terms of internal development and relationship with other positions on the main issues (including the imagination-hope theme), remains for future work.

between approbation and duty. Kant does not regard the Humean theory of the passions merely as pre-moral talk on the plane of pragmatic imperatives. For the problem of hope is there to suggest that many aspects of that theory are recovered at a transpassional, moral level in the Kantian conception of religion.

Still another incitement to fresh historical questioning of the sources comes from the consideration that Mill's elaboration of the function of hope cannot be grasped solely from a background in Hume and Kant. When Mill acknowledges a role for imaginatively sustained hope, he is drawing mainly upon his reading of romantic poets, his experiences with the Saint-Simonists, his study of Comte's philosophy, and his recognition at the outset of the Darwinian era that human evolution is now more cultural than biological. Thus a comparative analysis of Mill's notion of hope provokes many historical questions about how to interrelate the separate stories of romanticism and utopian socialism, positivistic prevision of humanity's future and the aspects of hope and futurity involved in Bergsonian and other evolutionary philosophies, as they move into the twentieth century. Whenever historians of modern philosophy look thus toward unfinished tasks, they are manifesting in practice their commitment to the open principle of the interpreting present.

3. Ways of the Responsive Interpreter: (ii) Appreciating the Middle-Range Philosophers and the Paraphilosophers

A skilled and creative historian of modern philosophy never permits his judgment of evaluation and comparative ranking to be determined exclusively by a philosopher's role within a specific from-to transition. Within such a framework, it is all too easy to assign the roles of being a middle-sized or minor thinker to philosophers involved in that relationship. These "middlizing and minorizing" judgments may be fair enough ways of signifying a man's functional contributions toward the structure of this particular from-to perspective. But they cannot be regarded as utterly definitive, both because that perspective itself is provisional and because his entire philosophical significance may not be expressed in terms of the criteria of importance holding for this context alone. Hence the historian must take methodic steps to listen for those uniquely insistent acts of philosophizing whose significance lies elsewhere than in the service of the dominant from-to span. If this methodological move receives support, not only from the philosopher's own source writings but also from some distinctive correlations between these writings and the philosophical interests of the historian's own time, then the effort to reach a more fair and adequate evaluation is notably facilitated.

The purpose of further historical research need not be to contrive any dramatic reversal of ranking. It is seldom that a philosopher usually regarded as being of middle or minor stature will suddenly emerge as a truly major mind. On the contrary, the aim may simply be to sift the philosopher's work and plural relationships more finely, in order to reach a firmer historical footing for regarding him comparatively as a minor thinker or one of intermediate rank.

In the process of improving these judgments of historical valuation, however, there are two consequences of great help for advancing our understanding of the history of modern philosophy. One is the proper appreciation of those philosophers who lie below the peak level defined by the very greatest men. To conclude, with some historical justice, that a certain philosopher falls short of being ranked alongside of Descartes and Hume, Kant and Hegel, does not entail any license to neglect that philosopher thereafter or to consider him only insofar as he ministers to some development involving these supreme modern thinkers. Quite to the contrary, such a judgment includes the historical imperative to examine and respect this thinker's methods and arguments in his own reach and meaning. We do not truly know the historical landscape in modern philosophy until we come to discern the values found upon the middle plateau and in the fertile lowlands, as well as those found on the highest mountains. The second consequence is that we learn to detect and prize the contributions made to modern philosophy by thinkers who may not themselves be philosophers in the professional sense, but whose historical influence as paraphilosophical thinkers is considerable and precious.

In the present section, our analysis will center upon the historian's responsibility toward philosophers of middle and minor rank and toward the paraphilosophers. Schopenhauer and Feuerbach are the significant instances considered here of the historical rehabilitation of middlesize and minor philosophers, respectively, whereas Kierkegaard and Hamann are religious thinkers who may nevertheless be viewed from our perspective as paraphilosophers. In all these functional approaches to historical understanding, however, our prime concern is to discover just how the co-factor of the interpreting present is decisively involved in quickening our historical appreciation of these four thinkers.

(a) Feuerbach and Schopenhauer. When they are treated primarily in reference to the Kant-to-Marx development, Ludwig Feuerbach emerges as a transitional, easily surpassable mind along the way, and Arthur Schopenhauer appears as a remote outsider, peripheral to the mainstream of modern philosophizing. Nevertheless, they are being studied and used by many more thoughtful workers in diverse fields today than might be expected from these measurements, as determined on the dominant Kant-to-Marx scale. It is not that exaggerated claims to major importance are being advanced for Feuerbach, or that Schopenhauer ceases to be taken as a philosopher of intermediate achievement. Rather, the new quality consists in a more exacting historical analysis of their writings and a more direct relating of their thought to some basic questions of our own time. These two thinkers are much

more alive for us in their own significance and just dimensions, now that their mode of philosophizing is not being routed entirely through their relationship with the movement from Kant to Marx.

In terms of the interpreting present, Feuerbachian studies have been kindled by the pioneer evaluations made by the personalist philosopher Martin Buber and the theologian Karl Barth. In a long autobiographical chapter on his indebtedness to Feuerbach and Nietzsche, Buber acknowledged the inspiration received in his youth from the former's maxim that "man with man—the unity of I and thou—is God."[16] This suggested to Buber that, within the religious relationship, man and God neither remain in rigid separation nor melt together, but come into interpersonal and dialogal union with each other. From this specific point of departure, Buber was led to read Feuerbach's *Principles of the Philosophy of the Future* with a sympathetic eye toward its generalization of the I-thou-it interpretation of all reality.

The two philosophers agreed that the soundest foundation for philosophy is furnished, not by the idealistic conception of the absolute spirit, but rather by "the real and whole being of man." Furthermore (in a passage which Buber hailed as being extraordinarily important for our present thinking in philosophical anthropology), Feuerbach located this integral human reality precisely in the interpersonal, I-thou community and not in the isolated thinker or moral agent.

[16] The passages quoted in this paragraph and the next one are from Ludwig Feuerbach, *Principles of the Philosophy of the Future*, principles 41, 50, 59, 60, 62 (pp. 59, 66, 71-72). See the chapter on Feuerbach and Nietzsche in Martin Buber, *Between Man and Man*, pp. 46-48; M. S. Friedman, *Martin Buber: The Life of Dialogue*, pp. 29, 48-51; R. E. Wood, *Martin Buber's Ontology*, pp. 5-6. Karl Barth's essay is printed as the Introduction to Feuerbach's *The Essence of Christianity*, pp. x-xxxii; and Feuerbach's most mature analysis of religion is found in his *Lectures on the Essence of Religion*. Historical interpretations sensitive to Feuerbach's many contemporary bearings are given by H. Arvon, *Ludwig Feuerbach, ou la transformation du sacré*, especially chapter 3 on the I-Thou relation; E. Kamenka, *The Philosophy of Ludwig Feuerbach*; and M. von Gagern, *Ludwig Feuerbach*.

> The essence of man is contained only in the community
> and unity of man with man; it is a unity, however, which
> rests only on the reality of the distinction between I and
> thou. . . . The true dialectic is not a monologue of a soli-
> tary thinker with himself; it is a dialogue between I and
> thou. . . . The community of man with man is the first prin-
> ciple and criterion of truth and generality.

By highlighting these Feuerbachian maxims and developing
their lead into a complex philosophy of his own, Buber compelled the interpreting present to devote more historical research to this German philosopher for his own thought, and
not solely for his ministrations to the Young Hegelians.

Similarly, Barth's sympathetic reading of Feuerbach's *The
Essence of Christianity* and *Lectures on the Essence of Religion* had repercussions reaching far beyond his immediate
theological purposes. He drew attention to the unique contribution of these books to our understanding of the general
process of individual and social alienation and the objectiviz-
ing projection of ideals, of which the religious modes are only
the most striking instance. By also stressing the positive appreciation of religious reality communicated in these source-
books, Barth did the history of modern philosophy the
distinct service of liberating them from being simply stereo-
typed as advancing a flatly materialistic theory of God and
the human soul.

Historians of philosophy have been encouraged by this
initiative from the interpreting present to revisit Feuerbach
and to conduct their analyses in much greater depth and
nuance. In the course of this historical reappraisal, certain
currently attractive aspects of his philosophy are being
brought out from the shadows. Feuerbach's thought is now
better appreciated for its correlation between experienced being and the integral response of man as a sensuous-reflective-
affective agency, for the distinctive role of my own body in
establishing interpersonal and other intramundane relationships, and for uncovering the human meanings invested in

many types of symbolic, conceptual, and institutional order. A philosopher, shown thus through improved historical questioning to speak sensibly to us on so many topics of contemporary concern, is undergoing a thorough revaluation instigated by the interpreting present.

Since the publication of the critical edition of his main works and his manuscript remains, Schopenhauer has proved his right to summon even more of the interpretive resources in history of philosophy. The tendency to permit his thought to slip down into the elaborate footnotes of modern philosophy has been decisively reversed. This valuative reversal can be traced quite directly to a reform in historical judgment based upon Schopenhauer's proven correlation with three basic rules of rehabilitation, as they are pressed home by the interpreting present. His claim to thoughtful consideration as a philosopher of middle ranking is being firmly regrounded.

The first rule of rehabilitation is that any philosopher who *markedly alters* a major pattern of historical comparison thereby earns the right for a more intensive examination of his own doctrines. We have just noticed how the classical German developments are being reconceived, as the result of treating Nietzsche as a new terminus in the speculations since Kant. But once Nietzsche enters prominently into this from-to inquiry, we can also perceive some freshly significant contributions being made by Schopenhauer. His relationship to the entire German situation radically affects our comparative understanding. He moves from the bankside (the position dictated by coordinates taken mainly from Hegel and Marx) into the main historical current, and does so on the strength of his intrinsic linkage with Kant at the headwaters and with Nietzsche at the estuary leading into the twentieth century.

Our historical recovery of Schopenhauer is being spurred by reflection upon the many enthusiastic references, in Nietzsche's early letters and books, to "my Schopenhauer" and "the spirit of Schopenhauer." Nietzsche's essay on "Schopenhauer as Educator" interprets his predecessor as the radical tutor of modern consciousness and modern philosophizing, as the witness who unblinkingly reveals our common predicament of having to bring forth human values in a world where God's shadow is shrinking to the vanishing point. Schopenhauer's influence is clearly marked in these statements appearing in Nietzsche's letters to his old friend from the Pforta schooldays, Carl von Gersdorff:

> Three things afford me relief, rare moments of relief from my work: my Schopenhauer, the music of Schumann, and solitary walks. . . . One has to have assimilated a great deal of Schopenhauer to sense how much of it all [Nietzsche's 1869 inaugural lecture at Basel] is subject to the decisive spell of his peculiar mode of thinking. . . . I really do stand now at a center from which Schopenhauerian threads reach out into all parts of the world.[17]

If in later years Nietzsche became critical of Schopenhauer, it was primarily the fad of a Wagnerized Schopenhauer which he satirized. We can discern the true historical import of Schopenhauer by attending to the reference made here to Robert Schumann's music. Nietzsche himself both sang in the chorus of Schumann's *Faust* music (composed 1844-53) and wrote a piano composition in the vein of Schumann's *Manfred* music (composed 1849). In these works and in his *Rhenish Symphony* (Third Symphony in E Flat Major,

[17] Nietzsche, *Letter of April 7, 1869, to Carl von Gersdorff*, in *Nietzsche: A Self-Portrait from His Letters* (Fuss-Shapiro, p. 3); and *Letter of September 28, 1869, to Carl von Gersdorff*, in *Selected Letters of Friedrich Nietzsche* (Middleton, p. 60). Moreover, the third essay in Nietzsche's *Untimely Reflections* is on "Schopenhauer as Educator," depicting his predecessor as a touchstone of heroic honesty in the modern philosophic life. After his break with Wagner, Nietzsche declares that his essays on Schopenhauer and Wagner "are really a series of self-disclosures, and above all solemn commitments, rather than genuine psychological studies of these masters (as much my kin as they are my antagonists)," *Letter of February 19, 1888, to Georg Brandes*, Fuss-Shapiro, p. 108. Nevertheless, Nietzsche is disclosing his mind and will in their genetic relationship to a Schopenhauer whose kinship associates him with Schumann, and whose assigned role of antagonist is correlated with Wagner.

1850), Schumann gave musical expression to man's struggle to integrate ideal form and pulsing vitality, cosmic structure and personal will, work and liberation, suffering and celebration. These were precisely the tensional themes whose philosophical development in Schopenhauer sank deeply into the young Nietzsche's mind and, through him, passed into the existential philosophers and artists of our century.

Furthermore, historians are finding it worthwhile to keep in proper perspective Schopenhauer's petty quarreling with Hegel. This personal foible cannot deflect them from undertaking a much more careful analysis of the sustained and perceptive Schopenhauerian critique of Kant. The direct relating of Schopenhauer to Kant visibly modifies our comparative understanding of both members of the relationship. For their conflict concerns, not superficial matters of personal polemics, but the root questions of the subject-object correlativity and the possibility of metaphysics, the power of evil and the presence of values in the world, and the replenishing operation of art (especially music) upon the human spirit. Schopenhauer's historical significance for us arises from his independent rethinking of these Kantian and humane issues, rather than from his reaction to Hegel and the academic world of his day.

A second rule of the interpreting present, considered as a re-evaluative tendency, is that the *radial influence* of a classical modern source upon several contemporary philosophers warrants a full scale historical reconsideration of that source itself. From this standpoint, it is worth attending to the joint impact which Schopenhauer has exerted upon the existentialists and Wittgenstein.[18]

---

[18] See Martin Heidegger, *An Introduction to Metaphysics*, p. 63, and idem, *Nietzsche*, I, 44-45, 126-128, and II, 92-93 (highly critical of Schopenhauer on will, pessimism, nihilism, and the Kantian meaning of disinterested beauty); Jean-Paul Sartre, *Being and Nothingness*, pp. 229, 231. That Schopenhauer studies are benefiting from interest in Wittgenstein's intellectual genesis, can be seen from these articles: B. F. McGuinness, "The Mysticism of the *Tractatus*," *The Philosophical Review*, 75 (1966), 305-328; A. S. Janik, "Schopen-

Although explicit treatments of his philosophy by Heidegger and Sartre are sparse enough, they do concern some fundamental problems. Schopenhauer's position has to be understood in order to capture the full significance of several existentialist themes. They are: the illusion of a purely objectivist attitude or "optical" metaphysics, the solipsist's futile effort to build a dam for stopping man's essential reference to the world, the unique meaning of my own body, and the powerful role of conscience in witnessing to man's practical opening to social reality. These pointers are quite sufficient to induce the modern historian to reread *The World as Will and Presentation* from the perspective of its effort to renovate ontology, on a basis more congruent with man's existential condition. Under such prompting from the interpreting present, philosophical attention centers upon the Schopenhauerian vision of man. He is portrayed as existing at the boundary situations of life-suffering-death, as discovering the unappeasable striving of will and its constitutive worldliness within himself, and as ever seeking to experience and communicate that which transcends the actual capacities of our concepts and language. This view of human reality strikes too many basic chords in our contemporary sensibility and re-

---

hauer and the Early Wittgenstein," *Philosophical Studies*, 15 (1966), 76-95; and S. M. Engel, "Schopenhauer's Impact on Wittgenstein," *Journal of the History of Philosophy*, 7 (1969), 285-302. An extended comparison is made by M. Michelletti, *Lo schopenhauerismo di Wittgenstein*. The intrinsic textual impetus for further historical study of Schopenhauer stems largely from the publication of his fertile and varied manuscript remains: *Der handschriftliche Nachlass*, ed. Arthur Hübscher. Between 1818 and 1860 (from completion of the original version of *The World as Will and Presentation* until his death), Schopenhauer engaged in intense underground reflections, preparing *ten* manuscript books (in Hübscher, vols. 3-4). They contain essays and sketches of his later editions and published works, metalogical studies and analyses of early evolutionary theories, *pensées* and polemics, moralizing travel notes and translations of the moralists-poets-philosophers-sages of every age and culture. See Wittgenstein: *Notebooks 1914-1916*, pp. 49-51, 72-89; *Prototractatus*, 5. 335-533552, 6. 41-7; *Tractatus Logico-Philosophicus*, 5. 6-5. 641, 6. 41-7.

flectivity to postpone a thorough historical reinterpretation of Schopenhauer's thought.

What makes him all the more indispensable for grasping the philosophical problems of our century, however, is the fact of his appeal—in these same features—to Wittgenstein as well as to the existentialists. As is becoming increasingly clear from the former's *Notebooks 1914-1916*, *Prototractatus*, and *Tractatus Logico-Philosophicus*, Wittgenstein incurred an early debt to Schopenhauer on at least six points.

(i) There is a distinction in principle between questions *framed within the world* and the question of *the sense of the whole world*. Whether or not the latter can ever be humanly formulated, it does incite men to launch out upon moral and religious quests which seek to transcend the totality of intramundane objectives. (ii) By distinguishing between the active, willing subject and the entire world structure, Schopenhauer opens up a possible reference to the basic stream of life. The latter affects all our relationships and uses of language, but is not restrictively identified with any particular form. (iii) One salutary effect of stressing that *the* world is always *my* world is to render the standpoints of skepticism and solipsism utterly acute and undodgeable issues. In relation to my own body, I can construe will as being my will in my world. Thus I am always seriously invited to make either a solipsistic withdrawal from the world or to indulge in skeptical description of what can amount to no more than my private impressions. Although I need not accept either invitation, I cannot conduct my reflections as though neither alternative is tempting, or as though no strenuous users of language have ever succumbed to them.

(iv) In a dislodging effort, Schopenhauer brings us right up to life's boundary situations. He uncovers not only the cognitive limits placed upon a deciphering of the world's encoded meaning but more especially those affective and practical limits placed upon a search after values and wholeness in life. (v) Yet the human agent accepts his suffering, keeps active in his life situations, and stubbornly squeezes out a modicum of happiness within the restrictions. Schopenhauer does not permit his metaphysics of the desiring will to suppress his analytic interest in mankind's intermediate range of responses in the moral, esthetic, and religious spheres. (vi) Nevertheless, a study of his thought enables us to feel a somber disillusionment with human goods, combined with a mystical attitude of always seeking something more and other than the world can offer. Amid many loquacious philosophers, the Schopenhauer of the concluding sections of *The World as Will* stands out through his ultimate appeal to silence as a way of indicating our unquenchable thrust beyond the world and its expressive languages.

It is not enough, however, for students of existentialism and Wittgenstein merely to record the many pathways leading toward Schopenhauer. These hints cannot be left in a vague and uninterpreted condition but must be made the occasion for historical comparisons, done with more awareness of his implications than heretofore. The aim of such comparative study is not only to improve our grasp upon the historical antecedents and suppositions of a Heidegger or a Wittgenstein. There is also the direct intention of furnishing a historically better founded evaluation of Schopenhauer's own achievement and relative position in modern philosophy. Our historical judgment will include the ranking of his philosophy somewhere between that of minor men and that of the greatest philosophers.

For such an evaluation to be made, there must be added to the previously stated rules of rehabilitation a third rule of demanding from the source thinker *a sustained systematic development* of the fundamental method and concepts in his mode of philosophizing. The modern philosopher of middle standing is one who not merely shows relevance for our problems but shows a quality of thorough analysis and synoptic comprehension in his own treatment of them. Here, there is a noteworthy difference between Feuerbach's program sketches and Schopenhauer's more intensive elaborations. Schopenhauer deserves a superior evaluation on the basis of his careful argumentation on the principles of knowing and being, his systematic development of the theme of universal will and its consequences for metaphysics and ethics, his close studies on freedom and character, his contributions to the esthetic philosophy of music and literature, and his unusual attempt to unify Eastern and Western accounts of man's religious and mystical experience. By satisfying this third criterion of a philosopher of middle standing, Schopenhauer research adds that the interpreting present includes its own requirement of self-criticism, distinguishing the resultant historical judgment from an undisciplined enthusiasm for current fashion.

(b) Paraphilosophers: Kierkegaard and Hamann. In further pursuit of the interpreting present, we will next consider the distinctive role of the paraphilosophers within history of modern philosophy. It is difficult to determine the exact sense in which a Pascal, a Hamann, or a Kierkegaard should be included in that history, although the need for their inclusion under some heading is clear. It will not do to classify them as minor philosophers. The question is not primarily one of relative gradation within the family of philosophers but of the family likeness itself, and in any case these men of genius fit uncomfortably into the minor and middling categories for formal philosophers.

To do justice to the whole situation, I will designate such men as paraphilosophical thinkers. As employed here, this is a methodological term having a threefold signification. It conveys the complex meaning: (i) that the source thinker has notably reshaped some methods and questions, concepts and living springs of evidence, in modern philosophy; (ii) that his chief orientation and activities lead him toward some other sphere of creativity; and (iii) that nevertheless a responsible historical judgment must recognize his philosophical influence and try to determine more precisely its basis and manifestations. Such an appraisal will not exhaust such a think-

er's significance for humanity, but it will specify the grounds
for reckoning with him in careful accounts of the development of modern philosophy and its contemporary usefulness.

Historical reckoning with the paraphilosophers is a notoriously tardy affair, as the classic case of Kierkegaard testifies.
Although we find Nietzsche (just before his breakdown) assuring the Danish critic Georg Brandes that he intends to look
into the problem of Kierkegaard, it is not until well into our
century that philosophers and historians of philosophy have
seriously acknowledged his importance. As a boundary thinker born out of due time, he had to await a ripening process
containing several elements. His writings had to be translated
and retranslated into the major philosophical tongues; the
relationships between his life and thought had to be sorted
out in all their ambiguities and elusive aspects; and his critical
position toward Hegel, Schopenhauer, and modern culture
had to be plotted with some accuracy.

But such labors also had to be motivated by a conviction
of their worthwhileness for philosophy and today's problems.
This assurance of Kierkegaard's philosophical bearing developed convergently from several quarters: from Heidegger's
use of his existential accounts of dread and conscience; from
Jaspers' coupling of Kierkegaard and Nietzsche as the polar
framework for discussing contemporary questions of meaning
and transcendence; from analytic interest in the Danish thinker's discoursing upon decisional freedom and the modal
spheres of existing; and from the independent research done
by the theologians, psychologists, and literary critics into his
ideas on God-self-and-stylistic-forms. This ripening process
can also be taken as a concrete symbol of the historical operation of the interpreting present. Kierkegaard came into his
own, as an important paraphilosophical thinker, through our
gradual recognition and use of his writings and life style in
their bearing upon the living issues of our day.

While doing the research and writing of *The Mind of Kierkegaard* in the nineteen-forties, I could not avoid being keenly

aware of the interconnectedness of my historical study with a multitude of other current tendencies.[19] The Danish edition of Kierkegaard's *Collected Works* and *Papers* had at last placed at our disposal the textual basis for a critical reading of his books and journals. Walter Lowrie, David Swenson, and Alexander Dru were presenting the first, heroic translations of his works in English, so that Kierkegaard was becoming an articulate voice within our language sphere. Simultaneously, the Danish, German, and French studies done on him respectively by Geismar and Bohlin, Haecker and Hirsch, Wahl and Mesnard, were supplying a preliminary orientation in the thicket of his writings. These scholars were relating Kierkegaard's intellectual and existential problems to the contemporary sense of conflict and estrangement in the erotic, moral, and religious spheres of life.

To increase the urgency of becoming familiar with Kierkegaard, the main existentialist philosophers were just being Englished in time to show how massively influential his thought was upon their own original work. Clearly, there was considerable contemporary motivation for examining the Kierkegaardian categories of the free individual existent and the instant, the interrelated spheres of existence and the leap of faith, as well as the prescient critique of dehumanizing social forces and anonymous opinion making. Otherwise, one would be at a severe disadvantage in grasping the precise nature of the language, problems, and alternatives which filled the books of Heidegger and Jaspers, Sartre and Marcel.

It was also clear to me, however, that *no* set of disposing cultural conditions, however powerful and impressive, should

---

[19] In *The Mind of Kierkegaard*, I try to center the interpretation around the philosophical themes, leaving historical room for such religiously and theologically oriented approaches as: Lev Shestov, *Kierkegaard and the Existential Philosophy*; Louis Dupré, *Kierkegaard as Theologian*; and Vernard Eller, *Kierkegaard and Radical Discipleship*. One functional way to describe a paraphilosophical thinker is, therefore, as a mind whose historical interpretation requires focal centers to be established, not only in his philosophical themes but also (and more fundamentally) in his other active meanings and aims.

be allowed to dictate the actual shape and philosophical significance of my Kierkegaard studies. Psychological and sociological influences did sustain a sense of contributing something toward currently important questions, but beyond this assurance of relevance they were not permitted to specify that "something" any closer. The philosophical standpoint and methodic limits of the approach, as well as its main themes and conclusions, called for some other basis of judgment than that of making a cultural fit with Kierkegaard's other aspects. My methodological commitment to the history of philosophy and its principle of the interpreting present required me to do more than respond sensitively to the going intellectual tendencies. It was necessary to reorder and reinterpret them in the light of the primary integration of this principle with the other components of historical understanding: the insistential sources in Kierkegaard himself and the general canons of interrogation, as adapted to these source writings.

Such research experience indicates that the ultimate controlling judgment about how to proceed and what significations to present, rests upon a very complex interrelation of all the co-factors determining the philosophical character and historical foundation of the whole study. Only on this basis was it possible to construe "the mind of Kierkegaard" functionally, that is, as an attempt to give a restricted view of his contributions to *philosophical* issues stemming from the naturalistic, romantic, and Hegelian problems of Kierkegaard's day. The result was far from being an exhaustive intellectual portrait of his thought, but it did specify those points at which his religious reflection was bound up with some modern philosophical themes, giving them a distinctive turn of argument and urgency for us. Kierkegaard the religious thinker was not converted into a philosopher thereby, but some pertinent reasons were advanced for regarding him as a modern paraphilosophical thinker whom the searching person cannot afford to ignore or treat cavalierly.

Johann Georg Hamann is another paraphilosopher who helps to cast light upon the operation of the interpreting present, since his import for modern philosophy is only now being established with the help of some correlations between his positions and our own predicaments. The modest centering of historical studies upon him brings home the point that, in order to qualify for paraphilosophical standing precisely in history of philosophy, a thinker must contribute significantly to the *philosophical* movements of his time and ours. What leads the historian of modern philosophy to Hamann is, first, his striking and still influential interpretations of Hume and Kant, and then the equally marked impact he in turn has had upon the German idealists, Kierkegaard, and existential personalism. Thus although his own intent is primarily religious, its actual mode of operation and historical implications have involved philosophical problems and continued to modify our understanding of philosophical developments since Hume and Kant.

Using the technique of transference of figure, Hamann presents a Hume who confronts the Enlightenment pretensions for human reason in a manner analogous to Socrates' confrontation of the Sophists. In Hamann's eyes, Hume is a stumbling block for his age, a philosopher of ignorance or *agnosia* who makes us intensely aware of the severe limitations placed upon every aspect of human knowing and planning. Through his moderate skepticism and artful use of doubt, he works as a counterspy and critic, smoking out the Enlightenment naïveté concerning the power of reason and its substitution for the faith attitude.

Using a phrase which is also given currency by Kant, Hegel, and Marx, Hamann bases his kinship with Hume upon the latter's ready courage in making "the descent into the hell of self-knowledge."[20] What Hume and Hamann discover in their

[20] The two quotations in this paragraph are taken respectively from the selections translated by R. G. Smith, *J. G. Hamann 1730-1788*, p. 87, and from Hamann's *Socratic Memorabilia*, tr. J. C. O'Flaherty, p. 167. W. M. Alexander, *Johann Georg Hamann: Philosophy and Faith*, balances the philosophical, religious, and esthetic intents. Harold Stahmer, *"Speak That I May See Thee!"*, pp. 68-105, relates Hamann to the religious and linguistic personalism of Buber and Ebner.

interrogation of the human existent is that formal reason depends essentially upon, and receives intrinsic limitations from, the living perceptual reality of our sensations and passions together (a cognitive and practical complex signified by Hamann's key term *Empfindung*). All our existential convictions and affirmations rest upon this perceptual-passional-practical basis, and hence must be recognized as acts of believing rather than of pure reasoning and demonstration. "Our own being-there [*Dasein*] and the existence [*Existenz*] of all things outside us must be believed, and cannot be determined in any other way." And when Hume and Hamann probe still further into the grounds of existential belief itself, they find it resting upon the workings of natural instinct and practical inclinations, rather than upon the claims of proof made by orthodox rationalist theologians. Reason is not banished from this anthropology, but it is required to become more closely integrated with the perceptual, sensual, and passional aspects of human nature, as well as to subordinate itself to the primary relationship of the believing agent to all reality.

The Hume who stands forth in this Hamannian perspective is not a hitherto unknown figure, indeed, but he does receive a special limning and accenting which relate him more closely with some skeptical-existential currents in the interpreting present. This portrait of Hume underscores his crucial role in modern skepticism and the advisability of extending that history in the direction of Hamann and Kierkegaard. Indeed, under the rubric of "Night Thoughts of a Doubter," Hamann presents a German translation of the famous last chapter in Book I of Hume's *Treatise of Human Nature*. The "wise man and worm of the north" is attracted to this passage, because it so perfectly expresses Hamann's own fideistic theme of the misery of man, taken in himself and as being only en route toward acceptance of God in faith.

The *intense* view of these manifold contradictions and imperfections in human reason has so wrought upon me, and heated my brain, that I am ready to reject all belief and reasoning, and can look upon no opinion even as more probable or likely than another. Where am I, or what? From what causes do I derive my existence, and to what condition shall I return? Whose favour shall I court, and whose anger must I dread? What beings surround me? and on whom have I any influence, or who have any influence on me? I am confounded with all these questions, and begin to fancy myself in the most deplorable condition imaginable, inviron'd with the deepest darkness, and utterly depriv'd of the use of every member and faculty. . . . In all the incidents of life we ought still to preserve our scepticism. If we believe, that fire warms, or water refreshes, 'tis only because it costs us too much pains to think otherwise. Nay if we are philosophers, it ought only to be upon sceptical principles, and from an inclination, which we feel to the employing ourselves after that manner. Where reason is lively, and mixes itself with some propensity, it ought to be assented to. Where it does not, it never can have any title to operate upon us.[21]

Hamann's main charge against the Enlightenment is that it will not permit this existential view of man to sink in deeply enough, will not look steadily and honestly enough upon the doubtfulness of the foundations of reason and its need for being mixed with "propensity," or the sensational-passional-practical inclinations of human nature.

Hamann's paraphilosophical standing depends also upon the distinctive standpoint from which he criticizes Kantian thought. His *Metacritique of the Purism of Reason* is an obscure and baffling essay, but under patient analysis it yields an important point, provided that its restricted historical sig-

---

[21] David Hume, *A Treatise of Human Nature*, I, iv, 7 (ed. Mossner, pp. 316-317). On Hamann's use of this text, see C. W. Swain, "Hamann and the Philosophy of David Hume," *Journal of the History of Philosophy*, 5 (1967), 343-351. Hamann's translations of Hume's *Dialogues concerning Natural Religion* and Shaftesbury's *Characteristics* are better known, but not more formative for his own thought, than the passages he renders from Hume's *Treatise*.

nificance is also acknowledged. Hamann is dealing only with the Kant of the first *Critique*; he treats Kant always in his function as the climax of the Enlightenment, rather than as its overcomer; and he assigns concrete competence solely to the Hume-Hamann reading of human nature for making a judgment upon the abstract theory of pure reason. Working under these qualifications, however, Hamann suggests that the Kantian critical effort belongs within the more comprehensive effort of the eighteenth-century world to achieve a threefold purification of philosophy.

The first purification of philosophy consisted in the partly misunderstood and partly unsuccessful attempt to render the reason independent of all tradition and belief in tradition. The second purification is even more transcendental, and results in nothing less than independence of experience [*Erfahrung*] and its everyday induction. . . . The third, chief, and as it were empirical purism concerns language, the only, the first and the last instrument and criterion of reason, with no other credentials but tradition and usage. But one has almost the same experience with this idol as the ancient philosopher had with the ideal of reason. The more one considers, the deeper and more inward is one's dumbness and loss of all desire to speak.[22]

[22] The complete translation of Hamann's *Review of Kant's Critique of Pure Reason* and his *Metacritique of the Purism of Reason* is given in Smith, *J. G. Hamann 1730-1788*, pp. 207-221 (with the passages quoted here found on pp. 214-215). The original text of these writings is available in Josef Nadler's historical-critical edition of Hamann's *Sämtliche Werke*, vol. 3: *Schriften über Sprache, Mysterien, Vernunft, 1772-1778*, pp. 277-289. A critical analysis of the argument is made by W. M. Alexander, "J. G. Hamann: Metacritic of Kant," *Journal of the History of Ideas*, 27 (1966), 137-144. In a *Letter of November 14, 1784, to Jacobi*, Hamann remarks: "All metaphysical studies have recently, on account of the *Critique of Pure Reason*, become almost as loathsome to me as they were formerly on account of Wolff's Latin *Ontology*. For me the question is not so much What is reason? as What is language? It is here I suspect the source of all paralogisms and antinomies can be found which are ascribed to reason: it comes from words being held to be ideas, and ideas to be things themselves" (letter translated in Smith,

Hamann speaks here as a forerunner of Hegel and other philosophers of concrete actuality who attack the march toward
an excessively abstract notion of human intelligence and its
instruments.

This metacritique contains three points. (i) Enlightenment
culture as a whole represents the first state of abstractive purification, insofar as it seeks to slough off *tradition and the historical* character of all our convictions. (ii) Kant himself
contributes to the second phase of abstractive removal from
human conditions, when he concedes a pure intuition of the
forms of sensibility and thus seems to liberate human knowing
from its fundamental dependence upon the *sensations and
passions* of concrete experience. (iii) And he also falls victim
to the third and climactic mode of abstractionism, embodied
in the ideal of a univocal formal language that is perfectly
transparent and receptive of the pure ideas of reason.
Hamann's contention is not that Kant ignores the linguistic
factor, but that he underestimates the essential *ambiguity of
language* and the contingent, historically qualified nature of
any stated theory of human knowledge and any assertion of
structural or functional necessity for the components in
Kantian epistemology.

What specially engages the interpreting present here is the
meta-standpoint of language which guides Hamann's groping
evaluation. In wording which anticipates Wittgenstein, he
warns that language can become a powerful idol and bewitch-
er of our intelligence, when it is cut loose from experiential
conditions and our critical self-understanding. But when developed in intimate conjunction with them, it is the principle
of wholeness in human existence and the healing basis for
hoping to surmount the chasms of subjectivity/objectivity
and idealism/realism. The *speaking and hearing word* helps

J. G. Hamann, p. 249). Clarification of the nature of language and
its relation with reasoning is one of Hamann's primary demands
upon the philosophers. For his adaptation of the parsimonious motto
of Persius, used in another letter to Jacobi and quoted below, see
Alexander, *Johann Georg Hamann*, p. 25.

us to achieve the concrete co-presence of four radically con-
stituent factors of human reality: sensuous-passional experience and rational analysis, historical growth of meanings and
openness to the God who speaks within the religious community of mankind. Philosophers of religion find that their
research on the sacredness of the word and the tensional communitarian nature of religious living gets enriched by
Hamann's conception of language. He hails it as the sacra-
mental bond uniting men with God, with each other, and with
the context of nature.

Amid all these lines of relevance for our philosophical
present, however, Hamann remains a paraphilosophical
thinker. His sense of a Socratic vocation leads him to retreat
into the background even as he is speaking, to make his com-
munications in a crabbed and cabbalistic style which is strong
in particularized allusions and concrete imagery—a clutched
fist of essays, whose precise significance is still being de-
ciphered by Germanic experts. In his opposition to pretentious systems of thought, Hamann conceives the existential
thinker's function to be that of communicating crumbs or
fragmentary gleams of meaning. But although in this respect
he anticipates Kierkegaard, he does not thematize his own
meanings from many perspectives and within some general
context of the modes of existing.

From Hamann's own standpoint, these traits do not constitute drawbacks but rather the proper signs of his personal
vocation in life. Making a distinctive use of Persius' motto:
"I work to know the least," he subordinates all his criticisms
of philosophers and all his reflections on language and reality
to a religious faith in Christ. In his own terminology, Hamann
is properly a philo-logian, a lover of the religious word coming from a revealing God and assimilated by a believing man.
History of modern philosophy draws whatever significance
it can from certain aspects and implications of this religiously
oriented work, but it does not pretend to assimilate Hamann
wholly or primarily to the sphere of human philosophizing.
Like all paraphilosophers, therefore, Hamann helps the in-

terpreting present to clarify its own nature and self-limitations, as a component within the distinctively philosophical order of knowledge and action which is not simply coeval with all human knowing and acting.

4. WAYS OF THE RESPONSIVE INTERPRETER:
(III) SERVING CURRENT THEORETICAL AIMS

Especially in trying to make a functional analysis of the interpreting present, it is necessary to delve into some quite particularized forms of historical knowing. Hence this portion of our move toward historical concreteness concludes with a brief look at those modes of utilizing the modern sources, where the foremost trait is the instrumental ordering of the historical factors toward some contemporary theoretical purposes. This ordination to the needs of current speculation stands out clearly in three areas: the revisability differential among various modern philosophers, the cultivation of "meditations in the spirit of" this or that modern philosopher, and the selective fate of continuative problems which come out of the modern centuries and move into the present scene. In each of these modalities, the interpreting present approaches toward the zone of strictly contemporary philosophizing just as far as it can go without breaking loose from its essential coordination with the demands of the modern sources and their interrogational canons, that is, without ceasing to function as a co-ingredient precisely in the historical way of knowing and using the modern philosophers.

(a) The revisability differential. Comparing the historical treatment of one modern philosopher with that of another, there is a quite noticeable difference in the judgment of revisability and the actual rate of revisionary work. With some source thinkers, we are content to make do with some well used, "standard" accounts of their philosophy, without yet feeling the urgency of breaking out of the schematic pigeonhole and making a basic reinterpretation. This is the case with Wolff and Bentham and Comte, who are held fast in their

respective categories of rationalism and utilitarianism and positivism, with only minor flurries of research aimed at reconsidering them from a fresh angle. Their fate can be contrasted with that of a philosopher roughly on a par with them: George Berkeley. There is general agreement that typing him as an idealist is too indeterminate to be accurate and informative, and hence that every facet of his historical significance has to be newly examined. His writings are being studied from every side, with the presumption that they have new meanings to yield in relation to some concerns of our own. Thus Berkeley research is being conducted within an explicit revisability situation, which does not yet prevail for those other modern philosophers.

Reflecting upon this situation enables us to specify the interpreting present in function of one concrete formation of it. Undoubtedly, Berkeley's pull upon investigators comes partly from his ability to work out a distinctive philosophical position in sufficient argumentative depth and communicative skill, within a relatively brief compass which fits different levels of university instruction in philosophy. To a not inconsiderable degree, the concrete focusing of the interpreting present upon one philosopher more than another depends upon this correlation between his mode of writing and current educational needs. Berkeley's *Principles of Human Knowledge* lends itself splendidly to the "text and critical essays" approach, which combines a historical grounding in modern philosophy with contemporary reassessments.[23] His treatise offers a model presentation of the difficulties of skepticism and solipsism, the problem of primary and secondary qualities, the distinction between understanding and will and their

[23] This is the case with Colin M. Turbayne's edition of George Berkeley, *Principles of Human Knowledge: Text and Critical Essays*. The historical studies which I inspect for their twofold sensitivity toward Berkeley's textual structure and toward the interpretive potential of present linguistic tools are: David M. Armstrong, *Berkeley's Theory of Vision*; Colin M. Turbayne, *The Myth of Metaphor*; and Gavin Ardley, *Berkeley's Renovation of Philosophy*. See also, P. J. Olscamp, *The Moral Philosophy of George Berkeley*, and W. E. Steinkraus, *New Studies in Berkeley's Philosophy*.

integration in an active notion of personality, the correlation between proofs of God and the rest of a philosophy, the suggestion that scientific laws are contingent, and the belief that moral obligation is addressed to a participating community of agents. On all these topics, Berkeley furnishes a literate and strongly argued text for introducing university students to the recurrent problems in modern and contemporary philosophy.

But what specially energizes the interpreting present is a realization that some basic meanings in Berkeley's thought can go unnoticed, until we learn to ask the liberating questions which bring them to the fore. His theory of vision has always seemed to be a peripheral theme, for instance, one that is too outmoded, psychologically and analytically, to yield much interest to ourselves. This assumption about its safe dismissal is nevertheless challenged by David Armstrong. He finds the Berkeleyan writings on vision to be eminently rich in materials for critical analysis and comparison with present discussions of the language and psychology of perception.

Prolonging this line of research, Colin Turbayne treats the theory of vision in an instantiating manner, by regarding it as Berkeley's one detailed application of a very comprehensive but elusive proposal. Negatively stated, that proposal consists in a movement away from the metaphor of the machine, from the camera model in the theory of perception and mind, and from the whole mechanistic world view of Descartes and Newton. Berkeley's positive suggestion is that we employ the metaphor of language as the reconstructive principle in philosophy and life. As interpreted by Turbayne, his program develops the model and idiom of language as a way of grasping the nature of mind and cognition. Indeed, a pervasive linguistic model underlies Berkeley's conception of the universal language of nature and the presence of God, considered precisely as speaking persistently in the patterns of nature and in man's spiritual experience of the self and the kingdom of persons.

In trying to make this prospect accessible to others through well written treatises and dialogues, Berkeley does much more than remove the mountain of absurdity contained in abstract talk about matter and quiddities. He returns to the homeland of commonsense ways of talking and thinking, not in order to apotheosize ordinary language but to make us more aware of the extraordinary philosophical potentialities it enshrines and that can still be methodically actuated. Gavin Ardley concentrates upon this Berkeley, who is neither a sheer innovator unsupported by human experience nor a purely descriptive analyst, content to point out the muddles and category mistakes of others, without himself engaging in basic reform. Rather, the proposal is that we view Berkeley as a *renovator* of the metaphysical and moral capacities of the working language.

This reforming and reconstructive intent becomes more understandable, when Ardley develops an analogy between Berkeley's situation and our own. In both ages, there is a danger that the philosopher will either surrender to the scientific community his entire task of interpreting the world and human reality or else will turn away from man's drive to grasp the metaphysical and moral relationships in our universe. Against the former danger, Berkeley develops his doctrine on scientific fictions and the only indirect reference of scientifically postulated entities to the experienced world. And against the latter dereliction, he keeps probing into the meaning of freedom and spiritual activity, as well as the persistent connotation that all responsible agents are drawn together in a metaphysical-moral bond of participation. By concentrating upon Berkeley as a renovator of language, our historical intelligence moves closer to the pervasive intent of the entire Berkeleyan corpus and its capacity to illuminate our present day study of the distinctive relations between science, commonsense, and philosophy.

From another arm of the historical compass, Berkeley studies are also being reshaped by cognate research in the development of American pragmatism. It is sometimes presumed that, after reviewing the Fraser edition of Berkeley's works, Charles Peirce assigned the Irish philosopher to an outer boundary of his concern. But this does not square with the retrospective memoranda and letters on the origin of pragmatism written by Peirce after 1900, even granting that they tell us more about the Peirce of this period than about the formative decades of pragmatism. In one note, he remarks that pragmatism "as a *practice*, had been, I think, best illustrated by Berkeley, especially in his two works on vision," which are precisely the ones so central in the historical reconsiderations made by Armstrong and Turbayne. Furthermore, in a 1903 letter to William James, Peirce concedes that "Berkeley on the whole has more right to be considered the introducer of pragmatism into philosophy than any other man, though I was more explicit in enunciating it."[24] Prodded on by such puzzling declarations, H. S. Thayer has been led to devote a separate appendix in his critical history of pragmatism to Berkeley's anticipations in practice.

Once more, the beneficiary is not solely the theory of pragmatism and the current appreciation of American philosophers but also the history of British empiricism. Keeping in mind the Berkeley-Peirce relationship as we revisit the familiar writings of the bishop of Cloyne, we are bound to

[24] These two remarks are quoted by H. S. Thayer, *Meaning and Action: A Critical History of Pragmatism*, p. 499 (see the entire Appendix Five, "Berkeley and Some Anticipations of Pragmatism," pp. 499-507). Their respective sources are: M. H. Fisch, "Was There a Metaphysical Club in Cambridge?" in *Studies in the Philosophy of Charles Sanders Peirce*, second series, ed. E. C. Moore and R. S. Robin, p. 28; and Peirce's *Letter of January 23, 1903, to William James*, in R. B. Perry, *The Thought and Character of William James* II, 425. William James bore Peirce's judgment in mind, both in the preparatory lectures where he referred to Locke, Berkeley, and Hume as "the first pragmatists" (Perry, II, 442) and also in the third lecture of *Pragmatism*, on "Some Metaphysical Problems Pragmatically Considered." There, he treated Berkeley's critique of matter paradigmatically: it is "absolutely pragmatistic" in seeking out the negotiable common meanings packed into matteristic talk. See *The Writings of William James*, ed. J. J. McDermott, p. 392. Thus there is a long American tradition behind the reinterpretation of Berkeley made by Roy Wood Sellars, *Lending a Hand to Hylas*.

search for a fresh glint of meaning. For we can now perceive the pragmatic implications of the Berkeleyan contention that matter is an operationally empty concept, that mind signifies an active relational principle, that scientific law has only practical-predictive import, and that philosophical meaning always leads to man's practical relationship with the course of nature toward God.

Since the interpreting present converges so persistently upon Berkeley in these respects, the revisability differential in history of modern philosophy inclines decidedly toward a revaluation of his thought. This quickening of historical research is reinforced by the hint that perhaps the last word has not yet been spoken by the dissenting participants in his famous dialogues. This point has been vividly made in R. W. Sellars' reformulation, entitled *Lending a Hand to Hylas*. Sellars strengthens the case for Hylas, or "Mr. Matter," by revising his contributions in *Three Dialogues between Hylas and Philonous*.

The updated Hylas is able to defend the meaningfulness of matter and its explanatory power in philosophy. This he does by using an emergent evolutionary conception of matter as an active reality; by introducing the view of many levels of organic life, in opposition to a flat contrast between spirit as a whole and the sensible world as an undifferentiated global entity; and by the realistic epistemology of treating cognition always as objectively referential and instrumental to orienting men in the living practical world. Henceforth, historical interpretation of Berkeley is unlikely to shut out the possibility of relating his dialogues to a more naturalistic and evolutionary kind of empiricism, looming just over the intellectual horizon of his explicit consideration. The work of historical understanding is pitched in a new key, when unexplored and unfinished aspects of Berkeley's mind are suggested to the interpreting present.

A purist may object that, in modifying the historical perspectives and terms of comparison in this fashion, we are moving away from the historical study of a philosopher into a purely abstract, a-historical restatement of his position. This danger is indeed present as an extreme limit placed upon the process of revision. But it cannot be invoked in such a manner that every reformulation responding to the interpreting present becomes illegitimate or, at most, only an extrinsic contributor to historical meanings. As long as we satisfy the condition of testing new approaches with the aid of the other components in a critical theory of historical understanding, we can profit from them even though they may not be directly historical in intent or stated outcome.

(b) Free thematizations. Such is the cautious use, for example, which historians can make of "meditations in the spirit of" this or that modern philosopher. Methodologically speaking, there are some unique meanings in Edmund Husserl's *Cartesian Meditations,* in Wilfrid Sellars' "Leibnizian Meditations," and in Frederick Sontag's *The Existentialist Prolegomena to a Future Metaphysics.*[25] By the authors' own

[25] Edmund Husserl, *Cartesian Meditations*; Wilfrid Sellars, *Philosophical Perspectives*, chapter six: "Méditations Leibnitziennes," pp. 153-181 (the sentence quoted below in our main text is from p. 153); and Frederick Sontag, *The Existentialist Prolegomena to a Future Metaphysics.* Each of these philosophers appreciates the tensile problem of meditating in a contemporary spirit upon a great modern source, and each one offers valuable suggestions for relating his own philosophical method to our theory of historical understanding of modern philosophy. (1) Husserl: "In this unhappy present, is not our situation similar to the one encountered by Descartes in his youth? If so, then is not this a fitting time to renew his radicalness, the radicalness of the beginning philosopher? . . . In a quasi-Cartesian fashion we intend, as radically beginning philosophers, to carry out meditations with the utmost critical precaution and a readiness for any—even the most far-reaching—transformation of the old-Cartesian meditations. . . . I start with those motifs in the *Meditationes de prima philosophia* that have, so I believe, an eternal significance and go on to characterize the transformations, and the novel formations, in which the method and problems of transcendental phenomenology originate" (pp. 1, 5, 6). (2) Sellars: "In the history of philosophy, as in philosophy itself, we must continually shift between analysis and synopsis, embracing the extremes of both. To stay at or near the middle is to be safe but uninspired. To give Kant's dictum one more twist: analysis without synopsis is blind, synopsis without analysis is empty" (p. 5). (3) Sontag: "Some years

declaration, they are not serving as mouthpieces for the great modern philosophers invoked in their titles and are not primarily interested in analyzing and restating the doctrine of these sources. Meditations conducted in the Cartesian spirit are not, and are not intended to be, a repetition of Descartes' act of meditative philosophizing; Leibnizian meditations do not give us a re-enactment of Leibniz's course of composing an opusculum; and the existentialist prolegomena carry no claim to provide a strict commentary upon Kant's *Prolegomena to Any Future Metaphysics*. Nevertheless, in each instance the correlation is far from being completely fanciful or vague, but repays the historian's attention with some valuable suggestions which perhaps cannot be obtained as readily through any other approach.

These writings belong in the class of free thematizations of issues drawn from the modern philosophers. What the contemporary author does is to develop a set of creative variations on a theme originally set forth, in another form and setting, in a modern philosophical classic. All three components in our general guiding hypothesis about historical understanding are present, but the modes of historical interrogation remain recessive while the dominant role is assigned to the interpreting present, working as directly as possible upon some salient points chosen from the source writing. The

---

ago, while teaching Kierkegaard to one group with my left hand and Kant's *Prolegomena* to another with my right, I ignored the biblical injunction and began to try to work the two together. Stated ever so simply, it seemed to me that Kierkegaard's literary and psychological writings had actually provided the empirical basis which Kant had demanded to have shown to him before he could license any new metaphysical construction. . . . Can existentialism mold from Kant's old injunctions a new path for metaphysics and then move on to provide from this a prolegomenon for our contemporary constructions? Have Heidegger, Sartre and Wittgenstein formed a holy alliance to open the way to new metaphysical construction?" (pp. 1-3). Insofar as phenomenologists, analytic men, and existentialists raise such questions, implicating both their own methodology and the argument of the sources, there is a presential aspect in the history of philosophy and a hopeful future for its work.

primary intent is not to improve our textual comprehension
of the source itself but to discern and select those themes
which, as elaborated by some current methods and in the context of our going problems, will make a definite contribution
to a contemporary way of philosophizing. Thus the historical
point of departure is used instrumentally to sharpen certain
issues and alternatives bearing primarily upon present theoretical discussions.

Nevertheless, the history of modern philosophy as well as
the contemporary argument profits from these free variations. For although the source structure and its internal
elucidation do not constitute the main object of such
thematization, they are by no means suppressed or treated
with utter irresponsibility. In the process of stimulating a contemporary advance in philosophy, the source itself receives
some sort of indirect illumination for having successfully
served in this function.

Thus Husserl's phenomenology is not the sole beneficiary
from his choice of Descartes' *Meditations on First Philosophy* as a point of departure. Through the comparative
process, the thematized problems in the latter work now stand
forth with new urgency for readers of Descartes as well as
those of Husserl. Cartesian scholars are impelled to look
more closely at Descartes' views on certitudinal assent and
personal perception of evidence, his account of the thinking
self's life world and its basis of identity, and above all at the
problem of the self and the wider community of men. The
very disproportion between Descartes' concise fifth meditation and Husserl's grand elaboration of the theme of solipsism
and the transcendental ego sharpens the historian's awareness
of the Cartesian conception of interpersonal relations.

There is multiple instructiveness, too, in Sellars' development of the Leibnizian thesis that "the world in which we live
is but one of many possible worlds, decidedly more numerous
than blackberries." When Sellars constructs the ideal figure
of a "Leibnoza" (who would like to blend Spinoza's necessary premises for the production of things with Leibniz's free

choice of this world, by contrast with other possible ones),
he gives imaginative direction to historical research. He
makes historians probe more closely into the actual grounds
upon which Leibniz rejected the charge that his system represents just such a "Leibnozan" compromise. And in formulating the principle of nameability—that every substance is
nameable, that the sense of a proper name (i.e. the individual
concept) must include a complete description of the substance properly named, and that in last analysis the names are
those which God has for every actual and every possible substance—Sellars does not draw us too far away from a textual
study of the *Discourse on Metaphysics*. Even when he employs the language of Frege's theory of proper names, he is
drawing upon the resources of the seventeenth-century philosopher and logician. Contemporary formalization of Leibniz does much more than sharpen certain issues in analytic
philosophy. It also renders his own thought more explicit,
suggests new grouping of his primary concepts, and encourages that kind of conspectus view of truth-time-and-life-plan
which marks a genuine advance in historical synthesis.

One does not use Sontag as a companion in Kantian study
in the way that one uses Paton and Heimsoeth on the first
Critique, Beck on the moral *Critique*, or Cassirer on the
Critique of Judgment. His intent is not to comment formally
upon the arguments of the *Prolegomena to Any Future Metaphysics*, comparing them with other formulations in Kant and
locating them within the governing concepts of the critical
philosophy as a whole. Rather, Sontag's concern is directed
toward the exegesis of man's esthetic, moral, and emotive
attitudes as presented by Kierkegaard and the existentialists.
Yet he suggests that these anthropological descriptions can
be correlated with the stages in Kant's own argument against
metaphysics, and that the existentialist analyses constitute
a reasonable case for reopening the possibility of metaphysics
and some limited philosophical theory of God. The historical
point is driven home that Kant was declaring only a moratorium upon metaphysics and not its demise, and that he re-

mained open to the subsequent existential modes of cultivating man's experiential subsoil.

One point to reconsider is Kant's own effort to differentiate among the several meanings of metaphysics, not all of which fall under the ban pronounced in the first *Critique* and the *Prolegomena*. Nevertheless, even after such differentiation is made, an intensive analysis of human existential attitudes and practical relations *need not* rehabilitate metaphysics, in the sense of a transcendent type of reasoning intended to yield speculative knowledge. For Kant will still ask about the precise sense in which literary and religious statements yield cognitive meanings. Sontag's essay at least goads historians into improving their comparative approach to Kant and Kierkegaard. There are some direct lines of communication running between these two thinkers which are overlooked, if their relationship is always mediated through reference to Hegel.

Historical understanding of modern philosophy cannot afford to impoverish itself by slighting the values offered by such thematizations.[26] Clearly, the thoughtful consideration of some major modern source by a contemporary philosopher develops a meaning which enjoys a certain leeway of interpretation and use. The thematic variation does indeed directly serve the present theoretical aims of a phenomenological or an analytic or an existential philosophy, but this service does not exhaust its potentiality for the philosophical community. It can also be made to contribute indirectly to the historical elucidation of the modern source itself, even though this further reach of meaning does not automatically actuate and recommend itself. So that our historical understanding can grow, the thematic variation must be reordered by becoming integrated with the polar insistencies of the source intent and

[26] Variations written *in the spirit of* this or that individual source philosopher remain distinct in kind from such broad historical generalizations about *the prevailing spirit of* an entire period or national approach as Josiah Royce's *The Spirit of Modern Philosophy* and John E. Smith's *The Spirit of American Philosophy*. The latter genre is much more directly and comprehensively concerned with the historical texts and actualities.

the general forms of historical query. Through such active re-orientation, the thematization is enabled to modify our sense of the problems and lines of comparison in the modern philosopher, thus affecting our historical judgment in some marked fashion. To achieve such judgmental difference is a sign that a speculative variation on a modern theme is being transformed into an aspect of the interpreting present, taken precisely as an ingredient principle of historical intelligence.

(c) Continuative problems. In our previous analysis of the general modes of historical interrogation, we saw that comparative relationships are often best brought out in function of the continuative problems which span and structure modern philosophy. It remains here only to recognize explicitly that the hold of such problems upon historical reality depends not only upon the implicational power of the sources and the generality of the questioning procedures but also upon the selective energizing of the issues, within a contemporary frame of reference. When a problem gets actually prolonged into present theorizing, its continuative character is further specified and secured. Especially in the case of a highly complex problem, current discussion is likely to involve many factors drawn from its previous stages of development, thus provoking interest in having that development more carefully investigated and restated in contemporary language. Thus a historian's choice of problem for sustained research often inclines toward that specific issue which is continuative in the intensive sense of showing its vitality within our own time of philosophizing.

One such question preoccupying twentieth-century philosophers of every sort is the meaning of the a priori.[27] It is

[27] The problem is studied from an analytic perspective in Arthur Pap's *Semantics and Necessary Truth*, and phenomenologically in Mikel Dufrenne's *The Notion of the A Priori*. The vast periodical literature is bibliographically summarized in *A Modern Introduction to Philosophy*, ed. P. Edwards and A. Pap, pp. 666-671. That the theme of the a priori is not purely logico-methodological but involves the theory of mind and action, is indicated by William James's judgment about our selective, futural, and subjective interests: "These

central to the work of Frege and Quine, C. I. Lewis and Wittgenstein, Carnap and Ayer, Husserl and Dufrenne. This major problem crosses the frontiers of every kind of contemporary philosophy. For it raises basic theoretical difficulties for naturalistic, analytic, and phenomenological thinkers alike, and affects their conceptions of scientific law, metaphysical statement, and ethical reasoning. But these ramifications are further complicated by the historical dimensions which enter into almost every treatment. Granted that (at least with respect to the mathematical a priori) there is a classic contrast between the positions of Kant and Mill, nevertheless numerous questions arise concerning the precise connotations and denotations for the usage of the a priori in these two sources. To meet the demands of elucidation on this score, the comparative historical study of Kant and Mill in respect to the continuative problem of the a priori recommends itself as a prudent choice for research.

Once the historical aspect of this question is raised, however, some unforeseen and not entirely palatable consequences follow for any present day references to its previous development. First, there is need for a more intensive study of the meanings of the a priori in Kant and Mill themselves than can be gathered from taking a quick look at the Introduction to the *Critique of Pure Reason* and at the set pieces in *A System of Logic*. Second, the Kant-Mill framework is much too narrow to incorporate the basic alternative theories of the a priori proposed during the nineteenth century. The investigation must be widened historically to include Hegel and the idealists, Nietzsche and the evolutionists, William James and the pragmatists—all of whom offered their own reformed meaning and explanation of the a priori factor in knowledge and experience.

---

interests are the real *a priori* element in cognition" (*Collected Essays and Reviews*, p. 50, note). On difficulties in Lockean studies which interchange "a priori," "analytic," and "necessary," see R. S. Woolhouse, *Locke's Philosophy of Science and Knowledge*, 10-32.

A third cautionary note, introduced by the historical approach to this continuative problem, is that it would be fatal to read back the standard Kantian sense into Descartes and Leibniz, Locke and Hume. Historical conscience warns against the common practice of making a retrospective Kantian reading of all analogues to the a priori published before 1781. There is something historically grotesque about imposing this anachronistic standard upon a Descartes or a Locke. To distinguish the seventeenth-century theories of apriority from both the Kantian doctrine and current analyses, the historical interpreter must follow his own teleology toward a presence that is historical and not purely contemporaneous.

Contemporary philosophers are free, of course, to avoid these historical complications by emptying out all historical references in their own treatment of the a priori, except as a clearly stated policy of rhetorical flourish. But to do so is to impoverish present theorizing on this continuative problem, by ruling out any accurate and adequate account of the reflections of modern philosophers of many sorts on this issue. It is wiser to keep the hearing open in principle to whatever these thinkers may have to offer, stipulating only that their views be presented *on the basis of* a historically reliable and thorough understanding, even though their positions may well be *reformulated in terms of* the various logical and epistemological positions of our own day.

Both for the health of present discussions and for historical purposes, the difference must be maintained between contemporary arguments and historical developments on a continuative problem. The interpreting present never collapses inwardly into the present act of theorizing, but always maintains its own integrity of active interrelation with the modern sources and all the instruments of historical questioning. Otherwise, there would be no genuine process of adapting the interpreting present and its correlates in historical understanding to some present needs in philosophical theory. There would only be an illusory identification, which would rob present theorizing of the salutary criticism and independent insistencies of the history of modern philosophy.

In concluding this chapter, we can observe that a relation of coherence and confirming support exists between our general analysis of the interpreting present and the more particularized ways of the responsive interpreter. This is most apparent in comparing the general canon of becoming critical about all previous historical accounts with the specific forms of self-criticism, developed in order to reform the accepted from-to perspectives. But the mutual adaptation between the general hypothesis and the specific historical practices is evident on other points as well. The reforming process can go on, and can be conjoined with fresh appreciations of middle-range philosophers and paraphilosophical thinkers, only because the historian remains radically open to the futural reference of the modern sources. It is his methodic search after their further significance which permits him to find, in contemporary philosophizing, some inciting reasons for working out new comparisons and acknowledging the importance of other thinkers than those in the main canon.

Finally, the distinctive way in which the interpreting present serves current theoretical needs, without ceasing to maintain its own historical identity, also helps to concretize the two remaining general features of this co-ingredient. For the reference to present philosophizing serves both as a concrete corrective against an archaicizing meaning for "the classical modern past" and as a concrete teleology toward historical presence. The attempt to respond to present theorizing, without reductively identifying the interpreting present with such theorizing, is an actual form of achieving historical presence. The presential act of historical understanding keeps the history of modern philosophy alive and serviceable today, without depleting its wellsprings in the source writings or its self-discipline in the historical modes of inquiry.

V

Kant Our Contemporary

The task of this chapter is to attempt to remedy a defect in the account given thus far of our historical understanding of modern philosophy. The elements in that theory have been considered primarily from the standpoint of their contribution to historical studies brought to completion in the form of books and other publications. It is proper to guide our basic analysis by these written and publicly available results, where the components in the guiding hypothesis can be observed and tested on the broadest basis of communication. But especially in a theory of historical understanding committed to the functional method, namely, to hewing close to the actual operations of research, this basis is not sufficiently inclusive. It takes only indirect account of the creative source for most major advances now being made in history of modern philosophy: the teaching and learning situation in the university seminar. Here is where we come closest to the historical intent in the making and where we can see the co-ingredients at work, under the unsorted but living conditions of the process of educating ourselves anew in the meaning and present bearing of philosophical sources.

No operational approach can afford to neglect or blur out the interpreting contribution to our historical understanding achieved through the common work of the members of a skillfully conducted seminar in modern philosophy. To make my examination of this perspective as concrete as possible, and yet also as widely representative of diverse educational situations as possible, I will consider some of the procedures and themes likely to emerge in a year's study of the philosophy of Kant in a university seminar today. At previous stages in the general theory, I have worked inductively through the historical study of Descartes and Leibniz, Locke and Berkeley, and the Hegel-to-Marx-to-Nietzsche passage. But Kant is so central in most college and graduate programs of instruction today, no matter where the university may be located or what its prevailing philosophical climate, that he offers a very representative basis of analysis. The historical traits exhibited in the Kant seminar will also characterize other joint efforts at understanding the modern sources, once the appropriate modifications are made for different philosophers.[1]

1. THE SEMINAR EXPERIENCE

Without always reflecting upon it, the seminar members have a lived comprehension of many fundamental aspects of historical understanding. Their very convening together in an atmosphere of expectation—of engaging in work that is to be exploratory rather than repetitive, a testing of new interpretations rather than a recall of old ones—tells something about the source under study. It affirms the essentially open texture and implicatory power of the Kantian text, its successful resistance to any effort to finish off its significance with an altogether definitive historical presentation. There is no topic in Kant, not even the much explained and repeatedly "overcome" distinction between the analytic and the synthetic, which does not hold a surprise for the next reading and pre-

[1] What John Dewey said ninety years ago, about the cardinal role of Kant's method of analytic and experiential reason, still holds good. "It was the suggestion of this method, it was the suggestion of so many means for its execution, it was the actual carrying of it out in so many points that makes Kant's 'Philosophy' the *critical* philosophy, and his work the *crisis*, the separating, dividing, turning-point of modern philosophy" (John Dewey, "Kant and Philosophic Method," in *The Early Works of John Dewey*, vol. I: *1882-1888*, p. 43). There are two good overviews of recent Kantian research: M. J. Scott-Taggart, "Recent Work on the Philosophy of Kant," in *Kant Studies Today*, ed. L. W. Beck, pp. 1-71; and Gerhard Lehmann, *Beiträge zur Geschichte und Interpretation der Philosophie Kants*.

sent a new visage in some other philosophical context. Thus the seminar's sense of expectation about new findings, yet to be made, in a much surveyed land, is the proper historical correlate of the original source's own classical nature and futural intent.

There is methodological significance also in the tacit recognition that an intellectual demand is being placed upon the seminar participants, that new insights into Kant have to be earned through arduous work. This is a concrete acknowledgment that the modes of interrogating the source are themselves never wholly fixed and standardized, but have to be refashioned and improved at every new session. The success of a particular meeting is never guaranteed beforehand, despite the reassuring presence of the sources and the record of previous research. Without the intervening labor and active reformulation of the present study group, Kant can fail to come alive for them in the significant sense of responding to their specific philosophical questions and interests.

Meetings in which the dead seem to be discussing the dead are nevertheless instructive for our theory of historical knowing. Criticized in retrospect, they make the participants more reflectively aware of the contingency of historical understanding and of its real dependence upon their own active interpreting, not solely upon the texts and the apparatus of scholarship. To live through the uneven journey of peaks and desert stretches in a year's Kant seminar constitutes an effective, if somewhat painful, way of translating the theory of historical co-ingredient factors into a personal comprehension of the conditions for living history of philosophy.

The seminar relationship enables the participants to experience concretely the work of the interpreting present. For it embodies, in an everyday manner, the distinction between simply *being contemporaries* (the common denominator among the seminar members) and *being rendered contemporary* through historical presence in our judgment (the intended relationship which Kant is to achieve in respect to the group, and in virtue of the communication worked out between his writings and their inquiries). Not at the outset but only as their eventual goal, does the seminar hope to be able to refer distinctively to "Kant Our Contemporary."

Perhaps an analogy with this historical intent can be perceived in the drama criticism of Jan Kott, who binds his studies under the theme of "Shakespeare Our Contemporary." Kott wonders, for instance, why *King Lear* has outlived the romantic theater to which it seemed so completely adapted, and has survived even the abortive efforts at a naturalistic transcription of the action.[2] He finds a way of grasping the play's vitality by re-thinking it in terms of Samuel Beckett's *Endgame*: in both works, the tragic and the grotesque views of life intermingle and jostle each other. Shakespeare in the setting of the absurd elicits fresh appreciation from us. Again, Kott sees in *Coriolanus* not obscure chronicle but perennial history, a symbolism of act which enables the soldiers quarreling over the carcass of a town to resound in our own age of spoliation. To help us grasp Shakespeare's vision of heroic and unheroic action, Kott asks us to bear in mind Berthold Brecht's conception of epic theater and his model of Mother Courage. In addition, Kott's notebook is filled with jottings on specific stagings and performances, lightings and intonations, which actuate the meanings of Shakespeare more concretely even than the comparisons with Beckett and Brecht can do. Participants in a Kant seminar can find in such literary work an encouraging analogue to their own complex engagement in the contemporanizing process.

Still another facet of historical understanding displays itself in each seminar member's readiness to pursue an inde-

---

[2] Jan Kott, *Shakespeare Our Contemporary*, pp. 127-168, "King Lear or Endgame." Analogous procedures for contemporanizing Kant are employed by the philosophers assembled in these two collective volumes: *The Philosophy of Kant and Our Modern World*, ed. C. W. Hendel, and *Kant: A Collection of Critical Essays*, ed. R. P. Wolff. Instead of current plays, Shakespeare performances, and literary theories, the philosophers use as their other pole of comparison the major twentieth-century philosophical methods and problems.

pendent line of inquiry, not only in a Kantian topic but also in his choice of a present-day frame of reference and procedure for examining that topic. The variation deliberately cultivated on these means of contemporary interpretation implies something beyond the point that a great philosopher, such as Kant, requires more than a one-channel, one-level, one-school explication. For in addition, the seminar situation teaches us that there is a crucial difference between reviewing different approaches on the part of a *single* interpreter, however capacious his mind and lively his criticism, and actively pursuing different approaches on the part of *several* interpreters. However cooperative and interdependent may be the work of the different participants, a new quality is introduced when each one initiates his own entry into Kant and assumes responsibility for the conduct of his own research.

What requires and justifies the seminar activity is our human need for developing many personal centers for the reading of Kant, not only many levels of his significance for any one reader. To apply here the favorite expression of Leibniz and Kant, historical understanding grows only out of a vigorously encouraged *concordia discors*. It is a richly complex convergence of the meanings of a philosophic source achieved through a maximal diversity and even divergence of interpreting minds, research instruments, and comparative contexts. Thus the seminar experience reinforces the conclusion that historical interpretation of modern philosophy is a community operation, and at the same time specifies that this inquiring community consists of the teachers and students bound together in a common work and not solely of the lone research writer.

Thus there is considerable wisdom in F. H. Bradley's remark that the conditions of historical knowing must be determined especially from examination of actual historical practice.

The historian, as he is, is the real criterion; the ideal criterion (if such an antithesis can be pardoned) is the historian as he ought to be. And the historian who is true to the present *is* the historian as he ought to be.[3]

Our previous treatment of the interpreting present shows, however, just how intricate and many-faceted is the meaning of "the present" as it functions co-constitutively to assure some historical understanding of modern philosophy. And when that key term is still more closely specified now in the seminar experience, we realize that fidelity to the present is actually subject to a threefold qualification. (a) Such fidelity is the communal achievement of many minds loyal to the governing ideal of *concordia discors*; (b) it requires their joint reference to a source text as the common testing ground for all the proposed interpretations; and (c) its presential quality depends upon a responsive integration of all the current methods shown to be capable of illuminating and evaluating the modern source. The purpose of a Kant seminar is to try to develop, under the guidance of these three canons, a new and more adequate proportioning between his writings and the many philosophical approaches and resources of our day. The ensuing sections of this chapter will consider how, in the course of improving the present perspectives on Kant, the seminar members also give a concretely visible and contemporary actuation to the permanent conditions of historical interpreting.

2. KANT AS CRITIC OF MATHEMATICAL AND SCIENTIFIC REASON

There is no better vantage point for observing the delicate, yet firm, correlation between the prevailing interpretation of a philosopher and developments in other disciplines than that afforded by Kant's standing in philosophy of mathematics and physical science. Using 1925 as a roughly approximate axial date, we can characterize the previous half-century as a time of disengagement from the Kantian philosophy, and the dec-

[3] F. H. Bradley, *The Presuppositions of Critical History*, ed. L. Rubinoff, p. 78.

ades since then as a time of gradual renewal of interest in Kant but upon different grounds. This is not a mere tidal phenomenon, not just the inevitable ebb and flow of judgments on a philosopher's worth. Rather, it is a specific and traceable instance of the essential revisibility of historical meaning insofar as it involves reference to one contingent intellectual context, which eventually gives way to another presential basis for reading Kant.

At the turn of the twentieth century, it became clear that the neo-Kantians had to pay a steep price for their formal interpretation of Kant as the epistemological theorizer of mathematics and classical modern science. So close a fit did they establish between the *Critique of Pure Reason* and the works of Euclid and Newton that every subsequent advance made in geometry, the foundations of arithmetic and logic, and relativity physics, could be taken as an undermining of this proportionment and a living refutation of the Kantian principles of knowledge.[4] The postulation of non-Euclidean conceptions of space, the analytic proof of small-number equations, and the function of different temporal frameworks were construed as having the philosophical implication of removing, or at least drastically shrinking, the basis for the claim of necessity and universality attaching to the Kantian forms and categories. The modes of knowledge supposedly explained by such machinery were being so radically transformed that liberation from Kant, rather than guidance from him, seemed to be the intelligent course for philosophers of science to follow.

And yet students of Kant today recognize that he is again at the heart of the philosophical interpretation of mathematics and science, and that this revised significance deeply affects our historical understanding of the intent and argument of his own writings. To trace out some of the factors which have made this change possible is a fitting project for some mem-

---

[4] This inverse recessional view of Kant is particularly strong among the logicians working during the period studied in G. D. Bowne's *The Philosophy of Logic 1880-1908*.

bers of the Kant seminar to undertake. It furnishes a lesson in the complimentarity between historical questioning in philosophy and the other forms of inquiry available in a particular era. This relationship can be seen as operative in the following three areas in the continuing revision of Kant's import.

(1) One very general reinterpretation can scarcely be made apart from the actual elaboration of two disciplines which were only rudimentarily present in Kant's own day: history of the sciences and specific logical analysis of this and that science or stage of a science.[5] Although he himself called for their development beyond the sketchboards of Bacon and D'Alembert, Kant also kept his own work carefully distinct from these desirable auxiliaries. The analogy which he drew between the question asked by Copernicus and his own critical question did not focus upon some particular content or function in the historical physiology of Copernicus, but upon the very general methodology for determining motions that do occur or appearances that do appear in nature, and those that do not. Such determinations depend upon analysis of the general structures of human subjectivity. Similarly, he did not give a point-by-point analysis of the reasoning in Euclid and Newton, since his purpose was not to replicate the internal

[5] Gerd Buchdahl's *Metaphysics and the Philosophy of Science: The Classical Origins, Descartes to Kant* uses historical and analytic resources to situate Kant within the evolution of early modern philosophy of science. In relation to his own successors, "Kant's influence is seen chiefly in his having established the *reflective* approach. The older cosmology and the philosophy of nature gave way, under the impact of positions influenced by him, to the study of the structure of our knowledge of nature. We speak not so much of matter as of the concept of matter and not so much of levels or forms in nature as of the role played by principles in theory construction. In this regard the 'critical' philosophy is still very much alive" (John E. Smith, "Kant's Doctrine of Matter," in *The Concept of Matter*, ed. E. McMullin, pp. 410-411). On Kant's own Copernican imagery for expressing his reorientational impact on our thinking about nature, see S. M. Engel, *Language and Illumination*, pp. 127-137, "Kant's Copernican Analogy: A Re-examination."

structure of these two sources but to probe into the presuppositions making their achievements possible as modes of knowledge.

We are now in a more favorable position to notice Kant's critical distancing from his noetic subject matter, because we can perceive the difference between his regressive and progressive methods of questioning and the actual procedures used today in history of science and regional logics of the sciences. The distinction between a current philosophy *of* mathematics and physical science, proportioned to such developments, and the Kantian inquiry into general principles of objectivity *for* mathematical and physical understanding of the world stands out more clearly to us than to the neo-Kantians and their critics. For we are in the situation of being able to compare the two treatments in historical fact.

(2) A seminar investigation into the critique of mathematical knowledge provides a second way of verifying the historical correlativity between the source text and one's interpreting context. The converging lines of research suggest that the Kantian meaning of "analyticity," "syntheticity," and the related family of terms, is highly complex and determined by several levels of intent that we can now more readily distinguish. With the work of recent mathematics and logic actually available for comparison, we can see that what is matter of formalized proof and demonstration within that framework can still be regarded as requiring an "intuitive" or synthesizing act of construction and exhibition, within the setting of Kant's own questions.

His approach to mathematics retains its distinctive historical configuration on several counts.[6] (a) He studies the

---

[6] See the critical expositions by C. D. Parsons, "Kant's Philosophy of Arithmetic," in *Philosophy, Science, and Method*, ed. S. Morgenbesser, P. Suppes, and M. White, pp. 568-594; and J. Hintikka, "Kant on the Mathematical Method," in *Kant Studies Today*, pp. 117-140. The most striking suggestion is in D. P. Dryer's *Kant's Solution for Verification in Metaphysics*, p. 320, is that "Kant is maintaining that in so far as it can obtain any knowledge, metaphysics is generalized

methods of Euclid and other mathematicians always as expressive patterns and instances of the general operations of human sensibility and understanding. (b) He pursues the use of these methods to the epistemologically significant point of the claim of truth and certainty made for them by their human users. And (c) the *Critique of Pure Reason* incorporates, rather than sheds, Kant's earlier effort at taming and pruning the rationalist claim for the mathematical way in physics and metaphysics. These three philosophical referents so thoroughly permeate Kant's thought and language that he never makes a logically isolated analysis of mathematics and never fails to include the mathematical intent within the larger aims of human knowing. We can better appreciate this distinctive matrix, if we sharpen our reading of the texts with the respective aid of a modern logic of existential statement, an epistemology of intential reference and verification, and a more detailed historical study of the classical rationalist meaning for the mathematical method in philosophy and Kant's lifelong challenge thereof.

(3) A third likely project for the Kant seminar is to come abreast with the reinterpretation of his critique of physical science. What underlies the growing conviction that this apparently well surveyed terrain must be revisited and seen in different proportions? The corrective judgment rests on a somewhat unexpected convergence of historical and theoretical work being done in philosophy of science, the bearing of which upon the Kantian position constitutes a new imperative for historical understanding. That the latter is a persistently revisionary process, operating in close interdependence with other research activities, is the reflective implication furnished by the reworking of our conception of what Kant is doing in this field.

---

geometry." Whether the intuitional-exhibitional method of geometrical verification encourages or misleads metaphysics, it does serve as one of Kant's primary means of criticizing dogmatic metaphysical judgments.

(a) Negatively, it is clear that his metaphor of man as law-maker of nature does not rest upon any foolish notion of arbitrary private legislation concerning natural happenings. Quite to the contrary, his account seeks to respect and explain the traits of objectivity and common intelligibility present in Newtonian physical theory, but not confined to that system. Certain components in the Kantian analysis have been separately thematized in our day. The lawlikeness of those statements which function as principles of physical knowledge is not a given trait or a slavish transcription. It is an active achievement of man's reason, which is just as dynamically operative here as in our determination of practical principles, although differences are to be respected. Along with the dynamism of human understanding as a constant factor, Kant also recognizes the specific need to shape the language of physics semantically so that there can be general categories and statements of law, holding for the entire physical world. Lawlikeness, intellectual dynamism, and semantic categorial reference—the more these themes are developed in contemporary philosophies of science, the more access routes are opened into Kant's thought and the more attractive his art of synthesizing them into a unified theory is seen to be for us.

(b) That the scientific inquiry consists in much more than determining some highly general laws and categorial concepts about the physical world is a strong, balancing judgment of Kant and an important modifier of his account of scientific method. Hence an important seminar objective is to study how our historical interpreting of Kant is being fired by more adequate research into his manysided relationships with eighteenth-century scientific work.[7] Kant's theory of science

---

[7] In addition to his *Elementi metodologici e metafisici in Kant* (see above, Chapter III, note 14), Giorgio Tonelli has studied the proximate scientific and philosophic setting for Kant's position on mathematical method, laws of nature, and causal relations: "Der Streit über die mathematische Methode in der Philosophie in der ersten Hälfte des 18. Jahrhunderts und die Entstehung von Kants Schrift über die 'Deutlichkeit,'" *Archiv für Philosophie, 9* (1959), 37-66; "La Nécessité des lois de la nature au XVIIIe siècle et chez Kant

did not flow tranquilly from an unmediated reflection on Newton's *Principia* or from a static abstraction called "the continental reception of Newtonism," but rather from his personal familiarity with the multiform, contentious process to which that label refers.

In his own early writings on cosmogenesis, tidal theory, and the inhabitation of other planets, Kant himself shared in the theoretical probings and disciplined use of imagination which are essential to the life of science. His correspondence with Lambert, Bernoulli, and other leaders in the Berlin Academy of Sciences gave him a concrete sense of the current revisions of Newton, the supporting arguments attending every generalization about the space-time world, and the variant methods for relating mathematical and experimental factors in natural philosophy, as an actually developing discipline. And throughout his reflections, Kant kept himself well informed of the advances being made in the life sciences and their philosophical interpretation by Buffon, Bonnet, Blumenbach, and a whole company of biologists who refused to regard their research as a mere spin-off from Newtonian physics. It is to determine the general critical conditions required by this many-leveled scientific study of the universe

---

en 1762," *Revue d'Histoire des Sciences, 12* (1959), 225-241; and "Die Anfänge von Kants Kritik der Kausalbeziehungen und ihre Voraussetzungen in 18. Jahrhundert," *Kant-Studien, 57* (1965-66), 417-456. Kant's own scientific speculations are skillfully related both to eighteenth-century concepts and to contemporary science, in the respective Introductions written by the editors of these two re-editions of the W. Hastie translation of Kant, *Universal Natural History and Theory of the Heavens*, ed. M. K. Munitz; and *Kant's Cosmogony*, ed. Willy Ley. Kant attempts to move beyond Newton by giving a physical account of the origin of the solar system and other systems, an interpretation of "nebulous stars" as being other galactic systems, a conception of the entire universe as a unified system of such galactic systems, and a shift from the static mechanical standpoint to that of evolutionary cosmogenesis. His own experience of thus moving beyond Newton leads him epistemologically to stress the synthetic, exploratory, and imaginative aspects of scientific thought, and to develop a theory of physical knowledge that by no means canonizes the Newtonian status quo.

that the Kantian analysis of knowledge is devoted, and only by reference to this operative intent can our historical comprehension be improved.

One important consequence of taking a comparative approach to Kant, seen in the light of the complex and changing scientific situation after mid-eighteenth-century, is a sharpening of philosophical interest in the role he accords to concept formation and hypotheses.[8] Only by devising, testing, and modifying new explanatory and unifying hypotheses, can the general categorial schemata be rendered functional for the actual process of scientific exploration and revision. Unlike the Kantian commentators of a half-century ago, current scholars are carefully weighing Kant's analysis of the kinds and norms of working hypotheses, as well as the probable aspects of physical knowledge and biological research which they are intended to support. *He* is enabled to communicate historically a further profile of his epistemology to us, because *we* are reshaping our interrogation procedures in response to a better understanding of his scientific setting and of the developmental side of every theory of science.

(c) The unterminating historical evolution of the source-and-interrogator relationship is nowhere more evident than in treatments of that most finely sifted section of the first *Critique*: the Transcendental Analytic. There are two shifts of emphasis in the contemporary interpretation of the Kantian philosophy of science which illustrate and clarify this relationship.[9] For one thing, although study of the first part of

[8] Here, the research articles of Robert E. Butts are helpful: "Hypotheses and Explanation in Kant's Philosophy of Science," *Archiv für Geschichte der Philosophie*, 43 (1961), 153-170; "Kant on Hypotheses in the 'Doctrine of Method' and the *Logik*," *Archiv für Geschichte der Philosophie*, 44 (1962), 185-203; "Kant's Schemata as Semantical Rules," *Kant Studies Today*, pp. 290-300. Concept formation is studied by George A. Schrader, "Kant's Theory of Concepts," *Kant-Studien*, 49 (1957-58), 264-278.

[9] This new emphasis, so pervasively characteristic of all the men and contemporary approaches studied in this chapter, concerns these sections in Kant's *Critique of Pure Reason*: his *Analytic of Concepts*, A 64-130: B 89-169 (N. K. Smith tr., pp. 102-175); and his *Analytic*

the Analytic (the "Analytic of Concepts," dealing with the methods for determining or deducing the categories) is in no degree diminished, there is an unusual growth of interest in the previously subordinated second part (the "Analytic of Principles"). We are beginning to grasp Kant's point that if categorial concepts are patterns of judging, then their meaning is fully grasped only when they are regarded operationally in the judgmental work of principles, as actually organizing a scientific mode of knowing.

The great problem faced in the Analytic of Principles is that of determining the methodic conditions which permit general categorial principles to function in the onward development of scientific inquiry. It is this face of Kant's theory of experience and objectivity which is being explored by commentators representing every philosophical standpoint today. Their appreciation of the Kantian discussion of the axioms, anticipations, and analogies of experience corrects a formalistic and static view of the categories. The Kant who culminates his conception of science with an analysis of guiding imagery and models, hypothesis-formation and controlled analogies,

---

of Principles, A 130-292: B 169-349 (Smith tr., pp. 176-296), including the important introduction and appendix. Historically sensitive here as elsewhere, Josiah Royce anticipates the move of interest from the first to the second part of the Transcendental Analytic: "But another set of problems remains, suggested also by the *Kritik* [*der reinen Vernunft*], and still very far from solution. These problems are concerned with the structure of knowledge. The space and time problem is one of them. The whole question of the Kantian 'Deduction of the Categories,' and of the 'Principles,' especially of the 'Analogies of Exper.,' is here involved." He made this prescient statement in a *Letter to William James, September 19, 1880*, in *The Letters of Josiah Royce*, ed. John Clendenning, pp. 87-88. Three recent studies which give prominence to the schemata, analogies, and postulates of experience are: Justus Hartnack, *Kant's Theory of Knowledge*; Friedrich Kaulbach, *Immanuel Kant*; and F. Grayeff, *Kant's Theoretical Philosophy*. There is a similar emphasis upon this portion of Kant's logic and methodology, but with more detailed analysis and comparison with contemporary logical and ontological problems, in M. S. Gram, *Kant, Ontology, and the A Priori*, and Walter Bröcker, *Kant über Metaphysik und Erfahrung*.

is brought much closer both to the scientific experience of every age and to the present contributions on a logic of scientific models. Out of just such firm conjunctions, emerge those new ways of reading a familiar source whereby the history of philosophy leaps ahead as a contemporary act.

In a second respect, historical developments must effect the seminar presentation of Kant's Analytic. His topic of analogies of experience centers upon those pervasive structuring principles which enable us to organize human experience in its permanent (substantial), temporally continuous (causal), and contextually active (communal, reciprocal) aspects. His direct concern is to examine this structuring and adaptive process in terms of the physical understanding of the world. Nonetheless, Kant is careful *not* to restrict every legitimate use of the respective categories of substance, causality, and reciprocity to their analogues in physics. Because he keeps open a core of meaning in these organizing categories, he also lays the foundation here for treating their valid as well as invalid employment in the other regions of experience. In the section below devoted to the Kantian theory of community, I will examine one such enlargement of categorial meaning and its contemporary resonance.

To read the Analytic in a new historical key means to perceive that it furnishes the common ground for Kant's basic approach to metaphysics and morals, as well as to physics. He does not postpone the discussion of metaphysical principles entirely for the Dialectic portion of the *Critique of Pure Reason*, but already initiates the question in the Analytic. The meanings which constitute both the valid and the invalid forms of metaphysical inference have their rooting in his transcendental logic as a whole, and are not wholly confined to its dialectical portion. Hence the import of such historical studies as *Kantian Physics and Metaphysics* (Vuillemin) and *Kant's Metaphysics of Nature* (Schäfer) is that physical and metaphysical issues are better related in terms of continuity of Kantian analysis than in those of sharp opposition. This reinterpreting of the categories and principles of experience is bound to broaden our working historical judgment of Kant as critic of natural science and ontology together.

(d) Finally, a Kant seminar should not miss the revisionary implications of the presently flourishing research upon the theme of nature.[10] At first glance, the problem of nature occupies only a minor niche in the first *Critique*, where it serves along with the correlative concept of world to resolve the antinomies uncovered in the dialectical study of cosmology. But just as the meaning of world has unsuspected reaches (to be considered in the next section), so does that of nature involve much more than a first outlining would suggest. It is one of Kant's basic instruments for situating his initial analysis of scientific knowledge within a broader context of methodic and conceptual continuities. Through its mediation, he can relate Newtonian science to morality (in the nature-freedom comparison in the *Critique of Practical Reason*), renew his foundational analysis of space-time-categories (in *Metaphysical Foundations of Natural Science*), and spell out the complexities in the humanistic relation between mechanism and teleology (a prime subject in the *Critique of Judgment* and the *Opus Postumum*). We are learning that the idea of nature is just as potent a binder of Kant's farflung investigations as it is of the philosophical outlooks of Whitehead and Collingwood, Husserl and Dewey.

---

[10] New impetus is given to historical study of Kant's theory of physical science and nature, when the textual basis for that theory is sought not only in the first *Critique* but also in *Critique of Judgment*, *Metaphysical Foundations of Natural Science*, and *Opus Postumum*. It can be expected that the J. Ellington translation of Kant's *Metaphysical Foundations of Natural Science* will modify our historical conception of the Kantian view on space and time, mechanics and dynamics, and physical phenomenology. This reinterpretation is already underway in: J. Vuillemin, *Physique et métaphysique kantiennes*; P. Plaass, *Kants Theorie der Naturwissenschaft*; L. Schäfer, *Kants Metaphysik der Natur*; H. Hoppe, *Kants Theorie der Physik*; G. Lehmann, *Beiträge zur Geschichte und Interpretation der Philosophie Kants*, part 3 (on the relation between the third *Critique* and the *Opus Postumum*); and the issue of *Synthese*, *23* (1972), on Kant and physical theory.

Coming to apprehend its synthetic power in Kant, not only improves our historical unification of his writings but also prompts a specific comparison with these twentieth-century philosophers of nature.

3. HUSSERL AND HEIDEGGER: LIFELONG STUDENTS OF KANT

One cannot penetrate very far into the genesis of phenomenology and existential ontology without realizing how radically these contemporary philosophies are involved with a reconsideration of Kantian issues, and hence how intimately their basic methods and concepts are shaped by that same Kantian involvement. At least one portion of the process of contemporanizing Kant can be functionally described as a specifying of the problems he posed for Husserl and Heidegger, along with a tracing of their critical responses and speculative reconstructions developed from rethinking his positions.[11] Insofar as Kant's philosophy is recognized as affecting our understanding and evaluation of their leading conceptions, it becomes effectively ingredient in the present forms of philosophizing. But is this contemporary ingredience attained only at the cost of stripping away those other requirements of textual fidelity and adaptive questioning which are essential for maintaining the historical basis of the Kant-and-phenomenology relationships? Is the act of incorporating Kantian thought into the most original centers of German

[11] Another lifelong existential grappler with Kant is Karl Jaspers, who reflectively reinterprets Kant through his own principles of philosophizing: "An understanding of Kant cannot be prescribed. Everyone who wishes to philosophize, at once on his own original ground and within the historic tradition, must open-mindedly immerse himself in Kant to see what ideas come to him in the process" (*Kant*, pp. 149-150). Jaspers distinguishes three stages in a critical revaluation of Kant: (1) pointing out errors of fact and limitations due to the level of scientific development in Kant's time; (2) questioning the logical consistency of his arguments and their relationship with the Kantian meaning of transcendental logic; and (3) attempting to penetrate Kant's general standpoint and relate it complexly to one's own basic orientation in the world and in philosophy.

philosophizing in our century a total dehistoricization of that classical modern source or a manner of fulfilling some of its properly historical potentialities?

At least a few aspects of this problem can be clarified in the Kant seminar. Here the chief emphasis is not upon working out the Kantian background for Husserl and Heidegger, but rather upon gaining from these later thinkers some new illumination on what Kant himself is doing and how his philosophical intent is still historically operative and accessible. There is some enlargement of our historical understanding of Kant, in the very operation whereby he is being instrumentalized and transformed to fit the methodologies of Husserl and Heidegger. The Kantian text is never entirely dissolved and swallowed up by the more recent configurations of philosophy, not only because of recalcitrance on the part of that text to submitting to dissolutional conditions but also because of a fundamental respect for it on the part of such vigorously original minds as Husserl and Heidegger. Although neither one pretends to be doing historical exegesis, each defines his approach to Kant in interpretive terms which encourage the partner in dialogue to retain and restate his own thought. This also gives the rest of us an opportunity to catch Kant's own voice in the contemporary effort at incorporating and surpassing him. A Kant seminar serves as the radar shell for detecting those Kantian themes and wordings which come to mean more to us than to previous generations of scholars, thanks to the mediation of philosophers who know the art of letting Kant be himself at the very time that they use him for aims of their own.

Although Kant studies are international in representation, the actual direction taken in English-speaking university seminars depends closely upon the availability and quality of translations. Previously, we noted this factor as it facilitated the opening-toward-us on the part of Kant and other modern sources. But historical understanding is also promoted, when the openings of contemporary philosophers toward Kant are themselves more widely communicated by translation into another language sphere. Thus although a Kant seminar in an American university will make some use of the Kantian studies of Husserl and Heidegger in the original German form, it will become much more demandingly occupied with the detailed arguments in these studies, once they become Englished. The effect of such translation programs is not only to make a Husserl and Heidegger the direct subject of philosophical analysis at every level but also—and most pertinently for any theory of the dynamics of historical intelligence —to make their Kant interpretations a lively part of the equipment and responsibility of all members of the seminar. Husserl-and-Heidegger-in-translation modifies the working horizon for the studying of Kant, by removing the language barriers from two entire ranges of methods and concepts which relate him to our own capacities of reflection.

In order to gauge just how deeply this changing situation concerns our theory of historical interpreting, we will concentrate here upon just one characteristic trait in the relationship. Both Husserl and Heidegger are *lifelong* students of Kant. A study of the latter's thought supplies a permanent impetus and focus throughout the long developments of each philosopher. Modifications in each one's position are partly *incited by*, and partly *reflected in*, their unfolding interpretations of Kant. Patient attention to these interpretations serves a threefold historical purpose. It supplies one guiding thread for a developmental approach to Husserl or Heidegger taken separately; it is one of the common grounds of critical interchange for the two philosophers and hence for our comparative study of their teachings; and it gives concrete and complex expression to two contemporary avenues into Kant's own philosophy and its continuing bearing on philosophical judgment. Our present interest lies mainly in the last of these consequences of their persistent return to the Kantian wellspring, since here we can relate the theme of Kant our contemporary with the general problem of how the history of philosophy continues to grow.

In some respects, Husserl philosophized along with Kant

more strenuously and radically than with his other two great forerunners in modern philosophy: Descartes and Hume. For Husserl was able to come directly and surely to grips with the actual course of thought in the French and British sources, without being unduly deflected by the view of Cartesians and Humeans in his own milieu. He could determine rather clearly (to his own satisfaction and in published communication) the precise contributions made to modern philosophy by Descartes as intimator of the life and apodictic evidence of the personal ego, as well as by Hume as intimator of how thoroughly the life of consciousness works intentionally to achieve the everyday and scientific worlds of objective meaning and relationship. But in the approach to Kant, there were special hurdles to overcome and critical clarifications constantly to be stated and re-expressed.

Husserl was painfully aware of what he called "a multicolored Kant, through the multiplicity of attempted interpretations and the reconstructions of neo-Kantianism."[12] Part of Husserl's instructiveness for historical methodology arises from his persistent efforts to reach the Kantian text as distinct from these neo-Kantian colorations, without in the least relaxing his own project of making an independent critical reading of that same text in terms of his phenomenology. Yet the complexity of understanding and transforming the work of Kant was found to be so massive and elusive, that he never succeeded in bringing his evaluation to the same sharply definitive form as his interpretations of Descartes and Hume, as set forth in Husserl's *First Philosophy, Cartesian Meditations*, and *The Crisis of European Sciences*. Although the relationship of Kant to transcendental phenomenology was

[12] Edmund Husserl, *The Crisis of European Sciences and Transcendental Phenomenology*, tr. D. Carr, p. 196. The most thorough comparative study is Iso Kern's *Husserl und Kant*, which not only analyzes the major texts of Husserl on Kant but also disentangles this historical relationship from Husserl's closely connected preoccupations with Natorp, Rickert, and Heidegger. The background is briefly sketched by E. Fink, "The Phenomenological Philosophy of Edmund Husserl and Contemporary Criticism," in *The Phenomenology of Husserl*, ed. T. O. Elveton, pp. 73-147.

also a crucial theme in all these writings, it was presented there in sketch and anticipatory judgment rather than in fully developed analysis and argument.

Nevertheless, a Kant seminar conducted in an effectively contemporary spirit is well advised to scrutinize Husserl's actual statements on that relationship, which reaches the heart of his own sense of philosophical tradition and unique vocation alike. In his 1924 bicentennial essay on *Kant and the Idea of Transcendental Philosophy*, he ponders the twin mystery of historical continuity and originality among philosophers, with concrete reference to Kant's significance for his own lifework. Husserl thematizes the problem of how a philosopher like himself, gradually becoming sensitized to the importance of history for philosophizing, can achieve his own integrity of mind through an independent following of Kant. Such a following does not consist in mimicking the terminology, repeating the methodology in venturesomeless fashion, or in adopting the system wholesale and making only some minor improvements. Rather, a philosophically and historically worthy filiation with Kant springs from the intent "to understand the ultimate sense of his revolution—and to understand it better than he himself, the trailblazer but not the completer, was able to do."[13] Probing after the ultimate

[13] Husserl, "Kant und die Idee der Transzendentalphilosophie," in his *Erste Philosophie (1923/24)*, Part One: *Kritische Ideengeschichte*, p. 286. As the subtitle of this book indicates, Husserl develops his method of critical history of ideas in Part One of *First Philosophy*. This is reformulated and further elaborated in *Crisis* as the teleological study of modern philosophy. In his lively reminiscences of Husserl's lectures and seminars in Göttingen and Freiburg-in-Breisgau (1912-1917), Roman Ingarden reminds us that Husserl gave courses on "History of Philosophy" and "Kant and Modern Philosophy," and that his seminars often centered around such classical modern philosophers as Descartes, Berkeley, Hume, Kant, and Fichte. Ingarden adds: "Yet withal, properly speaking there was no analysis of text and interpretation. Usually, the text was only a point of departure for Husserl's own reflections, which had as their primary aim to elucidate the problematic, about which it was treated in the text, and to mark out paths of a possible solution." Ingarden, "Meine Erinnerungen an Edmund Husserl," in Edmund Husserl, *Briefe an Roman Ingarden*, ed. Roman Ingarden, p. 111.

signification of Kant and other great modern sources is one of Husserl's primary occupations. As an aid, he develops a distinctive interpretive method for steering between the two extremes of a purely contingent historicist recital of the source's life and writings and a purely ideal genesis of his thought, apart from its historical concretion and textual expression.

Husserl calls his approach *the method of critical history of ideas* and that of *the teleological study of modern philosophy*. Together, these designations specify that a phenomenologically regulated investigation: (a) can and indeed (when it reaches reflective maturity) must examine the actual historical pathway followed by Kant and other basic predecessors; (b) can and must make a judgment of critical evaluation of these sources, considered as contributors toward phenomenology itself; and (c) is able to meet these historical and critical responsibilities by searching after and formulating the radical philosophical purpose of the forerunners—a purpose not always spelled out in the documents involved, but yet which is harmonious with their spirit and final intent. Indeed, it is from Plato and Kant that Husserl adopts the crucial term "ideas." It is used in this methodological context of "critical history of ideas," not as a description of plural and contingent meanings (what we ordinarily call "the history of ideas"), but rather as the organizing principle and active striving *telos* animating a philosopher's entire work and, in some measure, escaping his own reflective recognition. As a search after this operative and regulative ideal, insofar as it points toward the meaning of mankind and of modern philosophy as a whole, Husserl orders all his uses of historical sources. He is bound by the primary task of discerning, criticizing, and bringing to better selfawareness that common philosophical directedness of immanent teleology underlying the work of Descartes, Hume, and Kant.

Husserl's effort to capture the teleological sense of Kantian thought centers on the manner in which the latter did, and yet did not quite, place modern philosophy firmly upon its fulfilling course toward transcendental phenomenology. He insists strongly upon the revolution implicit in the three *Critiques* or, more precisely, upon the revolutionizing process which they initiated in our way of philosophizing. Kant opened up the transcendental question by seeking, within the forms and concepts of subjectivity, the ground of meaning and truth for the objective traits of the mathematical and natural sciences. By reorientating the main problems and expectations of modern philosophizing toward subjectivity as the soil of scientific laws and structures, he did thematize the transcendental foundations of certainty and rigorous knowledge, as the ideal for philosophy to attain. Yet in Husserl's estimation, Kant only pointed toward the promised land from afar: he launched reflection on the road toward transcendental philosophy but did not himself furnish the ultimate means and actuality of that purposive ideal. Playing with the pertinent metaphor, Husserl judges that Kant marks the decisive phase in the Copernican turning toward the constituting life of subjectivity and yet that "the Copernican turning," as the fully selfaware and executed transcendental turn of modern philosophy, is actualized only in Husserlian phenomenology.[14]

What will enrich a Kant seminar is to examine some grounds upon which Husserl bases this verdict, and then to see here certain aspects of the problem of historical understanding. For the Kant-Husserl relationship shows us how the evaluative judgment of a responsible successor, being made within his own framework, succeeds simultaneously in evoking implicit consequences of the source under interpretation and in enabling that source to maintain its effective integrity and own insistential act. Kant's resilience stands forth in the very process whereby Husserl assigns him, on at least four counts, to that "natural attitude" or not yet completely re-

[14] Kant is located well along the arc of the Copernican turning of modern awareness in Husserl's 1924 essay: "Kants kopernikanische Umdrehung und der Sinn einer solchen kopernikanischen Wendung überhaupt," in *Erste Philosophie*, Part One, pp. 208-229; cf. *Crisis*, p. 199. Kern, *Husserl und Kant*, pp. 276-285, discusses the complexities of Husserl's view here.

flective standpoint remaining to this side of the plenary awareness found in transcendental phenomenology. The Husserlian
criticism of Kant on these points is aimed at finally bringing
philosophy from the pre-discovery condition (being at the
threshold of the certitudinal and constituting life of subjectivity) to the condition of making actual entrance into, and discoveries concerning, that life activity.

(1) Palmary evidence of Kant's blindfolded relationship
with the transcendental sphere is sought in his treatment of
formal logic. Husserl interrupts the directly theoretical
analyses of his *Formal and Transcendental Logic* just long
enough to make what he terms a "historico-critical digression" on the development of the notion of a transcendental
logic. He acknowledges the Kantian contribution of seeking
a basis for the logical structures involved in the Newtonian
scientific statements about nature, as well as of discovering
more in formal logic than a conflation of syllogistics and
Humean associational bonds. Nevertheless, there is a halfway
character about Kant's exploration of the foundations of the
logic of science, since he fails to go absolutely to the foundations of formal logic as a whole.

> Kant is satisfied in resorting to formal logic in its apriori
> positivity or, as we should say, its transcendental naïveté.
> Formal logic is, for him, something absolute and ultimate,
> on which philosophy can be built without more ado. . . .
> He did not make his analytic Apriori a problem. . . . No
> one ventured, or had the courage to venture, to take the
> *ideality of the formations with which logic is concerned* as
> the characteristic of a separate, self-contained, *"world" of
> ideal Objects* and, in so doing, to come face to face with
> the painful question of how subjectivity can in itself bring
> forth, purely from sources appertaining to its own spon-
> taneity, formations that can be rightly accounted as ideal
> *Objects* in an ideal "world."[15]

[15] Husserl, *Formal and Transcendental Logic*, tr. D. Cairns, pp.
260-261, 265. Husserl refers to his critique of Hume and Kant (who
together lead us toward the transcendental question about the con-

The Husserlian Kant still uncritically accepts the ultimate givenness and objectivity of an ideal world of logical forms.

This pertinent, forcefully stated criticism can serve as a bridgehead in the contemporanizing of Kant. It gives bite and impetus to historical studies on the precise logical sources consulted by Kant and on the strenuous reinterpretation to which they were submitted by him, in order to serve as guiding clues (not as unaltered touchstones) for his theory of categories. It also sharpens a further reading of the first *Critique*, in order to discern how carefully Kant refuses the traits of noetic absoluteness and ultimacy to *all* logical forms. Husserl's criticism provokes a recognition of Kant's careful distinction between the objective ideality of logical formations, which can reduce to actively structuring consciousness, and the objectivity of a knowing act too complex for such reduction.

(2) A related topic where this historical polarization visibly develops is that of the meaning of "world." Under the tutelage of the leading neo-Kantians Natorp and Rickert, Husserl comes to appreciate the Kantian method of always dealing correlatively with the nature-spirit distinction. This has the advantage of rendering problematic the entire realm of nature as determined by the several sciences, since this meaning is also to be comprehended as an achievement of spirit. But in Husserl's mature estimate, the Kantian method remains too closely accommodated within the hard shell of meanings formed by nature and spirit, taken together in their mutual dependence and proportionality. This leads Kant to regard the purely rational idea of world as another high-level apriority, which remains unquestionable and which serves as a basis for the meaning of nature only in the sense of a scientifically investigated and determined nature. Correlatively,

---

stitution of logic, but who are reluctant to face and state the issue) as "historico-critical remarks" and "this historico-critical digression" (pp. 255, 266). Commentary on this section of his book is furnished by Suzanne Bachelard, *A Study of Husserl's Formal and Transcendental Logic*, pp. 197-204.

the meaning of spirit is probed only to the level where it employs the idea of world to develop the scientific account of the natural world.

Measured on the Husserlian scale of radicality, then, Kant's strength lies in opening out the life of consciousness always toward the forming of a meaning for world. But his shortcoming consists in stopping short at that I-pole which is completely conformed with the world-pole expressed in *scientific* categories. Thus he remains forever at the foyer of the life of pure subjectivity, the pure ego which works constantly to co-constitute and co-achieve *all* the senses of the world and of its correlatively immanent self, not merely those senses belonging to the scientific plane of world and self.

But what more can be questioned and discovered in the constituting process which gives meaning to the world? Curtly stated, Husserl's reply is that Kantian criticism naïvely accepts the given reality of the life world, whereas a genuinely transcendental philosophy investigates the genesis of the meaning of the life world and all its traits of obvious givenness.[16] Approached in our perspective of historical understanding, however, this reply stands in need of further explanation. It supposes the essential link which Husserl forges between his lifelong preoccupation with Kant and the theme of the *Lebenswelt* which so fills his later speculations.

In every Husserlian teleological study of Kant, the *Lebenswelt* topic performs two important historical functions. First, it must be judged to be formally missing in Kant, thus effectively sealing off his actual entrance into the domain of the transcendental. Next, its positive function is to supply the lead which ultimately brings Husserl himself into full possession of the transcendental-phenomenological method and

---

[16] On the critical and reconstructive aspects of the theme of the life world, which fills the pages of *Crisis*, see the analysis by Aron Gurwitsch, *Studies in Phenomenology and Psychology*, chapter 18: "The Last Work of Edmund Husserl," pp. 397-447. Gurwitsch also compares Kant and Husserl on intentionality and world, in chapter 9: "The Kantian and Husserlian Conceptions of Consciousness," pp. 148-174.

its goal. But despite these dialectical requirements of Husserl's teleology of ideas, his verdict has directed our historical attention to Kant's own critique of the life world. We can no longer slur over the texts in which Kant dissects standard perception and the Enlightenment appeal to "sound common understanding," or those in which he questions the conventional wisdom on moral and political, esthetic and religious issues. Somewhat unintentionally, Husserl enlivens the philosophical import of these points, whose restatement in terms of the life world's essential questionability is a distinct historical strand in rendering Kant our contemporary.

(3) A further point of explication bearing on historical methodology is that the Kant whom Husserl forbids to call into question the solidities of the life world is a *Kant-carefully-yoked-with-Hume*, in accord with the Husserlian strategy of critical history of ideas. Especially in determining the investigative failures of Kantian philosophy, Husserl shapes his interpretation by a view of Kant as the last great rationalist who reacted against Hume's official skepticism and atomism of sensory data, but who never grasped the deeper problem and genuine contribution made by Hume toward phenomenology.

> We must not pass over the fact that Hume, as he is understood by Kant, is not the real Hume. . . . [In the latter] we find nothing less than this universal problem: How is the *naïve obviousness* of the certainty of the world, the certainty in which we live—and what is more, the certainty of the *everyday* world as well as that of the sophisticated theoretical constructions built upon this everyday world—to be made comprehensible? . . . The world-enigma in the deepest and most ultimate sense, the enigma of a world whose being is being through subjective accomplishment, and this with the self-evidence that another world cannot be at all conceivable—that, and nothing else, is *Hume's problem*. Kant, however, for whom, as can easily be seen, so many *presuppositions* are "obviously" valid, presuppos-

tions which in the Humean sense are included within this world-enigma, never penetrated to the enigma itself.[17]

Thus the Husserlian Kant is again compounded of critical awareness and naïveté. He recognizes the accomplishing functions of subjectivity in constituting the world of scientific nature, but fails to perceive the need for these same functions to account for pre-scientific nature, everyday sureties, and the entire living web of validities woven into our cultural existence.

One way for a seminar to discover Kant's contemporaneity, then, is through a study of his intimate involvement in the phenomenological problem of the world. Husserl himself makes it clear that a historico-critical interpretation of the Hume-Kant relationship is an essential task for anyone seeking to grasp the development and purposive sense of his conception of transcendental phenomenology. To be able to view the world as *pre-given* (in the sense of founding all our modes of objective praxis, including that of theory-construction) and also to view the active life of subjectivity as a *pre-giving* of the same world (a specification of its presence as being there in several modes)—this supposes not only a readiness to perform the various Husserlian reductions but also a readiness to follow "our historically motivated path, moving from the interpretation of the interplay of problems between Hume and Kant."[18] Husserl's claim to actualize the immanent *telos* of modern philosophy rests upon his specific notion of the interplay between these two sides of the curved shield of philosophy's history. Consequently, an effective method of test-

---

[17] *Crisis*, pp. 95-97. Husserl's strategy of criticizing Kant, by means of shortcomings in comparison with Hume as radical questioner of the everyday and scientific worlds, is given due recognition by Paul Ricoeur, *Husserl: An Analysis of His Phenomenology*, chapter 7: "Kant and Husserl," pp. 175-201.

[18] *Crisis*, p. 147. The positive side of the Husserlian teleology for modern philosophy and modern history in general is examined by Ricoeur, *Husserl*, chapter 6: "Husserl and the Sense of History," pp. 143-174, as well as by J. J. Kockelmans, *A First Introduction to Husserl's Phenomenology*, pp. 250-280.

ing his claim to combine the critical strengths of both sources, while simultaneously transforming both areas of insensitivity to the active giving of meaning, is to evaluate Husserl's interpretation of Hume and Kant in the light of the historical requirements for textual insistency and interrogational range.

(4) Husserl is just as keenly disappointed as was Fichte with Kant's refusal to acknowledge an intuitive knowledge of the acting ego. He argues that Kant's failure on this score is correlated with, and indeed overmatches, his deficiencies in the analysis of the world. The Kantian method of regressive reconstruction of the conditions of possibility for judgments in the mode of scientific objectivity is lacking precisely in that intellectual intuition which could save it from becoming lost in objectivity, and could complete the turn toward the life of subjectivity. Hence there is no Kantian experience of the transcendental life of the ego, the I-actuality which is not just the ego-pole correlated with the objective world. By contrast, Husserl recommends his own philosophy as furnishing both the method for tracing the originative source of all meaning and synthesis and the reflective experience itself of the life of the pure ego. The clash between the Kantian and Husserlian conceptions of experience and philosophical method thus supplies an essential dynamism in the winning of philosophical minds to transcendental phenomenology.

Of considerable interest for our theme of historical interpreting is the manner in which this clash affects Husserl's treatment of three crucial features of Kantian thought. First, he underplays the role of the empirical and pure modes of sensuous intuition, especially those aspects concerned with temporality. This leads Husserl to claim that Kant is naïve about the obvious reality of sensible things and blind to the intuitive life of the active, temporalizing ego. Kant's own standpoint, however, is that of stressing the sensuous quality of human intuition and specifying the limits which this quality imposes upon all our knowledge-assertions.

Second, Husserl is disappointed with the Kantian theme of the transcendental unity of apperception, because it remains stubbornly within the frame of human limits upon a knowledge of the acting subjectivity. The carefully balanced Kantian synthesis between the apperceptive principle of mind or *Gemüt*, the self encountered in temporalization processes, and the limit-concept of the thing-in-itself, is disintegrated by Husserl. For he reduces each component to a separate mythical entity.[19] Husserl sees here nothing more than a compromise machinery, devised by Kant in order to ward off Humean skepticism, but unable to convert its intimation of the living subject into a certain and unifying insight. With the best of intentions, there is unavoidable disagreement over the

[19] Already in his early *Logical Investigations*, I, 214-15, Husserl states his basic critical strictures: "We are led back, in the most general terms, to Kant's distinctions between pure and applied logic. We may indeed approve of his most notable utterances on this point but only with suitable provisos. We shall naturally not accept Kant's confusing, mythic concepts of understanding and reason. . . . We agree with Kant in his main drift, though we do not find that he clearly espied the essence of his intended discipline, nor set it forth in accordance with its adequate content." Husserl's final verdict is that Kant makes a pre-discovery but not the actually penetrative discovery of the actively accomplishing life of subjectivity. "Our critical reflections on Kant have already made clear to us the danger of impressive and yet still unclear insights or, if you will, the illumination of pure insights in the form of vague anticipations while one is still working with questions posed on an unclarified ground (that of what is 'obvious'); and this also made comprehensible how he was forced into a mythical concept-construction and into a metaphysics in the dangerous sense inimical to all genuine science. . . . Kant does get involved in his own sort of mythical talk, whose literal meaning points to something subjective, but a mode of the subjective which we are in principle unable to make intuitive to ourselves, whether through factual examples or through genuine analogy. . . . As soon as we distinguish this transcendental subjectivity [in Kant] from the soul, we get involved in something incomprehensibly mythical" (*Crisis*, pp. 114, 118, 199). Hence Husserl proposes his transcendental phenomenology as the effective means of demythologizing Kant on the life of subjectivity, since it moves from a regressive method of analysis to one of phenomenological reduction, absolute experience, and intuitive exhibition (pp. 103-118). See the comparative essays by H. Wagner, "Critical Observations concerning Husserl's Posthumous Writings," and by L. Landgrebe, "Husserl's Departure from Cartesianism," in *The Phenomenology of Husserl*, ed. Elveton, pp. 204-306.

import and adequacy of a basic position in Kant. Whereas Husserl offers his transcendental philosophy as a *demythologizing* of a nest of Kantian faculties and entities, Kant himself might well consider this reinterpretation to be an instance of *visionary thinking*, that is, of intuitive exhibition that remains undisciplined by the human limits of experiencing and knowing.

Lastly, Husserl's strictures centering around the first *Critique* render him unduly reluctant to follow through the directedness of that work toward the *Critique of Practical Reason* and the *Critique of Judgment*. On his own behalf, Kant encourages us to persevere in a differentiating and synoptic study of his several meanings for objectivity and temporality, judgment and active mind. But Husserl hews to his basic strategy of building out from his theme of a special interplay between Hume and a Kant who manifests his thought primarily in the first *Critique*, and who does so there without either grasping the real nature of Hume's challenge or adequately foreshadowing Husserl's own response. Here, the interpreter's judgmental framework predetermines his stand not only on particular points of method and doctrine but on the comprehensive interrelation between a close-knitted series of source writings. By designating his approach as a *critico*-historical one, Husserl himself underlines the difficulty and opens a space for other, compensating readings of Kant's epistemological and metaphysical writings.

When such an independent interpretation did come in the form of Heidegger's *Kant and the Problem of Metaphysics*, however, there was considerable disagreement about its precise import and historical worth. The most severe public criticism came from Cassirer and other Kantian scholars, who judged the book to be arbitrarily concerned with Heidegger's own anthropological and ontological questions and not sufficiently responsive to Kant's theme of objective knowledge and values. Their objections, although serious, were never regarded by Heidegger as being radical and devastating enough to compel total revision of his interpretation.

In brief, he pointed out that the controverted topics on man and being *are* present in the Kantian writings, even though he sought to rework them in the original fashion befitting "a thoughtful dialogue between thinkers."[20] Heidegger expressed admiration for the neo-Kantians' recovery of the history of philosophy as a factual development, their careful exposition of the entire text of Kant, and their rescuing of the Kantian sense of objectivity and value structures from the leveling view of positivism. But he noted their own imbalance in downgrading the role of sensuous intuition, in failing to ponder the common root of intuition and thought, and thus in concluding too facilely that Kant sets aside the question of being. In the light of the voluminous lectures and working notes on ontological problems printed in the Prussian Academy edition of Kant, as well as the initial wave of historical studies on Kant as metaphysician, Heidegger concluded that there could be no "laying aside" of the question of being. At least this could not be done in the ordinary sense of ignoring the ontological theme in Kant or disposing of it with a few quick strokes.

But on three principal scores, he does admit that his version of Kant encounters peculiar difficulties. First, Heidegger is working out his break with Husserl, not only simultaneously with his interpretation of Kant but also in terms of it

---

[20] Martin Heidegger, *Kant and the Problem of Metaphysics*, p. xxv. The early critical reception is best stated by Ernst Cassirer, "Kant and the Problem of Metaphysics," in *Kant: Disputed Questions*, ed. M. S. Gram, pp. 131-157. It is perhaps with this dispute over "thoughtful dialogue" in mind that M. Merleau-Ponty declares: "Between an 'objective' history of philosophy (which would rob the great philosophers of what they have given others to think about) and a meditation disguised as a dialogue (in which we would ask the questions and give the answers) there must be a middle-ground on which the philosopher we are speaking about and the philosopher who is speaking are present together, although it is not possible even in principle to decide at any given moment just what belongs to each" (*Signs*, p. 159). This historical co-presence is the intention sought in the presential interpretation of the historian of philosophy, who *does* attempt to distinguish between what belongs to the source and what to the present speaker.

and in opposition to Husserl's own view of Kant. Hence the informed reader must appreciate this complex three-pronged relationship along with the textual problems. Second, Heidegger has a keen sense of the paradigmatic nature of his presentation of Kant, in respect to his treatment of other philosophical sources. In making his approach to Kant, he bears in mind its function as a model for understanding the path he takes toward other great philosophers. And lastly, he does not, and does not intend to, exhaustively discharge his interpretive responsibilities toward Kant in *Kant and the Problem of Metaphysics*. This is but the first of Heidegger's four major analyses of the *Critique of Pure Reason*, each of which takes a somewhat different perspective on the problems in the Analytic. Since these three internal difficulties can be related to some general traits in the historical interpretation of modern philosophy, they will repay a closer scrutiny by our Kant seminar.

(1) Part of the actual setting is supplied by Husserl's own response to the close linking of being and human temporality in Heidegger's *Being and Time*. That book seems to presuppose the pregiven reality of man, and thus to represent a slippage from Husserlian transcendental psychology to Cartesian philosophical anthropology and Kantian cosmology. But this criticism depends for its force upon some prior acceptance of the Husserlian method of reductions, only in terms of which the theme of human *Dasein* fails to rise above the level of the Cartesian ego and the psychology of personality and moods. Hence Heidegger is engaged in the process of dissevering the question of being from the context of phenomenological reduction. Both in his general study of being and in his exegesis of Kant, he feels justified in centering upon the nature of man's relationship with the world, without agreeing that this orientation leads to psychologism.

The disagreement becomes distinctive and radical, however, at that moment when Husserl employs the same language and argument against Heidegger as he had already used against Kant himself. The marginal notations in his copy of

Heidegger's first Kant book culminate in the judgment that all the talk there about the essence of being, the possibility of the concept of being, and the preconceptual understanding of being, is (in the philosophically most stringent sense) "mythical."[21] Just as Kant has recourse to mythical talk about the mind and the thing-in-itself as a means of avoiding the constitutive life of the pure ego, so does Heidegger lapse into the myth of being, as a cover against referring being and all its modes to the accomplishing operations of subjectivity and the context of the world.

In Husserl's calculation, the move into a *mythologizing* thought on being is made when Heidegger fails to acknowledge that a valid ontology (in its foundation and totality, as well as in its regional forms) always revolves around the relationship of beings *to* subjectivity, around the meaning-evidence-reality functions which they have *for* subjectivity and its transcendental constituting of the world. The dividing line is marked by the Heideggerian refusal to subordinate the question of man and being to that of the constitution of meaning. Thus Husserl invokes the same basic criterion to establish: (a) that Kant is only en route toward transcendental philosophy; (b) that Heidegger departs from the method and sense of problems in such philosophy; and hence (c) that both philosophers remain ultimately entangled in mythic thinking.

In reciprocal fashion, Heidegger ladens his interpretation of Kant with the additional duty of differentiating his own philosophy from Husserl's transcendental phenomenology. Every stage in the exegesis is guided by the carefully qualified thesis that "it was only Kant, in and with his *transcendental* method of inquiry, who could make the first decisive step since Plato and Aristotle toward an *explicit* founding of

[21] The texts are given in Kern, *Husserl und Kant*, pp. 189-191. The Husserl-Heidegger relationship should be studied from both standpoints: Herbert Spiegelberg, *The Phenomenological Movement*, I, 271-353; and Richard Schmitt, *Martin Heidegger on Being Human*, pp. 103-148, 261-263.

ontology."[22] That step consists in turning from the metaphysical realism of the external world to a concern about man, the basis of his finitude, and the relationship between his finitude and the question of being which he is ontologically structured and impelled to raise. Yet Kant is unable to do more than take this first step of seeking the meaning of being, through analysis of that distinctive presence which enables man to serve as the questioner and comprehender of being.

Why is the Heideggerian Kant barred, in principle, from actually achieving the fundamental ontology toward which his study of human existential structures points? In the broadest terms, the reason lies in Kant's inability or perhaps his ultimate reluctance to shake loose from the metaphysics of objectivity, from the assumption that the meaning of being is adequately determined in function of the relation of being-an-object-for-subjectivity. The second version of the Kantian deduction of the categories comes to a halt at the two-sided horizon of objectivity for the apperceiving subject.

> The analysis of the objectivity of possible objects is the "objective" side of the deduction. But the objectivity is formed in the self-orienting act of letting-stand-opposed, which happens in the pure subject as such. The question of the powers essentially participating in this orientation and of their possibility is the question of the subjectivity of the transcending subject as such a subject. It is the "subjective" side of the deduction. . . . In truth, it [modern metaphysics in its Kantian transcendental formulation] is concerned with the metaphysics of the object, that is, of being-as-the-opposed, of the object-for-a-subject.[23]

[22] Heidegger, *The Essence of Reasons*, p. 27, n. 14. The still continuing ontological revolution of Kant-Husserl-Heidegger is studied in part 3 of J. Vuillemin, *L'Héritage kantien et la révolution copernicienne*, and in the detailed historical comparison made by Henri Declève, *Heidegger et Kant*.

[23] *Kant and the Problem of Metaphysics*, p. 171 (for close comparative work, this translation must be thoroughly revised); and

Although the implication remains muffled in this passage, Heidegger is unmistakably suggesting that Kant's failure to reach the fundament of ontology stems from restricting the question of being to that of beings as they are constituted, under various modalities, by and for the pure transcending subject. In more explicit comparative language, Kant remains bound within the same suppositions as those operating in Husserl. Only in virtue of their common methodological limitations, can Heidegger draw the strong conclusion that there is a barrier, in principle, against reaching the foundation of ontology by way of either Kant or Husserl.

This three-cornered relationship between Kant, Hussserl, and Heidegger shows just how intimately the reading and evaluation of a modern source are intercoiled with the aims of contemporary criticism and philosophizing. We cannot understand the basis for Husserl's view of a mythologizing Kant, without realizing that this is a joint evaluation intended to apply also to Heidegger's proposals for fundamental ontology. Similarly, the full import of Heidegger's portrait of a Kant who never quite liberates the meaning of being from the subject-object context will escape us, unless we discern the lineaments of Husserl's mind in the background of that same portrait. In neither instance in Kant being considered apart from an essay in comparative philosophizing. Thus it is a Kant-coupled-with-Heidegger who fails to make the full transcendental turn and remains enveloped in mythic thinking. And it is a Kant-coupled-with-Husserl who is held so fast by the problem of the foundation of objectivity in the world that he never properly articulates the question of being. There remains the real problem, however, of determining the mode and degree in which this thoroughly comparative and specula-

---

Heidegger, *Vorträge und Aufsätze*, p. 75. The path from Kant's *ens imaginarium* and something-in-general to Heidegger's nought and time is traced by C. M. Sherover, *Heidegger, Kant and Time*, with a re-interpretation of the senses of "the Copernican revolution."

tive approach contributes significantly to our *historical* understanding of Kant himself as an insistential source.

(2) Heidegger does not sidestep this problem, indicating thereby that he does not regard its mere formulation as an indirect way of denying any historical value to his Kantian studies. And since those studies have an exemplar quality for his other investigations into the Greeks, Hegel, and Nietzsche, his treatment of the issue has general consequences for understanding his relationship to other philosophical sources. Just as Husserl admits that his teleological approach to Kant does some violence to the textual documents, so does Heidegger begin by granting that his ontological interpretation also wrenches the explicit text and strains the prevailing modes of historical interrogation.[24] If he simply left the matter at this admission, however, his views on Kant would cease to bear upon our quest for a theory of historical understanding. But in fact, he goes on to explain and defend his procedure on grounds which can be made more familiar, in terms of some cognate aspects of our general analysis of historical interpretation.

Our points of bearing can be drawn from the latent power of a classical modern source, the futural intent of its language, and the function of a changed intellectual situation for releas-

[24] Compare these statements: "Of course this most general concept of the 'transcendental' [building upon, but beyond, Kant] cannot be supported by documents; it is not to be gained through the internal exposition and comparison of the individual systems. Rather, it is a concept acquired by pondering the coherent history of the entire philosophical modern period" (Husserl, *Crisis*, p. 98). "It is true that in order to wrest from the actual words [of Kant] that which these words 'intend to say,' every interpretation must necessarily resort to violence. This violence, however, should not be confused with an action that is wholly arbitrary. The interpretation must be animated and guided by the power of an illuminative idea" (Heidegger, *Kant and the Problem of Metaphysics*, p. 207). A major responsibility of the historian of philosophy today is to resubmit the principles of Husserlian *coherent history* and Heideggerian *illuminative idea* to the many tests and corrective judgments of the insistential source itself and the full range of historical questioning.

ing that intent and rethinking it in new ways. Heidegger conceives of his relation with Kant primarily in these terms, without their being carefully modified by the other canons of interpretation. To justify taking the risks involved in an independent explicitation and reminting of previous philosophical thought, Heidegger appeals to the example set by Kant himself.

The Wolffian professor of philosophy at Halle University in Kant's time was J. A. Eberhard. Alarmed by the new edition (1787) of the *Critique of Pure Reason* and its rapid spread in German academic circles, he founded the *Philosophical Magazine* to defend the Leibniz-Wolff school against the critical philosophy. He tried to refute Kant by claiming that all the principles of knowledge treated in the latter's writings were already set forth by Leibniz. This gave Kant the occasion for stating his position on the interplay of tradition and originality in achieving philosophical progress. Heidegger quotes these passages from Kant's reply to Eberhard:

[1.] Herr Eberhard has made the discovery that "Leibnizian philosophy also contains a critique of reason just as the recent [Kantian] one, which, in addition, introduces a dogmatism based upon an exact analysis of the possibility of knowledge, which contains all the truth of the latter, but even beyond that contains a well-grounded enlargement of the sphere of the understanding." How it could happen that people had not long ago seen these things in that great man's philosophy and its daughter, the Wolffian philosophy, is not explained by him. But how many discoveries, taken as new, are now seen by some clever interpreters very clearly in ancient ones, after it had been indicated to them what to look for! . . . [2.] The *Critique of Pure Reason* may well be the real apology for Leibniz, even in opposition to his partisans whose words of praise hardly do him honor. It can also be an apology for many older philosophers about whom certain historians of philosophy, for all the praises they bestow, speak the purest nonsense.

They do not understand the intentions of these philosophers when they neglect the key to all explication of the works of pure reason through concepts alone, namely, the critique of reason itself (as the common source of all concepts), and cannot see, beyond the etymology of what these philosophers *have said*, that which they *have wanted to say*. . . . [3. Thus Leibniz's principle of sufficient reason is] a remarkable foreshadowing of investigations which were yet to be undertaken in metaphysics.[25]

These remarks do indeed constitute a remarkable *apologia* both for Kant's study of historical sources and for his speculative reinterpretation of them.

The first of these texts is ironical in tone. It underscores the foolishness of those who think that Leibniz's anticipations somehow detract from the originality of Kant's later explicit argumentation. They forget that their own hindsight account of earlier thinkers draws its strength and guidance precisely from the actual elaboration of Kantian critical philosophy. What we find in the sources depends, in important ways, upon the perspective and lines of interpretation afforded by our contemporary philosophizing.

Kant's second text distinguishes rather sharply between adulation and interpretation, as well as between a purely literal study of the express words of a philosopher and a sensitivity to his thematic intention and its latent meanings. What a classical source in philosophy needs, in order to display its

[25] Heidegger employs three texts from Kant's *Über eine Entdeckung nach der alle neue Kritik der reinen Vernunft durch eine ältere entbehrlich gemacht soll*, as given in E. Cassirer's edition of *Immanuel Kants Werke*, vol. 6: *Schriften von 1790-1796*, respectively pp. 3, 71, 68-69 (the work is printed in volume 8 of the Prussian Academy edition of Kant). The three texts are respectively quoted by Heidegger in: *What Is a Thing?*, pp. 79-80; *Kant and the Problem of Metaphysics*, pp. 206-207 (italics added to emended text); and *The Essence of Reasons*, p. 33. The historical and polemical context for Kant's *Reply to Eberhard* or *On a Discovery according to which All New Critique of Pure Reason is Made Dispensable by an Older One* can be found in H.-J. de Vleeschauwer, *The Development of Kantian Thought*, pp. 140-151.

continued vitality, is not unreflective praise but close analysis, criticism, and reworking in terms of the methodologies now being developed. Specifically, Kant suggests that his own vast exploration of pure reason and human experience furnishes the best working method and systematic context, in his own day, for reinterpreting Leibniz's principles and central ideas. Kant seeks to draw more from them than their author actually said, although perhaps not more than his unifying aim intended to say.

The third text gives one concrete instance in which the genuine case for esteeming Leibniz as a wellspring, laden with further meaning for coming generations in philosophy, is to be found in Kant's first *Critique*. This is so, *not despite* its close criticism of Leibniz on sufficient reason, its correlation of Leibniz with Locke and Hume for the warrant of sensuous intuition, and its integration of the principle of sufficient reason with the larger critical requirements for an empirical use of human understanding, but precisely *because of* such rethinking and through the act of such new judgment made upon Leibniz. As far as Kant is concerned, the futural intent of the Leibnizian speculation becomes historically actuated in this philosophical manner, rather than through the verbalism and timid repetitions of Eberhard and other partisan disciples. Hence he will not permit the latter to arrogate for themselves the entire sense of "history of philosophy," which in every age requires something analogous to that basic reconsidering of the sources which Kant's own "history of pure reason" renders possible.[26]

---

[26] Kant's schematic chapter on "The History of Pure Reason," *Critique of Pure Reason*, A 852: B 880–A 856: B 884 (N. K. Smith tr., pp. 666-669), has to be unpacked and tested by his other more specific treatments of philosophical sources. That his approach to Leibniz's *New Essays Concerning Human Understanding* (first published in 1765) has historical as well as critical worth, is coming to be recognized by such researchers as: Y. Belaval, "Sur un Point de comparison entre Kant et Leibniz," in *Kritik und Metaphysik*, ed. F. Kaulbach and J. Ritter, pp. 1-9; H. J. Paton, "Kant on the Errors of Leibniz," in *Kant Studies Today*, pp. 72-87; and G. Tonelli, "Early Reactions to the Publication of Leibniz's *Nouveaux*

What Heidegger then does with these three texts is to use the Kant-Leibniz relationship as a model for his own reappraisal and use of Kant himself. Thus his marginal comment on the first Kantian text specifies that every thoughtful dialogue with a source thinker must involve both a grasp of the same problem and a courageous rethinking of it in a new manner. "That which can already be found in the older philosophers is seen only when one has newly thought it out for himself. Kant spoke very clearly about this fundamental fact in the history of thought. . . . All great insights and discoveries are not only usually thought by several people at the same time, they must also be re-thought in that unique effort to truly say the same thing about the same thing."[27] A truly philosophical and historical approach will shun all facile claims of surpassing and moving beyond the great sources, since such claims usually rest upon an attempt to bypass the basic questions instead of reformulating them in new terms.

As Heidegger's notes on the second Kantian text indicate, a responsive rethinker is careful to search the very wording of the source writings for meanings not expressly stated there, yet suggested by the actual language.

> If an interpretation merely repeats what Kant has expressly said, then of course it is no explicating act, if the latter's set task remains that of rendering properly visible what Kant has brought to light, in the course of his laying of the foundation, beyond his express formulation. This, however, Kant himself was no longer able to say. Indeed, in every instance of philosophical knowledge, the decisive

---

Essais (1765)," to be published. In any case, Kant does not represent that extreme dichotomy between historical and transformational interpretations which is implied in Heidegger's schoolmaster-remark that "if we were to give out grades by the standards of the history of philosophy, Kant's historical comprehension of Aristotle and Plato would have to get a straight 'F.' Yet Kant and only Kant has creatively transformed Plato's doctrine of ideas" *What Is Called Thinking?*, p. 77.

[27] *What Is a Thing?*, pp. 79-80.

issue must become, not what it says in the expressed statements, but what it lays before our eyes as still unsaid, through what is said.[28]

However imperfect Heidegger's approach to Kant may be in execution, it does seek to achieve that delicate balance between the expressly formulated statement and the further reach of meaning which Kant somehow "brings to light" and "lays before our eyes," without being able to articulate it in explicit language. To reduce the arbitrariness of the interpretation as much as possible, the historically minded rethinker of what Kant *could not* say must nevertheless ground his own further suggestions in what Kant *did actually* say. For only through what is indeed textually said, can the power of philosophical language operate to evoke other authentic meanings, which are rendered unconcealedly present in our own thought by the interpreting judgment.

Finally, Heidegger's exegesis of the third Kantian text ties this entire discussion of historical interpretation with his own theory of truth and the teleology of western philosophy. Just as Kant treats the Leibnizian principle of sufficient reason as a remarkable foreshadowing of his own work on knowledge and metaphysics, so does Heidegger take an anticipatory view of the Kantian principle of the unity of all synthetic knowledge. "For the *problem* of the essential connection of being, truth, and reasons lies *concealed* in that principle."[29] Like

---

[28] *Kant and the Problem of Metaphysics*, p. 206. In line with this comment, Heidegger offers this functional criterion for a classical source: "Kant's *Critique of Pure Reason* is among those philosophical works which, as long as there is philosophy on this earth at all, daily become inexhaustible anew. It is one of those works that have already pronounced judgment over every future attempt to 'overcome' them by only passing them by" (*What Is a Thing?*, p. 61).

[29] *The Essence of Reasons*, p. 33. On the general problem of truth as emerging through the conflict-process of concealing and unconcealing itself in Kant, cf. W. B. Macomber, *The Anatomy of Disillusion: Martin Heidegger's Notion of Truth*, pp. 116-117, 154-168. The theme of Heidegger as philosophical retriever of Kant is developed by W. J. Richardson, *Heidegger: Through Phenomenology to Thought*, pp. 29-33, 106-160.

every original mind, Kant manifests and conceals a meaning in the same linguistic act. His philosophy is truth-ful, in the Heideggerian sense of that term, precisely because of its potent ambivalence in showing-and-hiding the basic sense of our human problems. That is why the "unsaid more" factor in Kant's thought arises out of what is actually said, obliging the interpreter to revisit the classic texts constantly for fresh draughts of meaning and leads toward truth.

It is for this same reason that Heidegger names his own interpreting of the Kantian philosophy a *Wiederholung*, which must be taken to mean both a retrieval and a repeating. It is a retrieval or recovery of the proper sense of the problem of being, in accord with the Heideggerian conception of western metaphysics as constituting a long tradition in the forgetting of being. Kant's critique stirs up and recalls the radical sense of being, because it reflects upon man's peculiar ability to open out to the presence of being, both in the form of the world and in that of humane values. Although Kant cannot leap over his own shadow in order to formulate the theme of being in the explicit sense of a fundament for ontology, his language does point in this direction and does make us dissatisfied with any lesser task for philosophy today. Thus the evocative power of Kant's language displays itself in the retrieving act or original interpretation on the part of his present-day readers, as they ask the ontological question in the light of his guiding clues.

Heidegger's study of Kant is also a creative repeating, although not a mere reiteration, since it rests upon frequent meditative returns to the original course of thought and the actual expressions of the source works. Even more fundamentally, there is a joint, mutually supporting return of one-self-as-interpreter and Kant-as-source-thinker to our common origins in human experience. The inquiry about being, as distinct from an inquiry about this or that particular being or zone of beings, makes a repeated cooperative demand upon all the historical sources and current theoretical resources of reflective mankind.

(3) Heidegger follows his own prescriptive rule of making frequent returns to the text of Kant, both in order to correct his own previous interpretations and to retrieve some new themes for reflection. The historian's concern to include a strong, self-correcting factor in his methodology finds analogous expression in Heidegger's practice of continually modifying his perspectives, as he makes different retrievals of Kant's meaning for ontology.

Not unlike the philosophers of science and the phenomenologists, Heidegger locates the heart of the first *Critique* in the part on the Analytic of Principles. In each of his Kantian studies he returns to these pages, but never from exactly the same standpoint or without effecting some significant revision of his earlier commentaries in the light of new reflections.

His basic strategy in *Kant and the Problem of Metaphysics* is to show that the truth about being arises out of some vital conflicts found in Kant. For that purpose, Heidegger concentrates upon the chapter in Kant dealing with "the schematism of the pure concepts of understanding," and treats Kant's theory of the transcendental imagination and its unifying function as a peak insight attained only in the first edition of the *Critique*. Kant is depicted as recoiling in fear, in the second edition, from the abyss of human subjectivity opened up by the schematizing imagination. This is reminiscent of the manner in which the Kant of Husserl also recoils fearfully from Hume.

In response both to the critics of this interpretation and to the internal requirements of his own method of variating retrievals, however, Heidegger turns his attention in later writings to that chapter in the *Critique* which treats of the "system of all principles of pure understanding." He progressively acknowledges the unique contributions on the problem of being which Kant makes in the second edition, including his distinctive notion of transcendental logic. The essential Kantian clue is to correlate this transformed view of logic with the problems of being and world.

Hence the pertinent sections in Heidegger's *The Essence of Reasons* make a return visit to Kant's theory of the world, without always nervously insisting upon the limits of that theory. Kant is seen to be engaged in reorienting the conception of world, so that it does not have a purely cosmic, impersonal signification but has an essential reference to human finitude. Man's practical, communitarian, and historical aims become more decisive in this approach to the Kantian sense of the world. The latter provokes us to think ontologically about the *Dasein* factor in man, as well as about the being-principle in man and cosmos alike.

> "World" serves as the name of the essence of human Dasein. This concept of world corresponds perfectly to Augustine's existentiell concept; only the uniquely Christian evaluation of "worldly" Dasein, of the *amatores mundi*, has dropped away. "World" now assumes the positive meaning of "fellow players" in the game of life.[30]

This Kantian humanistic conception of world builds bridges both to the life world of Husserl and to Wittgenstein's language games of life.

The major objective of Heidegger's *What Is a Thing?* is to determine more closely the Kantian sense of that elusive word "thing," as it is involved in the theory of world and as it leads us onward toward the meaning of being. Heidegger's two guiding axes of interpretation here are: first, that the theme

---

[30] *The Essence of Reasons*, p. 79. It is in *What Is a Thing?*, especially pp. 124-179, that Heidegger "makes up for what was lacking" in his 1929 Kant-book: by appreciating the second edition of the *Critique of Pure Reason*, by distinguishing Kant and his questioning of metaphysics from the position of the neo-Kantians, and by relating the Kantian theory of judgment to the unity of apperception. At the same time, Heidegger locates Kant even more firmly within the objective mathematical treatment of things and of truth (*What Is a Thing?*, pp. 55-61, 184-220). This issue is examined by L. Versényi, *Heidegger, Being, and Truth*, pp. 63-68; and T. Langan, "Heidegger: The Problem of the Thing," in *Heidegger and the Path of Thinking*, ed. John Sallis, pp. 105-115.

of thingness evokes the ideal of the "mathematical" treatment
of things as objects of scientific knowledge; and second, that
further reflection on the mathematical attitude discloses the
presence of human *Dasein*'s will to found and form this sort
of understanding of things. In the broadest sense of a mathematical taking of things in their objectivity for our mind, Kant
remains within the limits of the mathematical tradition of
Descartes, Leibniz, and (at least by implication) Husserl
himself. However, Heidegger also appreciates Kant's insight
into the experience of freedom and the deliberate fashioning
of theoretical and practical principles for interpreting the
things of experience. Kant's search for the principles upon
which we accept things, as reliably known or as involved in
moral action, serves as yet another foreshadowing of *Dasein*.
It is also an incentive for Heidegger to move from the "middle stretch" of Kant's halfway reflections on thing and world
to their ontological basis.

A final instance where Heidegger's development of Kantian
themes illustrates his revisionary activity is the essay entitled
Kant's Thesis on Being. This contains three matters bearing
upon the process of improving one's historical vision of Kant.
Heidegger admits, first of all, that it is insufficient to say that
Kant grounds the objectivity of the object in logic, as though
he reduces it to the readymade formal logic of the school
manuals. "The logic is no longer formal logic, but the logic
determined from the original synthetic unity of transcendental
apperception. Ontology finds a ground in such a logic."[31]
Having distinguished his own method sufficiently from that
of Husserl, Heidegger is now more ready than Husserl to

[31] Heidegger, *Kants These über das Sein*, p. 20; this opusculum is
also included in Heidegger's *Wegmarken* (Frankfurt: Klostermann,
1967). The impact of Kant's active, positional reinterpretation of being and existence upon contemporary ontology and existentialism is
brought out by Z. Adamczewski, "Kant's Existential Thought," in
New Essays in Phenomenology, ed. J. M. Edie, pp. 314-362. Heidegger's contrast between his thinking-of-being and the will-ful activism
of Kant, Nietzsche, and many existentialists is sketched in his
Nietzsche, II, 468-480, and in "Who is Nietzsche's Zarathustra?,"
Review of Metaphysics, 20 (1966-67), 411-431.

acknowledge the distinctive nature and ontological resource-fulness of the Kantian transcendental logic.

A second refinement is that Kant is not really satisfied with any purely thing-and-object-ordered conception of being. He directs philosophical attention to the positing act wherein being finds its proper meaning and ground. In our human experience there are different senses of to-be, precisely because there are different positing acts to signify the logical and the real, the transcendental and the experiential, bases of being. Kant's recognition of these different component sources of the meaning of being, in its humanly crucial sense of actually existing in some determinate relation to our experience, lies at the root of the several kinds of existential ontology.

Heidegger himself salutes the Kantian correlation between existential being and human thinking as the third contribution of this theory of being-as-positional-act, and the one which furnishes the motif for his own later reflections on the nature of thinking and being. But he also makes a firm transition, at this very point, from a historical interpreting of Kant's thesis on being to a philosophical criticism and judgment upon it. Their doctrinal differences stem from taking contrary positions on the unobtrusive connective word: thinking-*and*-being. For the word "and" is to be construed in accord with each philosopher's distinctive conception of how the human subject opens up a presence for being.

In the schematic criticism of Kant found in his book on *Nietzsche* and related essays, Heidegger tries rapidly and somewhat vaguely to distinguish Kantian will-activity from his own ontological waiting in expectancy, his attitude of letting being speak in our *Dasein*. Heidegger does not permit his historical interpretation to undergo further perspectival modifications on this core issue. He concludes his lifelong study of Kant with the rather rigid philosophical judgment that the relationship of Kantian subjectivity to being is too strenuously will-ful. This is an indirect way of affirming the philosophical originality of Heidegger's own theme of the disclosure of being in our free and reflective *Dasein*. Unfortunately, the historical reinterpreting of Kant remains frozen along the middle stretch of the road leading toward that welcome to being which is to come only in the Heideggerian form of ontological thinking, but which is already symbolized in the welcoming chairs, shoes, and pipes of a Van Gogh painting.

4. THE ONGOING ANALYTIC CONFERENCE ON KANT

Although history of modern philosophy develops through new appraisals of the source writings, it does so only under the express methodic condition of refusing to consider any one philosophical judgment as giving us the final word. For the source thinker still continues to offer other pools of meaning for our recognition and evaluation, provided that we will vary the philosophical contexts and not restrict our approach to but one intellectual and cultural tradition. The contemporanizing process includes as an essential working principle this imperative: *Look for still other* philosophical bases for reading the source work and releasing its many bearings upon our problems.

The experience of a Kant seminar yields a quite concrete formulation of the situation which this imperative is designed to meet. The very vigor and lifelong persistence with which Husserl and Heidegger conducted their investigation of Kantian philosophy have made their interpretation both an agency of historical understanding and a potential roadblock against its further development. There is a danger of contracting Kant's thought to those transformed aspects which are rendered commensurate with, and subordinated to theoretical evaluation in terms of, the philosophies of Husserl and Heidegger. It then becomes an explicit methodological task to unblock the path of historical inquiry in this region, to unfreeze the process of historical interpreting of Kant so that it can develop other illuminating themes and relationships. Otherwise, we cannot speak in any historically comprehensive and open sense about Kant *our integral contemporary*, but only about a Kant who is lopsidedly adapted to *only this* contemporary form of phenomenology or that of foundational ontology.

Thus those sessions of the Kant seminar which are devoted to the ongoing analytic approaches to Kant are of far more than incidental relevance for our general theory of historical understanding. For they furnish a case study in the complex work of opening up some new prospects on a major modern source, so that he can be made more readily responsive to a distinctive set of questions and methods. We cannot fully foresee the philosophical repercussions of relating Kant with the predominant aims of British and American analytic thinkers. But this fresh path of historical comparison and argumentation is unlikely to leave either the Kantian source or the Anglo-American philosophical world only lightly touched by the resulting interpenetrations. As in other movements of historical reorientation, all the component factors are being profoundly transformed by their respective engagement in the process. This can be verified by taking a seminar sighting along the lines marked by the progressively increasing impact of Kant upon Wittgenstein, Austin, and Strawson.

Ludwig Wittgenstein's Kantian background is sometimes sought by sewing together these two remarks from the *Tractatus Logico-Philosophicus*: "All philosophy is a 'critique of language,'" and "Logic is transcendental."[32] When conflated, these two statements suggest that the functions once performed by Kant's transcendental logic and deduction of categories are now supplied by Wittgenstein's logical analysis of language forms and the logic of the world, that is, by a critique of pure language or transcendental philosophy of language. This interpretation is useful as a retrospective view of Wittgenstein himself which relates his work to the present analytic interest in Kant. But it cannot be pressed

---

[32] Wittgenstein, *Tractatus Logico-Philosophicus*, tr. D. F. Pears and B. F. McGuinness, 4.0031, 6.13. Erik Stenius, *Wittgenstein's Tractatus*, depends largely upon these texts in chapter 11, "Wittgenstein as a Kantian Philosopher," pp. 214-226. A more thorough comparison is made by S. M. Engel, "Wittgenstein and Kant," *Philosophy and Phenomenological Research*, 30 (1969-70), 483-513.

very far as a historical comparison, without requiring some severe qualifications at every point.

Taken in context, the two statements have a definite and restricted reference. The first text borrows the term *Sprachkritik* from the pioneer linguistic research done by Fritz Mauthner, but transfers its present meaning to something similar to Bertrand Russell's point of contrasting the apparent and the real logical form of a proposition. Wittgenstein suggests that a critique of language is the positive remedy for the condition in which "most of the propositions and questions of philosophers arise from our failure to understand the logic of our language."[33] On Kant's part, there is a broadly similar recognition that philosophical disagreements follow a pattern discernible neither to dogmatism nor to skepticism, but only to a critical, transcendental logic.

As for the second text, the transcendental quality of logic consists in its showing forth of the logic of the world rather than being a content of doctrine by itself. For Wittgenstein, the transcendentality of logic also signifies its enclosure of mathematical equations as pseudo-propositions, and its self-surpassing consideration that "in philosophy the question, 'What do we actually use this word or this proposition for?' repeatedly leads to valuable insights." The Kantian dialectical reason does supply an analogue for Wittgenstein's conception of the active linguistic deceptions, just as there is a Kantian permeation of philosophical awareness with a sense of our reaching limits in human talk and judgment. But these similarities remain very general and do not warrant any direct, unmediated correlation between the two philosophers on determinate issues.

Hence it would be historically incautious to try to fit Wittgenstein's statements on solipsism and the world, the transcendental subject and the will, into a purely Kantian frame. This simplification overlooks the fact that, on such specific questions, Kant is always being mediated across the perspec-

[33] *Tractatus*, 4.003; the next quoted text is from *ibid.*, 6.211.

tive of Wittgenstein's early study of Schopenhauer. In our previous examination of the responsible interpreter, we noticed how the historical appreciation of such a middle-range philosopher as Schopenhauer develops, in our time, through his relationship with Wittgenstein on precisely these questions.[34] To understand Wittgenstein's position, his actual interpretation and adaptation of Schopenhauer must be taken into account before making any historical comparison which leads eventually toward Kant. Once this historical mediation is rendered definite, then there is a disciplined sense in which the Wittgenstein-Kant relationship bears some historical significance and also clarifies the work being done by the present generation of analytic philosophers.

Especially in his later developments, Wittgenstein approximated the Kantian way of philosophizing. There is a broad analogy between his topic of the bewitching effect of language and the Kantian description of the human mind's natural, inescapable attraction toward transcendent metaphysics and its dialectical illusions.[35] Kant noted how this tendency feeds upon the very dynamism of those completional analogies and

[34] See above, Chapter IV, section 3. The Schopenhauerian quality of Wittgenstein's conception of Kant is emphasized by David Favrholdt, *An Interpretation and Critique of Wittgenstein's Tractatus*, pp. 79-80, 101, 144-189.

[35] "Philosophy is a battle against the bewitchment of our intelligence by means of language" (Wittgenstein, *Philosophical Investigations*, tr. G. E. M. Anscombe, #109). The lulling and confusing effect of language in the service of uncritical metaphysics is prominent in Kant's account. Ordinary textbook metaphysics "favored conceit by venturesome assertions, sophistry by subtle distinctions and adornment, and shallowness by the ease with which it decided the most difficult problems by means of a little school wisdom, which is only the more seductive the more it has the choice, on the one hand, of taking something from the language of science and, on the other, from that of popular discourse—thus being everything to everybody but in reality nothing at all" (Kant, *Prolegomena to Any Future Metaphysics*, tr. L. W. Beck, p. 132). The problem of Kant's own style is discussed by D. W. Tarbet, "The Fabric of Metaphor in Kant's *Critique of Pure Reason*," *Journal of the History of Philosophy*, 6 (1968), 257-270, especially his use of the metaphors of flight and battle, science and jurisprudence.

metaphors which form the heart of human language, including philosophical style. Critically untamed language has the power to entice us to fill out the relationships saluted in words, to convert our craving after completeness and generality of expression into a claim to have a homogeneous body of knowledge realizing these same traits. Both philosophers sought to devise methods for uncovering and disciplining this linguistically charged drive toward noetic overstatement and misstatement, even though they did not hope to extirpate it.

Wittgenstein also finds an instructive exemplar in Kant's preoccupation with how the world is related so multifariously to our human ways of living and talking. That philosophy dwells properly at-and-within the limits of human life and language, is a common theme for which each thinker supplies his own variations. When Wittgenstein "puckishly" compares himself with Kant on the related matter of attending carefully to the ordinary talk and judgments of practical people around him, the parallel is well taken.[36] For both men make philosophy move from the deceptively smooth surface of theoretical constructions to the rough terrain and massive difficulties of practical actions. Hence there is an insuppressibly irritant factor incorporated into their respective notions of human inquiry, a sense of never wholly comprehending in their philosophical expressions the many actual relationships between man and nature. The philosopher is bound to stop short in his conceptual analyses, take note once more of their inadequate footing in human actualities, and try again to understand what men are saying about themselves and the

---

[36] Wolfe Mays, "Recollections of Wittgenstein," in *Ludwig Wittgenstein: The Man and His Philosophy*, ed. K. T. Fann, p. 82; cf. p. 27, on the "only occasional glimpses of understanding" which Wittgenstein said he got from Spinoza, Hume, and Kant. Yet there is a methodological similarity, even if no historical link, between Kant's determinate analysis of the components in each different cognitive sphere and Wittgenstein's contrast between an *Erklärung* of a language-game through our experiences and a *Feststellung* of this language-game itself as the primary thing upon which to think (*Philosophical Investigations*, #654-656). See below, note 41.

world. Between Kant's de-rhapsodizing critique and Wittgenstein's un-captivated eye or spirit, there is at least an illuminating comparison even when there may be no strict genesis or historical dependency, apart from the Schopenhauerian filter.

The working engagement of analytic philosophy with Kant becomes somewhat more specific and defined in the writings of J. L. Austin. He is very critical of the conventional handling of epistemological themes through an obsessive repetition of just a few words, facts, and examples treated as the standard fonts of wisdom. His main remedy is to attend more carefully to the distinctions operative in our ordinary forms of speech, foreswearing both the *ivresse des grandes profondeurs* resounding in the "deep thinkers" and also the facility displayed by the "masters of a certain special, happy style of blinkering philosophical English" (as found in Berkeley and Hume, Russell and Ayer).[37] In exploring after a good site for doing field work in philosophy, Austin follows two criteria. He looks for some theme where our ordinary language is rich and subtle in its expressions; and he seeks a field which has not been trodden into bogs that permit no sustained analysis, or into rutted tracks of precedent from which the philosopher cannot arise to take an original sighting of the relation between words and the world. In this respect, analytic philosophers are placed on their guard against fitting their work comfortably into any established pattern of history and against regarding their relationship with past philosophies as one of mere prolongation, instead of the revolution which the analytic method makes possible.

Yet Austin actually develops his criticism in a reflective manner that compels the analytic mind to recognize the reality of philosophical tradition and the intellectual obligation to grapple with the authentic arguments of its leading representatives (for him: Plato and Aristotle, Leibniz and Kant). Thus in his metaphor of finding a good site for field work in

[37] J. L. Austin, *Philosophical Papers*, p. 179; and Austin, *Sense and Sensibilia*, p. 4.

philosophy, he makes it clear that one can profit only so far by examining the ordinary sources of talk about the problem of excuses, for instance, and that one cannot impoverish that theme by obliterating the original contributions made by the great philosophers. It is true that "we can discuss at least clumsiness, or absence of mind, or inconsiderateness, even spontaneousness, without remembering what Kant thought, and so progress by degrees even to discussing deliberation without for once remembering Aristotle or self-control without Plato."[38] But the penumbral awareness remains of what these sources *do* have to offer, so that eventually the analysis must achieve a new conjunction between the best in ordinary speech and the best in the philosophical tradition.

That is why Austin refrains from indulging in wholly unbuttoned remarks about the confusions and mistakes of the central philosophers. "In philosophy, there are many mistakes that it is no disgrace to have made: to make a first-water, ground-floor mistake, so far from being easy, takes one (*one*) form of philosophical genius." Criticism of originative philosophers places the burden upon us to understand their arguments precisely, to appreciate the large consequences that follow from their principles, and to be ready to back up in present discourse the grounds for regarding past conceptions as mistakes at the ground-floor relationship of language with realities perceived by us.

---

[38] *Philosophical Papers*, p. 183; the words *at least, even*, and *without for once*, indicate that it requires disciplined effort *not* to advert to these philosophical sources on such topics. The next quoted text is from *ibid.*, p. 205, where Austin makes the footnote-remark that "Plato, Descartes, and Leibniz all had this form of genius, besides of course others." Austin's criticism of, and yet continuity with, historical tradition in philosophy can be seen in different perspectives: Stuart Hampshire, "J. L. Austin, 1911-1960," and Stanley Cavell, "Austin at Criticism," both in *Symposium on J. L. Austin*, ed. K. T. Fann, pp. 33-46, 59-75. Cavell observes that, in assessing a philosophical tradition, "the first step would be to grant to philosophers the ordinary rights of language and vision Austin grants all other men: to ask of them, in his spirit, why they should say what they say where and when they say it, and to give the *full story* before claiming satisfaction" (p. 73). This is basic counsel for any work in history of philosophy and in historical aspects of any problem.

Were it not for the pretentious sound, Austin would have been willing to call his philosophical coordination of word-study with perception of things around us a type of "linguistic phenomenology." And similarly, were it not for the connotation of uncritical respect and mindless repetition so often attached to the term, he might have conceded that his method-in-use includes some measure of "historical understanding of philosophy," especially of Kant. Before plunging into the specific knots of problems and distinctions comprising his William James Lectures, he offered this highly compressed but informative acknowledgment of Kant as a forerunner, and thus of a definite historical component in his own view of the analytic turn in philosophy:

> First, and most obviously, many "statements" were shown to be, as KANT perhaps first argued systematically, strictly nonsense, despite an unexceptionable grammatical form: and the continual discovery of fresh types of nonsense, unsystematic though their classification and mysterious though their explanation is too often allowed to remain, has done on the whole nothing but good. Yet we, that is, even philosophers, set some limits to the amount of nonsense that we are prepared to admit we talk: so that it was natural to go on to ask, as a second stage, whether many apparent pseudo-statements really set out to be "statements" at all. . . . Here too KANT was among the pioneers. We very often also use utterances in ways beyond the scope at least of traditional grammar. It has come to be seen that many specially perplexing words embedded in apparently descriptive statements do not serve to indicate some specially odd additional feature in the reality reported, but to indicate (not to report) the circumstances in which the statement is made or reservations to which it is subject or the way in which it is to be taken and the like.[39]

[39] Austin, *How to Do Things with Words*, pp. 2-3. Austin's second stage corresponds almost exactly with Kant's interpretation of the history of metaphysics, from the time of Leibniz and Wolff to his own day, as being a development from unqualified assertions about entities (regardless of human ways of cognition), to statements in-

This is a deft instance where a philosopher's judgment about a revolution going on in philosophy includes two familiar operations of historical reinterpretation: (a) altering the from-to perspective, and thereby (b) reinforcing a continuative problem.

(a) Under the first heading, Austin invites us to read Kant in yet another light, in a line of descent that does not follow the more familiar path through the romantic philosophers and Hegel, or even that through Schopenhauer and Nietzsche. He alters the from-to perspective sufficiently for us to perceive the different Kantian seeding which the analytic revolution seeks to bring to maturity. In outgrowing the dogmatic rigidities of logical positivism, Austin proposes a continuation of the general sort of inquiries launched by Kant. For the German philosopher proposes both *the radical questioning about sense and nonsense* which constitutes the first phase in every analytic inquiry and also that *awareness of plural intentions*, on the part of the statement fashioner, which sets the tasks for the second phase of analytic work. To establish a completional relationship between Kant as pioneer and the analytic group, as present developers of the two stages of philosophizing, is Austin's distinctive way of making a difference in the historical from-to perspectives, involving Kant as point of departure.

(b) A historically responsible interpreter must also specify those aspects of the modern source which become ingredient in his own investigations, and which thereby comprise the present stage of some continuative problem in history of modern philosophy. Austin makes a very brief beginning at meeting this second historical requirement. What he

---

tended to include overt reference precisely to the human conditions of intention, desire, and limitation of knowledge. See Kant, *Welches sind die wirklichen Fortschritte, die die Metaphysik seit Leibniz'ens und Wolff's Zeiten in Deutschland gemacht hat?* (Prussian Academy edition of Kant's *Gesammelte Schriften*, vol. 20, pp. 259-351). This work, along with the *Reply to Eberhard* (above, note 25), shows Kant making critical use of Leibniz and other sources to orient his contemporaries in the new way of looking at metaphysical statements.

calls Kant's contribution to the problem of sense and nonsense finds a broad textual basis in the first *Critique*, especially the procedures in the Dialectic of pure reason. There, Kant takes in hand the many volumes written on general ontology and the special metaphysical fields of cosmology-psychology-theology. Such volumes are filled with grammatically unexceptionable sentences, which claim to be conveying inferential knowledge. Yet under epistemological challenge, they cannot meet the standards of humanly ascertainable sense, at least not those found to prevail in mathematical and physical knowledge.

But what chiefly interests Austin is Kant's refusal simply to rule out all human talk that does not conform with the statemental standards set in these latter fields of knowledge. The continuative influence of Kant is felt especially in his sensitivity toward other intents of utterance and judgment, which he designates as the shift from meanings about the physical order to meanings about the human modes, aims, and limits of inquiry. Austin finds that the critical philosophy's treatment of the language of belief and freedom, responsibility and hope, has a latent power not fully recognized until it becomes incorporated into the linguistic and conceptual setting of contemporary analytic methods. It is through this latter network that a significant portion of the contemporanizing process operates to secure Kant's effective historical presence among us.

We noted previously how every reinterpretation of a major modern source involves a reverse criterion of philosophical worth. That is, the new historical alignment tells us almost as much about the relative adequacy of the contemporary basis of interpreting as it does about the source thinker in question. To the extent that Wittgenstein and Austin include some rethinking of Kant within their scope, they raise a legitimate query about just how thoroughly *their* approaches can illuminate the Kantian text and cope with the range of Kantian problems and concepts. This pertinent challenge is being faced by the present generation of analytic philosophers, who find it necessary to plunge into a direct and sustained study of Kant, on a scale and in a manner going far beyond the scouting expeditions of Wittgenstein and Austin. Once the reverse criterion is activated, the task of analyzing Kant becomes more explicit, detailed, and comprehensive in its demands.

There is a qualitative escalation of historical and present theoretical issues together, in P. F. Strawson's *The Bounds of Sense: An Essay on Kant's Critique of Pure Reason*. Whatever criticism its specific arguments require, this book does define the major conditions for another stage in the ongoing analytic conference on Kant and in the evolution of Kant-interpretations. Strawson moves beyond general allusions and comparisons to point-by-point argumentation. But in doing so, he strives to avoid the twin deficiencies inherent in his philosophical heritage: isolating a particular text so that it receives no modifications from its context and long range direction, and then querulously finding that the source abounds in confusions and elementary fallacies. Strawson recognizes that these moves are interdependent, and also that they issue in a quite attenuated appraisal of Kant which is neither convincing history nor sound theory.[40]

The three remedial measures taken in this situation are reciprocally beneficial for the historical understanding of Kant and for the development of analytic thought. First, Strawson rights the imbalance between taking short soundings of the Kantian text and paying unbounded attention to ordinary locutions. Just as one determines the theoretical im-

---

[40] Strawson says of his book: "It is by no means a work of historical-philosophical scholarship," and yet "I have tried to present a clear, uncluttered and unified interpretation, at least strongly supported by the text as it stands, of the system of thought which the *Critique* contains" (*The Bounds of Sense*, p. 11). In his concern for the actual text, the system of thought, and a unified interpretation, Strawson shows a distinctively analytic responsiveness to historical canons. He also modifies his previous distinction between descriptive and revisionary metaphysics (*Individuals: An Essay in Descriptive Metaphysics*; see above, Chapter I, note 7), which he now refines in the light of criticism and of his lectures on Kant.

port of ordinary ways of using words only through a patient, sensitive, and varied approach, so one comes to grasp a modern philosopher's use of language only *by hearing him out at length* and in his several modulations. An interpreter who respects this requirement of equal justice is not only more faithful to the analytic tradition but also closer to the meaning of Kant and other philosophical sources. For he is responding to one primary rule of historical understanding: to cultivate the listening ear and thus achieve a fuller presence for the insistential meaning of the text.

That this rule does not mean a supine enregistering of source statements, but rather a vigorous rethinking and revaluation of them, is evident from Strawson's persistent relating of particular arguments to the general question of metaphysics. This second corrective procedure removes the illusory autonomy from isolated analyses by connecting Kant's position, at every point, with his underlying theme of the problem of metaphysical cognition. Strawson's personal interest in this broad question has not handicapped his reading of the *Critique of Pure Reason*, but rather has enabled him to interpret it more pertinently and comprehensively than would be otherwise possible. His own distinction between descriptive and revisionary metaphysics permits him to respond, this time *contextually and thematically*, to Kant's careful distinctions among the kinds of metaphysics. It is this respect for the contextual and thematic requirements of historical interpretation which endows the Strawsonian Kant with enough textual bearing to instruct other Kantian scholars.

Strawson suggests that there are three primary Kantian meanings for "metaphysics," which he correlates with his own proposals for that term. (a) There is a legitimate metaphysics of experience, analyzing the general conditions of human experiencing and knowing. This finds its counterpart in Strawson's constructive phase of a descriptive metaphysics, which inspects the concepts and methods required for an immanent study of human experience. (b) Both Kant and

Strawson are opposed to a transcendent metaphysics, which would discourse about entities supposed to lie beyond our experience, without reckoning with the manner and limitations of all human knowledge. The Kantian analysis of the unverifiable claims of dialectical-speculative reason and the Strawsonian restrictions upon descriptive metaphysics are alike intended to curb this transcendent tendency. (c) But there is a parting of the ways between source and interpreter over what Strawson regards as an unfounded attempt of Kant to do metaphysics in the revisionary style. Kant is not resolute enough in drawing the bounds of human sense and respecting its closure within the realm of appearance. His long-range attempt to prepare the way for practical convictions of noumenal reality is criticized by Strawson, under the rubric of a metaphysics of transcendental idealism or transcendental subjectivism. He indicates, but does not argue in detail, that this third meaning of metaphysics is vitiated by a defective model of mind-made nature and an unintelligible theory of the mind as a process of making nature. At this point, further progress would depend upon a renewed examination of Kant's remarkably tenacious qualifications on every kind of belief, as well as upon a comparative study of the constitution of the meanings of "nature" in Kant, Husserl, and Heidegger. Strawson's accomplishment is to bring the analytic interpretation of Kant within range of a responsible comparative evaluation, involving discussion of the best historical, phenomenological, and ontological studies of the issues he raises.

As his third corrective principle for analytic narrowness on historical issues, Strawson admits the meaningfulness of questions about the subject-object relationship in general. He broadens the empiricist grooves of analytic inquiry sufficiently to ask about the constitutive factors for objectivity and the limiting principles for subjectivity. Thereby, he enables analytic philosophy *to receive the Kantian dimension* of the range of problems which determine the direction of much philosophical work today. Wittgenstein had already prepared the way for this enlargement of scope, with his unresolved references to the world in general and the limitation of languages in that respect. And Austin's contribution came in his admission that, although mistaken, there is a Kantian transcendental way of asking about the basis of possibility and relationships, in our sensing of things.[41]

Objects of discourse are never sufficiently analyzed in terms of the sense-data theory, if only because the latter theory is itself enclosed within a tissue of other questions about the perceptual act and the conditions for having a world of objects. Strawson, no less than Husserl, counts as a real gain Kant's study of the conditions of possibility for distinguishing between the temporal flow of our perceptions, the order of objects of these perceptions, and the general relational structures in the objective domain of nature. Insofar as Strawson maintains that a "truly empiricist philosophy" of human meaning must include such critical questions about this wider context of our statements, he testifies to the still revolutionary capacities in Kantian thought and their transforming impact upon the analytic frame of reference. We have not yet heard the last word in the dialogue between Hume and Kant, as it continues to resound through the work of contemporary analysts and phenomenologists.

5. A FOCUS IN KANTIAN COMMUNITY

We have already drawn the distinction, in general terms, between taking a conspectus approach to a philosopher in preliminary survey fashion and then returning to that approach at the end of a historical inquiry, as a means of attaining some unifying synthesis of his thought. When a seminar centers around the philosophy of Kant, this further effort at unification is seen to be demanded both by the source think-

---

[41] In *Philosophical Papers*, pp. 34-36, Austin distinguishes and criticizes two types of transcendental argument: Kantian presuppositional inquiry and ontological transcending toward another, universal sort of entity. For his part, Strawson allows some sense of Kantian presuppositional inquiry, which (in Wittgenstein's terms) need not be construed as a transcending *Erklärung* that dissipates the force and specificity of a *Feststellung* of perceptual language.

er's own theme of the systematic unity of reason, examined in its several modalities, and by the difficult, partial perspectives opened up along the main routes. The seminar members are likely to feel, toward the close of their research, that they are well acquainted with this or that parcel of Kant's arguments but that a sense of the wholeness of his mind still eludes them. Historical comprehension of Kant does aim at such a unifying act, and yet refuses to base it upon any facile and fraudulent claim of having discovered "the key" to his philosophy. Historical unification must arise *out of* the actual research situation and *in fulfillment of* its intrinsic tendencies of convergence, or it will not come in any form that can survive the scrutiny of methodically varied modes of interrogation.

But the problem of attaining a mature conspectus of Kantian philosophy can be stated in more specific terms. Whereas every preliminary survey moves easily from one *Critique* to the next—from theory of knowledge and metaphysics to ethics and esthetics, and to theory of history and religion—this movement of tranquil passage becomes the first victim of the advanced Kant seminar. In one sense, the loss means historical gain. Closer study of Kant and sharper variation of present-day bases of interpretation reveal to us that the transition from one region of Kantian reflection to another is not easily made, and that some distance always remains between systematic unity as a program intended by Kant and as a gradually achieved movement of his thought. Furthermore, our own contemporanizing standpoints serve to exacerbate the difficulty. The precise manner in which to conceive the passage from one phase of critical philosophy to another differs concomitantly with the different bases of interpretation and present reorientation involved in the study of Kantian texts.

Indeed, if a Kant seminar were conducted along the lines suggested thus far in the present chapter, it would have the added educational effect of sharpening the problem of conspectus as it confronts the most promising philosophical approaches to Kant in our time. For it would not escape the attention of seminar participants that there is a trailing off of historical comprehension, on the part of all three main centers of interpretation, precisely on the issue of *continuity* between the first *Critique* and Kant's other critical writings. (a) The findings on Kant as philosopher of science have not yet been rethought in their application to his moral, esthetic, and religious doctrines. (b) From the standpoint of phenomenology and foundational ontology, these moral domains remain a puzzle and are rapidly criticized, as bringing only superficial alleviation of Kant's basic theoretical defects concerning objectivity and the world. (c) And in the present state of analytic studies of Kant, there is a persistent cleft between those which seek an enclosure of meaning and metaphysics within the perceptual world and those which independently assess the strength and pertinence of Kantian moral philosophy. In such a dichotomous situation, the theory of historical interpreting can best contribute by maintaining an unremitting search after all the interpretant goals, especially after Kant's synoptic meaning as well as his separate analyses.

For a seminar group, it is more effective to find a synthesizing principle *already at work* in the primary centers of interpretation than to invoke one from some considerations extrinsic to these working bases of Kantian research. One such internally operative and available center of unification is *the principle of community*. It is a prominent generalizing theme in several philosophers concerned with rethinking Kant—an indication that the plurality of contemporanizing standpoints does not work solely toward the fragmentation of Kantian philosophy but also contains the grounds for its reintegration in our historical understanding and philosophical evaluation.

There is a broad working base of convergence here between the logical studies of Jaakko Hintikka, Wilfrid Sellars' analytic realism, and Paul Ricoeur's phenomenology. They find some common ground, not simply in the writings of Kant as a constantly fruitful subject matter, but specifically in the topic of community as a guide and binding factor in these writings. To trace out the implications of such an immanently generated principle for achieving historical conspectus, is a project agreeing both with the spirit of Kant himself and with the dispositional capacities of a seminar group already employing the resources of logical, analytic, and phenomenological methods of contemporary interpretation of Kantian thought. That certain aspects of the community theme are becoming central in the research of many textually oriented Kantian scholars today is both a reassurance about the historical soundness of this joint emphasis and a futural intent that, from a meeting of the several components, there will develop a more adequately synoptic and continuative understanding of Kant's philosophy.

There is no sudden, dramatic recognition of the Kantian theory of community as providing an intrinsic transition from the metaphysico-epistemological standpoint of the first *Critique* to the principles of practical cognition and action. Here as elsewhere, progress in historical understanding comes quietly, incrementally, and convergently. For it depends upon the steady transformation of our emphases and questioning wrought by an entire generation of independent Kantian investigations. Hence a major objective of a historically grounded seminar must be to identify some common tendencies operative in widely separated Kantian studies, showing how so many newly staked-out paths of inquiry lead eventually to Kant's philosophy of community.

The scientific, phenomenological, and analytic studies of Kant during the past generation have accomplished a threefold preparatory work toward perceiving the potentialities in the community theme.[42] First, they jointly call attention to the loose fit between Kant's most general principles and conditions of knowledge and any specific body of epistemic state-

[42] That the three following interpretations of the community theme are historically well grounded in Kant's own treatment of moral, religious, and historical aspects of human reality, is documented by James Collins, *The Emergence of Philosophy of Religion*, pp. 114-117, 163-164, 181-204, 409-416; also by A. W. Wood, *Kant's Moral Religion*.

ments, such as Newtonian natural philosophy. There is no
need to remain imprisoned, however, in the sartorial logic of
close and loose fits. Kant is not concerned with loosening the
rigor of his principles, but rather with *establishing their analogical power*. His categorial concepts and principles of judgment are not rigidly set premises of deduction, but are guides
and safeguards for the many specific tasks of cognitive inquiry. The relevant point is that the analogical meaning of the
community principle—its guiding and criticizing function—
gets developed not only in the direction of physical knowledge of the world but also in that of the moral, historical, and
religious relationships among men. To move beyond the first
Critique does not mean to flee beyond the pale of disciplined
cognitive procedures and principles, then, but to continue the
actualization of meanings and the recognition of cognitive
limits in still other modes of human inquiry.

A second cooperative achievement of these centers for con-
temporaring Kant is their recognition that, in the four
classes of categories (those of quantity, quality, relation, and
modality), the most complex and far-reaching questions concern *the relational and modalizational categories*. The open
texture of categorial meaning stands forth most strongly in
relational questions (concerning substance, cause, and community) and in modality assertions (involving possibility,
existence, and necessity). These are the areas in Kant that are
most responsive to logical and metaphysical analyses today,
but they are also the areas that orient the critical mind toward
moral and other actional topics. Reflection upon the relational and modalizational concepts, including that of community itself, involves one in the distinctively Kantian process
of penetrating simultaneously into the foundations of physical nature and those of moral freedom. The three *Critiques*
symbolize distinct phases in this multidirectional radiation
from a common center, this orderly study of categorial meanings in their analogical uses and limitations.

Thirdly, there is remarkable unanimity among the diverse
interpreters about the crucial nature of Kant's move from the

Analytic of Concepts to the Analytic of Principles. For only through a reflective study of principles-in-use, can he distinguish effectively between a visionary expansion of categorial meanings (which is heedless of the inherent differentiations and bounds of human experience) and a disciplined exploration of their various implications. The Analytic of Principles constitutes one such approach, since it treats of the schematizing patterns and unifying analogies needed to achieve that "closer fit" of the Newtonian conception of nature. Just as important as following these exploratory uses of scientific understanding, however, is recognizing that these specific acts do not exhaust the process of careful schematization and analogical unification. This is an evolving activity, one which Kant considers to be already ordered toward some practical forms of experience. What he achieves in the Analytic of Principles is but the first sketch of *the multi-form schematizing and analogizing of human meanings*, a complex process which he reconsiders, in a new light, in each of the subsequent *Critiques* and in his essays on history and religion.

In all these latter regions, moreover, he seeks to elucidate the difference between wishful dreaming and philosophically critical judgment. He kindles the sense of self-criticism in practical regions, by prolonging into them his findings on categorial analysis. The operation of schematizing and analogizing does not enjoy any autonomy, although it does make for diversification of experiential relations and modes of cognitivity. What become schematized and analogized are the perceptual and categorial meanings, especially those involved in the judgments of relation and modality. Thus the model established in the first *Critique* is never abandoned, even when it is being revised.

This persistent critical control is quite evident in Kant's theory of community. The judgment of reciprocity and community belongs among his relational categories, and his third analogy of experience is that of viewing it in this relation of reciprocity and community. Hence every assertion concerning physical or social communities must be scrutinized for the modality of that assertion and the grounds, shown in analysis of our modes of experiencing, for accepting the assertion under this concretely schematized and analogized form. The theory of schematism and analogy of principles serves, not as a license for speculative and practical rhapsodizing about societal forms, but as an instrument of control and criticism of the human mind's development of many modes of societal meaning and truth. By the same token, this theory serves as one of the unifying bases of Kant's entire philosophy in its synoptic aim.

Viewed in the light of this gradually prepared background, Jaakko Hintikka makes a contribution to some logical aspects of the theme of community. This theme keeps meeting him at the end of several distinct roads of inquiry. Notably, in trying to show the radical (and not just Quine's canonical) translatability of quantifiers, especially of the existential quantifier, he considers them in their meaning-in-use. This is to view the quantifiers in the context of the communal human activities of searching-looking-finding.

When existence is treated contextually, Hintikka states its meaning thus: "To be is to be (capable of being) an object of search."[43] There are two general implications of this concept of the ontic commitment. The connection between use of quantifiers and the activities of searching and finding requires: (a) that some underlying common field of search is understood as being given, and (b) that there is some mutual knowledge of what counts as finding the kind of object for which the search is made. It is not surprising that these implications should resemble the Kantian conception of the

---

[43] Jaakko Hintikka, "Behavioral Criteria of Radical Translation," in *Words and Objections: Essays on the Work of W. V. Quine*, eds. D. Davidson and J. Hintikka, p. 75. In a related essay, Hintikka amends the Kantian transcendental argument on space and time with these two contextual propositions: "The process by means of which we come to know the existence of individuals is that of searching for them. . . . The structure of a logical argument is due to the structure of the processes of searching for and finding" (Hintikka, "Kant on the Mathematical Method," *Kant Studies Today*, ed. Beck, p. 140).

physical and social worlds as developing their meaning through our human methods and activities, a meaning that is guided by the several senses of objectivity for which we seek. This resemblance is present, since Kant is also treating statemental meanings in their use and their setting of human activities. Community is a basic analogical way of conceiving a field of search and the interrelation of many such fields.

The parenthetical phrase in the above quoted statement reinforces the connection between the relational category of community and the modality of possibility. Hintikka notes that one common human sort of searching and finding consists in recognizing the same individual under different circumstances, courses of events, and other relational matrices. The individual's identity is not given in atomic isolation, but is discovered through different ways of profiling, cross-identification, or recognition of the same individual as belonging in different possible worlds or community contexts. This proportion between the individual's cross-world identity and the individuating functions in different possible worlds is a restatement, in modern logic, of Kant's respective analogies of substance and community in human experience.

Hence Hintikka refers to his concept of the individual as "a semantic neokantianism," which signifies a rethinking of Kant's own Analytic of Principles itself more than an extension of nineteenth-century neo-Kantianism.

> These "possible worlds" and the supply of individuating functions which serve to interrelate their respective members may enjoy, and in my view do enjoy, some sort of objective reality. However, their existence is not a "natural" thing. They may be as solidly objective as houses or books, but they are as certainly as these created by men (however unwittingly) for the purpose of facilitating their transactions with the reality they have to face. Hence my reasoning ends on a distinctly Kantian note. Whatever we say of the world is permeated throughout with concepts of our own making. Even such *prima facie* transparently sim-

ple notions as that of an individual turn out to depend on conceptual assumptions dealing with different possible states of affairs.[44]

We find Hintikka (in company with Husserl, Heidegger, and Strawson) establishing a contemporanizing relationship with Kant, as soon as he inquires about the suppositions required to make sense out of our ordinary and scientific conceptions of world, individual, and objectivity. Between the extreme poles of a purely logical analysis of these notions and their actual usage in life and specialized research, the task of philosophers in a Kantian tradition is to determine how the conceptual framework becomes adapted to our general judgments of objectivity, individuality, and existence. That is why the first *Critique* sections on the mind's activities of schematizing and analogizing are being so intensely scrutinized from different methodological standpoints today.

Although he has made some subtle correlations between Kant's noumenal-phenomenal distinction and his own distinction between the scientific and the manifest images of the world, Wilfrid Sellars' chief contribution to our theme lies in relating the theoretical framework to the practical and moral aspects of community. He characterizes this relationship in four ways, as being: thematic, mutually implicatory-and-coherent, ordered toward practical and morally categorical reasonableness, and interpretive of the functional meaning of humanity for Kant and our own age. Each of these traits helps to specify the philosophical theory of community and, at the same time, to give us a better historical grasp upon the Kantian source thereof.

(1) When Sellars subtitles his book on *Science and Metaphysics* as a set of "Variations on Kantian Themes," he is using the latter phrase in a somewhat extraordinary sense, not unrelated to Husserl's talk about *thematizing* a topic in Kant. This subtitle serves two related purposes. It characterizes at

---

[44] J. Hintikka, *Models for Modalities*, pp. 108-109, in the concluding section entitled: "Toward a Semantic Neokantianism."

least this portion of Sellars' own analytic work as "an attempt to exhibit the, to me at least, astonishing extent to which in ethics as well as in epistemology and metaphysics the fundamental themes of Kant's philosophy contain the truth of the variations we now hear on every side."[45] This is a way of stating our reverse historical criterion: to attain the sense and truth of many contemporary philosophical fragments, they must be replaced in their unifying contextual source and measure in Kant. This rule holds with special force for the often separated areas of epistemological and ethical problems, which Kant does show to be intimately correlated even when the details of his own mode of reintegrating them may be challenged.

This same subtitle also signifies the role of at least one intermediary philosopher between Kant and ourselves, thus suggesting a fresh line of historical genealogy and comparison. In referring to Charles Peirce as "this gifted composer of variations on Kantian themes," Sellars does more than recall the biographical fact of Peirce's early dedication to the writings of Kant and the indelible impression which such close study left upon every corner of the Peircean corpus itself. He also opens up a distinctive from-to path of historical continuity leading from Kant to the leading American philosophers since mid-nineteenth century. Peirce, James, and Royce were strongly attracted toward the Kantian conception of community and were careful to shape their own methodologies in a manner that would permit them to rethink Kantian community, and to do so with full recognition of its theoretical and practical interconnections.

(2) By bringing Kant into constant comparison with the Peircean tradition and restating them both in this joint perspective, Sellars engages in some historical as well as

[45] W. Sellars, *Science and Metaphysics: Variations on Kantian Themes*, p. x; the next quoted text is from *ibid.*, p. vii. For the American philosophical tradition on community, see P. L. Vetter, "The Theory of Community in Charles S. Peirce" (unpub. diss.); and James Collins, "Josiah Royce: Analyst of Religion as Community," in *American Philosophy and the Future*, ed. M. Novak, pp. 193-218.

analytic revisions. Often, Kant's statements on the effective presence of pure practical reason already in the elaboration of epistemology and metaphysics are treated—against his own intent—as an admission of the self-serving and arbitrary nature of theoretical systems and their concept formations. But instead, this involvement brings out (for Kant and Sellars alike) the value quality of scientific reasoning and the pervasive normative character of the standards of theoretical research and truth. The relationship of truth and normative value is one of *mutual implication and coherence*. There are ought-to-be's and ought-to-do's in the life of theoretical reason, just as there are imperatives in the sphere of practical reason, and the philosopher's aim is to work out a basis for their ultimate harmony and mutual penetration.[46]

When Sellars argues for an everyday life which feels the challenge of theoretical research and truth standards, as well as for a mode of theoretical inquiry which recognizes epistemic valuations and human agency, he is also recovering the historical intent of Kant. Nature and freedom are not sealed-off spheres but methodologically distinct aspects of our total human experience, aspects which make a demanding interpenetration of each other. Kant's *Critique of Judgment* sets this task of communication between nature and freedom for our reflective philosophical judgment; Peirce strives to develop a set of categories and interpretive principles embracing enough to achieve the relationship; and the ideal of their interpenetration prompts the central emphasis that Sellars places upon the epistemic-and-ethical community.

(3) Just as there is a Kantian presence of practicality in the theoretical order, so there is a Kantian presence of rea-

---

[46] *Science and Metaphysics*, pp. 175-176. On the epistemological and teleological basis for the Kantian communication between theoretical rigor, imperativity, and free action, cf. W. H. Bossart, "Kant's Doctrine of the Reciprocity of Freedom and Reason," *International Philosophical Quarterly*, 8 (1968), pp. 334-355; A. C. Genova, "Kant's Complex Problem of Reflective Judgment," *Review of Metaphysics*, 23 (1969-70), 452-480; and J. D. McFarland, *Kant's Concept of Teleology*.

sonableness in the practical and moral order. In reconstructing the Kantian moral point of view, Sellars probes into the
reasonableness of moral intentions, that is, the basis upon
which they carry a claim on the practical assent of rational
agents. There are two presuppositions supporting the reasonableness of intention in our moral judgment. Practical intending involves a claim to the assent of rational beings, because
of the intersubjective or communitarian form of the intending
act, as a practical judgment about what we together intend
to do. Thus *intersubjectivity* is one basic requirement for
moral reasonableness, but it is there along with a note of
value *imperativity*. The valuing acts of the sharers of the
intersubjective intention ought to agree with each other: the
reasonableness in question is not only practical but categorical, in respect to moral values sought together. Moral
intention is based upon practical reasonableness, or the intersubjectivity among men, and upon categorical reasonableness,
or the universality of making evaluations as members of a
community where there should be agreement. The community
of human action is, therefore, a jointly *practico-categorical*
meaning and reality.[47]

This Sellarsian theory of intersubjective and categorical
moral intention is a thematic variation on Kant's conception
of moral belief and his plural formulations of the categorical
imperative itself. The contemporary theory enables us to perceive more readily the philosophical import of Kant's defense
of moral belief against the charge of irrational wish-fulfill-
ment. Kantian belief must manifest its reasonable quality
through the practical openness and requiredness for the community of moral agents. Sellars gives a formalized restatement
of these traits, as the basic determinants of moral intention.

Moreover, there is a historical filiation between Kant,
Peirce, and Sellars in comparing the scientific community and
the ethical community. Both forms of community seek the
intended value of agreement among personal researchers and

[47] *Science and Metaphysics*, pp. 208-223.

moral agents, as incorporated into their respective centers of evaluation. Although the personal viewpoint is never eradicated, it is educated into making judgments as a community member, as one of us gathered together in actuation of the scientific and the moral intention. Kant himself expresses *this self-education into the community frame of reference* in terms of universal principles of legislation, impartial judgment, and pervasive natural laws. Peirce gives to laws of nature a long-run social connotation for science and morality. Sellars helps to translate these social aims into the present forms of analytic and phenomenological treatment of community structuring.

(4) Kant interweaves his themes of the intersubjectivity, practicality, and normativeness of experience through the practical ideal of *humanity*. This unifying conception is also kept alive in Sellars' remark that "roughly, to value from a moral point of view is to value *as a member of the relevant community*, which as far as the present argument is concerned, I shall assume to be mankind generally."[48] But he encounters difficulty in working out the two conditions under which the intersubjective intention can be securely construed as establishing the community of all rational beings in a moral union, such as the Kantian kingdom of persons as ends or members of the interpersonal community of humanity.

The fully humane intentional relationship would consist of *the epistemic and the ethical community* in synthesis. Sellars concedes to Kant and Peirce that all rational beings think of themselves as subject to common epistemic oughts, and hence as members implicitly of an epistemic community. But he does not find Kant and Peirce cogent enough on the real-

[48] *Science and Metaphysics*, p. 220; on pp. 223-229, Sellars questions the actual convergence of the epistemic and humanity-wide ethical imperatives. But Kant relies upon the common interpersonal nature of the scientific, ethical, and all other human forms of community. The pertinent Kantian argument rests on the correlative, analogical meanings of theoretical and practical objectivity and subjectivity, as studied by Bernard Rousset, *La Doctrine kantienne de l'objectivité*, and by Heinz Jansohn, *Kants Lehre von der Subjektivität*.

ity of a moral fact of reason. Sellars questions whether an agreement on the imperative to promote epistemic welfare also implies the intersubjective intention to promote human welfare as such and in its moral values. In daily life and human history, the moral conflicts and clashes of practical values prevent any easy acceptance of the conclusion that rational beings must also think of themselves as belonging implicitly to an ethical community of all mankind.

To bring this question again into the foreground of inquiry is a service to history of Kantian philosophy, as well as to ethics. For it prompts a more careful reading of Kant on the practicality of the idea of man and the unifying function of the question about man. Epistemic welfare itself is vulnerable, unless one is satisfied with a purely formal definition of a rational being or of relevant membership in the scientific community. When the epistemic intention and ought are attacked, *human values* are under threat, not only epistemic values. Indeed, epistemic welfare is already included within the conception of human welfare, which affords a common ground for the scientific and the ethical intentions of humanity. The Kantian demanding fact—whether of physical experience or of moral reason and freedom—is always mediated by converging reference to the practical ideal of humanity. Our acknowledgment of this reference can be beclouded and hindered, especially under the needs of practical living. But the intellectual resilience of Kantian philosophy, specifically its capacity for re-expression by means of pragmatic and analytic methods, stems from its unflagging concern for the theoretical and practical modes of developing the ideal of humanity.

That our adhesion to this ideal is subject to beclouding and hindrance, repudiation and renewal, however, furnishes the ground for considering the historical and religious sides of the question. Paul Ricoeur's distinctive accent can be detected here, since he shows that the Kantian critical philosophy is incompletely understood and inadequately related to contemporary methods, apart from its culminating treatment of man's historicity and religiousness. These latter topics have a direct bearing on the meaning of community and humanism, insofar as that meaning is open, in principle, both to setbacks and to growth. Both in his examination of Husserlian phenomenology and in his bridgemaking comparison between that philosophy and analytic procedures, Ricoeur returns to Kant for support and historical orientation. One way to conceive a closer relationship between the phenomenological and analytic approaches is to define for them a common task of learning, from Kant, to prolong the theme of the human community into its historical and religious interpretation of the evils and hopes of concrete living.

Just as the Kantian categories of relation receive their fruitful theoretical elaboration and empirical employment through the operations of schematizing and analogizing, so also they receive practical scope and power through the images furnished by history and religion. This practical concretizing enriches especially the meaning of human community, which cannot be abruptly halted at the most general level of the kingdom of ends or systematic interconnection of reasonable agents under intersubjective laws. Kant spurs a search for philosophically disciplined analyses of the *human family* developing in historical time, struggling with *radical evil* as an infection of human agency, and taking hope from the conception of itself as the *people of God*. These images of the human community in its moral freedom can no more be overlooked by a critical methodology than can the concrete ways of viewing man in relation to physical nature and the living environment.

Ricoeur seeks to make a cautious interpretation of the practical dimensions of human community, "with the guidance of that sense of limits which is perhaps the soul of the Kantian philosophy."[49] Under such guidance, speculative

---

[49] Ricoeur, *Husserl*, p. 176. Kant's doctrine on the concrete schemata and syntheses in our theoretical and practical life is a basic referent in Ricoeur's *Fallible Man*, pp. 63-121, just as the Kantian theory of human finitude under historical conditions of seeking truth permeates Ricoeur's *History and Truth*.

theories of history are always chastened by the reminder that, considered as a Kantian regulative idea, history sets a practical task for humanity that is never totally conceptualizable and achievable in social realities. The master conceptions of history are always analytic syntheses, that is, unifying but limited results of analysis of the community structures and tendencies of an age. That is why there is no wholly definitive formulation of historical processes and teleologies, which continue to remain plural and to conflict with each other at vital points. In this respect, Ricoeur finds that the historical study of Kant gives a judgmental basis for placing some epistemological limitations upon the Husserlian teleology of history, and for incorporating every speculative generalization about human history within a critically regulative framework.

Yet the Kantian sense of limits also operates to clarify the practical activities which do bind men together in ethical community, not solely under theoretical and technological ties. Hence to Sellars' account of the premises required for enlarging the demands of epistemic welfare to include those of human welfare inclusively considered, Ricoeur would add the practical act of a *Grundlegung*. This is Kant's term for *the foundation laying of recognition of others as free persons* having an intrinsic, not wholly instrumentalizable, value in themselves and in the union of humanity.

> The notable thing [in Kant] is his not having sought a "situation" for the person other than in his "belonging" (as member or as leader) to a practical and ethical totality of persons. Outside of this, one is no longer a person. One's existence can only be a value-existence. . . . Through respect the person is seen to be directly situated in a field of persons whose mutual otherness is founded on their irreducibility to means. Should the Other lose the ethical dimension which Kant calls his dignity (*Würde*), or his absolute price, should sympathy lose its quality of esteem, then the person becomes nothing more than a "merely natural

being" (*blosses Naturwesen*) and sympathy merely an animal affect.[50]

In its analogical forms, a Kantian *Grundlegung* internally constitutes both the field of research (Hintikka), the epistemic community (Sellars), and the field of persons (Ricoeur).

For Kant as philosopher of religion, the community of persons is not only practical and ethical but also religious. Respect for the interpersonal community can be lost or deliberately attacked, or else confused with those affective states which enjoy intense peaks but show little staying power of a moral quality. Hence the Kantian foundation laying of the ethical relationship among persons leads, by its own internal dynamism and the stresses of the human condition, toward a religious interpretation of the human community. When the conception of the kingdom of God is interpreted within a critical sense of limits, it enables men to continue regarding themselves as fellow members of an interpersonal community. Men of religious faith are still jointly subject to the costing ideal of moral humanity, even under the historical forms of diverse religious communities and churches.

At the outset of this chapter, I proposed the seminar experience as a symbol of the need for many ways of rendering Kant our contemporary. This significance is borne out by the complementary relationships between the scientific, phenomenological, and analytic restatements and criticism of his philosophy. In the process of living through such a seminar experience, however, we are likely to discover that something more than a plurality of contemporary modes of questioning is needed for historical knowledge of modern philosophy. At least two further traits of such historical understanding are

[50] Ricoeur, *Husserl*, pp. 199-200. The Kantian moral conception of person and humanity is closely analyzed by J. Schwartländer, *Der Mensch ist Person: Kants Lehre vom Menschen*, and is shown to have a strong socio-political aspect by J. G. Murphy, *Kant: The Philosophy of Right*.

rendered visible: the plural character of the source thinker's own insistential openings toward us, and the distinctive community of language and intention realized throughout common research and discussion on the source texts. It is not only that *we* must follow several routes for interpreting the mind of Kant, but that this mind *itself* can convey its meaning to us only through its many facets and many problematic openings toward the questions of today. Hence it belongs to the cautious historian to refuse the illusion of expecting some one utterly definitive contemporary mode of presenting Kant, just as it belongs within his office to give careful hearing to even the most indirect and partial contemporary analyses of Kant.

As a historical presence, the seminar understanding of Kant lives in the work of research and interchange of evaluations on the part of a representative company of interpreters. Together, they must specify the linguistic role of their use of language, its intention to co-explore and historically co-signify the arguments and unity of the source. Thus the Kant seminar serves to actuate a specific linguistic-cognitive community, unified by its common aim of relating the Kantian text historically to a wide circle of our own methods and problems. And once the theme of community is brought around to a fully reflexive application in Kant's case, this seminar pattern gains a more general signification for the other modern philosophers whom we also seek to explore more thoroughly in contemporary thought and language.

VI

Teleology of Historical
Understanding

In this concluding chapter, I will make a final try at probing
the knowledge pattern developed in history of modern philosophy. Until now, the emphasis has fallen upon the elements in our general theory and their unification in actual
historical writings and the learning situation. Were we to stop
the examination at this point, however, we would be omitting
one essential requirement and one distinctive viewpoint upon
the entire process of understanding the modern sources. For
the co-ingredient factors show their significance not only in
reference to some forms of their actual unification and expression but also in reference to the purposive ideals of the
historical interpreter himself. He has some abiding general
goals in mind, which shape the sense in which he will approach the specific source materials, the recognized procedures of research, and the contemporary points of
reference. Our conception of historical understanding would
be incomplete, then, without some formal treatment of those
historical purposes and values which appreciably affect the
entire work of interpretation.

We are shifting the perspective now from the order of specific actualization to that of possibility. Our concern is not
with a purely logical and definitional possibility, but rather
with that powerful medium of the comprehensive ideals and
aims which incite, sustain, and always surpass the results of
particular historical investigations. For historians of philosophy consistently measure any particular instance of using
the sources and framing the questions by standards also set

in terms of teleology. There is a teleological reference operating in their discipline to reinforce their adherence to proper research procedures, to unify their particular findings into a distinctive work of historical knowledge, and to urge them back into the modern sources once again for a more informed and pertinent reading. The historians' sense of never being fully faithful to the sources or fully serviceable to contemporary students expresses this comparison between achievement and unrealized purpose. Far from inducing discouragement, however, the teleological principle functions as a recuperative and newly spurring influence upon all members of the interpreting community. What Kant names as the regulative principle of knowledge is a very real factor, one which is experienced by every working historian of modern philosophy.

There will be no attempt here to make a full inventory or draw a complete picture of the telic considerations at play. The intellectual freemasonry among historians of philosophy encourages them to share in many common aims, without requiring them to do so in identical pattern and measure. Our general theory only requires us to recognize the presence of some recurrent aims and widely shared historical values, which are effectively realized in widely different forms and relationships. Most of these teleological factors have already been mentioned in passing, at different stages of the previous analysis, but they gather strength and consistency by being considered explicitly and together.

It is likely that the individual interpreter of modern philosophy will be responsive to some synthesis of the following five long-range purposes, around which our teleological analysis revolves. He will find himself seeking: to render the past thinkers more alive for present philosophical concerns; to take into account the full range of interpretant considerations in his research situation; to clarify what it means to be a great philosopher and to test some leading claimants to that name; to conduct the investigation in accord with the demands of the intent to do justice to all factors involved; and to keep

open and well travelled the northwest passage between history of modern philosophy and the fundamental meaning and
needs of humanity. No one can dictate to the historian that
he must subscribe to each of these aims or how he must unify
them, in the pursuit of his own historical project. But in one
form and relationship or another, most of them do become
functionally ingredient in his interpretation in virtue of the
general methodology and kind of knowledge involved. Hence
they serve to incorporate the many restricted and variant intentions of historians into that general purposive intent which
marks the tradition of modern philosophizing and its historical study.

1. OUR PHILOSOPHICAL PAST: FROM BURDEN TO RESOURCE

Historians of philosophy share with other historians the
problem that, whereas a study of the past may well provide
support and guidance for men today, it can also have the
effect of dampening their hopes and sense of original activity.
Neither potentiality of the historical mode of thinking can be
glossed over as being inconsequential for an understanding
of that aspect of philosophy. To recognize the ambiguity of
the historical principle in our philosophizing is to take the
first salutary step toward developing a realistic response to
the problem. For the ambiguity signifies that we are not fore-
doomed to be laden down by the modern philosophical tradition, since we retain sufficient freedom of interpretation to
insure that its presence will become resourceful rather than
burdensome for us. The teleological principle inclines us to
grapple with this alternative and to present the modern
sources in a nonstifling fashion, as far as present philosophical creativity is concerned.

It is useful to notice that the great modern philosophers
themselves had to face this same question of relating some historical past to their own philosophical plans. Hume's essays
are filled with the topic of the ambiguity of one's historical

heritage in every field of endeavor. The following long passage formulates in everyday language his dialectic between the weightiness and the sustenance of history, whether considered in literature or science or philosophy.

> A man's genius is always, in the beginning of life, as much unknown to himself as to others; and it is only after frequent trials, attended with success, that he dares think himself equal to those undertakings, in which those who have succeeded have fixed the admiration of mankind. If his own nation be already possessed of many models of eloquence, he naturally compares his own juvenile exercises with these; and, being sensible of the great disproportion, is discouraged from any further attempts, and never aims at a rivalship with those authors whom he so much admires. A noble emulation is the source of every excellence. Admiration and modesty naturally extinguish this emulation; and no one is so liable to an excess of admiration and modesty as a truly great genius. . . . If we consider the shortness of human life, and our limited knowledge, even of what passes in our own time, we must be sensible that we should be for ever children in understanding, were it not for this invention [of history], which extends our experience to all past ages, and to the most distant nations; making them contribute as much to our improvement in wisdom, as if they had actually lain under our observation. A man acquainted with history may, in some respect, be said to have lived from the beginning of the world, and to have been making continual additions to his stock of knowledge in every century.[1]

Here, Hume is proposing the problem of how we can pass from the condition of being "children in understanding" in

[1] David Hume, *Essays Moral, Political and Literary*, pp. 136-137, 561. Hume's crucial role in stating the problem of historical tradition and creative originality, and in preparing for the romantic cultivation of imagination and personal perceptiveness, is set forth in W. Jackson Bate's *The Burden of the Past and the English Poet*, pp. 80-107. Hume's historical realism looms large in Gay, *The Bridge of Criticism*, pp. 39-47, 159-61.

our discipline to being men of historical experience in it, without suffering the atrophy of our sense of originality, our sense of confidence in being able to surpass the previous achievements. In the specific terms of our inquiry, he asks how to reconcile historical study of philosophical sources with that spirit of "noble emulation" which impels us to bring forth fresh methods and conceptual patterns, marking an advance in philosophical understanding.

Hume warns against falling victim to a menacing idol of our own creation: that of a philosophical past which enjoys a monopoly upon all creative energies and hence which can only depreciate and snuff out our independent efforts. The remedy is neither to surrender our initiatives to this idol nor to flee from all historical considerations, but rather to engage in a twofold act of self-education. First, our liberating imagination enables us to regard earlier philosophers as our older companions and teachers. They enter our presence in order to enable us to share in mankind's developing experience, especially as it reaches the form of reflective methods and argumentation. To relate ourselves with the philosophical tradition as we do with more experienced friends and teachers, is to regard it as a source of educative reflection and not of granitic imposition upon us.

The other imaginative act is to relocate the entire philosophical activity, in its present theorizing as well as its historical reconsidering, upon what Hume calls "a fresh soil." We must search for an intellectual terrain and mode of communication which will establish a new "league between the learned and conversable worlds," that is, between the philosopher's formal and historical modes of reasoning and the experience of everyday living and conversing.[2] The conversable world—the domain of daily experience and discussion—constantly opens up problems and perspectives which

[2] Hume, *Essays Moral, Political and Literary*, pp. 138, 569. That philosophers must give due regard to their forms of expression, in order to bind together the learned and conversable worlds and the literatures of knowledge and moral power, is the theme of Brand Blanshard's essay *On Philosophical Style*.

provoke new philosophical responses to the historical sources as well as to current theories. A mind that grows historically, along with the human community of philosophers of many ages, is better prepared for perceiving the new philosophical opportunities which arise in everyday experience. Between the learned world of history of philosophy and the conversable world of existence today, there can develop (although it is not inevitable) a cooperative relationship which will enable contemporary philosophers to strengthen their originative thinking and contributions.

A linguistic sign of such fruitful cooperation is that we can cease to speak abstractly and uncritically about "*the* philosophical past" and can learn, rather, to refer to "*our* philosophical past." This more intimate, social-incorporative usage manifests the historian's teleology, his goal of achieving a historical presence and presential act for the modern sources. It is not enough to distinguish between the dated-and-passed present, belonging uniquely to the source thinker, and his communicational presence for us and our philosophizing. The careful historian also tries to determine the precise sense in which some modern philosopher's method, principles, and arguments can become historically ours as well as being originatively his own.

They do not become historically ours through any invasion or immediate, dominating entrance into our act of philosophizing. Rather, the source contributions come to us through a certain analogy worked out in the course of a historical interpretation. The skilled historian helps us to envision a similarity between the traits and problems of human experience, as they provoked the response of a source philosopher, and those traits and problems which are incitive of our own philosophical methods and arguments. Such recognition of similarity amid the differences supposes that we are conducting our own philosophical inquiries in that historical spirit which will permit a free and responsible relationship with the modern sources to develop. Through the mediating theme of "our philosophical past," then, these sources encourage our present theorizing and do not render it in any way superfluous.

Two philosophers of the just recently passed generation—Maurice Merleau-Ponty and J. L. Austin—can serve as our instructors on this facet of historical teleology. The former views the move from an oppressive to an enlightening past from the standpoint of the historian's exercise of discriminating judgment, as he represents the bond of encouraging likeness and liberating difference between source philosophers and ourselves.

> Rather than "explaining" a philosophy, the historical approach serves to show how its significance exceeds its circumstances, and how as an historical fact it transmutes its original situation into a means of understanding it and other situations. . . . What counts certainly is that thinking life called Descartes, whose fortunately preserved wake is his works. The reason why Descartes is present is that—surrounded by circumstances which today are abolished, and haunted by the concerns and some of the illusions of his times—he responded to these hazards in a way which teaches us to respond to our own, even though they are different and our response is different too.[3]

The concrete facts and concerns of a Descartes' original situation are not purely incidental, either to his own shape of thought or to the problems encountered in our historical interpretation of that thought. We have used the situational determinateness of the Cartesian theory of order as a case study, in our previous analysis of the insistential nature of source texts. This situational determinateness does not block our efforts to gain some historical understanding of the Cartesian theory of order, but it does require us to specify the meaning and bearing of that theory in such fashion that they

---

[3] Merleau-Ponty, *Signs*, pp. 128, 130. Speculative problems concerning the nature of the past and its self-surpassing move toward the present are the central theme of Paul Weiss's *History: Written and Lived*, Part I: "The Recovery of the Past," pp. 23-110.

become related to our own reflections as a historical presence, not as an invading force. In the very act of gaining some historical comprehension of Descartes on the meaning of order, we also perceive that the freedom of present philosophizing about order is thereby strengthened, instead of being inhibited.

Austin's contribution consists in showing, from the standpoint of the originative minds themselves, that a certain self-limiting intention operates to respect the temporal differences and the need for new departures on a continuing theme in philosophy: "Although I am not sure importance is important: truth is. . . . I dreamt a line that would make a motto for a sober philosophy: *Neither a be-all nor an end-all be*."[4] Invested as they are in Austin's typical ambiance of stringency and simplicity, these statements are instructive not only about his analytic approach but also about a position widely shared by modern philosophers and their historians. Hence his words are relevant for our general theory of historical understanding.

It is a question here of how the search for truth involves a correlative act of self-restriction concerning one's own claim of contributing to philosophical truth. What sets off the philosopher decisively from braying men is his ruthless subordination of the quest for importance to the quest for truth. It is this sane ordering of objectives which kindles the affinity between ourselves and some past thinker, as we observe in him this same tug of motivations and this eventual subordination of other considerations to truth.

Amid all the vaunting claims of a philosopher and all the Dionysan celebrations of his followers, there is a quiet moment when he espouses in full strength the motto: *Neither a be-all nor an end-all be*. His thought cannot equate itself with the whole of philosophy and cannot claim to bring philosophical inquiries on truth to a halt. This motto is a good symbol of a philosopher's rockbottom acceptance of the discipline of community inquiry, plural conflicting interpreta-

---

[4] Austin, *Philosophical Papers*, p. 271 and note 1.

tions, and the continuous historical growth of new conceptions. No philosophy (whether in its originative act or in its historical configurations and influence) adequately exhausts our human potentiality for reflective work, and hence no philosophy is a terminus beyond which there can be opportunity only for reiteration, manicuring, and the ultimate death of philosophical creativity.

How does the historian of modern philosophy incorporate this self-limiting and self-opening intent of the source thinkers into his methodology? He does so in a manner comparable to Kant's procedure for stating the several formulations of the categorical imperative. Just as Kant takes pains to qualify each such statement with the general directive: *Act in such a manner that,* so the reflective historian qualifies every procedural statement with the general direction: *Interpret in such a manner that.* Along with the analysis of this or that component in historical understanding comes the connotative requirement that the component must be taken as serving, rather than as thwarting, the general teleological program of transforming our philosophical past from the condition of burden to that of a present resource. A teleologically well instructed historical judgment will relate the sources and the contemporary philosophizers in such fashion that the integrity of each is respected, at the same time as their mutual bearing is established. Negatively, this means an avoidance of the categories of conquest and oppression, whether from the side of the source or from that of the most recent theorizing mind. And positively, the manner of interpreting should teach us how to comport ourselves in a perpetuating company of fellow inquirers, where the insistential minds in the modern tradition serve intentionally as guides for our contemporary speculation.

The imperative for always making a liberating interpretation of the historical presence of sources is best observed in action, as the historian employs the modes of interrelation. We have designated these interdependencies under the headings of: the radial thinker, the from-to span, and the continuative problem. These relationships can be studied woodenly or with historical perceptiveness, depending upon whether the liberative sense of the injunction *to interpret in such a manner that,* is disregarded or kept central. Only under the latter condition, do these forms of historical interrogation conjointly satisfy the teleology of the interpreting process and meet the needs of contemporary theorizing.

There are two ways of strengthening the theme of the radial mind, in order to vivify the source relationship. First, we can move beyond the initial point of finding some striking illustrations of this quality to the more searching task of determining the sense in which *every* modern philosopher realizes it, in his peculiar fashion. Leibniz is indeed preeminently radial in his theory of finite minds, his study of sources, and his correspondence with contemporaries. But the radial quality is present in some manner and degree in the other modern philosophers as well, so that the interrelational questioning based upon it cannot be omitted anywhere in the historical study of modern sources. Once the question about radiality is seen to qualify the historical mode of interpreting as such, the distinctive forms of interconnection stand forth and encourage the working hypothesis that the radial striving reaches as far as the source philosopher's bearing upon our present discussion of problems.

The second step can then be taken, namely, to show that such radial relationships help to establish the categories of continuant freedom, rather than those of oppressive destiny, as the appropriate ones for grasping the modern philosophical tradition. The seed of free discussion and integrity of contesting minds is already planted in a modern philosopher's relationship with his own contemporaries. He may judge them harshly and be impatient under the lash of their criticism; he may emphasize everything that is distinctive and as yet unfamiliar about his method; and he may treat opposing theories as being special regions within his embracing system. And yet the other philosophers *do* retain their originative energy and their own active orientations. There is an intersection of differing horizons and organizing visions, each of which benefits from the interchange without suffering the loss of its own creativity. Hence we may infer that when a source philosopher's radiating significance prolongs itself into our presence, it will increase the vigor of contemporary philosophizing and not shrivel it.

It is the historian's duty, furthermore, to draw more methodological significance from the from-to type of comparison than the first-level description of connections requires. When we agree to study a philosophy in the historical spirit and not as a collage of abstract theses, we find it to be already deeply involved in the process of being mediated, qualified, and reoriented in one respect or another. For this is the living process which furnishes the historical grounds for taking the from-to approach to that philosophy. Its capacity to educate us in an understanding of its problems and ours does not suddenly manifest itself to the present generation of students. The judgment about a source's latent capacity of meanings and its accessibility for subsequent minds rests upon that source's *gradual* achievement of continuing historical presence, that is, upon its involvement already for some time in the kind of interpretive relationships which underlie the from-to interrogation of a historian. Thus the historical intelligibility of modern sources is neither an arbitrary postulate nor an over-benevolent conception of historical presence, but a general way of acknowledging the fabric of interrelations which a from-to analysis is designed to explore.

Several times in the course of the general theory, we have used the distinction between actual genetic dependence and theoretical comparability among philosophies originating in different times. The usefulness of this distinction testifies to the tenacity with which productive philosophers (whether personally of a historical bent or not) pursue one kind or another of interrelational interpretation of the modern sources. Should a limit be reached in the strictly genetic form of a from-to relationship, then there would be no reluctance in framing other questions based on a typology of methods and doctrines rather than upon direct interdependence among the sources. This is the functional counterpart, in present theoretical practice, to the distinction we have drawn between the from-to question and the continuative problem. This distinction not only serves the purposes of historical interpretation but also places the outcome of such interpretation at the intellectual disposal of contemporary philosophizing.

We can now offer a teleological meaning for "continuative problem," insofar as this category bridges the difference between historical work and present theorizing. The language and problems of historical continuity do not concern a completed and distanced past, one which would (if somehow bodily transported) compete with and menace our original philosophizing. Rather, a study of continuative problems is an effective means of participating in the continuing life of our philosophical past. It permits us to follow the course of human reflections on such central themes as space and time, perception and truth, ethical rules and values, and to learn that this tradition courses its way into our own wondering on the same themes. With the help of historical interpretations of these continuative problems, we are introduced to the experiential bases, the diverging and converging positions, and the steady growth of a family language—all of which flux into our own reflections and belong among the factors to be weighed in any new interpretations. Realization of this abiding influence of historical sources is likely to lead us to reformulate the problem of overburdening our minds. What becomes really burdensome and dampening on human energy is not the historical approach, but rather any treatment of continuant problems which fails to recognize the historical dimension and to make full use of developmental findings.

In addition to the main issue of relating history and present philosophizing, there is also a reflexive difficulty confronting historians of philosophy. Are not their own historical projects smothered under the long shelves of monographs and multivolume works, articles and dissertations, constituting the record of historical research in modern philosophy? Even without making a formal comparison between the historical work done in the nineteenth and the twentieth centuries, it is evident that previous accomplishments have not stifled the creativity of historians in our century.[5] There has been a steady evolution of new study methods and modes of historical synthesis, suggesting that the historiography of modern philosophy is just as open-ended as is the development among the modern philosophers themselves.

Indeed, there is a close mutual bond between growth of new philosophical theories and the possibility of new historical conceptions. One reason why the history of philosophy has made the turn into contemporary thought is that the analytical and naturalistic, the phenomenological and existential, philosophies which define that turn are also engaged in releasing new instruments for questioning and explicating

[5] Compare L. Geldsetzer, *Die Philosophie der Philosophiegeschichte im 19. Jahrhundert*, and the twentieth-century essays edited by E. Castelli, *La filosofia della storia della filosofia*. Drawing upon his own mature experience as a historian of modern philosophy, Martial Guéroult identifies the central problem as that of reconciling the historicity and the truth-orientation of all forms of philosophy. He reaches these conclusions on the foundation for historical interpretation of all philosophical sources. "1. Every philosophy, even in the act of breaking from the past which affirms its advent, cannot separate itself from that collection of relationships which links it to the universe of the philosophical systems and makes both interdependent. 2. Unlike the scientist, the philosopher cannot initiate himself in philosophy except through its history; it is by going to school to past philosophers that he becomes a philosopher himself. 3. Whereas historical and scientific interests are radically separated, philosophical and historical interests are intimately intermingled. The most original philosopher can pose or renew philosophical problems only by referring to past philosophies he opposes. Hence his necessary interest in history. If the historian of philosophy turns historian, it is in view of what past doctrines may be harboring of immanent philosophical content. His philosophical interest cannot be dissociated from his historical interest" ("The History of Philosophy as a Philosophical Problem," *The Monist, 53* [1969], 583). Thus the specific conditions of creativity in philosophy demand, rather than exclude, the work of historical interpretation, just as the latter leads toward and not away from philosophical judgments concerning the meaning and truth of things.

the historical sources. The prospects for creative work in history of philosophy are delicately calibrated with those which continue to emerge in every type of philosophical method and conceptual scheme. Thus if historical studies can make some contribution to current philosophizing, this debt is more than repaid by the new potencies of interpretation which this philosophizing makes available (whether deliberately or inadvertently) to the aware historian of philosophy.

Our previous analysis of the ways of the responsive interpreter supplies some internal grounds for concluding that historical work in modern philosophy has scarcely begun to realize its diverse forms and capacities. The historian must remain responsive not only to advances made in philosophical methods but also to the scientific, artistic, and societal developments in our century. A new physical concept, an innovation in music or writing, a change in social behavior and interrelations among peoples—each such development brings along with it a wake of suggestions and questions which may have unsuspected bearings upon our ways of reading and representing the modern philosophers. Whether these possible clues will actually lead anywhere in historical interpretation, is the responsibility of historians to discover through their actual tries at a new understanding. There is always an experimental dimension to historical work in modern philosophy, undermining the appearance that repetition and routine govern all approaches.

Indeed, the historical mind is always rescanning the prose of the historical world of modern philosophy, always striving to render anew its basic significance and the analogy of its problems with our own.[6] Interpretations cannot remain rigid and immobile, operating like a standard vise which clamps down upon our eyes as we begin to study a philosophical

---

[6] An analogy is suggested here with M. Merleau-Ponty's fragmentary project, *The Prose of the World*, tr. John O'Neill, with acknowledgment made to Hegel's use of the phrase. My theme of "the prose of the historical world of modern philosophy" relates the insistential modern sources to the continuing tradition of their historical interpreters.

source. The best interpretations remain essentially open to re-seeing and re-saying, not because they are vague and only loosely founded in the texts, but because the texts themselves maintain a perennial insistency of their own and refuse to close off their discourse with the now living generation of men. The insistential thought of the source philosophers is constantly repoising itself for shaping another relationship with developing mankind. Yet the new significance does not automatically express itself, apart from the act of interpretation. This is the authorization for new work on the part of historians. They must continue to rethink and restate the prose of modern philosophy, for only through their activity can that prose utter still another living word and become a living historical presence for a new generation of men.

2. THE HISTORIAN OF PHILOSOPHY AND HIS INTERPRETANTS

In defense of his own art, the sculptor Isamu Noguchi makes this observation:

They say in Japan that the end interest of old men is stone —just stone, natural stone, ready-made sculptures for the eyes of connoisseurs. This is not quite correct; it is the point of view that sanctifies; it is selection and placement that will make of anything a sculpture, even an old shoe.[7]

Something similar holds between the student of history of philosophy and the works which he comes to prize. These works are not just natural stones strewn along the beach and imposing their shapes of thought upon him. For in our human world there is no *philosophie trouvée*, no body of reflective work just lying there to be beheld, but rather there are textual sources standing in need of our historical "selection and placement." Not only are judgment, interpretation, and art required for the original statement to appear, but these same acts are the necessary conditions for establishing our his-

[7] Isamu Noguchi, *A Sculptor's World*, p. 39.

torical relation of comprehension and evaluation in respect to the philosophical work. Each interpreter must achieve his own perspective and compare it with other ways of taking the original meaning, so that the act of philosophizing continues itself into the art of historical interpreting. In philosophy and its history, the point of view does illuminate, even though it may not sanctify.

The establishing, amending, and interrelating of respective points of view upon the modern philosophical sources furnish the functional basis and testing grounds for the present theory of historical understanding. It will now be helpful to discover how many aspects of that theory can survive an independent appraisal, made with the help of Charles Peirce's conception of semiosis and the kinds of interpretants. He worked out this doctrine in three mature writings of the years 1906-1909: his *Monist* article on "Prolegomena for an Apology for Pragmaticism," his unpublished manuscript entitled "A Survey of Pragmaticism," and his correspondence with Lady Welby.[8] Peirce confessed to Lady Welby that, in tackling the problem of interpretants, he was a pioneer or, more precisely a rude backwoodsman and first-comer into this intellectual territory. Although he had spent a lifetime in the study of other aspects of sign theory, he found himself groping at this point and conceded that he could not yet bring his thought about interpretants entirely out of the mist. Perhaps it is for this very reason that his reflections, although coming from his ripest years, also carry the fertile power of the *Grundgedanke* which Schelling advises us to seek in the formative expressions of a philosophy. In any case, Peirce's theme lends itself to transformations and analogous use in other contexts, in-

---

[8] *Collected Papers of Charles Sanders Peirce*, ed. C. Hartshorne, P. Weiss, and A. Burke: 4.536 (from "Prologomena for an Apology for Pragmaticism," *The Monist*, 16 [1906], 492-546); 5.470-491 (from "A Survey of Pragmaticism"); 8.184-185 (manuscript note intercalated in a review of Lady Welby's *What is Meaning?*); 8.343 (partial draft of a letter to Lady Welby); and *Charles S. Peirce's Letters to Lady Welby*, ed. I. A. Lieb, pp. 25-32 (*Letter of December 23, 1908*), pp. 34-40 (*Letter of March 14, 1909*).

cluding our working hypothesis on historical searching for the intent and import of modern philosophy.

Weaving together his several scattered expositions, we can express his position through the following outline as adapted for our own purpose of clarifying the nature and methodic elements in historical understanding.

A Peircean Theory of Interpretants

I. Interpretants: proper significate effects or outcome of action of signs, determining an interpreter toward objects thus signified.

II. Kinds of Interpretants:

  1. *Immediate*: peculiar interpretability of each sign, its own possibility of specifying an interpreting process.

  2. *Dynamical*: direct effect actually produced upon the individual interpreting mind or minds, distinctive actual uses of signs as:

    (a) *emotional*: feeling of recognition and familiarity.

    (b) *energetic*: action, especially mental effort with signs.

    (c) *logical*: development of meaning of intellectual general concepts, telically ordered toward ultimate interpretant.

  3. *Final or Ultimate Logical*: self-analytical habit deliberately formed, that effect which a sign would produce on any mind if the sign were sufficiently considered, worked out, and brought to fully developed meaning. Teleological unity of immediate and dynamic interpretants in a continuing, unrestricted community of interpreters.

III. Semiosis: action of signs, their influence upon the interpreter as achieved through the several kinds of interpretants.

Our present purpose is neither to make a close exegesis of Peirce's own justifying texts for their own sake nor to attempt a reconciliation of his various statements with each other and the rest of his philosophy. Instead, we will use this rough framework as a basis of commentary upon our general theory of historical interpretation, viewing its teleological aspect in the light of the Peircean interpretants and semiosis.

I. Our special concern is with interpretants in their historical functions. Peirce provides us with a general way of conceiving the difference between considering modern philosophies as so many "Japanese natural stones strewn along the beach" and considering them precisely as involved in the historical operations of analyzing, criticizing, and appreciating on the part of the interpreters. A source philosopher's basal act of philosophizing realizes itself in spoken and written words, in all those textual forms through which he succeeds in communicating. Like all other signifying realities, his surviving writings (what Merleau-Ponty memorably terms his "fortunately preserved wake") are mediating principles of meaning. They tell something *about* his method and consequential pattern of reflective argument, and they tell this *to* the investigating mind of an interpreter.

Peirce's own concise statement on this mediating and communicating function cannot be surpassed: "I define a Sign as anything which is so determined by something else, called its Object, and so determines an effect upon a person, which effect I call its Interpretant, that the latter is thereby mediately determined by the former."[9] There is a textual opening from the source philosophy in its insistential act, responding to which is an interrogative and judgmental opening toward the source philosophy on the part of the inquiring reader. The historical interpretant is not a separate entity apart from source and inquirer, but is a distinct aspect in the factorial analysis of this sign relationship in historical understanding. We attain to the historical interpretant at that point in the analysis when we learn to consider the textual writing *as a complex sign-source* engaged in achieving its historical presence, that is, precisely as determining the inquirer to under-

---

[9] Peirce, *Letters to Lady Welby*, p. 29. Analyses of Peirce's theory of interpretants are made by George Gentry, "Habit and the Logical Interpretant," in *Studies in the Philosophy of Charles Sanders Peirce*, first series, ed. P. P. Wiener and F. H. Young, pp. 75-90; J. J. Fitzgerald, *Peirce's Theory of Signs as Foundation for Pragmatism*, pp. 71-90; and A. J. Ayer, *The Origins of Pragmatism*, pp. 122-136, 156-168.

stand something about the originative philosophy under investigation.

In two specific respects, the notion of a historical interpretant helps to sharpen the methodological and epistemological issues. For one thing, this notion stresses the *actional* basis of every relationship constituting the interpretation of sources. It is not accidental that the statement of our general theory of historical interpretation is saturated with active verbal forms: the insistential, demanding, manyshaping acts of the source thinker, as well as the interrogating, comparing, and synthesizing acts of the interpreter. This language is appropriate to an actional relationship, whose general formal properties are stated in the theory of historical interpretants.

As a second contribution, this theory explicitly includes the condition of there being *plural* forms of actional influence of signs upon the interpreter. Even a highly general semiotic must study the varieties of sign-actions and hence the various modes of interpretant determinations. This rings true to the more concrete situation presented by historical studies of modern philosophy. There is no singularly privileged, one-channel path of interpretation linking a source philosophy with a historical inquirer. At every turn in our analysis, we have found the modes of signification to be various and deliberately variated, whether they come from the source thinker's fertile use of arguments and modes of expression or from the historian's ways of questioning and interrelating. Whether based upon functional reflection of the actualities of historical interpretation or upon a general logical analysis of the significate outcome of sign action, therefore, a theory of historical understanding requires that the historical interpretants be both actional and multiperspectival in nature.

II. 1. It is not the aim of *an immediate kind of historical interpretant* to smuggle in some note of intuitional immediacy, which would be foreign both to Peirce's philosophy and to our historical theory and its experiential basis. Rather, the immediate interpretant simply designates a restricted phase in our analysis of the bond of meaning which develops between the originative source and its interpreter. The philosophical source offers itself as a historical presence under these definite conditions: concrete distinctiveness, possible meaning-conveyance, and prospect for continuing interpretation. And reciprocally, the interpreter's search for historical presence is specified in an initial, and as yet unanalyzed, openness to the source and its conditions of signifying itself. The immediate historical interpretant is a way of considering, in conjunction, both the potential giving of the source fundament to the inquirer and the potential giving of the inquirer to the task of interpreting this fundament.

The sign-complexus which is *this* source work, rather than some other one, already presents itself with some concrete definiteness to the interpreter. It makes a difference in his expectation and preparation that he is setting out to study the *Meditations* of Descartes rather than the *Phenomenology* of Hegel. His background work and the kind of questioning being brought into a state of readiness are already becoming differentiated by the historical shape of the former work and its context. Moreover, the rich context of Cartesian studies suggests, by anticipation, that the *Meditations* bears the promise of interpretability in the philosophical mode. This work comes in the form of a *proposal* that it may offer philosophical meaning and thus furnish an opportunity for a specifically philosophical sort of historical interpretation, rather than some other kind of response to its historical shape. The *Meditations* offers itself as a philosophic fundament, requiring certain methodological and analytical acts on the interpreter's part in order to comprehend its specific significance. The immediate interpretant characterizes the joint achievement of source and investigator, in constituting the fundamental recognition that here is an open possibility for working out a specific historical meaning in the philosophical order.

Insofar as it combines the notes of distinctive concretion and invitation to interpret, a source work such as the *Meditations* begins its second life as a historical determinant in the tradition of interpreting minds. There is historical wisdom, and not only categorial rule, impacted in Peirce's account of the immediate interpretant. It constitutes "the total unanalyzed effect that the Sign is calculated to produce, or naturally might be expected to produce; and I have been accustomed to identify this with the effect the sign first produces or may produce upon a mind, without any reflection upon it."[10] In the case of the historical type of immediate interpretant, the "natural" basis of expectation concerning the possible nature of the meaning of the sign-source arises from the tradition of historical interpretation of that source work, within the history of philosophy. Within this context, we are already predisposed to treat the *Meditations* as a resource in the philosophical order, even before we reflect formally on this identification and begin to test its soundness. The actual stages of historical interpretation would never get underway in the particular instance, were there not this general orientation of the interpreter in the presence of a source work as belonging in the matrix of historical interpretability within a philosophical tradition.

II. 2. The *dynamical interpretants* are the heartland of the actual interpreting work in history of philosophy. A preliminary orientation in possibility is attained through the immediate interpretant, just as a teleological ideal becomes operative through the final or ultimate logical interpretant. But the everyday tasks and values of historical research emerge most clearly and properly in the form of dynamical interpretants. For this is the realm of actual response given by the individual interpreter and the supporting community of historians of philosophy. The devising and employing of methods, the performance of analytic inspection and criticism, the acts of synoptic unification and evaluation, and the gradual flowering of historical understanding of the sources— these are the specific kinds of sign determination which constitute the dynamic interpretants. The major responsibility

[10] Peirce, *Letters to Lady Welby*, p. 35.

of historians is to keep improving those dynamical interpretants which give historical access to the modern sources and their contemporary implications.

This complex development of interpretants can be understood only through some distinctive lines of factorial analysis, signified by the subdivisions of the dynamical interpretants. The subkinds of dynamical interpretants permit us to distinguish and follow certain aspects in the growth of historical meaning, but without authorizing any inference that these subkinds are separate entities or successive stories in a chronicle. On the contrary, the types of historical dynamic interpretants refer to some traits which pervade our *entire* relationship with the modern philosophical sources, and do not refer to different regions or serial episodes in the interpretation of these sources.

II. 2 (a). One feature of the historical mind is finely delineated in Peirce's *emotional interpretant*. He describes this significate effect of sign action as "that feeling of recognition," or again as "a feeling which we come to interpret as evidence that we comprehend the proper effect of that sign." It is "such familiarity as gave a person familiarity with a sign and readiness in using it or interpreting it. In his consciousness he seemed to himself to be quite *at home* with the Sign. In short, it is Interpretation *in Feeling*."[11] In his early articles on pragmatism, Peirce assigns the elucidation of this feeling as the first grade of clearness or the first step in the clarification of meaning. But the emotional interpretant is not a lower rung that is eventually left behind. For Peirce intends to view it in terms of his category of firstness, which remains incorporated as a permanent spring of freshness in every growth of knowledge. Hence in his mature theory of interpretants, he states explicitly not only that the emotional interpretant persists but also that every other mode of dynamic interpretant develops through its medium and ministration.

[11] Peirce, *Collected Papers*, 5.475, and 8.185.

We do not have to reflect very long upon the experience of doing work in modern philosophy, before we discover the bearing thereon of Peirce's emotive historical interpretant. A student does not remain forever on the threshold marked by only the possibility of discovering meaning in a source work, but soon plunges into the actual work of interpreting it. His first aim is to become somewhat familiar with this work and its structure of theory. That process is personal and different for each inquirer but, whatever his individual pace and approach, he waits for a time when he can say that he is beginning to feel at home with the chosen philosopher and his texts. It is just as important for an interpreter to come to feel at home with his sources as it is for any of us to feel at home in the world, however differently we may designate that world through our own interests and activities.

There are many modes of familiarity achieved in the historical study of modern philosophy. There is the initial sense of entering into a distinctive philosophical presence and textual structure, the sense of finding one's way around for the first time in this region. This is the prelude of gaining sufficient preliminary orientation and confidence to begin a closer reading, to launch out upon an advanced plan of research and criticism. We must experience and reflect upon this basic feeling of at-homeness with our source, before we gain the assurance required for making an original interpretation of the philosopher. And that feeling of at-homeness is never abandoned, only corroborated and deepened with every further act of study.

If the historian persists in his work and is fortunate, then the sense of familiarity will mature into the act of recognition, similar to the condition of returning to a friend's home after an absence. And should our return visit be sufficiently prolonged and intensive, the historical emotional interpretant may manifest itself in a truly comfortable feel for the source philosopher's language, his understanding of problems, and his characteristic use of methods and principles for attacking them. We sometimes express this deepened emotional interpretant in a phrase indicating historical companionship with (for instance) "our friend John Locke," even though we may be just as strenuously critical of Locke's philosophy as were the Stillingfleets and Leibnizes of his own day. We interpret such determinations and their expression as evidence of our attaining sufficient comprehension of Locke's philosophy so that, thereafter, we can make our own historical interpretation and independent assessment of it.

A similar process of familiarization is followed in studying the comparative aspects of history of philosophy. Here, one must gradually grope around in the complex signification of Locke as a critic of Descartes, or of Locke's specific contributions to the continuative problem of certainty and opinion, or again of the ingrediency of Lockean thought in the subsequent argumentation of a Berkeley or Hume. The cautious student must first find his own way around in these interrelations and in the practice of interrelational questioning, using the landmarks of previous historical interpretation as well as the pertinent source writings. From the educational standpoint, then, a major purpose of the seminar in history of philosophy is to furnish the setting and specific instruments for developing familiarity with the interconnections among modern philosophies. When the seminar members come to see that certain meanings cannot be properly apprehended in the isolated philosopher or in a purely abstract formalization, but require a specifically comparative mode of consideration, they are responding to a mature actuation of the emotive interpretant of the historical relationships among the philosophies under investigation.

II. 2 (b). The historian's response must be made not only in the medium of feeling and presentiment but also in that of action, which is the domain of the *energetic* type of dynamical interpretants. The language used in explicating our general theory of historical understanding again provides a clue about the general sign situation. The precision which we can now make is that historical interpretation is not only actional, but a mode of human activity performed under conditions of *obstacle and effort*, and hence one that requires the relationships specified by the energetic interpretants.

Our thematic term "access" recommends itself precisely as connoting the need for persistent striving toward the goal of historical understanding. We have to struggle constantly to open new routes for analyzing the modern philosophical sources and comprehending their relationships. Our historical praxis contains an acknowledgement of the energetic interpretant, which is a formal way of considering the intellectual labor involved in re-editing and retranslating the sources, reforming the established perspectives, and realigning old principles with new questions. Indeed, the transformation of history of philosophy from burden into resource is a concrete parable, on the grand scale, of how much the interpretive process owes to the energetic interpretant. It is this significate presence which impels us to engage in the revisionary acts which alone prevent the modern sources from lapsing into the status of antiquarian remains, reliquaries which would render our interpretive work futile and spiritless.

Peirce regards the energetic interpretant as the pragmatic core of his entire theory of interpretation: it is also the pragmatic component in every realistic analysis of historical understanding of modern philosophy. Bringing students to the condition of self-knowledge where they realize imaginatively the work involved in the historian's calling, is another service of the historical seminar. For the making or unmaking of a historian of philosophy depends upon his reflective acceptance of *the act of labor*, his readiness to relate himself toward the sources in terms of the intellectual, imaginative, and indeed muscular efforts required to improve our historical comprehension. Along with the familiarity of feeling and the finesse of method, interpretation moves ahead through actional modes of cooperative work among researchers. Thus the theme of the energetic interpretant endows with quite literal sense our talk about the working community of interpreters of modern philosophy, since that community is constituted by actional effort as well as intentional reference in regard to the source writings.

II. 2 (c). Peirce delays his exposition of the nature of the *logical* kind of dynamical interpretant, until a firm setting has been prepared for it through his presentation of the other interpretants. It is as though our sign-determination toward the logical interpretant is so powerful and well suited for formalization as a method, that it carries the danger of lopsidedly dominating and distorting all other interpretant contributors to historical meaning. Once the precaution is taken to give due acknowledgement to the surrounding interpretants, however, we can safely consider the field of the logical interpretant. Here, the question concerns the proper influence of intellectual concepts as signs and hence also the meaning of general concepts. Peirce is able to restate the results of his lifelong preoccupation with the logic of inquiry and meaning in terms of this logical interpretant. It is not surprising that he should establish some internal differentiations among the forms and relations of logical interpretants, or that at this point his theory should be specially detailed in its bearing on our general view of historical understanding.

There are five features of the Peircean doctrine which have definite analogues in our account of the interpretation of modern philosophy. First, the growth of a logical interpretant begins in the mode of suggestion and conjecture. This is a formal statement of a trait already observed in the practice of historians. The art of historical questioning is fructified by a constant influx of new interpretive hypotheses, new suggestions about how to explore the fundament and trace the interdependencies among philosophers. Without this mine of conjectural logical interpretants, there could be no fresh orientations of research and revision.

Second, the logical interpretant incorporates the values of the emotional and energetic factors, since general meanings emerge only from exploring imaginative situations and steadily modifying all the accepted historical judgments.

Peirce's concise account of this aspect of the logical interpretant's impact could stand as a phenomenological description of how we continually educate ourselves in an understanding of the historical sources.

We imagine ourselves in various situations and animated by various motives; and we proceed to trace out the alternative lines of conduct which the conjectures would leave open to us. We are, moreover, led, by the same inward activity, to remark different ways in which our conjectures could be slightly modified. The logical interpretant must, therefore, be in a relatively future tense.[12]

The creative historian tries out several imaginative approaches, varies the proportions of analysis and synthesis, and thus always presses toward those slightly altering and slightly more illuminating conceptions which keep his interpretation of the textual source futurally alive and incremental for historical understanding. In so doing, he manifests his vital hold upon the logical interpretant and its distinctive influence upon the explication of philosophical sources. This interpretant trait manifests that power of human language both to achieve a continuant tradition and to foster a forward dynamism in philosophy requiring expression always "in a relatively future tense."

---

[12] Peirce, *Collected Papers*, 5.481. The pioneer Vico seeks to identify a historical knowing that is neither deductive nor inductive, neither purely perceptual nor utterly fantastic. What this human capacity signifies, "above all in the recovery of the past not as a collection of factual beads strung on a chronicler's string (or of 'ideas,' arguments, works of art, similarly treated by the taxonomists and antiquaries of the humanities), but as a possible world, a society which could have had such characteristics whether it had precisely these or not—the nature of this kind of knowing is Vico's central topic. The past can be seen through the eyes—the categories and ways of thinking, feeling, imagining—of at any rate possible inhabitants of possible worlds, of associations of men brought to life by what, for want of a better phrase, we call imaginative insight" (Isaiah Berlin, "A Note on Vico's Concept of Knowledge," in *Giambattista Vico: An International Symposium*, ed. G. Tagliacozzo and H. V. White, p. 376).

Peirce's third point is that the growth of a logical interpretant is quite similar to, although not provenly identical with, a modification of personal consciousness. He does not merely psychologize the pattern of sign action upon the interpreter, and yet he also does not want to squander that experiential analogy which most closely resembles the dynamics of the logical interpretant. Our historical awareness is forever altered, as we engage in firsthand interpretation and change our conception of some modern philosophy through improvement of the logical interpretants. This personal experience of the growth of historical sensibility gives us an untrodden insight into the sources, together with a potent means of testing every established theory of historical interpretation. This fact of the human condition does not reduce the theory of interpretants to a psychological description, any more than it reduces the general account of historical understanding to a purely empathetic meaning of *Verstehen*. The principles of interpretation retain their methodological and epistemological sense, while remaining functionally related to the actual modifications in our historical understanding which they serve to illuminate in general patterns.

The fourth and fifth traits of the logical interpretant are closely intertwined, both in the Peircean exposition and in their hermeneutic bearing upon our topic of historical access. These traits signify respectively that the logical interpretant seeks to establish *a habit of inquiring and judging*, and that this habit consists in *a disposition to frame statements of futural generality*, in the conditional mood. This twofold dynamism of the logical interpretant secures the general meaning of the intellectual concepts involved in historical interpretation, and hence both aspects are incorporated into our theory of historical understanding.

The habit of inquiring and judging is methodologically expressed in the interrogational functions which bring the interpreter into relationship with his sources. It is his responsibility to exercise the modes of questioning in such a manner that they lead to historical judgments and evaluations, which have definite meaning along with their openness to alteration under proper criticism. The futural intent and conditionality of many historical judgments become most visible in the interpretive meanings concerned with interrelations. Especially in the case of from-to spans and continuative problems, the conditional type of statement is very appropriate to the complex meanings under consideration. For the interpretation concerns a likely structure of relationships between philosophers, or between different phases in the development of a persistent philosophical theme. The likelihood of these general patterns is not that of a mere guess, and yet it is not just a summation of factual reports. Interrelational historical judgments are deeply qualified by the interpretive perspectives, and hence remain essentially subject to the conditional considerations underlying the proposal to use this, rather than that, working approach and relational viewpoint.

II. 3. How can we insure that acceptance of revisibility will not become a facile gesture, never leading the interpreter to make any painful actual revisions in his historical statements? This leading question about the danger of historical calcification may help us to grasp the pertinence of Peirce's *final or ultimate logical interpretant*. He is not violating the whole spirit of his philosophy by proposing any cut-off for the process of interpretation, since the ultimate interpretant is not intended to designate any separate content or fixed state of knowledge. Rather, its function is to suffuse the immediate and dynamic interpretants of every sort and function with a teleological sense of the *normative* aspects of an inquiry. To foster their own integrity and further development, all our interpretant feelings, actions, and logical concepts need to be influenced by the presence of more demanding standards and ideals. In Peirce's carefully weighed words, the ultimate or final logical interpretant is

the effect the Sign *would* produce upon any mind upon which circumstances should permit it to work out its full effect. . . . The Final Interpretant is the one Interpretative result to which every Interpreter is destined to come if the Sign is sufficiently considered. . . . The deliberately formed, self-analyzing habit—self-analyzing because formed by the aid of analysis of the exercises that nourished it—is the living definition, the veritable and final logical interpretant.[13]

Peirce employs conditional and futural language here, in order to press home the ideal of seeking comprehensive meanings and laws of reality, through longterm community efforts at interpretation and reflective development of sign situations of every sort.

Throughout our theory of historical interpreting, we have recognized this need for methodic spurs which render us fruitfully dissatisfied with any achieved results of historical interpretation and with any present form of methodology itself. The Peircean final interpretant is a logical guarantor that this sense of discrepancy between accomplishment and ideal will operate as a teleological principle of growth for every phase and instrument in the historical study of modern philosophy. There are, indeed, three observable ways in which the drive toward still more adequate interpretation of the sign-sources is given concrete form in the historical investigation of modern philosophy.

A first expression of this teleological ideal comes in the working imperative *to employ all* the methods of historical study and to improve their relevance for the sources and ourselves. The experienced historian knows most vividly that this remains a never fully realized standard. Indeed, it is this comparison between a plenary conception of methodology and his own past approximations to it that frequently sets the historian back on the research path once again, in order to follow his own teleology more faithfully.

A second source of creative measurement derives from relating one's own work to the activity of the *entire community* of historians of modern philosophy. This interpretive

[13] Peirce, *Collected Papers*, 5.491; and *Letters to Lady Welby*, pp. 35, 36.

community is itself historical in nature. It embraces the tradition coming from past historical research, the discussions and critique of the contemporaneous generation, and the futural tendencies announcing the possibility of improved historical perspectives, yet to come. The reflective historian learns to relate his own work to all these points of demanding reference, and to do so in a manner that will discipline his self-esteem without damaging his historical plans and hopes.

And finally, the historian of philosophy seeks to practice his craft in a *truly philosophical spirit*. Hence he must guard against becoming so lost in his particular research materials that he fails to become reflective about the general nature of historical understanding and about the many ties of meaning which bind him to the general questions and concerns of mankind. He must allow the teleology of his philosophical discipline to exert its proper influence upon his mind, so that he will feel the demand of unresolved questions concerning the methods and cognition in history of modern philosophy, together with those broader problems of human existence and values facing men in every age. Deliberate exposure to these unsettling matters is a third way in which the reflective historian acknowledges the ideal demands made upon his work, under the rubric of Peirce's final logical interpretant.

III. Whereas the interpretants themselves are the proper significate effects or outcome of the action of signs, that action itself constitutes the nature of *semiosis*. This is Peirce's name for the active influence of signs upon the interpreter, an operation which works through the interpretants and gives the interpreter some access to the signified object itself (under the aspect of some specified ground or quality). It is then possible to define semiotic as the reflective theory of the essential nature and basic variety of possible modes of semiosis. The attention of logicians is directed mainly toward Peirce's theory of semiotic, but his conception of semiosis itself deserves to be considered in its own right. As far as our general theory of historical understanding of modern philosophy is concerned, indeed, it is more necessary to focus upon the sign-action process itself or the semiosis. For this latter conception permits us to connect the analysis of historical interpretants with the teleological principle in the historical study of philosophy.

In the text given above on the meaning of the final logical interpretant, Peirce refers indeterminately to the "full effect" of a sign's working upon the mind, and to the interpretive result accruing if the sign is "sufficiently considered." Our problem is to specify more closely (with the resources of our general theory of historical understanding) the criterion behind these quoted phrases. What would serve as sufficient consideration of a philosophical source viewed as a sign-complexus, and under what conditions could we judge that it had worked its full effect upon the interpreting mind?

The answer cannot be framed in quantitative terms, or even after the analogy of matching one's interpretation against a master die. In order to determine a judgment of interpretive adequacy within a historical context, we scrutinize the interpreter's basic relationship with his sources. The quality we seek is his steady purposive openness to *the full range of the source work's semiosis*, along with his skill in using all relevant methods for examining and communicating this semiosis. We test for his effectiveness in developing interpretant meanings that are immediate and dynamic, emotive and energetic, conceptual and normative, in their influence upon his historical judgment.

Thus in our actual evaluation of historical studies, sufficiency of consideration and full working out of signs are ways of expressing the teleological bond between the interpreting mind and the integral semiosis of the sourcing texts and any other sign factors. Any judgment of comparative valuation, gauging the historian's integrity and powers of comprehension and communication, can be translated ultimately into an estimate of how central and operative is the purposive ordering of his interpreting activity toward an understanding of all the modes of semiosis afforded by his designated source.

This is an extremely complex relationship to determine,

and yet its two poles help us to verify the basic valuative judgment in history of philosophy. These poles of reference are: the sourcing fundament and the historical interpreter. In the two following sections, we will make a separate examination of an important evaluative judgment about the source philosophers and one about the historians themselves. In the first case, we will try to fathom the sense in which some source thinkers are regarded as great philosophers. And then we can turn to the problem of what is meant in saying that a good historian tries to do historical justice to his sources.

3. THE MARK OF A GREAT PHILOSOPHER

A teleological presence sometimes manifests itself through the gradual elaboration of a master theme, which is actively at work from the outset of an inquiry but whose precise nature and ramifications can be grasped only in the closing phase. Such is the case with the theme of "a great philosopher." I have frequently used this term throughout the study, but have postponed its formal consideration until this final position. It does carry sufficient sense, in transference from other usages, to be employed at previous stages in the general theory of historical understanding. But its direct connection with the teleological aspect of such understanding provides an opportunity for looking more directly at its methodological significance and at the problem of its sparing, disciplined employment in history of modern philosophy.

Historians of philosophy do not serve as contest judges, making flat decisions and awarding medals to different classes of modern philosophers. But they do engage in comparative analysis and interconnective viewing of the different methods, leading principles, and synoptic visions found among these sources. By the nature of their work, therefore, historians must make judgments of evaluation and comparative ranking as an integral portion of the kind of understanding sought in their discipline. Such judgments share fully in the general traits of corrigibility and futural reference to a philosopher's changing impact upon some contemporary situation. But within the qualifying limits, many specific instances of comparative evaluation stand up well enough in the historical tradition and contribute toward the general interpretation of modern philosophy. They testify to our abiding teleological interest in recognizing the mark of a great philosopher, and in being able to furnish the historical warrant for asserting its presence in this or that source mind.

Indirectly, our general theory has already touched at two points upon this issue. The ranking process is involved, first, in that phase of the interpreting present which assures our appreciation of philosophers of the middle range, relatively minor ones, and the paraphilosophers. We were careful to state there that the comparative ranking intends no depreciation of the philosophies thus ordered, but only pursues their analysis in every direction, including that of their interrelations and interordering. Similarly now, the topic of great philosophers must expressly include the intent of respecting the integrity and distinctive value of every other philosophical mind, from which the note of greatness is withheld. The historical judgment of greatness carries with it no baleful claim that a few peak minds monopolize the methodological and conceptional significance of modern philosophy, eliminating the men of lesser rank from careful consideration and appreciation. Quite to the contrary, a philosopher is adjudged to be great only on the basis of certain definite criteria, which themselves suppose and require the co-presence of the entire company of philosophical sources variously contributing to the full meaning and context of modern philosophizing.

The second preparatory step is taken in our previous discussion of philosophical classics. What obliges us to reject any done-and-forever-settled connotation of a classical work is, primarily, the recurrent and self-renewing power of those minds from which we cannot withhold the title of "great philosophers." They are not alone in their ability to keep unsettling our accepted philosophical positions and perspectives, since this quality characterizes in some degree all the modern philosophical sources. But the writings of great philosophers do display this continuing creativity in greater concentration, variety of expression, and radical consequences for later modes of speculation. Hence although the writing of a philosophical classic is not confined to those philosophers denominated as great, this ability does get realized more consistently and amply in their case. Whereas a philosopher of middle or minor standing may be noted for a classical book or two, the great philosophers come to us with a fuller sheaf of classical works and a correspondingly severer demand upon our own interpretive resources.

We can rightfully expect a conscientious historian of philosophy to exercise caution in applying the judgment of greatness, and eventually to clarify the criteria under which it is made. For at stake are both the integrity of his method and a broad range of practical educational consequences. He cannot afford to make this evaluative judgment carelessly and with softbrained benevolence, since indiscriminate use deprives it of historical significance and claim upon our acceptance. The name of "great philosopher" includes the methodological assurance that it is being employed at the outcome of a rigorous testing process, at least as far as its usage in history of philosophy is concerned. If the conditions of comparative judging are met, then this historical judgment helps to determine many educational decisions concerning the subject matter of introductory courses in modern philosophy, as well as the direction to be taken in advanced study, research, and publication.

I have introduced the qualifying phrase "at least as far as its usage in history of philosophy is concerned," since of course the relative reputation of modern philosophers is decided on many other grounds as well, not all of which come within the disciplining criticism of our historical theory of inquiry. One need only consult the general encyclopedias and dictionaries of national biography in order to see how influential are the nonphilosophical grounds for recognizing the greatness of a Descartes or a Locke or a Leibniz. But the historian of philosophy takes responsibility for the evaluative judgment of greatness in the precise degree that it intends to determine relative *philosophical* significance, on some historically warranted grounds of appraisal. From this standpoint, the judgment of greatness is thoroughly functional to the method and modes of knowing which underlie the general theory of historical interpreting of modern philosophy.

In order to perceive how this judgment is formed and constantly reformed, we will trace the ideal path which a reflective historian might well follow in weighing the historical grounds for regarding Hegel as a great modern philosopher. The general working rule is that, if Hegel's hold upon this rank were sound, then his writings would engage the entire range of historical questioning and would place an extraordinary demand upon every mode of interpretive activity. This functional test is sufficiently pliable to admit of many creative variations for other philosophers, and yet it is also sufficiently definite and linked with our general theory of historical understanding to regulate the verificational process.

In the case of Hegel and other great philosophers, the correlation between the semiosis of their writings and the interpretive acts of the historian is unusually comprehensive, energetic, and implicatory. It is only by attending to the qualities of this relationship that the reflective historian can understand and justify his judgment of greatness about Hegel's philosophy. *What* these interpretive methods and judgmental acts are and just *how* variously they are actuated for Hegel in comparison with other philosophers, are determinate questions which pertain to our general theory and its teleological import. That is why the theme of greatness has to be postponed until we acquire some historical experience in modern philosophy, as well as some grasp upon the specific factors involved in our general theory of historical interpreting. We are now better positioned to follow the workings of six criteria of philosophical greatness, as they help to test our historical judgment about Hegel's stature.

1. Biographical soundings on a philosopher need not report the presence of dramatic happenings or momentous actions, at least not in the political and social sense of greatness. Yet however quiet and even-paced may be the life of a putatively great philosopher, we can expect it to reveal a broad sensitivity toward the many modes of human experience and their attendant problems. This quality of *widely ranging concern and knowledgeableness* is markedly present in Hegel's life style.[14] He is thoroughly but not narrowly academic, since he views the educational process as the comprehensive cultural formation of a people in the ways and values of human living.

He himself experiences love and domestic attachment, the pleasure of travel as well as the responsibility of stable institutional service, the heat of revolutionary ideals and the prosaic workings of legislative bodies and the bureaucracy. He feels both the tug of belief and the need for skeptical purification of all our affirmations and theologies. His esthetic judgments rest upon personal appreciation of the artistic traditions of mankind, especially Greek literature and Shakespeare. And his very uneasiness about new scientific and social tendencies reflects his study of them, along with his attempt to wrest some anticipative philosophic sense from them. With all his warts and blind spots included, Hegel maintains an incessant quest for the rose of wisdom in the gnarled and thorny texture of human existence and history.

2. It is not necessary for philosophical greatness that an entire industry be built around the editing, translating, and otherwise better presenting of the source writings. Sometimes, these matters are handled with ease and dispatch, but such is not the case with the Hegel corpus. There are peculiar difficulties here, stemming from the state of his manuscripts, his lifelong revising of his published books, and the editorial policies of the first generation of his students. Yet certain

---

[14] A presentation of Hegel from this standpoint is made by G. E. Mueller, *Hegel: The Man, His Vision and Work.*

aspects of the unusual concentration of Hegelian scholarship upon textual and translational questions do furnish a reliable index of his greatness.

Hegel has already been cited as an extraordinary instance of the philosopher's futural intent and *ability to employ the latent resources of language*. He makes deliberate comparisons between the different traditions of philosophical usage and ordinary usage; he forges his own meanings out of very closely inspected linguistic materials; and he strives to state the particular phases of an argument in a manner that will carry over into subsequent problems. The very vigor of his internal shaping of language compels students to follow every turn of the text and hence to demand better textual readings and editorial presentations of his words. A philosopher's greatness becomes manifest in his engagement with the languaging act, corresponding to which is the whole series of problems raised for a critical edition of his writings.

Another sign to notice is the growth of a tradition of translating the philosopher into the main languages, and of retranslating his books at intervals set by new philosophical conditions in the adoptive language area. No matter how intimately proportioned a great philosopher is to his own national tradition and language, his significance cannot remain forever confined to their boundaries. Sooner or later (a qualification which keeps all our comparative historical valuations fallible and revisible), the worth of his thought for the rest of humanity is recognized and affirmed through translation work. Even the homely maxim about translators being traitors cannot prevent the universally human significance of his philosophy from communicating itself, with increasing effectiveness, in a tradition of translations.

There may be some highly contingent or even faddish reasons for doing new translations, but in the case of the great modern philosophers there is also a coordination between their thought and new currents of philosophizing. When we examine the successive retranslations of Hegel by French, Italian, and English-speaking scholars, we find a Hegel who is being adapted now to a dominant idealism, now to an existentialist or phenomenological audience, and now to readers sensitive to linguistic and conceptual analysis. The more recent versions build upon the older ones, offer philosophical as well as philological reasons for making a new rendition, and soon begin to function as handbooks involved in some contemporary methodology and argumentation. Hence the translational efforts devoted to Hegel constitute a pragmatic form of recognition of his greatness, both for his own age and for ours.

His philosophical stature is also co-affirmed by the results of studies on the forms of his writings. He satisfies the criterion of making distinguished use of several bands of the communicational spectrum, without seeming to exhaust his inventiveness in the actual forms of presentation. By its own organizing pattern, Hegel's *Phenomenology of Spirit* gives a uniquely appropriate form to the voyage of human experience and philosophical reflection. Both the *Phenomenology* and the *Science of Logic* retain their power of surprising us at each rereading, because of some previously unnoticed implications and their total structuring. His prefaces and introductions to these books comprise an intellectual world of their own, in addition to their function within the specific work. Along with introducing us to the meaning of Hegelian phenomenology and speculative logic, these sections repay close parsing in their own right. Hegel's amplitude of mind and style can be further observed by comparing the numbered paragraphs of his *Encyclopedia of the Philosophical Sciences* with the more flowing form of his different lecture series. And moving beyond the academic genres, his creativity also finds expression in book reviews and reading notes on a constitutional convention, in poems and in a steady stream of letters to friends and philosophers. Hegel exhibits that restless, exploratory, diversifying spirit of a great philosopher endeavoring to work out his thought in the many modern forms of self-education and communication.

3. When we probe into Hegel with the aid of questions

concerning genesis-system-conspectus, he does not disappoint us. Indeed, the history of Hegel scholarship warns us not to be content with any simplified view of "the young Hegel." His formative mind can be reached only at the center of a forest of reflections on his Germanic predecessors in philosophy and theology, as well as of observations on the economic and social life of his age. In his youthful manuscripts and mature treatises alike, he invites us to plunge into their study as deeply as we can—without there being any fear on his part that we will wring his meanings dry, or any reasonable basis of concern on our own part about scraping bottom and finding no more challenges to interpret. Like other great philosophers, Hegel conveys a sense of confidence in the continuing interpretability of his writings, their power of always offering good grounds for revisiting them, under our changing philosophical circumstances.

Hegel also schools us well in that trait of philosophical greatness which depends upon *combining organizational unity with implicational fruitfulness in a system of thought*.[15] Reflection upon this characteristic helps us to formulate three leading questions, which not only test his own standing but also can be propounded analogously to other claimants of philosophical greatness.

(a) Is the philosopher sufficiently open to and challenged by philosophical methods other than his own, to the point where he engages in a close analysis, evaluation, and incorporation of their best aspects? Hegel is careful to develop his speculative method with the help of studies in formal logic, empirical methodology, Kantian transcendental method, and the believer's way of immediacy. He does not thereby set a standard pattern, but he does suggest that a certain openness to the plurality of methods is a basic requirement for a great philosopher.

(b) Is there a salutary tension between method and doc-

[15] See G. R. G. Mure, *The Philosophy of Hegel*; I. Soll, *An Introduction to Hegel's Metaphysics*; and Q. Lauer, *Hegel's Idea of Philosophy*.

trinal content at every stage in the development of the philosophy, so that the methodological qualifications placed upon every doctrinal statement stand forth and the speculative implications of every methodic move are spelled out? Because it maintains these reciprocal relationships, Hegel's thought is a highly flexible center which remains attractive for our own explorations in method-making and judgmental formation.

(c) Does the philosophy furnish us with principles of argument and interpretation sufficiently proportioned to the modes of human experience that they can surpass the defects of the philosopher's own intellectual age, and show their analogous relevance for our own? The structuring principles of Hegelian philosophy enjoy this primary ordination to a reflective understanding of human experience, so that the serious defects in their particular forms of elaboration do not bind them down to their original situation. After duly criticizing the Western-oriented and serially related stages in Hegel's philosophy of history, for instance, we still recognize the resourcefulness of his theme of the constant human search for freedom and the wisdom of his fusion of all elements in a culture into the intellectual shape or spirit of an entire mode of perceiving-valuing-striving.

If we discover that the philosopher under investigation responds in some strongly affirmative way to these test questions, then we have some presumptive grounds for including him in the small company of great philosophers. Each one will respond in his own accent, of course, as is apparent from listening a bit longer to Hegel's own treatment of the three questions. (a) Great philosophers do not suppose that there will be instantaneous understanding and acceptance of their basic method and principles. That is why Hegel is under no illusion that one brilliant exposition of his speculative method will suffice. He keeps re-examining it, now in the perspective of phenomenology and now in that of ontological logic and the history of the spirit. Consequently, his use of different forms of style and organization in his books is not motivated by literary virtuosity but by the forcefulness of his philosophical reflection and exposition.

(b) There is a significant correspondence between shifts in Hegelian method and those in the fundamental Hegelian doctrine of spirit. Spirit is not related extrinsically to methodology, but is the living agency which reflects upon itself precisely in the form of this or that register of method. Hegel's philosophic greatness does not rest upon an ingenious arrangement of conflicting partial viewpoints or upon an encyclopedic coverage of topics, because taken by themselves these are exercises better performed by minor dialecticians and encyclopedists. His specific genius comes through, rather, in his teleological ordering of everything else to the interpenetration of method and spirit. He is great in his own fashion, through the recognition of this interpenetration and its potentialities for every aspect of his philosophizing.

And (c) Hegel prefers the term "spirit" as the organizing principle of his philosophy, on the basis of its manifold connotations in the many philosophical, religious, and social traditions of mankind. It keeps his thought strategically open to the different modes of experiencing, the different arts and sciences, and the whole diversity of human cultures. A great philosopher is likely to choose some such key word, which can be given strict methodological interpretation and yet which remains in touch with the more informal uses which relate his thought with other centers of reflection. Once a Descartes fixes upon *cogito*, or a Kant upon *critique*, or a Hegel upon *spirit*, the meaning of these widely used terms is indelibly altered to include the unifying employment found in these great philosophers, who use them to synthesize experience and reflection.

4. Hegel furnishes a particularly striking image of how a great philosopher becomes involved in the comparative relationships which sustain the history of philosophy. He is not merely a subject matter for interrelational questioning, but himself takes the *initiative in philosophizing along inter-*

relational and historical lines. His interest in historical studies marks Hegel as a *stella hians et radians* of primary brightness, in some Leibnizian galaxy of philosophical minds. He goes out to welcome the works of others on the meaning of substance and the basis of relationship, the passional factor in history and the purposiveness of all modes of thought. Through his critical analyses of skepticism and empiricism, rationalism and romantic idealism, he makes the first move toward establishing connective and developmental ties with these philosophies. Hence the historian does not have to force Hegel into the harness of comparative questioning but, instead, finds that this great source thinker has already set the comparisons in motion.

It is instructive to notice the way in which Hegel fits into the framework of a historical from-to transition. No matter where his philosophy figures in such a relationship, it never becomes *totally submerged* in the transition. Although Hegelian thought is decisive for the development of German philosophy, it is not dwarfed by this developmental comparison but retains its own orienting axis of method and concepts. A great philosopher's work is fundamental enough to count heavily in any comparative interpretation, but it also affirms its own unity of significance. In such a presence, historians are not tempted for very long to conclude that the philosopher's chief contribution lies in being a functional segment within some from-to span. If our general theory emphasizes the irreducible fundament or originative mind, this is done in response, first of all, to this lesson so strenuously taught us by the great modern philosophers themselves.

In Hegel's specific case, we have examined several aspects of his involvement in the work of reforming the from-to perspective on modern German philosophy. We noted that the development cannot be halted with the Kant-to-Hegel comparison; that Hegel can be reconsidered as the start of a further evolution leading to Marx; and that he also fills a role as an intermediate phase in the entire Germanic movement leading from Leibniz and Wolff to Nietzsche and Heidegger.

But what our present topic of the great philosopher compels us to add, now, is that Hegel's comparative roles do not add up to an exhaustive account and reckoning with his philosophy, and that he himself furnishes much of the impetus for the subsequent phases of comparison. There is no more danger of historical reductionism when Hegel is viewed as a starting point or a waystation in a from-to relationship than when he is considered as a relative terminus. All these perspectives help to work out the relational implications of his philosophy, and none of them—taken individually or together—are able to weaken his philosophical integrity and greatness. The from-to relationships permit us to grasp the implications of his thought for the community and continuity of modern philosophy, without diminishing our assessment of his originative mind.

5. In testing the ascription of greatness to a modern philosopher, we must also use the negative criterion of *what his loss would mean for our historical understanding*. If the removal of his work would open up some deep crevasses in the philosophical landscape and would unravel some basic patterns in our historical understanding of modern philosophy, then that work is likely to belong in the group of great contributions. In Hegel's case, the gap resulting from a cancellation of his writings would nullify many foundational meanings, not just some details and variant expressions. We would be deprived of an entire major path in philosophizing, one that thematizes the meaning of historically developing spirit in the various shapes of human experience.

To account for many great themes on the estrangement and historicity of the human spirit which occupy modern philosophers since 1831, we would be forced to posit some invisible star. It would lie beyond our intellectual sightings, but not beyond our detection of its massive philosophical consequences. There would be an unbearable strain placed upon our historical understanding, as developed in terms of continuative problems, were we unable to include the originative work of Hegel in our comparative study of the methods, concepts, and language of philosophy during the last century and a half. A philosopher whose presence or absence makes such a fundamental difference in historical judgments exercises a firm, operational grip upon the rank of great philosopher.

Expressed in affirmative language, great philosophers are those who transform the problems and methods in philosophy so deeply and permanently that we come to perceive human life differently, and to interpret the course of philosophical reflections from another perspective than before. Hegel's *Phenomenology of Spirit* and other writings exert just such a radical modification in our experience and historical consciousness, thus furnishing a functional meaning for his greatness. Yet the responsibility of the historian of modern philosophy is not to make similar evaluations of "other Hegels," but to discern the grounds upon which some other philosophers realize the quality of greatness *otherwise* than did Hegel. For philosophical greatness also signifies a deeply ramifying differentiation in the basal act of philosophizing, not a conformity with some exhaustive and univocal model.

6. Having mentioned the practical educational consequences of the ranking among modern philosophers, we must now specify the sense in which this sign enters into the verificational procedure. What counts is not the factual incidence of courses and readings in a philosopher, but rather the quality of the intellectual relationship aroused between students and this source. Our tie with a great philosopher is not merely a case of filling a chronological gap or a gestalt form of possible kinds of philosophy. We come into his presence for the serious business of learning to philosophize along with an extraordinarily demanding, yet helpful, master.

And in a sense, a great philosopher is *more approachable*, forthright, and singleminded in his own intent of leading us toward a method of philosophizing, than are lesser minds who may have regard for incidental considerations. However difficult may be the path of reflection and the terminology of a great philosopher, he gives us assurance that the inquiry's the thing, and that every effort of ours will be philosophically very worth while. A great philosopher personifies the intrinsic values of philosophizing for us. He attracts and rewards a wide circle of students, whether they are professionally engaged in philosophy or not, and hence he establishes a maximally liberative relationship within the university community.

As the chapter on the Kant seminar sought to show, a great philosopher invites and sustains our best cooperative efforts. When a Kant or a Hegel is the central source for the philosophy seminar, he calls forth new interpretations and educates us in the meaning of the unfailing resourcefulness of a great thinker.[16] We do not fear that such a mind will have no more to offer us, or that what we can now judge about him will settle his significance in philosophy forever. Although something similar can be said about philosophers in the middle and lower ranges, we make this judgment of unflagging originality and helpfulness much more readily and comprehensively about a great philosopher. Hence, one purposive aim of historical work is to hone and test our evaluative judgments, taking a lead from our experience of the unusual abundance of a great philosopher's gifts to the reflective community of men and women.

4. THE INTENT TO DO HISTORICAL JUSTICE

Having just employed the components in our general theory to elucidate the judgment of ranking among modern philosophers, we can now test this theory's capacity to elucidate the judgment of approbation about historians of modern philosophy themselves. About the best men in that field, we sometimes say in recognition and recommendation: "They can be relied upon to do historical justice to their theme."

---

[16] Various combinations of these six criteria of philosophical greatness are operative in the following bicentennial symposia: *Hegel and the Philosophy of Religion*, ed. D. E. Christensen; *New Studies in the Philosophy of Hegel*, ed. W. E. Steinkraus; *The Legacy of Hegel*, ed. L. C. Rice; and analogously, the *Proceedings of the Third International Kant Congress*, ed. L. W. Beck.

From their past work and operating standards, we judge them to be masters of their craft, men of probity in all phases of historical interpretation. Phrased as it is in the third-person or qualified-observer terms, such an appraisal signifies that the historians in question have lived up to the best ideal of the community of historians of modern philosophy. What we must examine is the nature of this ideal, insofar as it affords insight into the working teleology of historical inquiry and permits us to assess the general quality of work done by those who accept its attraction. The teleological meaning of doing historical justice brings us close to that abiding historical-intent-in-the-making which animates every phase of research and reflection, teaching and writing, in which we develop the reality of history of modern philosophy.

Teleology toward Doing Historical Justice

1. Imperativity of our historical experience.
2. Justice toward the sources:
   (a) in their own pursuit of truth.
   (b) in their critical generosity toward predecessors.
   (c) in their demand for consequential envisioning.
3. Justice toward the present bearings of the sources.
4. Justice toward the modes of historical inquiry.
5. A working ideal: to develop a faithful and pertinent image of modern philosophy that somehow illuminates our humanity.

1. In defense of the use of a method of functional analysis for developing the general theory of historical understanding, I have remarked that the analytic and ontological approaches to historical knowing always remain at a somewhat higher altitude than the actual formative principles governing the study of modern philosophy. A prime condition for closing this gap is to learn how the problems of historical method and knowledge look from the distinctive standpoint and practice of the field workers in history of modern philosophy. Seen from that standpoint, the general dialectic of subjectivity and objectivity of historical knowledge is only remotely and potentially related to the actual intent of historical inquirers.

Abstract problems about facticity and objectivity, historicity and subjectivity, have to be retranslated and rendered more concretely pertinent to the actual operations and teleology of historical work.

Much closer to the intent and language of actual historians of modern philosophy is the theme of intending to do historical justice, so that a direct analysis of the main facets of this theme will help to bridge that interval. The historical inquirer does not set himself in the position of a judge, exalted above the parties in a court proceeding. His intent to do justice means that he resolves to render, in full, all the interpretive judgments bearing upon a designated subject of inquiry, using the proper source materials and modes of interrogation and correlation with present philosophizing. All these components of historical relationship contain an *aspect of requiredness*, a demand that he use and relate them as precisely, discernedly, and artfully as he can. If his actual interpretation responds to this demand, then it realizes one form of the pervasive imperativity of historical experience and research.

Although C. I. Lewis is not specifically concerned with historical understanding, he does recognize the demanding character of all experiential situations and does reformulate the meaning of objectivity in terms of this trait.

> We have to "move ourselves" in order to be what we call sensible or rational in our acting toward an objective fact which is signalized by, but not realized in, our experience as presently felt. This sense of experience as signifying something beyond its immediate content is the sense of reality. And the imperative to respect that reality which portentous feeling portends, not by the measure of the feeling which portends it, but in the full measure of it as it will or would be felt when realized—that imperative is implicit in or essential to the recognition of any fact as objective or any reality as genuine but beyond the here and now. . . .
> The first imperative is the law of objectivity: recognize that

your experience signifies a reality beyond your present feeling of it, and act appropriately to that reality you recognize and not merely in response to the immediately felt quality.[17]

The sign character of every source work in modern philosophy consists in its ability to dispose us to recognize the presence of something more, the reality of the sourcing mind's basal act of philosophizing and methodically developed meanings which affect the wider philosophical community.

In discussing Peirce's theory of interpretants, we have called this signification the basic interpretability of the source texts, their capacity to signify something more through our use of interpretive questioning. Now it is necessary to add that there is an imperative or disciplining note attached to this sense of interpretability. The interpreter is under call to make the most thorough and responsive use of all his instruments of inquiry, so that his interpretation will measure up to the philosophical reality being presented. He is being required to conduct his work with historical appropriateness and justice to the complex situation. By the very teleology of historical understanding, he is under the imperative of rendering due and plenary interpretation of some portion of the world of modern philosophy.

2. Working responsively within the commitment, an inquirer soon discovers that his so-called historical "materials" are not indifferent to the quality of the interpretive relationship, but make a definite contribution of their own to his intent of doing justice. If we make a teleological examination of the basal philosophizing of some modern source thinkers, we will find them conspiring to elicit and retain this intent at its demanding maximum.

---

[17] C. I. Lewis, *Values and Imperatives*, ed. John Lange, pp. 134-135. The bearing of the objectivity-subjectivity problem upon history of philosophy and its search after more fully significant reality and truth is treated explicitly, from the standpoint of a phenomenology of such recognition of further meaning, by Paul Ricoeur, *History and Truth*, pp. 21-77.

(a) The sign situation engaging the historian is precisely that one which expresses a source philosopher's own *pursuit of the truth*. His dedication to the central problem of truth, its meanings and its modes, is sometimes fiercely affirmed by the philosopher in the face of other interests and influences. Its costing nature comes across to us in a revealing notation of even that moderate man of the world, John Locke. In the same private journal which records his successive drafts of the essay on human understanding, he makes these normative observations about his philosophical work:

> Our first and great duty, then, is to bring to our studies, to our enquiries after knowledge, a mind covetous of truth, that seeks after nothing else, and after that impartially, and embraces it how poor, how contemptible, how unfashionable soever it may seem. This is that which all studious men profess to do, and yet it is that where I think very many miscarry. Who is there almost that hath not opinions planted in him by education time out of mind, which by that means come to be as the municipal laws of the country which must not be questioned, but are here looked on with reverence as the standards of right and wrong, truth and falsehood; when perhaps these so sacred opinions were but the oracles of the nursery, or the traditional grave talk of those who pretend to inform our childhood, who received them from hand to hand without ever examining them? . . . These ancient preoccupations of our minds, these revered and almost sacred opinions, are to be examined if we will make way for truth, and put our minds in that freedom which belongs and is necessary to them. . . . Here, therefore, we had need of all our force and all our sincerity; and here 'tis we have use of the assistance of a serious and sober friend who may help us sedately to examine these our received and beloved opinions.[18]

[18] John Locke, "Of Study," in *The Educational Writings of John Locke*, ed. J. L. Axtell, pp. 415, 417.

Locke's recommendation of singlemindedness and radicality in examining received views and pursuing truths holds good as a norm for historians of philosophy, as well as for the modern philosophers themselves. Historical interpretation must be approached in this same spirit of a ceaseless struggle to achieve critical reflectivity, a deliberate consultation with friends and the community of historians of philosophy, and a free resoluteness in holding to the true consequences of research.

If there is a certain moral and even passional overtone in Locke's account of our first and great duty, this is not alien at all to the historian's own mode of responding to his teleological ideal. There is a moral, as well as a theoretical, quality in the intent to render historical justice to one's sources: the imperative response includes a sense of vocation which pervades the whole personal experience of the historical interpreter. Hence it is not amiss to refer to his conscientiousness and to give a value connotation to the integrity of his purpose and the soundness of his work. The ideal of doing historical justice shapes not only a methodology but also a personal mind using a method, a human interpreter seeking to achieve some complimentarity with the mind of Locke and other philosophical pursuers of truth.

(b) Not all the modern philosophers enjoy a broad and untroubled relationship with their own predecessors. Philosophers respond in a wide variety of ways to their antecedents: sometimes by concealing and sometimes by acknowledging their debt to a resourceful philosophical past; by avoiding or else by critically examining the specific forms of argumentation proposed by earlier philosophers; and by presenting their own originality either in terms of discontinuity with the historical tradition or by some continuity with it. Amid all this variance, however, it is noteworthy that those philosophers who are able to overcome a purely abstract conception of "previous work," and to engage in close study of actual texts of preceding philosophers, usually show *a marked generousmindedness* toward their own sources. They suggest that their originative thought is not endangered, but rather is enriched, by patient study and assimilation of earlier modes of theorizing.

This habit of joining generosity with rigor of appraisal is specially manifest in such a radial thinker as Leibniz. His experience with source studies is sufficiently sustained and varied to earn him the right of influencing the purposiveness of historians of modern philosophy. That he is fully cognizant of alternative responses to source traditions and of the normative character of his own approach, is seen in these three texts which differ in circumstance but nevertheless converge in their common advocacy of a generous spirit to be maintained by the careful interpreter.

[1.] The "foretaste" of a history of philosophy which you [Leibniz's teacher Jacob Thomasius] have written has set all our mouths to watering more than I can tell you, for it shows clearly how great a difference there is between a mere enumeration of names and such profound reasons as you give for the interconnections between doctrines. You know that I am no flatterer. But wherever I hear people who understand these matters speak of your essay [on the Greek historical origins of philosophy], they are unanimous in saying that there is no one from whom we can better hope for the entire history of philosophy than from you. Most of the others are skilled rather in antiquity than in science and have given us lives rather than doctrines. . . . I wish, indeed, that you would produce both a style and a method for this new age and warn our unseasoned youth that it is wrong to give our moderns credit either for everything or for nothing. . . . [2.] I read books, not in order to censure them but to profit from them. This leads me to find something good everywhere, but not equally everywhere. . . . [3.] My remarks on M. Gassendi, Father Malebranche, M. Descartes, Spinoza, and Mr. Locke serve to prepare minds. I cannot always explain myself amply, but I always do try to speak what is just.[19]

Leibniz speaks here as a practised hand in the interpretation of other philosophers, so that his words carry some authority for including the note of generosity in the historian's intent to do justice to source thinkers.

The first text expresses an open welcome, rather than closed hostility, toward history of philosophy. Leibniz wants every historical inquiry to be ordered in a philosophically profitable way, with the stress falling upon doctrinal analysis and interrelational problems rather than upon biographical facts by themselves. He asks historians to furnish something more mature than a précis description of the individual philosophical work and an episodic view of philosophical schools. If history of philosophy does give us an internally organized conception of a philosopher's thought and an interconnective understanding of a philosophical tradition of problems, then it is an ally for the philosophizing mind and a source of balanced appreciation. The just balance between tradition and contemporaneity is well stated in Leibniz's memorable sentence: "It is wrong to give our moderns credit either for everything or for nothing." Responsible historical interpretation enables us to avoid the two extremes of ahistorical self-congratulation and erudite despair.

[19] G. W. Leibniz, *Letter of April 20/30, 1669, to Jacob Thomasius*, in *Philosophical Papers and Letters*, ed. L. E. Loemker, p. 93; *Letter of December 10, 1696, to A. Morell*, in *Textes inédits*, ed. G. Grua, I, 103; manuscript annotation at Hannover, transcribed by E. Bodemann, *Die Leibniz-Handschriften der königlichen öffentlichen Bibliothek zu Hannover*, p. 58, and quoted in Y. Belaval, *Leibniz, critique de Descartes*, p. 535. A good instance of Leibniz's own evenhandedness is found in his manuscript remarks on stylistic differences between Descartes and Malebranche: "M. Descartes speaks with exactness. Father Malebranche has clothed his thoughts in an orator's style, which I do not blame at all. For when once one has thought justly, figurative expressions are useful to win over those to whom abstract meditations are painful. Nevertheless, while one has indulgence for metaphors, he should guard himself well against giving in to illusions" (*Die Leibniz-Handschriften*, ed. Bodemann, pp. 56-57).

Leibniz's second and third texts together give his actual personal witness to the spirit of historical inquiry, not just his hope for the work of others. He is no Dr. Pangloss of the seminar in history of philosophy. No philosopher excels Leibniz in ability to detect fatuous thinking and fallacious argument, on the part of venerable sources. He is the master of those who can forcefully join particular points of criticism with a radical overhaul of the basic principles operating in another philosophy. Yet he does not expose or criticize in a denigrating manner, and never pretends to do his own speculative reconstruction entirely apart from historical origins and suggestions. The sound elements which he finds "everywhere, but not equally everywhere," are deliberately sought and generously acknowledged. They are required to prove their philosophical soundness and declare their limits by reference to the Leibnizian principles, but they are never totally divorced from their historical origins and their reference to the agelong work of the community of philosophers.

Nothing less than a similar discerning generosity can be demanded of the practising historian of philosophy. Like a Leibniz, he will be sufficiently sensitive to the difference between an antiquarian treatment of the modern sources and one that renders their methods and doctrines historically present and available for philosophers today. His teleological bent will be toward preparing minds through a precise and accessible interpretation of source thinkers, rather than toward a censorious or uncommunicative presentation. And in every attempt at historical understanding and evaluation, he will learn from Leibniz both the necessity of speaking justly and the liberality of weaving a thread of magnanimity into every historical pattern.

(c) It is quite possible to make accurate summaries of the individual arguments in a philosopher's writings, and nevertheless fail to do historical justice to their context and function within that philosopher's own development and comprehensive vision of life. These latter considerations serve to modify and unify all his statements, so that their proper presentation belongs among the chief aims of the responsive interpreter. Historical re-envisioning of a philosophy requires that the purposive unity of meanings be respected, along with their separate argumentative structure.

On this teleological integration as on other requirements of the just historical approach, we receive some basic counsel from the modern philosophers themselves. Among those who have reflected upon the canons of unificational adequacy in our historical understanding are Edmund Husserl and William James. Their testimony is all the more welcome as coming from powerful conjunctive minds, who themselves help to prolong modern philosophy into the contemporary world. Their reflections about the purposive nature of thinking and its telic continuity in temporal experience belong not only to their general conception of mind but also to their account of their own manner of philosophizing, They imply that any just historical interpretation of their work or of other philosophies ought to be concerned with these same properties of temporal continuity and unifying purposiveness.

Husserl makes his contribution to this aspect of the general theme of historical justice in his report about repeated efforts to complete his last major work, *The Crisis of European Sciences*, which has already occupied us in treating his lifelong study of Kant. A manuscript note entitled "Foreword to the Continuation of the *Crisis*" deals quite vividly with the problem of interruption and discontinuity, as experienced by the creative philosopher who is trying to fulfill his own philosophical purposes.

> Herewith appears, unfortunately very much delayed, the continuation of this work which was begun in the first volume of [the journal] *Philosophia* with two introductory sections. Insurmountable inhibitions, the effects of my faltering health, forced me to neglect drafts which were long since ready. With this there arose a pause which is dangerous for the understanding of the teleological-historical way attempted here to the conception of the idea and

method of transcendental phenomenology. The resulting situation has become somewhat similar to that which would arise if the presentation of a great musical work were to break off with the conclusion of the overture, and indeed in such a way that the actual work (the opera itself) to which it points the way, and which it has created a vital readiness to understand, was then to be performed sometime later without repetition of the overture.[20]

Apart from its biographical and genetic significance for the study of Husserl's own philosophy, this remarkable passage contains some valuable suggestions for historical methodology and understanding in general.

We may well ponder the musical analogy used here. It sharpens our historical concern for the interdependencies among the sections of a total work, the thematic continuity intended by its author even in the midst of interruptions, and the need for taking the work as a purposive whole in our own interpretative act (whether it be a musical performance or a historical exposition). Husserl's remark about the function of a well conceived introduction to achieve "a vital readiness to understand," on the part of a listener or reader, is another reminder of the skill required for making introductory statements and their valuable contribution to an understanding of the entire work. There would be a breakdown of historical interpretation, were the introductory statement of problems, methods, and principles divorced from the main body of the treatise by isolative analysis. Even a prolonged pause in the consequential or follow-through movement of interpretation could be just as dangerous for historical understanding as an overlong pause would be for the appreciation of an opera or symphony. Precisely *how* to proportion and time the relationship between parts in a complex historical account of a modern philosophy, belongs to the art and practice of historical judgment in unifying the appropriate interpretants.

William James develops a similar theme, yet not from the

---

[20] Edmund Husserl, *The Crisis of European Sciences*, p. 102.

standpoint of the creative mind struggling to realize its own purposiveness, but rather from the standpoint of an author watching his achieved works being dissected and dismembered by an apprentice interpreter. In 1909, the year before he died, James read a doctoral dissertation on his philosophy which met one set of standards but emphatically not those of historical comprehension of his thought. With characteristic vigor and friendliness combined, he placed his finger on the reason for this failure in historical insight.

> I like greatly the objective and dispassionate key in which you keep everything, and the number of subdivisions and articulations which you make give me vertiginous admiration. Nevertheless, the tragic fact remains that I don't feel wounded at all by all that output of ability, and for reasons which I think I can set down briefly enough. It all comes, in my eyes, from too much philological method—as a Ph.D. thesis your essay is supreme, but why don't you go further? You take utterances of mine written at different dates for different audiences belonging to different universes of discourse, and string them together as the abstract elements of a total philosophy which you then show to be inwardly incoherent. This is splendid philology, but is it live criticism of anyone's *Weltanschauung*? Your use of the method only strengthens the impression I have got from reading criticisms of my "pragmatic" account of "truth," that the whole Ph.D. industry of building up an author's meaning out of separate texts leads nowhere, unless you have first grasped his center of vision, by an act of imagination. That, it seems to me, you lack in my case. . . . Not by proving their inward incoherence does one refute philosophies—every human being is incoherent—but only by superseding them by other philosophies more satisfactory. . . . For only by such experiments on the part of individuals will social man gain the evidence required.[21]

[21] William James, *Letter of May 26, 1909, to Miss S.*, in *The Letters of William James*, ed. Henry James, II, 355-356. Internal reference to an article of Bertrand Russell (published in April, 1909)

This is not an obscurantist's blast against doctoral dissertations and the philological-analytic method, but a philosopher's living cry that justice be done to his central vision and the organic unity of his thought. James is speaking out on the pitfalls of a method insensitive to the originative mind's purposive context of meaning, a context which is evacuated by what he calls in this same letter the "vicious abstractionism" of building up a total philosophy out of discrete theoretical elements.

Even the most seasoned historian of philosophy should submit his work to the examination of historical conscience proposed by William James. Does he disregard the temporal relationships, the different audiences, and the specific intentions of the source philosopher's many textual statements? Does he thread together a pile of abstractly regarded statements into a theoretical reconstruction of the original philosophy, and then expose the formal fallacies and obscurities in this straw-man creation of his own? Is he lured by the notion of a neat and definitive refutation of a source philosopher, who has been thus reassembled into an axiomatic system? Is it his practice to disregard the problem of teleological phasing and unification of meaning, on the ground that it rests upon a hopelessly vague appeal to a philosopher's *Weltanschauung* (a word whose present connotation is that of a formless emotive attitude, whereas William James correlates it with the philosopher's "center of vision," as grasped "by an act of imagination")? And does he overlook the philosopher's distinctive contribution to the evolving experience of mankind, a contribution which becomes superseded only in the sense of improving the total human fund of reflectiveness and intelligent action beyond its own human limits?

If an investigator of modern philosophies is obliged to answer most of these questions in the affirmative, then he is equivalently admitting his failure to do historical justice to

suggests that this letter should be dated 1909, not 1900. There are resonances from Peirce and Royce in this letter.

these philosophies. His work may be otherwise useful in philosophical discussions, but it cannot count directly as a historical interpretation or as enlarging our historical resources. Its precise bearing upon the source philosophy in question can eventually be determined, but that determination has its own complexities and leads only to an oblique relationship with the historical sense of the original argumentation.

3. It is sometimes supposed that the intention of doing historical justice refers only to our treatment of sources. But in fact, this intent encompasses all the components in the interpreting process. Hence in the context of our general theory, there must also be a reading of the sources which has due regard for their reference to the interpreting present. The imperativity of historical experience comes not only from the source thinkers but also from the situation and problems in contemporary philosophy.

A sense of this twofold requiredness becomes manifest in the very language we use to state our ideal expectations from historical studies in modern philosophy. We hope that they will be *at once veracious and valuable*, that is, faithful to the sources and also effectively related to our own philosophical inquiries. There is wisdom in this standard, not only in its separate parts but especially in the synthesizing recognition that the one part cannot be achieved properly without the other.

There can be a deadening sort of fidelity or accuracy concerning the thought of modern philosophers. It consists in that sort of formalist precision which transcribes past lines of argument, but which recognizes no interpretive obligations toward living minds today. It can make statements about source thinkers, but is unable to achieve their historical actuality and presence for us. At the other extreme lies that converse approach which seeks contemporary significance for the modern sources, but does so at the cost of a historically grounded presentation of their thought in its own context and mode of philosophizing. In the former case, memory is served while present theorizing starves; and in the latter case, our present theorizing is fraudulently stoked with fuel, which does not come from the mines which are claimed to be supplying it. In seeking to avoid these opposite causes of failure in historical comprehension, we discover (sometimes with painful slowness) what it means to honor the full intent of doing justice to sources and current philosophizing alike.

4. I give separate formulation to that facet of the just intent which applies reflexively to the methodology itself of historical inquiry. The historian's conscientiousness and self-criticism are heightened by checking his work against the full range of historical questioning. This is an important practical consequence of developing an explicit general theory of historical understanding: it furnishes specific criteria not only for conducting our research but also for testing its integrity and adequacy. The historian's readiness to incorporate such self-evaluation into his working life is an index of the presence there of the ideal of justice. This is a salutary presence in two senses: it saves the historian from becoming uncritically complacent about his own research, and it keeps him open to the contribution of others working both in history of modern philosophy and in the other disciplines.

Explicit commitment to the purpose of doing justice to his own methodological requirements lies at the heart of the historian's intellectual wellbeing. This is what keeps him honest in judgment, artful in showing how a philosophical source still communicates with us, and creatively ready to conceive new tasks of historical interpretation. The reflective historian of philosophy is sympathetic toward the following declaration made by Anton Chekhov to his friendly critic and editor, A. S. Suvorin: "One must work, and to hell with everything else. The important thing is that we must be just, and all the rest will come as a matter of course."[22] Chekhov made this resolve upon his return from the Siberian prison camp on

---

[22] Anton Chekhov, *Letter of December 9, 1890, to A. S. Suvorin*, quoted in E. J. Simmons, *Chekhov: A Biography*, p. 234. Simmons observes that Chekhov wanted to write a book which would be "a picture of Sakhalin that would be at once scientific and artistic" (p. 234). The result was Chekhov's *The Island: A Journey to Sakhalin*.

Sakhalin Island. He was filled with the horrors of the place, with notes on his research and observations, and with a desire to present a report that would not only accurately analyze the situation but also move his contemporaries to reform it. Physician and playwright, reporter and reformer, all these sides of his personality were fused in Chekhov's wholehearted giving of himself to the ideal of doing justice to all the factors involved in his purpose.

Any historian of philosophy would be fortunate to achieve some distantly analogous fusion of his own sense of his craft, the situation in the source thinker, and his obligation to modify the quality of contemporary living and reflecting. He would be eager to subscribe to Chekhov's statement that what counts is to be just and that then all else will follow. And standing on his own soil, the historian of modern philosophy might well devise as his motto: *Fiat justitia ut floreat historia philosophiae.*

5. The just historical measure becomes realized in that act of interpreting which does synthesize the prime considerations, as symbolized by the Chekhov letter, into a careful and accessible study. This brings us almost full circle in our investigation. We began with a working hypothesis, and we now conclude by stating its correlative working ideal. In the perspective of the theme of the intent to do historical justice, all the methods and acts of inquiry are teleologically directed toward developing a faithful and pertinent image of modern philosophy, one that will somehow *illuminate our humanity in its historical and contemporary reality.* Our general hypothesis tries to formulate and test the component principles and procedures which will bring our actual historical understanding closer to realizing this ideal purpose. There is one last feature of this purpose, however, which remains to be examined. If the historical study of the modern philosophical sources is intended to cast some light upon the meaning of humanity, then we must consider briefly the concatenation between history of philosophy and a better understanding of humanity.

5. HUMANITY AND HISTORY OF PHILOSOPHY

One question raised, but held in abeyance until now, concerns the wider applicability of the theory of historical understanding proposed here. Does it hold also for the historical study of ancient and medieval, renaissance and eastern, philosophies? Its broadest traits are likely to be matched by similar procedures and modes of cognition in the interpretation of these other source centers. But I suspect that there are also some profound differences, which come to light only in the actual process of relating these sources with the interpreting mind of the historians in these fields. A common terminology concerning texts and translations, biographical and genetic questions, systematic and comparative viewpoints, cannot conceal the distinctive problems encountered and modes of response undertaken in relating the pre-modern Western and the Eastern philosophies to ourselves. But we must leave the task of determining the precise likenesses and differences in historical interpretation to those investigators who have prolonged working experience in these areas.

From within the modern perspective itself, however, there are two considerations which suggest that the differences will not be found to be merely superficial. One point is the uniquely intimate relationship between the modern philosophical sources and our contemporary act of philosophizing. There is a *prolonging relationship* of intellectual continuity here, which does not find its equal in comprehensive pertinence and challenge anywhere else in the philosophical source relationships with our interpreting present. The phrase "our philosophical past" applies most determinately and completely to the classical modern philosophies, just as the study of how they become a resource for us constitutes the primary model for examining the transformation process in respect to the other temporally and culturally designated philosophies of mankind. Although we make direct and fruitful studies of the Greek dialogues, the Hindu scriptures, and the medieval disputations, we usually do so across an interpretive background of comparison with the modern sources, especially when we seek to establish the philosophical character and relevance of research in the former writings.

The second distinguishing mark is the altogether central position occupied by the theme of human reality and the meaning of humanity, within the conjunction of modern and contemporary philosophies. The problem of man is basic in all periods of philosophy, but it serves as the primary organizing principle and teleological aim of the modern and contemporary philosophers. Here we can discern the peculiar mutuality between the modern and the contemporary ways of philosophizing. It is in virtue of their education in the modern sources that philosophers today are so ready to organize their work around the problems and values of humanism, studied in its various modes and relationships with the other thematic principles. Although it goes sometimes unnoticed, this abiding and encompassing reference to the study of human nature characterizes every use of method and every act of understanding achieved in the history of modern philosophy and its reference to contemporary theorizing.

The theme of humanity constitutes a sur-teleology for the historical study of modern philosophy. It is a further teleological deepening and specifying of the intrinsic teleology of history of modern philosophy, not another storey added extrinsically to that center of historical understanding. Our inquiry into the modern source philosophers aims at *such* an interpretation of their thought as will illumine and improve the meaning of humanity among us. This more comprehensive purpose does not inevitably propose itself to, and impose itself upon, individual historians of modern philosophy. Furthermore, it dictates nothing determinate and exclusive about *how* the reality of man is to be explored, the meanings of humanism to be related and ranked, or the sense of humanity among us to be enhanced for practical responses. These matters have to be determined in accord with the internal procedures and interpretive modes of history of modern philosophy. But the teleological dynamism of these procedures and interpretive acts points toward the meaning of humanity as the unifying center of reference for all specific investigations. And it is the pivot whereby historical inquiries can be given practical significance for human action today.

As far as the general theory of historical understanding is concerned, it is better to inspect this sur-teleology explicitly than to leave its operative presence in an implicit and uncriticized condition. On at least three counts, it makes a noticeable difference in our comprehension and evaluation of historical work in modern philosophy, to know that such work includes an ultimate ordination toward clarifying the meaning of humanity. This telic reference underlines the humanistic influence of history of modern philosophy within university education; it elucidates the recurrent need for diversification in the modern sources and in the modes of their historical interpretation; and it brings us firmly into the working context of the community of modern philosophers and their historians. Our general theory receives its final testing and strengthening from a consideration of these three aspects.

Ideally, *the university study of philosophy* should join rigorous adherence to methods of inquiry with lively concern for the problems of men and all the values achieved through the other disciplines. Sometimes in practice, however, the latter concern is discouraged through a technique of isolating the professional interests in philosophy from the broader aims of education. The humanistic quality of the philosophical strand in university education does not get actualized effortlessly and without discussion. One way to secure its effective presence is to cultivate the history of modern philosophy in its plenary teleological interest in the question of man.

When historical studies are permeated with the theme of humanity, they enable the contemporary forms of philosophizing to remain open to the full range of humane problems and values. If developed in this spirit, the history of modern philosophy serves as a humanizing force which binds together the philosophical and the other components in university education. All these uses of intelligence are quickened by being compared with each other and by inclining the university community toward the common task of reflectively analyzing, appreciating, and improving human reality in all its modes.[23]

A reflexive benefit also accrues to our general theory of historical access, once the connection is perceived between the theme of humanity and *the methodic drive toward diversification* of the means and patterns of interpreting. A proximate reason for such variation lies, of course, in the complexity of the modern source writings and in the constant developments at the contemporary pole of reference for historical understanding. But such complexity and developments are themselves an appropriate response to the teleological ideal of reflecting upon and further actuating the meaning of humanity. Thus the diversifying process in historical studies is fundamentally proportioned to this purposive ideal acknowledged by the modern philosophers.

John Stuart Mill offers a lively argument for the entailment relation between the theme of humanity and the pluriformity of philosophies and interpretive methods in history. His 1859 essay *On Liberty* can be instructively transposed from the setting of political philosophy to that of historical methodology in philosophy, especially since he himself maintains a synoptic conception of the pattern for "political and philosophical theories" in coadaptation. This essay is itself a notable example of delayed influence and cross-fertilization among philosophers in different modern traditions. For the theoretical crux of his argument, Mill draws heavily upon Wilhelm von Humboldt's *The Limits of State Action*. This latter treatise was composed during the springtide of German

---

[23] "The humanist alone can establish humanity's dialogue with its own unconscious or semiconscious drives, because he alone considers man a free being who has to do with himself before and after he has to do with conditions and results" (Eric Weil, "Humanistic Studies: Their Object, Methods, and Meaning," *Daedalus*, Spring 1970: *Theory in Humanistic Studies*, p. 254).

idealism (1791-92), was published as a complete text only in 1852, and was issued in English translation (under the somewhat grandiloquent title *The Sphere and Duties of Government*) just five years before Mill published his own essay.

Mill chose the following sentence from Humboldt as the epigraph for *On Liberty*: "The grand, leading principle, towards which every argument [hitherto] unfolded in these pages directly converges, is the absolute and essential importance of human development in its richest diversity." This is a principle which holds good for diversification in philosophies and historical interpretations, as well as in the political order. Mill strengthened his argument for intellectual pluralism by selecting key phrases from this declaration of his German source:

> The true end of man, or that which is prescribed by the eternal and immutable dictates of reason, and not suggested by vague and transient desires, is the highest and most harmonious development of his powers to a complete and consistent whole. Freedom is the first and indispensable condition which the possibility of such a development presupposes; but there is besides another essential—intimately connected with freedom, it is true—a variety of situations. . . . This individual vigour, then, and manifold diversity, combine themselves in originality; and hence, that on which the whole greatness of mankind ultimately depends—towards which every human being must ceaselessly direct his efforts, and of which especially those who wish to influence their fellow-men must never lose sight: individuality of energy and self-development.[24]

Humanity's development requires freedom along with variety of situations. Mill insisted that variety of situations holds

[24] Wilhelm von Humboldt, *The Limits of State Action*, ed. J. W. Burrow, pp. 16-17, 51 (revision of the 1854 Coulthard tr. used by Mill). Compare the selective thematic use of Humboldt in Mill's *On Liberty*, as contextually presented in *Prefaces to Liberty: Selected Writings of John Stuart Mill*, ed. Bernard Wishy, pp. 239, 301.

as stringently for free variation in the modes of thought as it does for social and political processes.

His own summary of the argument discloses that we must look to a study of human nature for the grounds supporting the principle of maximum diversification of philosophical and social-political positions.

> First, if any opinion is compelled to silence, that opinion may, for aught we can certainly know, be true. To deny this is to assume our own infallibility. Secondly, though the silenced opinion be an error, it may, and very commonly does, contain a portion of truth; and since the general or prevailing opinion on any subject is rarely or never the whole truth, it is only by the collision of adverse opinions that the remainder of the truth has any chance of being supplied. Thirdly, even if the received opinion be not only true, but the whole truth; unless it is suffered to be, and actually is, vigorously and earnestly contested, it will, by most of those who receive it, be held in the manner of a prejudice, and with little comprehension or feeling of its rational grounds. And not only this, but, fourthly, the meaning of the doctrine itself will be in danger of being lost or enfeebled, and deprived of its vital effect on the character and conduct. . . . [A fifth and summary point is that] the only way in which a human being can make some approach to knowing the whole of a subject is by hearing what can be said about it by persons of every variety of opinion, and studying all modes in which it can be looked at by every character of mind. No wise man ever acquired his wisdom in any mode but this; nor is it in the nature of human intellect to become wise in any other manner.[25]

[25] Mill, *On Liberty*; in *Prefaces to Liberty*, pp. 261, 296; the next quotation is from p. 289. See J. M. Robson, *The Improvement of Mankind: The Social and Political Thought of John Stuart Mill*, for the underlying humanistic conception and its connection with Mill's logic of the moral sciences and his practical view of philosophizing. A linguistic and poetic interpretation of the diversification principle, operative in humanity, is advanced in Stéphane Mallarmé's *Crisis in Verse*: "The diversity of idioms on earth prevents anyone from utter-

In this simple language and realistic thought, Mill presents some home truths about our actual human nature and the paths to wisdom. And in virtue of the teleology of philosophy toward the study of man, his arguments spell out the pluriform conditions for philosophizing and historical interpreting.

His first point reminds us that the principle of fallibilism, governing philosophical inquiry and its history, is not arbitrarily stipulated but gives normative statement to the reality and experience of fallible man. The requirement of diversification in philosophies and historical interpretations arises from the self-assessment of the human race, not from either a failure of nerve or a predilection for novelty for its own sake. History of philosophy continually and by policy enables many kinds of considered opinions to break their silence, to speak once more to us, and thus to regain their chance of conveying some neglected truth to our minds.

Mill's second consideration rests on the fragmentary quality of even our most systematically developed philosophies and, in complimentary relation, the presence of sound meanings in even the most contracted and oblique readings of human existence. This impels a careful historian to pay scrupulous attention to modern philosophers of middle and minor standing, as well as to look for something enlightening for his own discipline in even the least history-minded sort of contemporary philosophy. Mill himself notes that "in the human mind, one-sidedness has always been the rule, and many-sidedness the exception. Hence, even in revolutions of opinion, one part of the truth usually sets while another rises." A distinctive service of history of philosophy to man-

---

ing the words which otherwise would be, by a single impression, materially the truth itself. This prohibition exists on purpose so that in nature (we come up against it with a smile) there may be no valid reason for thinking oneself God" (*Mallarmé*, ed. and tr. by Anthony Hartley, p. 166). Francis Bacon's phrase, quoted below, is taken from the Preface to *The Great Instauration*; see *The Philosophical Works of Francis Bacon*, ed. J. M. Robertson, p. 247.

kind is, therefore, to liberate it from an inexorable alterna-
tion of intellectual sunrises and sunsets. The pluralism of historical judgments is there to insure that new methods and
conceptual schemes will not be taken so absolutely as to dull
our appreciation of still other ways of perceiving, reflecting,
and appreciating.

The third and fourth arguments of Mill thematize the
fragility of our hold upon meanings and truths, as well as the
positive function of differences and oppositions among philosophies. We are always sliding from a direct judgmental
relation with a statement and its supporting grounds to a relationship based on memory and uncontested tradition, as
Locke has already observed. This inclination cannot be constructively disciplined simply by reducing ourselves to a
momentary and ahistorical mode of thinking. Rather, the
countermeasure consists in becoming critically reflective
about the tradition-making process itself. A thorough historical study of the diversity of philosophical traditions and
the need for comparing and criticizing them in the light of
one's own experience helps to keep human meanings alive,
not consigned to imposing mausoleums. Our earlier contrast
between the dead past and our living historical past is thus a
methodological way of meeting Mill's difficulty on the en-
feebling and distorting effect of a settled tradition of opinions, especially if they become as sacrosanct and unquestionable as what Locke calls satirically "the municipal laws of the
country." The transformation of philosophical sources from
a burden into a resource signifies not only a move within history of modern philosophy but also a general move required
by our human nature.

In his summary point, Mill establishes a basic proportion
between the actual collision among philosophical methods-
principles-syntheses and the human manner of attaining wisdom. Fallible men can indeed rectify their onesided opinions
through further experience and argument, but not through
experience alone if it is insulated from the bite of reasoned
disagreements and discussions. In some sense compatible with

their freedom, men have to be compelled to shed their comfortable intellectual blinkers, and this can be done only through the patient and publicly recorded argumentation of free and diverse minds. History of philosophy brings such argumentation into full focus and communicative form. It furnishes the developmental and interrelational aspects which do help men to open their minds to the insights of others, thus achieving the humane quality of manysidedness.

In history of modern philosophy, the conflict of interpretations—whether among the source thinkers or among their historical interpreters—is not a disaster but the normal and essential condition for any growth in meaning and truth. Under Mill's insistence, however, it must now be stated explicitly that diversity and methodic strife among philosophers is fruitful because it is an important mode of the diversity and strife required everywhere for mankind's development and wisdom. Thus the teleological reference of historical understanding toward the meaning of humanity is not an idle afterthought, but the basic condition for attaining a further clarification of what constitutes good and useful historical work. The human good itself—what Francis Bacon calls the *utilitas et amplitudo humana*, in a thematic phrase found noteworthy by Descartes and Vico, Kant and Mill—spurs the unremitting search of historians of modern philosophy after better textual bases, better modes of investigating them, and better forms of communication in contemporary language.

Finally, if modern philosophy accepts the teleology of developing the meaning of humanity, then it requires *the entire community of historians of philosophy* to grasp and interpret the many forms of this teleological development. All the methods and modes of knowing incorporated into our general analysis of historical understanding participate in this context of the interpreting community of historical inquirers. That is why there are no definitive closures and no entirely insular efforts in the historical interpretation of modern philosophy. The interpreting community, embracing past efforts and present modalities and the futural tendencies of historical understanding, keeps every individual line of investigation open to revision, support, and innovation.

Since there is some artistry involved in the act of historical interpreting of the philosophical conceptions of humanity, here at the end it may be permissible to surmise about a visual image which might convey the community relationship among the modern philosophers. Perhaps a latter-day Raphael will depict the spirit of modern philosophy in as perceptive a manner as Marc Chagall visualizes the spirit of modern music, in his glowing *Paris Opera Ceiling* (1964).[26]

The composers are drawn from every period and culture, from every form and style of music. Here are Rameau and Gluck, Mozart and Beethoven, Verdi and Wagner, Tchaikovsky and Stravinsky, Debussy and Ravel. They belong in an interrelated company, so that the values of the one can modify and enrich us along with the values of the other. Each musical source can be identified through some public forms, but Chagall maintains his free interpretive presence by interweaving his own images and connotations. Moreover, all the figurative motifs of music are embodied in the color zones and shadings, the perspectives and dynamisms, proper to the art of painting. Thus Chagall conveys a sense of the musical interrelations among composers at the same time as he suggests, through the power of his own mode of expression in painting, that analogies hold together the several arts and put them at the common service of our humanity. It is not difficult to find here a kindred assurance to our recurring theme of the di-

[26] For a developmental account of this great painting, see Izis Bidermanas and Roy McMullen, *The World of Marc Chagall*, chapter 12, "The Paris Opera Ceiling," pp. 206-237. Chagall's working principle that "a thing has to be allusive to other things in order to acquire its true identity" (p. 122), is a sound analogue of the historian's methodological principle that contextual and genetic, interdevelopmental and problem-centered, modes of questioning (the clues to philosophical allusiveness) are indispensable for reaching the living meaning of a philosophical source.

versity and intercommunication among modern philosophers, their availability to the art of historical interpreting and interdisciplinary analogies, and their joint teleology toward the self-understanding and further evolving of humanity.

Let me assign the last word, however, to two representative modern philosophers themselves. Royce and Kant are not primarily historians of philosophy, but each in his day and manner has appreciated the purpose and uses of historical studies. This quality of appreciation knits together the source philosophers and their historical interpreters, today as in previous years. In the midst of an argumentative letter to Charles Peirce, Royce makes this forthright statement: "I myself am a lover and teacher of the history of philosophy. I believe most ardently that *only* this history can help us out."[27] In view of the theory of historical understanding proposed here, it is advisable to attach two qualifications to this welcome declaration. First, the "us" who are helped by history of philosophy is a term whose reference cannot be confined to the ranks of professional philosophers, but must include all reflective men and women who are seeking their self-education in the meanings and ways of humanity. And second, the educative value of history of philosophy invites and requires the contribution of every other discipline, historical and otherwise, for the purpose of improving the possibilities for human cognition, valuation, and action.

The persistent teleology of modern philosophy and its history, joining just estimates with generosity and hopefulness for man, also shines through this private reflection penned by Kant:

> In judging the writings of others, one must choose the method of participation in the general cause of human reason. From the endeavor to seek out that which belongs to the whole, one finds it worth the try to lend a helping hand to the author, or rather to his best representative, and to

[27] Josiah Royce, *Letter of November 18, 1891, to Charles S. Peirce*, in *The Letters of Josiah Royce*, ed. John Clendenning, p. 285.

treat the defects as secondary matters. To destroy everything is depressing for reason as a whole.[28]

It is altogether fitting to bring the present study to a close with this Kantian coda. For amid all the complex aims and particular procedures uncovered through our functional reflection upon the historian's work in modern philosophy, there is also a pervasive sensitivity to the general interests of humanity. The teleological sense of this alliance between the interpreting of modern philosophy and the enriching of humane reasonableness in all its modes is captured in Kant's memorable phrase: *die Methode der Teilnehmung an der allgemeinen Sache der menschlichen Vernunft*—the method of participation in the general cause of human reason.

[28] Kant, *Reflexionen zur Metaphysik*, no. 4992, ed. E. Adickes; in the Prussian Academy edition of Kant's *Gesammelte Schriften*, vol. 18, pp. 53-54. Kant's reflection, made in reference to his use of other philosophers while still hewing to his distinctive plan in the composition of *Critique of Pure Reason*, is used as a guiding maxim in Ernst Cassirer's already cited essay on Heidegger: "Kant and the Problem of Metaphysics," in *Kant: Disputed Questions*, ed. M. S. Gram, p. 136. Kant can look with equanimity on any objection that the philosophical rigor of his critique deprives people of valuable convictions. "The loss affects only the *monopoly of the schools*, in no respect the *interests of humanity*," which remain paramount for critical philosopher and critical historian together (*Critique of Pure Reason*, Preface, B xxxii; Smith tr., p. 30).

BIBLIOGRAPHY

Bibliography

(For additional entries see p. 451.)

1. BOOKS

Adams, H. P., *Karl Marx in His Earlier Writings*. London: Allen and Unwin, 1940.

Alexander, W. J., *Johann Georg Hamann: Philosophy and Faith*. The Hague: Nijhoff, 1966.

Allen, R. E., ed., *Studies in Plato's Metaphysics*. New York: Humanities Press, 1965.

Anscombe, G. E. M., and P. T. Geach, *Three Philosophers*. Ithaca: Cornell University Press, 1961.

Ardley, Gavin, *Berkeley's Renovation of Philosophy*. The Hague: Nijhoff, 1968.

Armstrong, David M., *Berkeley's Theory of Vision*. Melbourne: Melbourne University Press, 1960.

Arvon, H., *Ludwig Feuerbach, ou la transformation du sacré*. Paris: Presses Universitaires, 1957.

Asveld, P., *La Pensée religieuse du jeune Hegel*. Louvain: Nauwelaerts, 1953.

Austin, J. L., *How to Do Things with Words*. New York: Oxford University Press, 1962.

———, *Philosophical Papers*. Second edition. New York: Oxford University Press, 1970.

———, *Sense and Sensibilia*. Oxford: Clarendon Press, 1962.

Avineri, Shlomo, *The Social and Political Thought of Karl Marx*. New York: Cambridge University Press, 1968.

Ayer, A. J., *The Origins of Pragmatism*. San Francisco: Freeman, Cooper, 1968.

———, ed., *Logical Positivism*. Glencoe: Free Press, 1959.

Bachelard, Suzanne, *A Study of Husserl's Formal and Transcendental Logic*. Evanston: Northwestern University Press, 1968.

Bacon, Francis, *The Philosophical Works of Francis Bacon*, edited by J. M. Robertson. New York: Dutton, 1905.

Baldini, A. E., *Il pensiero giovanile di John Locke*. Milan: Marzorati, 1969.

Balz, A. G., *Cartesian Studies*. New York: Columbia University Press, 1951.

————, *Descartes and the Modern Mind*. New Haven: Yale University Press, 1952.

Barrett, W., and H. D. Aiken, eds., *Philosophy in the Twentieth Century*. 2 vols. New York: Random House, 1962.

Bate, W. Jackson, *The Burden of the Past and the English Poet*. Cambridge: Harvard University Press, 1970.

Baudelaire, Charles, *Selected Verse*, translated by Francis Scarfe. Baltimore: Penguin Books, 1961.

Bauer, Gerhard, *"Geschichtlichkeit"*: *Wege und Irrwege eines Begriffs*. Berlin: Gruyter, 1963.

Bausola, Adriano, *Metafisica e rivelazione nella filosofia positiva di Schelling*. Milan: Vita e Pensiero, 1965.

————, *Lo svolgimento del pensiero di Schelling*. Milan: Vita e Pensiero, 1969.

Bayle, Pierre, *Historical and Critical Dictionary*, edited by R. H. Popkin. Indianapolis: Bobbs-Merrill, 1965.

Beck, Lewis W., *Early German Philosophy*: *Kant and His Predecessors*. Cambridge: Harvard University Press, 1969.

————, *Studies in the Philosophy of Kant*. Indianapolis: Bobbs-Merrill, 1965.

————, ed., *Kant Studies Today*. La Salle: Open Court, 1969.

————, ed., *Proceedings of the Third International Kant Congress*. Dordrecht: Reidel, 1971.

Belaval, Yvon, *Leibniz, critique de Descartes*. Paris: Gallimard, 1960.

Bennett, Jonathan, *Kant's Analytic*. New York: Cambridge University Press, 1966.

Bentham, Jeremy, *A Bentham Reader*, edited by M. P. Mack. New York: Pegasus Press, 1969.

Berkeley, George, *Principles of Human Knowledge*: *Text and Critical Essays*, edited by Colin M. Turbayne, Indianapolis: Bobbs-Merrill, 1969.

————, *The Works of George Berkeley, Bishop of Cloyne*, edited by A. A. Luce and T. E. Jessop. 9 vols. New York: Nelson, 1948-1957.

Bidermanas, Izis, and Roy McMullen, *The World of Marc Chagall*. New York: Doubleday, 1968.

Bigo, Pierre, *Marxisme et humanisme*. Paris: Presses Universitaires, 1954.

Billicsich, F., *Das Problem des Übels in der Philosophie des Abendlandes*. 3 vols. Cologne: Sexl, 1952-1959.

Blanshard, Brand, *On Philosophical Style*. Bloomington: Indiana University Press, 1954.

Bloch, Ernst, *The Principle of Hope*. New York: Herder and Herder, forthcoming.

Boas, George, *The History of Ideas*. New York: Scribners, 1969.

Bodammer, Theodor, *Hegels Deutung der Sprache*. Hamburg: Meiner, 1969.

Boelen, B. J., *Existential Thinking*. Pittsburgh: Duquesne University Press, 1968.

Bonno, G., *Les Relations intellectuelles de Locke avec la France*. Berkeley and Los Angeles: University of California Press, 1955.

Borges, J. L., *Other Inquisitions*. Austin: University of Texas Press, 1964.

Bourke, V. J., *Will in Western Thought*. New York: Sheed and Ward, 1964.

Bowne, G. D., *The Philosophy of Logic 1880-1908*. The Hague: Mouton, 1966.

Bradley, F. H., *The Presuppositions of Critical History*,

edited by L. Rubinoff. Chicago: Quadrangle Books, 1968.

Brand, Myles, ed., *The Nature of Human Action*. Glenview: Scott, Foresman, 1970.

Brazill, W. J., *The Young Hegelians*. New Haven: Yale University Press, 1970.

Bruaire, Claude, *Schelling, ou la quête du secret de l'être*. Paris: Seghers, 1970.

Buber, Martin, *Between Man and Man*. London: Routledge and Kegan Paul, 1947.

Buchdahl, Gerd, *Metaphysics and the Philosophy of Science: The Classic Origins, Descartes to Kant*. Cambridge: Massachusetts Institute of Technology Press, 1970.

Burgin, Richard, *Conversations with Jorge Luis Borges*. New York: Holt, 1969.

Busson, Henri, *La Pensée religieuse française de Charron à Pascal*. Paris: Vrin, 1933.

Cairns, H., *Legal Philosophy from Plato to Hegel*. Baltimore: Johns Hopkins Press, 1967.

Callot, Émile, *La Philosophie de la vie au XVIIIᵉ siècle*. Paris: Rivière, 1965.

Calvez, Jean, *La Pensée de Karl Marx*. Paris: Seuil, 1956.

Campo, M., *La genesi del criticismo kantiano*. Varese: Magenta, 1953.

Cassirer, Ernst, *Das Erkenntnisproblem in der Philosophie und Wissenschaft der neueren Zeit*. Volumes 1-3. Berlin: B. Cassirer, 1906-1920.

————, *The Logic of the Humanities*. New Haven: Yale University Press, 1961.

————, *The Platonic Renaissance in England*. Austin: University of Texas Press, 1953.

————, *The Problem of Knowledge: Philosophy, Science, and History since Hegel*. New Haven: Yale University Press, 1950. [Volume 4 of *Das Erkenntnisproblem*.]

Castelli, Enrico, ed., *La filosofia della storia della filosofia*. Milan-Rome: Bocca, 1954.

Cavell, Stanley, *Must We Mean What We Say?* New York: Scribners, 1969.

Chekhov, Anton, *The Island: A Journey to Sakhalin.* New York: Washington Square Press, 1967.

Christensen, D. E., ed., *Hegel and the Philosophy of Religion.* The Hague: Nijhoff, 1970.

Collingwood, R. G., *The Idea of History.* New York: Oxford University Press, 1946.

———, *The Idea of Nature.* New York: Oxford University Press, 1960.

Collins, James, *Crossroads in Philosophy.* Chicago: Regnery Gateway, 1969.

———, *Descartes' Philosophy of Nature.* Oxford: Blackwell, 1971.

———, *The Emergence of Philosophy of Religion.* New Haven: Yale University Press, 1967.

———, *God in Modern Philosophy.* Chicago: Regnery Gateway, 1967.

———, *The Mind of Kierkegaard.* Chicago: Regnery Gateway, 1965.

Comte, Auguste, *Introduction to Positive Philosophy*, translated by F. Ferré. Indianapolis: Bobbs-Merrill, 1970.

Copleston, Frederick, *A History of Philosophy*, vol. 5: *Hobbes to Hume*, and vol. 8: *Bentham to Russell.* Westminster, Maryland: Newman Press, 1959, 1966.

Cornu, Auguste, *Karl Marx et Friedrich Engels.* 3 vols. Paris: Presses Universitaires, 1955-1962.

———, *The Origins of Marxian Thought.* Springfield, Illinois: C. C. Thomas, 1957.

Cottier, G. M., *L'Athéisme du jeune Marx.* Paris: Vrin, 1959.

Cowley, Fraser, *A Critique of British Empiricism.* New York: St. Martin's Press, 1968.

Cranston, Maurice, *John Locke.* New York: Macmillan, 1957.

Crocker, L. G., *Jean-Jacques Rousseau: The Quest (1712-1758)*. New York: Macmillan, 1968.

Croxall, T. H., *Kierkegaard Commentary*. New York: Harper, 1956.

Curley, Edwin M., *Spinoza's Metaphysics*. Cambridge: Harvard University Press, 1970.

D'Alembert, Jean Le Rond, *Preliminary Discourse to the Encyclopedia of Diderot*, translated by R. N. Schwab and W. E. Rex. Indianapolis: Bobbs-Merrill, 1963.

Danto, A. C., *What Philosophy Is*. New York: Harper and Row, 1968.

Davidson, D., and J. Hintikka, eds., *Words and Objections: Essays on the Work of W. V. Quine*. New York: Humanities Press, 1969.

Delaney, C. F., *Mind and Nature: A Study of the Naturalistic Philosophies of Cohen, Woodbridge and Sellars*. Notre Dame: University of Notre Dame Press, 1969.

Descartes, René, *Discourse on Method, Optics, Geometry, and Meteorology*, translated by P. J. Olscamp. Indianapolis: Bobbs-Merrill, 1965.

——, *Entretien avec Burman*, edited by Charles Adam. Paris: Boivin, 1937.

——, *Oeuvres de Descartes*, edited by Charles Adam and Paul Tannery, vol. 7: *Meditationes de Prima Philosophia*. Paris: Vrin, 1964.

——. *Oeuvres philosophiques*, edited by F. Alquié. Vols. 1-2 (to date). Paris: Garnier, 1963, 1967.

——, *Philosophical Essays*, translated by L. J. Lafleur. Indianapolis: Bobbs-Merrill, 1964.

——, *Philosophical Letters*, translated by Anthony Kenny. New York: Oxford University Press, 1970.

——, *The Philosophical Works of Descartes*, translated by E. S. Haldane and G. R. T. Ross. Corrected edition. 2 vols. New York: Cambridge University Press, 1968.

——, *Philosophical Writings*, translated by E. Anscombe and P. T. Geach. New York: Nelson, 1954.

————, *Philosophical Writings*, translated by N. K. Smith. New York: Modern Library, 1958.

————, *Regulae ad directionem ingenii*, edited by G. Crapulli. The Hague: Nijhoff, 1966.

Dewey, John, *The Early Works of John Dewey*, vol. I: *1882-1888*. Carbondale and Edwardsville: Southern Illinois University Press, 1969.

Dewhurst, Kenneth, *John Locke 1632-1704, Physician and Philosopher: A Medical Biography*. London: Wellcome Historical Medical Library, 1963.

Dibon, P., ed., *Pierre Bayle, Le Philosophe de Rotterdam*. Amsterdam: Elsevier, 1959.

Diderot, Denis, *Rameau's Nephew and Other Works*, translated by Jacques Barzun and R. H. Bowen. New York: Doubleday Anchor, 1956.

Dilthey, Wilhelm, *Pattern and Meaning in History*, edited by H. P. Rickman. New York: Harper Torchbook, 1962.

Dray, W. H., ed., *Philosophical Analysis and History*. New York: Harper and Row, 1966.

Dreyfus, H. L., *A Critique of Artificial Reason*. New York: Harper and Row, forthcoming.

Dryer, D. P., *Kant's Solution for Verification in Metaphysics*. Toronto: University of Toronto Press, 1966.

Dufrenne, Mikel, *The Notion of the A Priori*. Evanston: Northwestern University Press, 1966.

Dunn, John, *The Political Thought of John Locke*. Cambridge: Cambridge University Press, 1969.

Dupré, Louis, *Kierkegaard as Theologian*. New York: Sheed and Ward, 1963.

Edie, J. M., ed., *New Essays in Phenomenology*. Chicago: Quadrangle, 1969.

Edwards, P., and A. Pap, eds., *A Modern Introduction to Philosophy*. Revised edition. New York: Free Press, 1965.

Einaudi, M., *The Early Rousseau*. Ithaca: Cornell University Press, 1967.

Eller, Vernard, *Kierkegaard and Radical Discipleship*. Princeton: Princeton University Press, 1968.

Elveton, T. O., ed., *The Phenomenology of Husserl*. Chicago: Quadrangle, 1970.

Engel, S. M., *Language and Illumination*. The Hague: Nijhoff, 1969.

Fabro, Cornelio, *God in Exile*: *Modern Atheism*. Westminster: Newman Press, 1968.

Fackenheim, Emil, *Metaphysics and Historicity*. Milwaukee: Marquette University Press, 1961.

Fain, Haskell, *Between Philosophy and History*. Princeton: Princeton University Press, 1970.

Fann, E. T., ed., *Ludwig Wittgenstein*: *The Man and His Philosophy*. New York: Dell, 1967.

————, ed., *Symposium on J. L. Austin*. New York: Humanities Press, 1969.

Favrholdt, David, *An Interpretation and Critique of Wittgenstein's Tractatus*. Copenhagen: Munksgaard, 1965.

Feuerbach, Ludwig, *The Essence of Christianity*. New York: Harper Torchbook, 1957.

————, *Lectures on the Essence of Religion*. New York: Harper and Row, 1967.

————, *Principles of the Philosophy of the Future*. Indianapolis: Bobbs-Merrill, 1966.

Fichte, J. G., *Science of Knowledge (Wissenschaftslehre)*, translated by P. Heath and J. Lachs. New York: Appleton-Century-Crofts, 1970.

Findlay, J. N., *Hegel*: *A Re-Examination*. New York: Macmillan, 1958.

Fitzgerald, John J., *Peirce's Theory of Signs as Foundation for Pragmatism*. The Hague: Mouton, 1966.

Friedmann, G., *Leibniz et Spinoza*. Revised edition. Paris: Gallimard, 1962.

Friedman, M. S., *Martin Buber*: *The Life of Dialogue*. New York: Harper Torchbook, 1960.

Fromm, Erich, *Marx's Concept of Man*. New York: Ungar, 1961.

Fuhrmans, Horst, *Schellings Philosophie der Weltalter*. Düsseldorf: Schwann, 1954.

Gagern, Michael von, *Ludwig Feuerbach*. Munich: Pustet, 1970

Gallie, W. B., *Philosophy and the Historical Understanding*. New York: Schocken, 1968.

Gardiner, Patrick, ed., *Theories of History*. Glencoe: Free Press, 1959.

Gay, Peter, *The Bridge of Criticism*. New York: Harper Torchbook, 1970.

Geldsetzer, L., *Die Philosophie der Philosophiegeschichte im 19. Jahrhundert*. Meisenheim: Hain, 1968.

Görland, I., *Die Kantkritik des jungen Hegel*. Frankfurt: Klostermann, 1966.

Gouhier, Henri, *La Pensée métaphysique de Descartes*. Paris: Vrin, 1962.

————, *Les Premières Pensées de Descartes*. Paris: Vrin, 1958.

Gram, M. S., *Kant, Ontology, and the A Priori*. Evanston: Northwestern University Press, 1968.

————, ed., *Kant: Disputed Questions*. Chicago: Quadrangle, 1967.

Grayeff, F., *Kant's Theoretical Philosophy*. New York: Barnes and Noble, 1970.

Green, F. C., *Jean-Jacques Rousseau*. Cambridge: Cambridge University Press, 1955.

Grene, Marjorie, *The Knower and the Known*. New York: Basic Books, 1966.

Grua, Gaston, *Jurisprudence universelle et theodicée selon Leibniz*. Paris: Presses Universitaries, 1953.

Guéhenno, Jean, *Jean-Jacques Rousseau*. 2 vols. New York: Columbia University Press, 1966.

Guéroult, Martial, *Descartes selon l'ordre des raisons*. 2 vols. Paris: Aubier, 1953.

————, *Spinoza*. 2 vols. Paris: Aubier, 1970-71.

Gurwitsch, Aron, *Studies in Phenomenology and Psychology*. Evanston: Northwestern University Press, 1966.

Guttmann, Julius, *Philosophies of Judaism*. New York: Holt, 1964.

Hallie, Philip, *Maine de Biran, Reformer of Empiricism 1766-1824*. Cambridge: Harvard University Press, 1959.

Hamann, J. G., *Sämtliche Werke*, vol. 3: *Schriften über Sprache, Mysterien, Vernunft, 1772-1778*, edited by J. Nadler. Vienna: Herder, 1951.

————, *Socratic Memorabilia*, translated by J. C. O'Flaherty. Baltimore: Johns Hopkins Press, 1967.

Hamlyn, D. W., *Sensation and Perception: A History of the Philosophy of Perception*. New York: Humanities Press, 1961.

Hammond, Albert L., *Ideas about Substance*. Baltimore: Johns Hopkins Press, 1969.

Harrison, J., and P. Laslett, *The Library of John Locke*. Oxford: Oxford University Press, 1965.

Hartmann, Klaus, *Die Marxsche Theorie*. Berlin: Gruyter, 1970.

Hartnack, Justus, *Kant's Theory of Knowledge*. New York: Harcourt, Brace, 1967.

Hegel, Georg Wilhelm Friedrich, *Gesammelte Werke*, edited by Otto Pöggeler. Hamburg: Meiner, 1968 ff.

————, *Hegels Vorreden, mit Kommentar zur Einführung in seine Philosophie*, edited by Erwin Metzske. Heidelberg: Kerle, 1949.

————, *On Art, Religion, Philosophy*, edited by J. Glenn Gray. New York: Harper Torchbook, 1970.

————, *Philosophy of Right*, translated by T. M. Knox. New York: Oxford University Press, 1967.

————, *System und Geschichte der Philosophie*, edited by J. Hoffmeister. Leipzig: Meiner, 1955.

Heidegger, Martin, *Being and Time*. New York: Harper and Row, 1962.

————, *The Essence of Reasons*. Evanston: Northwestern University Press, 1969.

————, *Hegel's Concept of Experience*. New York: Harper and Row, 1970.

————, *An Introduction to Metaphysics*. New Haven: Yale University Press, 1959.

————, *Kant and the Problem of Metaphysics*. Bloomington: Indiana University Press, 1962.

————, *Kants These über das Sein*. Frankfurt: Klostermann, 1963.

————, *Nietzsche*. 2 vols. Pfullingen: Neske, 1961.

————, *Vorträge und Aufsätze*. Pfullingen: Neske, 1954.

————, *Wegmarken*. Frankfurt: Klostermann, 1967.

————, *What Is a Thing?* Chicago: Regnery, 1967.

————, *What Is Called Thinking?* New York: Harper and Row, 1968.

Heimsoeth, H., *Studien zur Philosophie Immanuel Kants*. Cologne: Kölner Universitäts-Verlag, 1956.

————, ed., *Studien zu Kants philosophischer Entwicklung*. Hildesheim: Olms, 1968.

Hendel, C. W., ed., *The Philosophy of Kant and Our Modern World*. New York: Liberal Arts Press, 1957.

Hintikka, J., *Models for Modalities*. New York: Humanities Press, 1969.

Hofmann, J. E., *Die Entwicklungsgeschichte der leibnizschen Mathematik während des Aufenthaltes in Paris (1672-1676)*. Munich: Leibniz Verlag, 1949.

Hohlenberg, Johannes, *Søren Kierkegaard*. New York: Pantheon, 1954.

Holger, K., and others, *Personenindex zu Kants gesammelten Schriften*. Berlin: Gruyter, 1969.

Hollingdale, R. J., *Nietzsche*. Baton Rouge: Louisana State University Press, 1965.

Hook, Sidney, *From Hegel to Marx*. New York: Humanities Press, 1950.

Hoppe, H., *Kants Theorie der Physik*. Frankfurt: Klostermann, 1969.

Humboldt, Wilhelm von, *The Limits of State Action*, edited by J. W. Burrow. Cambridge: Cambridge University Press, 1969.

Hume, David, *Dialogues concerning Natural Religion*, edited by N. K. Smith. Indianapolis: Bobbs-Merrill, 1963.

Hume, David, *Essays Moral, Political and Literary*. New York: Oxford University Press, 1963.

————, *The Letters of David Hume*, edited by J. Y. T. Greig. 2 vols. Oxford: Clarendon Press, 1932.

————, *New Letters of David Hume*, edited by R. Klibansky and E. C. Mossner. Oxford: Clarendon Press, 1954.

————, *A Treatise of Human Nature*, edited by E. C. Mossner. Baltimore: Penguin, 1969.

Husserl, Edmund, *Briefe an Roman Ingarden*, edited by Roman Ingarden. The Hague: Nijhoff, 1968.

————, *Cartesian Meditations*. The Hague: Nijhoff, 1960.

————, *The Crisis of European Sciences and Transcendental Phenomenology*. Evanston: Northwestern University Press, 1970.

————, *Erste Philosophie (1923/24)*, Part I: *Kritische Ideengeschichte*, edited by R. Boehm. The Hague: Nijhoff, 1956 (*Husserliana*, vol. 7).

————, *Formal and Transcendental Logic*. The Hague: Nijhoff, 1969.

————, *Logical Investigations*. 2 vols. New York: Humanities Press, 1970.

Hyppolite, Jean, *Logique et existence*. Paris: Presses Universitaires, 1953.

————, *Studies on Marx and Hegel*. New York: Basic Books, 1969.

Jähnig, Dieter, *Schelling*: *Die Kunst in der Philosophie*. 2 vols. Pfullingen: Neske, 1966-1969.

James, William, *Collected Essays and Reviews*. New York: Longmans, Green, 1920.

————, *The Letters of William James*, edited by Henry James. 2 vols. Boston: Atlantic Monthly Press, 1920.

————, *The Writings of William James*, edited by J. J. McDermott. New York: Random House, 1967.

Janke, W., *Leibniz*: *Die Emendation der Metaphysik*. Frankfurt: Klostermann, 1963.

Jansohn, Heinz, *Kants Lehre von der Subjektivität*. Bonn: Bouvier, 1969.

Jaspers, Karl, *The Great Philosophers: The Foundations*. New York: Harcourt, Brace, 1962.

——, *Kant*. New York: Harcourt, Brace, 1962.

——, *The Origin and Goal of History*. New Haven: Yale University Press, 1953.

——, *Schelling: Grösse und Verhängnis*. Munich: Piper, 1955.

Jones, W. T., *The Sciences and the Humanities*. Berkeley and Los Angeles: University of California Press, 1965.

Julia, Didier, *La Question de l'homme et le fondement de la philosophie (Réflexion sur la philosophie pratique de Kant et la philosophie speculative de Fichte)*. Paris: Aubier, 1964.

Kabitz, W., *Die Philosophie des jungen Leibniz*. Heidelberg: Winter, 1909.

Kamenka, Eugene, *The Philosophy of Ludwig Feuerbach*. New York: Praeger, 1970.

Kant, Immanuel, *Critique of Pure Reason*, translated by N. K. Smith. New York: St. Martin's Press, 1965.

——, *Immanuel Kants Werke*, vol. 6: *Schriften von 1790-1796*, edited by Ernst Cassirer. Berlin: B. Cassirer, 1923.

——, *Introduction to Logic*. New York: Philosophical Library, 1963.

——, *Kant's Cosmogony*, W. Ley's edition of W. Hastie's translation. Westport, Connecticut: Greenwood, 1968.

——, *Metaphysical Foundations of Natural Science*, translated by J. Ellington. Indianapolis: Bobbs-Merrill, 1970.

——, *Philosophical Correspondence, 1759-99*, translated by A. Zweig. Chicago: University of Chicago Press, 1967.

——, *Prolegomena to Any Future Metaphysics*, translated by L. W. Beck. Indianapolis: Bobbs-Merrill, 1950.

——, *Reflexionen zur Metaphysik*, edited by E. Adickes. Vol. 18 of Prussian Academy edition of Kant's *Gesammelte Schriften*. Berlin: Gruyter, 1928.

Kant, Immanuel, *Universal Natural History and Theory of the Heavens*, M. K. Munitz's edition of W. Hastie's translation. Ann Arbor: University of Michigan Press, 1969.

————, *Vorlesungen über philosophische Enzyklopädie*, edited by G. Lehmann. Berlin: Akademie-Verlag, 1961.

Kaufmann, Walter, *Hegel*. New York: Doubleday, 1965.

————, *Nietzsche*. Third edition. Princeton: Princeton University Press, 1968.

Kaulbach, Friedrich, *Immanuel Kant*. Berlin: Gruyter, 1969.

————, and J. Ritter, eds., *Kritik und Metaphysik*. Berlin: Gruyter, 1966.

Keeler, L. W., *The Problem of Error from Plato to Kant*. Rome: Gregorian University Press, 1934.

Kelly, Donald R., *Foundations of Modern Historical Scholarship*. New York: Columbia University Press, 1970.

Kenny, Anthony, *Descartes*. New York: Random House, 1968.

Kern, Iso, *Husserl und Kant*. The Hague: Nijhoff, 1964.

Kluback, William, *Wilhelm Dilthey's Philosophy of History*. New York: Columbia University Press, 1956.

Kockelmans, J. J., *A First Introduction to Husserl's Phenomenology*. Pittsburgh: Duquesne University Press, 1967.

Kojève, Alexander, *Introduction to the Reading of Hegel*. New York: Basic Books, 1969.

Kolakowski, Leszek, *Toward a Marxist Humanism*. New York: Grove Press, 1969.

Kott, Jan, *Shakespeare Our Contemporary*. New York: Doubleday Anchor, 1966.

Koyré, Alexandre, *From the Closed World to the Infinite Universe*. Baltimore: Johns Hopkins Press, 1957.

Krikorian, Y. H., ed., *Naturalism and the Human Spirit*. New York: Columbia University Press, 1944.

Kroner, Richard, *Speculation and Revelation in the History of Philosophy*. 3 vols. Philadelphia: Westminster Press, 1956-1961.

————, *Von Kant bis Hegel*. 2 vols. Tübingen: Mohr, 1921-1924.

Kwant, R. C., *Critique: Its Nature and Function*. Pittsburgh: Duquesne University Press, 1967.

Lazerowitz, Morris, *The Structure of Metaphysics*. New York: Humanities Press, 1955.

————, *Studies in Metaphilosophy*. New York: Humanities Press, 1964.

Leeuwen, H. G. Van, *The Problem of Certainty in English Thought 1630-1690*. The Hague: Nijhoff, 1963.

Lehmann, Gerhard, *Beiträge zur Geschichte und Interpretation der Philosophie Kants*. Berlin: Gruyter, 1969.

Leibniz, G. W., *The Leibniz-Arnauld Correspondence*, translated by H. T. Mason and G. H. Parkinson. New York: Barnes and Noble, 1967.

————, *The Leibniz-Clarke Correspondence*, edited by H. G. Alexander, New York: Philosophical Library, 1956.

————. *Die Leibniz-Handschriften der königlichen öffentlichen Bibliothek zu Hannover*, edited by E. Bodemann. Hannover and Leipzig: Hahn, 1895. Reprinted, Hildesheim: Olms, 1966.

————, *Malebranche et Leibniz: Relations personelles*, edited by André Robinet. Paris: Vrin, 1955.

————, *Philosophical Papers and Letters*, translated by L. E. Loemker. Revised second edition. New York: Humanities Press, 1970.

————, *Textes inédits*, edited by G. Grua. 2 vols. Paris: Presses Universitaires, 1948.

Lenoble, R., *Esquisse d'une histoire de l'idée de nature*. Paris: Michel, 1969.

Leroy, A.-L., *George Berkeley*. Paris: Presses Universitaires, 1959.

Lewis, C. I., *Values and Imperatives*, edited by John Lange. Stanford: Stanford University Press, 1969.

Leyden, W. von, *Seventeenth-Century Metaphysics*. New York: Barnes and Noble, 1968.

Locke, John, *An Early Draft of Locke's Essay*, edited by R. I. Aaron and J. Gibb. Oxford: Clarendon Press, 1936.

——, *The Correspondence of John Locke and Edward Clarke*, edited by B. Rand. Cambridge: Harvard University Press, 1927.

——, *The Educational Writings of John Locke*, edited by J. L. Axtell. Cambridge: Cambridge University Press, 1968.

——, *Epistola de Tolerantia: A Letter on Toleration*, edited by R. Klibansky and J. W. Gough. Oxford: Clarendon Press, 1968.

——, *Essay concerning Human Understanding*, edited by J. W. Yolton. Revised edition. 2 vols. New York: Dutton, 1964-1965.

——, *Essays on the Law of Nature*, edited by W. von Leyden. Oxford: Clarendon Press, 1954.

——, *Locke's Travels in France 1675-1679*, edited by John Lough. Cambridge: Cambridge University Press, 1953.

——, *Two Tracts on Government*, edited by P. Abrams. Cambridge: Cambridge University Press, 1967.

——, *Two Treatises of Government*, edited by P. Laslett. Second edition. Cambridge: Cambridge University Press, 1967.

——. *The Works of John Locke*. Tenth edition. 10 vols. London: Johnson, 1801.

Lovejoy, A. O., *Essays in the History of Ideas*. Baltimore: Johns Hopkins Press, 1948.

——, *The Great Chain of Being*. Cambridge: Harvard University Press, 1936.

——, *The Reason, the Understanding, and Time*. Baltimore: Johns Hopkins Press, 1961.

Löwith, Karl, *From Hegel to Nietzsche*. New York: Holt, 1964.

Lowrie, Walter, *Kierkegaard*. New York: Oxford University Press, 1938.

Luce, A. A., *Berkeley and Malebranche*. New York: Oxford University Press, 1934.

————, *Berkeley's Immaterialism*. New York: Nelson, 1945.

————, *The Dialectic of Immaterialism*. London: Hodder and Stoughton, 1963.

Lukács, Georg, *La Destruction de la raison*, 2 vols. Paris: Arche, 1958-1959. [German edition, 1954.]

————, *Der junge Hegel und die Probleme der kapitalistischen Gesellschaft*. Berlin: Aufbau-Verlag, 1954.

McFarland, J. D., *Kant's Concept of Teleology*. Chicago: Aldine, 1970.

McKinnon, Alastair, ed., *The Kierkegaard Indices*. Leiden: Brill, 1970 ff.

McMullin, Ernan, ed., *The Concept of Matter*. Notre Dame: University of Notre Dame Press, 1963; and revised, 2-volume paperback edition.

McRae, Robert, *The Problem of the Unity of the Sciences*: *Bacon to Kant*. Toronto: University of Toronto Press, 1961.

Macomber, W. B., *The Anatomy of Disillusion*: *Martin Heidegger's Notion of Truth*. Evanston: Northwestern University Press, 1967.

Mallarmé, Stéphane, *Mallarmé*, translated by Anthony Hartley. Baltimore: Penguin, 1965.

Mann, Thomas, *Death in Venice and Seven Other Stories*. New York: Knopf, 1936.

Manuel, Frank E., *Shapes of Philosophical History*. Stanford: Stanford University Press, 1965.

Maréchal, Joseph, *A Maréchal Reader*, edited by J. Donceel. New York: Herder and Herder, 1970.

Martin, Gottfried, *Leibniz*: *Logic and Metaphysics*. Manchester: Manchester University Press, 1964.

————, ed., *Allgemeiner Kantindex*. Berlin: Gruyter, 1967 ff.

Marx, Karl, *Writings of the Young Marx on Philosophy and Society*, edited by L. D. Easton and K. H. Guddat. New York: Doubleday Anchor, 1967.

Matheron, A., *Individu et communauté chez Spinoza*. Paris: Minuit, 1969.

Mazlish, Bruce, *The Riddle of History*. New York: Harper and Row, 1966.

Meiland, J. W., *Scepticism and Historical Knowledge*. New York: Random House, 1965.

Melsen, A. G. Van, *From Atomos to Atom*. New York: Harper Torchbook, 1960.

Merleau-Ponty, Maurice, *Phenomenology of Perception*. New York: Humanities Press, 1962.

————, *Signs*. Evanston: Northwestern University Press, 1964.

————, *The Visible and the Invisible*. Evanston: Northwestern University Press, 1968.

Michelletti, M., *Lo schopenhauerismo di Wittgenstein*. Bologna: Zanichelli, 1967.

Mill, John Stuart, *Autobiography*, edited by J. J. Coss. Indianapolis: Bobbs-Merrill, 1957.

————, *The Earlier Letters of John Stuart Mill, 1812-1848*, edited by F. E. Mineka. 2 vols. Toronto: University of Toronto Press, 1963. Vols. 12 and 13 of University of Toronto edition of Mill's *Collected Works*.

————, *The Early Draft of John Stuart Mill's Autobiography*, edited by Jack Stillinger. Urbana: University of Illinois Press, 1961.

————, *John Stuart Mill and Harriet Taylor*, edited by F. A. Hayek. Chicago: University of Chicago Press, 1951.

————, *The Letters of John Stuart Mill*, edited by H. S. R. Elliot. 2 vols. London: Longmans, Green, 1910.

————, *Mill's Essays on Literature and Society*, edited by J. B. Schneewind. New York: Collier Books, 1965.

————, *Mill's Ethical Writings*, edited by J. B. Schneewind. New York: Collier Books, 1965.

————, *Prefaces to Liberty*, edited by Bernard Wishy. Boston: Beacon Press, 1959.

Moltmann, Jürgen, *Theology of Hope*. New York: Harper and Row, 1967.

Moore, E. C., and R. S. Robin, editors, *Studies in the Philosophy of Charles Sanders Peirce*. Second series. Amherst: University of Massachusetts Press, 1964.

Morgan, George W., *The Human Predicament: Dissolution and Wholeness*. Providence: Brown University Press, 1968.

Morgenbesser, S., P. Suppes, and M. White, editors, *Philosophy, Science, and Method*. New York: St. Martin's Press, 1969.

Mueller, Gustav E., *Hegel: The Man, His Vision and Work*. New York: Pageant Press, 1968.

Mure, G. R. G., *The Philosophy of Hegel*, New York: Oxford University Press, 1965.

Murphy, J. G., *Kant: The Philosophy of Right*. New York: St. Martin's Press, 1970.

Nash, R. H., ed., *Ideas of History*. 2 vols. New York: Dutton, 1969.

Newman, John Henry, *The Philosophical Notebook*, edited by E. J. Sillem and A. J. Boekraad. 2 vols. New York: Humanities Press, 1969-70.

Nietzsche, Friedrich, *Basic Writings of Nietzsche*, translated by Walter Kaufmann. New York: Modern Library, 1968.

————, *Nietzsche: A Self-Portrait from His Letters*, translated by Peter Fuss and Henry Shapiro. Cambridge: Harvard University Press, 1971.

————, *Schopenhauer as Educator*, translated by J. W. Hillesheim and M. R. Simpson. Chicago: Regnery Gateway, 1965.

————, *Selected Letters of Friedrich Nietzsche*, translated by Christopher Middleton. Chicago: University of Chicago Press, 1969.

Nietzsche, Friedrich, *Thus Spoke Zarathustra*, translated by R. J. Hollingdale. Baltimore: Penguin, 1961.

Nivelle, Armand, *Les Théories esthétiques en Allemagne de Baumgarten à Kant*. Paris: Les Belles Lettres, 1955.

Noguchi, Isamu, *A Sculptor's World*. New York: Harper and Row, 1968.

Novak, Michael, ed., *American Philosophy and the Future*. New York: Scribners, 1968.

Pap, Arthur, *Semantics and Necessary Truth*. New Haven: Yale University Press, 1958.

Pascal, Blaise, *Pascal's Pensées*, translated by Martin Turnell. New York: Harper, 1962.

Passmore, J. A., *Hume's Intentions*. New York: Basic Books, 1968.

————, ed., *The Historiography of the History of Philosophy*. The Hague: Mouton, 1965. (*History and Theory*, Beiheft 5.)

Paterson, A. M., *The Infinite Worlds of Giordano Bruno*. Springfield, Illinois: Charles C. Thomas, 1970.

Peirce, Charles Sanders, *Charles S. Peirce's Letters to Lady Welby*, edited by I. C. Lieb. New Haven: Whitlock's, 1953.

————, *Collected Papers of Charles Sanders Peirce*, edited by C. Hartshorne, P. Weiss, and A. Burks. 8 vols. Cambridge: Harvard University Press, 1931-1958.

Peperzak, A. T., *Le Jeune Hegel et la vision morale du monde*. Revised second edition. The Hague: Nijhoff, 1969.

Perry, R. B., *The Thought and Character of William James*. 2 vols. Boston: Little, Brown, 1936.

Peters, Richard, *Hobbes*. Second edition. Baltimore: Penguin, 1967.

Peursen, C. A. van, *Leibniz*. New York: Dutton, 1970.

Philonenko, Alexis, *La Liberté humaine dans la philosophie de Fichte*. Paris: Vrin. 1966.

————, *Théorie et praxis dans la pensée morale et politique de Kant et de Fichte en 1793*. Paris: Vrin, 1968.

Pieper, Josef, *Hope and History*. New York: Herder and Herder, 1969.

Plaass, P., *Kants Theorie der Naturwissenschaft*. Göttingen: Vandenhoeck and Ruprecht, 1965.

Popkin, Richard H., *The History of Scepticism from Erasmus to Descartes*. New York: Harper Torchbook, 1968.

Preller, Victor, *Divine Science and the Science of God: A Reformulation of Thomas Aquinas*. Princeton: Princeton University Press, 1967.

Préposiet, J., *Spinoza et la liberté des hommes*. Paris: Gallimard, 1967.

Randall, J. H., Jr., *How Philosophy Uses Its Past*. New York: Columbia University Press, 1963.

Rescher, Nicholas, *The Philosophy of Leibniz*. Englewood Cliffs: Prentice-Hall, 1967.

Rice, Lee C., ed., *The Legacy of Hegel*. Forthcoming.

Richardson, W. J., *Heidegger: Through Phenomenology to Thought*. The Hague: Nijhoff, 1963.

Ricoeur, Paul, *Fallible Man*. Chicago: Regnery Gateway, 1965.

———, *History and Truth*. Evanston: Northwestern University Press, 1965.

———, *Husserl: An Analysis of His Phenomenology*. Evanston: Northwestern University Press, 1967.

Rivaud, Albert, *Histoire de la philosophie*, vol. 5: *La Philosophie allemande de 1700 à 1850*. 2 parts. Paris: Presses Universitaires, 1968.

Robson, J. M., *The Improvement of Mankind: The Social and Political Thought of John Stuart Mill*. Toronto: University of Toronto Press, 1968.

Rotenstreich, Nathan, *Jewish Philosophy in Modern Times: From Mendelssohn to Rosenzweig*. New York: Holt, 1968.

Rousseau, Jean-Jacques, *The First and Second Discourses*, translated by R. D. Masters. New York: St. Martin's Press, 1964.

Rousset, Bernard, *La Doctrine kantienne de l'objectivité*. Paris: Vrin, 1967.

————, *La Perspective finale de "L'éthique" et le problème de la cohérence du spinozisme*. Paris: Vrin, 1968.

Royce, Josiah, *The Letters of Josiah Royce*, edited by John Clendenning. Chicago: University of Chicago Press, 1970.

————, *The Spirit of Modern Philosophy*. New York: Braziller, 1955.

Russell, Bertrand, *A Critical Exposition of the Philosophy of Leibniz*. Second edition. London: Allen and Unwin, 1937.

Ryan, Alan, *John Stuart Mill*. New York: Pantheon Books, 1970.

Ryle, Gilbert, *Plato's Progress*. Cambridge: Cambridge University Press, 1966.

Sallis, John, ed., *Heidegger and the Path of Thinking*. Pittsburgh: Duquesne University Press, 1970.

Sartre, Jean-Paul. *Being and Nothingness*. New York: Philosophical Library, 1956.

Sayre, Kenneth M., *Plato's Analytic Method*. Chicago: University of Chicago Press, 1969.

Schäfer, L., *Kants Metaphysik der Natur*. Berlin: Gruyter, 1966.

Schelling, F.W.J., *Bruno*. Hamburg: Meiner, 1954.

————, *On University Studies*. Athens, Ohio: Ohio University Press, 1966.

————, *Werke*, Ergänzungsband 6: *Philosophie der Offenbarung*, new ordering by M. Schröter. Munich: Beck and Oldenbourg, 1954.

Schilpp, Paul A., ed., *The Philosophy of Rudolf Carnap*. La Salle: Open Court, 1963.

Schlanger, Judith, *Schelling et la realité finie*. Paris: Presses Universitaires, 1966.

Schmitt, Richard, *Martin Heidegger on Being Human*. New York: Random House, 1969.

Schneewind, J. B., ed., *Mill: A Collection of Critical Essays*. Notre Dame: University of Notre Dame Press, 1969.

Schopenhauer, Arthur, *Der handschriftliche Nachlass*, edited by Arthur Hübscher. 5 vols. Frankfurt: Kramer, 1966-71.

————, *Essays and Aphorisms*, translated by R. J. Hollingdale. Baltimore: Penguin, 1970.

Schumann, K., *Die Grundlage der Wissenschaftslehre in ihrem Umrisse: Zu Fichtes "Wissenschaftslehren" von 1794 und 1810*. The Hague: Nijhoff, 1969.

Schulz, Walter, *Die Vollendung des deutschen Idealismus in der Spätphilosophie Schellings*. Stuttgart: Kohlhammer, 1955.

Schwartländer, J., *Der Mensch ist Person: Kants Lehre vom Menschen*. Stuttgart: Kohlhammer, 1968.

Seeberger, W., *Hegel, oder die Entwicklung des Geistes zur Freiheit*. Stuttgart: Klett, 1961.

Sellars, Roy Wood, *Lending a Hand to Hylas*. Yellow Springs, Ohio: FRH Library, 1968.

Sellars, Wilfrid, *Philosophical Perspectives*. Springfield, Illinois: Charles C. Thomas, 1967.

————, *Science and Metaphysics*. New York: Humanities Press, 1968.

Serres, Michel, *Le Système de Leibniz et ses modèles mathématiques*. 2 vols. Paris: Presses Universitaires, 1968.

Shestov, Lev, *Kierkegaard and the Existential Philosophy*. Athens: Ohio University Press, 1969.

Simmons, E. J., *Chekhov, A Biography*. Boston: Little, Brown, 1962.

Simon, J., *Das Problem der Sprache bei Hegel*. Stuttgart: Kohlhammer, 1966.

Singer, D. W., *Giordano Bruno: His Life and Thought*. New York: Schuman, 1950.

Smith, John E., *The Spirit of American Philosophy*. New York: Oxford University Press, 1963.

Smith, Norman K., *The Philosophy of David Hume*. New York: St Martin's Press, 1964.

Smith, R. G., *J. G. Hamann 1730-1788*. New York: Harper, 1960.

Soll, Ivan, *An Introduction to Hegel's Metaphysics*. Chicago: University of Chicago Press, 1969.

Somerhausen, Luc, *L'Humanisme agissant de Karl Marx*. Paris: Richard-Masse, 1946.

Sontag, Frederick, *The Existentialist Prolegomena to a Future Metaphysics*. Chicago: University of Chicago Press, 1969.

Spiegelberg, Herbert, *The Phenomenological Movement*. Second edition, 2 vols. The Hague: Nijhoff, 1965.

Spink, J. S., *French Free-Thought from Gassendi to Voltaire*. London: Athlone Press, 1960.

Spinoza, Benedict, *The Correspondence of Spinoza,* translated by A. Wolf. New York: Dial Press, 1928.

————, *Earlier Philosophical Writings*, translated by F. A. Hayes, Indianapolis: Bobbs-Merrill, 1963.

————, *Oeuvres complètes*, translated by Caillois-Francès-Misrahi. Paris: Gallimard, 1954.

————, *Opera*, edited by C. Gebhardt. 4 vols. Heidelberg: Winter, 1925.

————, *The Political Works*, translated by A. G. Wernham. Oxford: Clarendon Press, 1958.

Stahmer, Harold, *"Speak That I May See Thee!"* New York: Macmillan, 1968.

Steinkraus, W. E., ed., *New Studies in Berkeley's Philosophy*. New York: Holt, 1966.

————, ed., *New Studies in the Philosophy of Hegel*. New York: Holt, 1971.

Stenius, Erik, *Wittgenstein's Tractatus*. Ithaca: Cornell University Press, 1960.

Strawson, P. F., *The Bounds of Sense*: *An Essay on Kant's Critique of Pure Reason*. New York: Barnes and Noble, 1966.

———, *Individuals*: *An Essay in Descriptive Metaphysics*. New York: Doubleday Anchor, 1963.

Tagliacozzo, G., and H. V. White, eds., *Giambattista Vico*: *An International Symposium*. Baltimore: Johns Hopkins Press, 1969.

Thayer, H. S., *Meaning and Action*: *A Critical History of Pragmatism*. Indianapolis: Bobbs-Merrill, 1968.

Tilliette, Xavier, *Schelling: une philosophie en devenir*. 2 vols. Paris: Vrin, 1970.

Tonelli, Giorgio, *Elementi metodologici e metafisici in Kant dal 1745 al 1768*. Turin: Edizioni di Filosofia, 1959.

Tucker, Robert, *The Marxian Revolutionary Idea*. New York: Norton, 1969.

———, *Philosophy and Myth in Karl Marx*. New York: Cambridge University Press, 1961.

Turbayne, Colin M., *The Myth of Metaphor*. New Haven: Yale University Press, 1962.

Tymieniecka, A. T., *Leibniz's Cosmological Synthesis*. Assen: Van Gorcum, 1964.

Versényi, L., *Heidegger, Being, and Truth*. New Haven: Yale University Press, 1965.

Viano, C. A., *John Locke*: *Dal razionalismo all'illuminismo*. Turin: Einaudi, 1960.

Vico, Giambattista, *The Autobiography of Giambattista Vico*, translated by M. H. Fisch and T. G. Bergin. Ithaca: Cornell University Press, 1944.

———, *The New Science of Giambattista Vico*, translated by T. G. Bergin and M. H. Fisch. Revised edition, Ithaca: Cornell University Press, 1968.

Vleeschauwer, H.-J. de, *The Development of Kantian Thought*. New York: Nelson, 1962.

Volkmann-Schluck, K.-H., *Mythos und Logos*: *Interpretationen zu Schellings Philosophie der Mythologie*. Berlin: Gruyter, 1969.

Vrooman, J. R., *René Descartes, A Biography*. New York: Putnam, 1970.

Vuillemin, J., *L'Héritage kantien et la révolution coperni-cienne*. Paris: Presses Universitaires, 1954.

———, *Physique et métaphysique kantiennes*. Paris: Presses Universitaires, 1955.

Walsh, W. H., *Philosophy of History*. New York: Harper Torchbook, 1960.

Watson, James, *The Double Helix*. New York: Atheneum, 1968.

Watson, R. A., *Cartesian Studies*. Privately issued. St. Louis: Washington University, 1968.

———, *The Downfall of Cartesianism 1673-1712*. The Hague: Nijhoff, 1966.

Weiss, Paul, *History: Written and Lived*. Carbondale: Southern Illinois University Press, 1962.

Whitehead, A. N., *The Aims of Education*. New York: New American Library, 1949.

Wiedeburg, P., *Der junge Leibniz*. 2 vols. Wiesbaden: Steiner, 1962.

Wiener, P. P., ed., *Dictionary of the History of Ideas*. New York: Scribners, forthcoming.

———, and F. H. Young, eds., *Studies in the Philosophy of Charles Sanders Peirce*. First series. Cambridge: Harvard University, 1952.

Wild, Christoph, *Reflexion und Erfahrung: Eine Interpretation der Früh- und Spätphilosophie Schellings*. Munich: Alber, 1968.

Wisdom, J. O., *The Unconscious Origins of Berkeley's Philosophy*. New York: Hillary House, 1957.

Wittgenstein, Ludwig, *Philosophical Investigations*, translated by G. E. M. Anscombe. Third edition. New York: Macmillan, 1968.

———, *Tractatus Logico-Philosophicus*, translated by D. F. Pears and B. F. McGuinness. New York: Humanities Press, 1961.

———, *Zettel*, edited by G. E. M. Anscombe and G. H. von Wright. Berkeley and Los Angeles: University of California Press, 1967.

Wolff, R. P., ed., *Kant: A Collection of Critical Essays*. New York: Doubleday Anchor, 1967.

Wood, A. W., *Kant's Moral Religion*. Ithaca: Cornell University Press, 1970.

Wood, R. E., *Martin Buber's Ontology*. Evanston: Northwestern University Press, 1969.

Yolton, J. W., *Locke and the Compass of Human Understanding*. New York: Cambridge University Press, 1970.

————, ed., *John Locke: Problems and Perspectives*. Cambridge: Cambridge University Press, 1969.

Zac, S., *L'Idée de vie dans la philosophie de Spinoza*. Paris: Presses Universitaires, 1963.

2. ARTICLES

Alexander, W. M., "J. G. Hamann: Metacritic of Kant," *Journal of the History of Ideas, 27* (1966), 137-144.

Ayers, Michael R., "Substance, Reality, and the Great, Dead Philosophers," *American Philosophical Quarterly, 7* (1970), 38-49.

Bossert, W. H., "Kant's Doctrine of the Reciprocity of Freedom and Reason," *International Philosophical Quarterly, 8* (1968), 334-355.

Butts, Robert E., "Hypotheses and Explanations in Kant's Philosophy of Science," *Archiv für Geschichte der Philosophie, 43* (1961), 153-170.

————, "Kant on Hypotheses in the 'Doctrine of Method' and the *Logik*," *Archiv für Geschichte der Philosophie, 44* (1962), 185-203.

Cross Currents, 18 (1968), 257-335: symposium on "Hope."

Danto, A. C., "Basic Actions," *American Philosophical Quarterly, 2* (1965), 141-148.

Day, J. P., "Hope," *American Philosophical Quarterly, 6* (1969), 89-102.

Dunn, John, "The Identity of the History of Ideas," *Philosophy, 43* (1968), 85-104.

Engel, S. M., "Schopenhauer's Impact on Wittgenstein," *Journal of the History of Philosophy, 7* (1969), 285-302.

———, "Wittgenstein and Kant," *Philosophy and Phenomenological Research, 30* (1969-70), 483-513.

Faurot, Jean H. "What Is History of Philosophy?" *The Monist, 53* (1969), 642-655.

Genova, A. C., "Kant's Complex Problem of Reflective Judgment," *Review of Metaphysics, 23* (1969-70), 452-480.

Gleiman, L., "The Challenge of Nietzsche," *Thought, 42* (1967), 52-68.

Guéroult, Martial, "The History of Philosophy as a Philosophical Problem," *The Monist, 53* (1969), 563-587.

Hamburg, Carl H., "A Cassirer-Heidegger Seminar," *Philosophy and Phenomenological Research, 25* (1964-65), 208-222.

Heidegger, Martin, "Who is Nietzsche's Zarathustra?" *Review of Metaphysics, 20* (1966-67), 411-431.

Janik, A. S., "Schopenhauer and the Early Wittgenstein," *Philosophical Studies, 15* (1966), 76-95.

Krausser, Peter, "Dilthey's Revolution in the Theory of the Structure of Scientific Inquiry and Rational Behavior," *Review of Metaphysics, 22* (1968-69), 262-280.

Kristeller, Paul O., "History of Philosophy and History of Ideas," *Journal of the History of Philosophy, 2* (1964), 1-14.

Levi, A. W., "The Writing of Mill's Autobiography," *Ethics, 61* (1951), 284-296.

Leyden, W. von, "Philosophy and Its History," *Proceedings of the Aristotelian Society*, n.s. *54* (1954), 187-208.

McGuinness, B. F., "The Mysticism of the *Tractatus*," *The Philosophical Reivew, 75* (1966), 305-328.

McKinnon, Alastair, "Kierkegaard's Pseudonyms: A New Hierarchy," *American Philosophical Quarterly, 6* (1969), 116-126.

Marti, Fritz, "Schelling on God and Man," *Studies in Romanticism, 3* (1964-65), 65-76.

Marx, P., and J. Simon, "Jorge Luis Borges: An Interview," *Commonweal, 89* (1968), 107-110.

Osler, M. J., "John Locke and the Changing Ideal of Scientific Knowledge," *Journal of the History of Ideas, 31* (1970), 3-16.

Perl, M. R., "Physics and Metaphysics in Newton, Leibniz, and Clarke," *Journal of the History of Ideas, 30* (1969), 507-526.

Popkin, Richard H., "Berkeley and Pyrrhonism," *Review of Metaphysics, 5* (1951-52), 223-246.

———, "David Hume: His Pyrrhonism and His Critique of Pyrrhonism," *Philosophical Quarterly, 1* (1950-51), 385-407.

———, "Kierkegaard and Scepticism," *Algemeen Nederlands Tijdschrift voor Wijsbegeerte en Psychologie, 51* (1959), 123-141.

———, "The Sceptical Precursors of David Hume," *Philosophy and Phenomenological Research, 16* (1955-56), 61-71.

———, "Scepticism in the Enlightenment," *Studies on Voltaire and the Eighteenth Century, 26* (1963), 1321-1345.

Rotenstreich, Nathan, "The Essential and the Epochal Aspects of Philosophy," *Review of Metaphysics, 23* (1969-70), 699-716.

Rubinoff, L., "Collingwood's Theory of the Relation Between Philosophy and History: A New Interpretation," *Journal of the History of Philosophy, 6* (1968), 363-380.

Schrader, George A., "Kant's Theory of Concepts," *Kant-Studien, 49* (1957-58), 264-278.

Sherover, C. M., "Kant's Transcendental Object and Heidegger's *Nichts*," *Journal of the History of Philosophy, 7* (1969), 413-422.

Sokolowski, Robert, "Fiction and Illusion in David Hume's Philosophy," *The Modern Schoolman, 45* (1967-68), 189-225.

Swain, C. W., "Hamann and the Philosophy of David Hume," *Journal of the History of Philosophy*, 5 (1967), 343-351.

Synthese, 23 (1972), issue on Kant and physical theory.

Tarbet, D. W., "The Fabric of Metaphor in Kant's *Critique of Pure Reason*," *Journal of the History of Philosophy*, 6 (1968), 257-270.

Tonelli, Giorgio, "Die Anfänge von Kants Kritik der Kausalbeziehungen und ihre Voraussetzungen im 18. Jahrhundert," *Kant-Studien, 57* (1965-66), 417-456.

————, "La Necessité des lois de la nature au XVIIIᵉ siècle et chez Kant en 1762," *Revue d'Histoire des Sciences, 12* (1959), 225-241.

————, "Der Streit über die mathematische Methode in der Philosophie in der ersten Hälfte des 18. Jahrhunderts und die Entstehung von Kants Schrift über die 'Deutlichkeit,' " *Archiv für Philosophie, 9* (1959), 37-66.

Weil, Eric, "Humanistic Studies: Their Object, Methods, and Meaning," *Daedalus*, Spring 1970: "Theory in Humanistic Studies," pp. 237-255. (*Proceedings of the American Academy of Arts and Sciences, 99*, no. 2.)

3. DISSERTATIONS AND OTHER

Duschesneau, F., *Les Sources de l'empirisme de Locke*. Unpublished doctoral dissertation, University of Paris, 1970.

Haley, M. A., *Mathematics and Method in Leibniz's Metaphysics*. Unpublished doctoral dissertation, Saint Louis University, 1971.

Lineback, R. H., ed., *The Philosopher's Index*. Bowling Green, Ohio: Philosophy Documentation Center, 1967 ff.

Penderecki, Krzysztof, *Passion according to St. Luke*. RCA recording VICS-6015 (Library of Congress card number R67-3744).

Vetter, P. L., *The Theory of Community in Charles S. Peirce.* Unpublished doctoral dissertation, Saint Louis University, 1968.

BIBLIOGRAPHICAL ADDITIONS

1. BOOKS

Bennett, Jonathan, *Locke, Berkeley, Hume: Central Themes.* New York: Oxford University Press, 1971.
Bröcker, Walter, *Kant über Metaphysik und Erfahrung.* Frankfurt: Klostermann, 1970.
Declève, Henri, *Heidegger et Kant.* The Hague: Nijhoff, 1970.
Ghiselin, Michael T., *The Triumph of the Darwinian Method.* Berkeley and Los Angeles: University of California Press, 1969.
Janke, W., *Fichte: Sein und Reflexion.* Berlin: Gruyter, 1970.
Lauer, Quentin, *Hegel's Idea of Philosophy.* New York: Fordham University Press, 1971.
Mandelbaum, Maurice, *History, Man, and Reason: A Study in Nineteenth-Century Thought.* Baltimore: Johns Hopkins Press, 1971.
Marx, Karl, *Critique of Hegel's 'Philosophy of Right.'* Edited by Joseph O'Malley. New York: Cambridge University Press, 1970.
Merleau-Ponty, Maurice, *The Prose of the World.* Translated by John O'Neill. Evanston: Northwestern University Press, forthcoming.
Olscamp, Paul J., *The Moral Philosophy of George Berkeley.* The Hague: Nijhoff, 1970.
Ryle, Gilbert, *Collected Papers.* 2 vols. New York: Barnes and Noble, 1971.
Sherover, Charles M., *Heidegger, Kant, and Time.* Bloomington: Indiana University Press, 1971.
Wittgenstein, Ludwig, *Notebooks 1914-1916.* Edited by G. H. von Wright and G. E. M. Anscombe. New York: Harper, 1961.

Wittgenstein, Ludwig, *Prototractatus*. Edited by B. F. Mc-
    Guinness, T. Nyberg, and G. H. von Wright. Ithaca:
    Cornell University Press, 1971.
Woolhouse, R. S., *Locke's Philosophy of Science and Knowl-
    edge*. New York: Barnes and Noble, 1971.

2. Article

Mandelbaum, Maurice, "The History of Ideas, Intellectual
    History, and the History of Philosophy," *History and
    Theory*, 4, Beiheft 5 (1965), 33-66.

Index

access to sources, 29f, 369f
act of philosophizing, 48-52, 93, 197, 360, 362f, 389f, 406; as labor, 369-75
Acta Eruditorum, 114
Adam, C., 104ff
Adams, H. P., 129
Adoratsky, V. 142
agnosia, 246
Alquié, F., 106
analogizing power, 331-33
analysis and synthesis, 65-72, 77, 137n, 145, 148-54, 179n, 182, 191f, 268, 327-30, 365, 403f
analytic thought and history, 10-12, 16-18, 21f, 26, 110ff, 131-37, 209-11, 219, 240f, 260f, 287n, 314-43, 357-59, 395-98, 403ff, 413
apriority, 263ff
Aquinas, St. Thomas, 224f
Ardley, G., 225
Aristotle, 5, 9, 17, 21, 85, 158, 165, 202, 224, 300, 307n, 319f
Armstrong, D., 254, 256
Arnauld, A., 74, 114, 160, 164
art factor, 76-94, 101f, 132f, 151, 164, 168f, 184f, 187, 193f, 220f, 237-42, 270, 359f, 370f, 400, 404f, 411n, 415f
Asveld, P., 129
Augustine, St., 4n, 10, 99, 158, 311
Austin, J. L., 319-24, 327, 351f
auto-and-allo references, 58n, 205
autobiography, 54, 72, 120-25, 237f, 381
Avineri, S., 148
Ayer, A. J., 264, 319

Ayers, M. R., 21f

Bacon, F., 40, 54, 88, 94, 114, 121, 181, 214, 274, 414
Baillet, A., 130
Baldini, A. E., 28
Balz, A. G., 167f
Barth, K., 234f
basal acts, 50-53, 362f, 389
Baudelaire, C., 194n
Bauer, B., 172n
Bausola, A., 216f
Bayle, P., 113f, 134, 159, 223
Beck, L. W., 225, 261
Beckett, S., 187, 270
Beethoven, L. van, 415
Belaval, Y., 162-64
Bentham, J., 122, 184f, 252f
Bergin, T. G., 121
Bergson, H., 93, 140, 149, 231
Berkeley, G., 22, 81f, 93, 128f, 214, 221, 223, 287n, 319, 368; *Commentaries*, 133-36; *Dialogues*, 87, 257; genetic study, 130-31, 133-36; *Principles*, 82f, 133, 135, 253; revision, 253-57
Berlin, I., 371n
Bernier, F., 114
Bernoulli, J., 278
Berryman, J., 187
Bible, 76
biodoctrinal analysis, 110-25, 141-48
biography, 110-25, 381
Blanshard, B., 349n
Bloch, E., 230
Blumenbach, J. F., 278
Boas, G., 13
Bohlin, T., 244
Bonnet, C., 278

Borges, J. L., 187f
Boscovich, R., 162
Boyle, R., 114, 116f, 121
Bradley, F. H., 271f
Brandes, G., 243
Brazill, W. J., 172n
Brecht, B., 270
Brentano, F., 19
Browning, R., 90
Bruno, G., 40, 54, 85f, 86n, 88, 180
Buber, M., 225, 234f
Buchdahl, G., 169, 274n
Buffon, G. L., 278
burden of history, 3-5, 32-34, 97f, 347-59, 369, 395-97
Burman, F., 74ff
Busson, H., 168
Butler, J., 93

Callot, É., 183
Calvez, J., 148
Campo, M., 128
Carnap, R., 6, 19ff, 264
Cartesianism, 54ff, 113f, 163, 167f, 221-23, 258ff
Cassirer, E., 179f, 417n; and Heidegger, 201-03, 297f
Cassirer, H., 261
categories, 16f, 20f, 331ff, 338, 354, 365-77
Cavell, S., 195n, 320n
century-based studies, 182-84
Chagall, M., 415
Charron, P., 39, 114
Chekhov, A., 404f
Christianity, 39, 63, 114, 170, 251
Clarke, S., 161f
classical works, 23, 48, 142, 190, 192-96, 266, 303-06, 308n, 378-90
Cobb, J., 219
co-factors of ingrediency, 30-34, 101f, 188-90, 204, 208, 213, 245, 259f, 266f, 345ff, 353-77, 390-405
Cohen, H., 171
Coleridge, S. T., 90

Collingwood, R. G., 16n, 26, 195n, 282
Collins, A., 120
communication, 76-96, 100n, 202f, 382f, 413f
community of inquirers, 15, 43-44, 95-96, 155-84, 191, 234f, 267-72, 274ff, 281, 329-44, 346-59, 369-75, 395, 398, 404f, 414-17
comparative viewpoint, 154-84, 226-31, 264f, 299-319, 368, 373, 386-88, 395f, 406f; and interdependence, 171, 177, 319, 355f
componential analysis, 30-34, 207
computer research, 45-48
Comte, A., 26, 92f, 95, 122, 129, 231, 252f; futurity, 198
concentration-expression-origination, 156f
concordia discors, 271f
conspectus, 148-54, 327-30, 384
contemporanizing, 269f, 283, 329ff, 335, 343f
contextual meaning, 102f, 105f, 144, 151f, 166f, 169f, 183, 192, 199-203, 226, 243-45, 274-79, 325f, 333-35, 358, 379ff, 398-405, 408f; and allusiveness, 415n
contingency, 115-17, 143, 269, 273, 382f, 394f, 413
continuant index, 165
continuative problem, 155, 177-84, 322f, 329-44, 356, 368, 372
continuity, 155-84, 200ff, 287ff, 328f, 354f, 399-403
Copernicus, see Kant
Copleston, F., 166
Cordemoy, G. de, 114, 168
Cornu, A., 129
correspondence, 74, 86n, 94n, 121n, 159-62, 237, 256, 280n, 401, 404, 416
Cottier, G. M., 129
counter-initiatives, 164f
Cranston, M., 111
Crapulli, G., 106

creativity, 33f, 97f, 124, 199-203, 348-59, 395-97; as noble emulation, 348f
Croce, B., 187
Crocker, L. G., 128
crossover relationships, 228f
Croxall, T. H., 153n, 154
Cudworth, R., 114
Curley, E. M., 107n
Cusanus, N., 54, 180, 218

D'Alembert, J., 91f, 95, 274
Danto, A. C., 50n
Darwin, C., 180, 206f, 231
Dasein, 247, 299, 311-13
Day, J. P., 229f
Debussy, C., 415
Dedalus, Stephen, 97
Descartes, R., 4, 9, 11n, 40, 49n, 50, 94f, 113, 116, 121, 128, 134, 136, 161, 228, 230, 254, 258-60, 265, 312, 320, 351f, 368, 379, 386, 414; and Leibniz, 162-64, 396f; Cartesius, 56; demanding text, 53-76; Discourse, 54, 72f, 91; from-to analysis, 168f, 222f; futurity, 198f; genetic study, 130, 132-33; Meditations, 57, 69, 72ff, 258-60, 364f; on order, 57-71, 351f; Principles, 73, 81; Replies, 74f; Rules, 105f; structured writings, 71-76; translations, 104-06. See also Cartesianism
developmental study, 41, 126-48, 153, 176, 386-88
De Volder, B., 160f
Dewey, J., 70, 172n, 220, 268n, 282
dialogue, 85-88, 298, 307, 349
Diderot, D., 87, 183
Dilthey, W., 27, 35ff; The Dream, 95-96
discourse, 91-93
dispersion technique, 8-14
double helix, 52-53, 188f
Dove, K. R., 109
Dream of Dilthey, 95-96

Dru, A., 244
Dryer, D. P., 275n
Dufrenne, M., 264
Du Vair, G., 39

Eberhard, J. A., 305-06
editing and translating, 104-09, 123n, 124, 130f, 141f, 244, 284f, 369, 381-83, 414
Einaudi, M., 128
Elizabeth, Princess, 74
empathy, 38, 43, 134, 372
empiricism, 112ff, 223, 227ff, 256f, 327
Enlightenment, 87, 114, 144, 167, 169, 223, 226, 294; and Hamann, 246-50
Epicureanism, 63, 114
Episcopius, Simon, 113
epistemology, 112, 115-19, 159, 174, 179-82, 190, 263ff, 275, 314-27, 336-40, 372
Erasmus, D., 87n, 222
Erklärung and Feststellung, 318n, 327n
essay, 88-91
Euclid, 39, 66, 77, 273-76
Euler, L., 162
evolutionism, 206f, 231, 257, 278n
examination of conscience, 402-03
existentialism, 9f, 238f, 243-45, 247f, 259n, 261f, 283, 357f
experience, 79, 112, 144, 201n, 249, 280f, 332f, 349f, 381, 385f
explicatio Dei, 218

Fabro, C., 180f
fallibilism, 40, 120, 382, 412
familiarity, 366-68, 389f
Faurot, J. H., 11n
Feuerbach, L., 144, 171, 172n, 175; futurity, 198, 234; revalued, 233-36, 241-42
fiat justitia, 405
Fichte, J. G., 93, 171, 214, 287n, 295; and Kant, 175f

Findlay, J., 147
Fisch, M., 121
Fontenelle, B., 183
foreshadowing and fulfillment, 146ff
Foucher de Careil, L. A., 130
Fraser, A. C., 130
Frege, G., 261, 264
Freud, S., 225
Friedmann, G., 162, 164-65
from-to span, 155, 165-77, 212-31, 322, 336, 355f, 372, 386-88
Fuhrmans, H., 217f
full story and hearing, 320n, 325, 376
fundament inquiry, 101-54, 184, 189f, 364, 377, 387f
futurity, 94, 190, 196-203, 303-06, 309, 330, 372-77, 414f

Galileo Galilei, 40, 116, 180
Gassendi, P., 63ff, 70, 74, 113f, 121, 396
Gebhardt, C., 107
Geismar, E., 244
generosity, 396-98, 416-17
genesis and system, 126-48, 214, 384-86
Gersdorff, C. von, 237
Gilson, É., 105, 132, 167n
Gluck, C., 415
God, 60f, 69f, 86ff, 164, 170f, 172n, 180f, 218f, 234f, 254, 341-43
Görland, I., 129
Gouhier, H., 105, 127f, 132
great philosophers, 10, 17, 149f, 232, 377-90
great-works syndrome, 138f, 142-45
Grotius, H., 121
groundlevel description, 163
Grua, G., 137n, 157
Grundgedanke, 140, 146, 360
Grundlegung, 342f
Guéroult, M., 357n
Guttmann, J., 170

Haecker, T., 244

Haldane, E. S., 104f
Hallie, P., 151-53
Hamann, J. G., 93, 242; para-philosopher, 245-52
Hamlyn, D. W., 228
Hartmann, K., 147n, 148
Hartshorne, C., 219
Hegel, G. W. F., 4f, 12ff, 20, 26, 50, 54, 70, 87, 92f, 95, 129, 150, 223, 238, 243, 246, 250, 262, 264, 303, 322; and Jewish philosophers, 170f; Encyclopedia, 12, 84, 108, 146, 383; from-to analysis, 171-76, 213f, 224f; futurity, 198; genetic study, 141-45; language, 199f; logic of filiation, 173-76; Phenomenology, 12, 78f, 84, 109, 141f, 146, 175, 201n, 364, 383, 389; philosophical greatness, 380-90; Philosophy of Right, 84, 108; Science of Logic, 84, 109, 142, 146, 383; system and history, 176; translations, 108f
Hegelians, Young, 172n, 224, 235. See also Hegel
Heidegger, M., 9, 27, 93, 195n, 225, 243f, 259n, 286n, 387; and Cassirer, 201-03; and Kant, 283-314, 326, 335; and Schopenhauer, 238f, 241
Heimsoeth, H., 162, 225, 261
hell of self-knowledge, 246
Herder, J. G., 26, 86n, 88, 170
hermeneutic canon of co-consideration, 161
Hintikka, J., 329-35, 343
Hirsch, E., 244
historical turn, 3-24, 33f
historical understanding, 30-32, 35-38, 48-53, 186-88, 196, 200, 203-07, 259, 267-72, 321, 324f, 327-30, 343f, 345-417
historicity and general theories of history, 25n, 27, 97f, 341f, 391f
history of ideas, 8, 12-14, 178n, 288

history of philosophy: chiasmal relation, 48, 52-53, 134, 188-90, 362f; community of historians, 375f, 414-17; correlation of research phases, 145f, 243-52, 329-43, 384-86; extrinsic and intrinsic contingency, 115-17; human grounding, 103; human language basis, 199-203; insistential reality, 48-54, 171-73, 386ff, 393-403; intelligibility, 51-53, 362f; *lingua et interrogatio franca*, 100-01; method and doctrine, 384-86; open research, 165, 180f, 190-92, 197-203, 212-52, 304-09, 314f, 328, 336-43, 353f, 374ff, 414ff; problem orientation, 177-84, 204, 230f, 263-65, 315-27, 329-43; rethinking, 305-09, 323f, 369f; searching, 99ff, 333-35, 358f; telic ideals, 345-417; unification, 94-96, 327-30, 398-403; veracious and valuable, 186n, 403f

Hobbes, T., 40, 54, 66, 74, 93, 114, 120f, 134, 149; conspectus, 151f

Holbach, P.-H. T. d', 183

Hölderlin, F., 210

Hollingdale, R. J., 124

Hook, S., 172

Hooke, R., 117

hope, 94-96, 229-31, 323, 397

Huet, P.-D., 114

humanism and humanity, 9, 19, 23f, 39, 76, 81, 89-92, 114, 120, 122, 142-45, 157f, 171, 200, 213ff, 238-41, 248-52, 288, 311-14, 339-43, 375, 402, 405-17

Humboldt, W. von, 409f

Hume, D., 11, 19, 89, 211, 223, 225, 228-31, 256n, 318n, 319, 368; and Hamann, 246-48; and Husserl, 286-97; and Kant, 286-97, 306, 310, 327; conspectus, 151-54; *Dialogues*,

86f; *Inquiries*, 89; *My Own Life*, 121f; on history, 347-49; *Treatise*, 81, 89, 228, 247f

Husserl, E., 6, 223, 228, 264, 282; and Kant, 283-314, 326f, 335, 342; *Cartesian Meditations*, 258-60, 286ff; *Crisis*, 286ff, 296n, 303n, 399f; *First Philosophy*, 9, 10n, 286ff; *Logical Investigations*, 296n; *Transcendental Logic*, 291f

Hutcheson, F., 152

Huyghens, C., 116

Hyppolite, J., 143n, 146f

I and thou, 234f, 337-43

idealism, 5, 171-75, 220

imperativity, 337-40, 353f, 373-77, 392f

inciting cultural origin, 217ff, 243ff

indirect-instantial approach, 24-28

informal view, 120f

Ingarden, R., 287n

ingressive relation, 196

insistency of sources, 30f, 35-96, 121, 134, 189f, 197f, 279, 289-97, 304-09, 344, 354f, 359, 386-88, 393-403

intent as central and textual, 46-53, 102f, 140, 284, 287, 305-09, 324f, 344, 345ff, 390-405

interpretants, 360-77

interpreting: act of community labor, 369-75, 404-05; aided by sources, 64, 67f, 72-94, 171-73, 197f, 279, 304-08, 362-65, 386ff; basal act, 52-53; comparing, 154-84, 226-31, 283-34, 368, 386ff; complexity, 126, 271f, 299, 353-39, 362f, 404f, 409-14; conjecture, 370ff; doing historical justice, 390-405; esthetic delight, 184, 359f, 415f; futural meaning, 197-203, 303-06, 372-77; harmonizing, 95, 137n, 145f, 271f; historical presence, 204-10, 272;

interpreting: *cont.*
imagination, 370ff; incremental, 330, 371; interplay of genesis and system, 127-48, 384-86, 402; interpretability, 361-65, 384, 393; interrogating work, 101-85, 279f, 322ff, 363-73; judgmental act, 204-07, 210f, 231f, 236, 263, 307-08, 351, 359f, 362, 372-77, 384f, 400, 413; longrange aims, 345-417; multiformity, 136f, 162ff, 176, 180f, 199, 207-10, 271f, 286, 314f, 322, 329, 343, 352f, 363, 374, 385f, 409-14; ranking, 231-42, 376-90; retrieving, 309; revising, 212-58, 306-14, 358f, 369f, 373-75; selection and placement, 359f; seminar center, 267-72; thematizing, 163f, 168f, 177ff, 258-63, 335f; violence in, 303, 401f
interpreting present, 30-32, 186-266, 378, 403f
interrelation modes, 101f, 154-85, 353-39, 368, 386ff, 395-98
interrogatio franca, 100-01
interrogation poles, 99-102, 189f, 370, 377
intersubjectivity, 234-35, 260, 338-43
introductory materials, 80-85, 108, 156, 383, 399f

Jacobi, F., 86n
Jähnig, D., 220
James, William, 4n, 93, 256, 263n, 264, 336, 399-402
Janus-faced colossus, 186-88, 194
Jaspers, K., 9f, 25n, 225, 243f; on Kant, 283n; on Schelling, 218f
Jena University, 141
Johnston, G. A., 131
Journal des Savants, 114
Joyce, J., 97, 225
Judaism, 170f, 191
justice motif, 390-405

Kabitz, W., 128
Kafka, F., 187
Kant, I., 4f, 6, 11, 17, 19, 22, 26, 70, 90, 93, 95, 128f, 139, 149, 201f, 218n, 258n, 346, 353, 384, 386f, 390, 399, 414; and Eberhard, 304-06; and Hamann, 246, 248-51; and Hume, 286-97; and Jewish philosophers, 170f; and Leibniz, 159, 162, 321n; and Mill, 228-31, 264f; and Schopenhauer, 238, 317; as seminar theme, 268-72; community theme, 327-44; conspectus, 153; Copernican turn, 6, 83, 274n, 289, 302n; *Critique of Judgment*, 83f, 169f, 183, 282, 297, 337; *Critique of Practical Reason*, 83, 282, 297, 329-43; *Critique of Pure Reason*, 83, 153, 162, 174, 226, 249f, 261f, 276, 279-82, 291, 297, 299-313, 323ff, 329-35; from-to analysis, 171-75, 182, 225f, 233f; humanity, 416f; in analytic thought, 314-27; in Heidegger and Husserl, 283-314; mathematics and physical science, 272-83; philosophizing act, 49; *Prolegomena*, 259, 261f, 317n
Kaufmann, W., 108n, 124, 224
Kern, I., 286n
Kierkegaard, S., 4n, 94, 115, 123, 125, 153n, 154, 223, 247, 251, 259n; and Kant, 261-62; paraphilosopher, 242-45
Knox, T. M., 108
Kojève, A., 142n
Kott, J., 270
Koyré, A., 169
Kristeller, P., 178n
Kroner, R., 172, 224

Lafleur, L. J., 106
La Forge, L. de, 168
Lambert, J. H., 278
La Mettrie, J. O. de, 183

La Mothe le Vayer, F. de, 114
Lamy, F., 114
language, 45f, 65, 82, 199-203, 241, 249-51, 254f, 305-09, 315-22, 325, 344, 356, 371, 382f, 386
Lasson, A., 142
latency in sources, 42, 99f, 164f, 194-96, 196-203, 210f, 268ff, 303-14, 323, 355, 359, 364, 382f
Lazarus, M., 171
Lazerowitz, M., 22
Le Clerc, Jean, 113, 119
lecture courses, 92f, 109, 258, 282f, 298, 321, 383
Leeuwen, H. G. van, 118n, 181
Leeuwenhoek, A. van, 117
Le Grand, A., 168
Leibniz, G. W., 40f, 86n, 93, 95, 114, 128, 130, 171, 195, 211, 225, 258-61, 271, 312, 319ff, 379, 387; and Kant, 304-08; and Pascal, 157f; *Discourse on Metaphysics*, 78, 160, 261; futurity, 198f; generosity, 396-98; genetic study, 136f; *Monadology*, 40; *New Essays*, 158f; radial thinker, 156-65, 354; *Theodicy*, 158f
"Leibnoza," 260f
Lenin, V. I., 20
Lessing, G. E., 170
Lewis, C. I., 264, 392f
Ley, W., 278n
Leyden, W. von, 182f, 186n
Leyden University, 75
"life and writings," 125f, 148
Limborch, Philip van, 113
Linnaeus, C., 183
Lipsius, J., 39
Locke, J., 4f, 81f, 128, 134, 159, 181, 223, 228f, 256n, 264n, 265, 306, 368, 379, 396; bio-doctrinal study, 110-20; *Essay*, 82, 110-19; pursuit of truth, 394f, 413
logic of filiation and surpassing, 173

Lovejoy, A. O., 12f
Lovelace Collection, 111
Löwith, K., 225
Lowrie, W., 244
Luce, A. A., 128, 131
Lucian, 87n
Lukács, G., 129, 172, 215f

Mach, E., 19
Maine de Biran, M. F., 151-53
Malebranche, N., 87, 114, 134, 158, 221; and Leibniz, 161, 396f
Mallarmé, S., 411n
Mandelbaum, M., 13n, 183f
Mann, T., 194f
Manuel, F. E., 26
Mapletoft, John, 117
Marcel, G., 244
marked judgmental alterations, 236ff, 262-63, 388f
Marti, F., 218n
Martin, G., 162, 165
Marx, K., 20, 26, 129, 171, 172n, 173, 175, 213f, 225, 233f, 246, 387; *Capital*, 142, 148; genetic study, 141-45; *Manifesto*, 141; *Political Economy*, 142
master work, 76-80, 192f, 383
mastery language, 42f, 52, 56, 353
Maupertuis, P., 183
Mauthner, F., 316
McRae, R., 182
means test, 208ff
meditation mode, 64-68, 258-63, 298n
Meiland, J. W., 195n
Meinong, A., 11
Mémoires de Trévoux, 115
Mendelssohn, M., 171
Merleau-Ponty, M., 53, 196, 226-28, 298n, 351f, 358n, 362
Mersenne, M., 57f, 74
Mesnard, P., 244
Metacritique of Purism, 248-51
metaphor, 81, 118f, 186-89, 317f, 397n

metaphysics, 16f, 19-21, 60-65, 84f, 160, 171, 182f, 201, 238f, 258-63, 281f, 317, 325ff; and ontology, 297-314
method of functional reflection, 28-34, 37, 98-102, 127, 154f, 267, 363, 372, 380, 391f, 404-05
middle-range and minor philosophers, 152f, 231-42, 266, 317, 378f
Mill, H., 121n
Mill, J. S., 89f, 195, 214, 228-31, 264f; *Autobiography*, 121f; *On Liberty*, 90, 409-14; *System of Logic*, 264
Miller, A. V., 108f
miniaturization, 175
Moltmann, J., 231
Montaigne, M., 39, 88, 114
Montesquieu, C. L., 93, 183
Montpellier University, 119
moral philosophy, 89-92, 152, 171, 229-31, 281f, 329-43
More, H., 158
Morgan, G. W., 186n
Morris, C., 20
Mozart, W. A., 415
"municipal laws," 394, 413
Munitz, M., 278n
mystique of young thinker, 138ff, 142-45
mythical thinking, 296f, 300, 302

Natorp, P., 291
naturalism, 5, 257, 357f
nature, 274n, 277-83, 326f, 331f, 337
Naudé, G., 114
neither a be-all, 352
Newman, J. H., 134n
Newton, I., 81, 83, 89, 114, 116, 134, 161f, 174, 180, 226, 228, 254, 273-82, 290, 331f
Nicole, P., 114
Nietzsche, F., 42, 93, 123f, 171ff, 175, 214, 234, 264, 303, 313, 322, 387; and Schopenhauer,

236-38; revalued, 223-26; *Zarathustra*, 78ff
Nivelle, A., 170
Noguchi, I., 359
Nohl, H., 142
nostalgia and escape, 195f

Oakeshott, M., 195n
objectivity and subjectivity, 393f
Ockham, W., 165
Olscamp, P. J., 105f
open-ended realignment, 221-26, 323f, 357-59
order, 57-71, 351f
originality as surprising and steady, 149, 383-85
Oxford University, 112, 119f

paraphilosophical thinker, 242-52
Pascal, B., 93, 113f, 121, 242; and Leibniz, 157f
Passion according to St. Luke, 185
Passmore, J. A., 153n, 154, 209n
past philosophy, 193-96, 203-07, 266, 347-59, 395-98, 406f, 413
Paton, H. J., 261
Peirce, C. S., 21, 56n, 256f, 336-39, 402n, 416; theory of interpretants, 360-76
Penderecki, K., 185
pensée, 93, 157f
Peperzak, A. T., 129
perception, 226-28, 247, 254f, 327; "my perception," 62-64
periodization, 38-40, 166f, 216-20
Persius, 251
Peters, R., 151f
Petry, M. J., 108
phenomenology, 79, 219, 226-28, 260, 283-97, 321, 329-43, 357f, 393n
philosophie trouvée, 359, 363
Pico della Mirandola, Giovanni, 91
Plato, 9ff, 87, 158, 165, 187, 224, 288, 300, 307n, 319f

Plotinus, 10
pluriformity and unity, 30, 40f,
    88, 94-96, 136f, 143f, 154,
    162-81, 207-10, 271f, 286,
    314f, 322, 352f, 363, 374,
    385f, 398-403, 409-14
Pöggeler, Otto, 108n, 109
Popkin, R. H., 168, 222f
Pragmatic theme, 255f, 369, 383,
    401, 414
Pragmatism, 255-57
presential act, 203-07, 224f, 265f,
    272, 298n, 350-59, 363-69
prevailing spirit, 183f, 262n
principles, 70-71, 160, 331
problem studies, 177-84, 252-66
prose of historical world, 358-59
psychologizing, 38-46, 123-25,
    299f, 372
purist split, 14-22
Pyrrhonian crisis, 222f

questioning, 30f, 95-185, 363-73
Quine, W., 264, 333

radial center, 155-65, 238-41,
    353-55, 396-98
Rameau, J. P., 415
Raphael, 95, 415
Ravel, M., 415
reciprocity of initiative, 180f,
    195n
Régis, P.-S., 168
religion, 86f, 114, 170f, 180f,
    216ff, 229, 234ff, 245-52, 340-
    43
Renaissance, 12, 39, 87, 133,
    165, 179
reversal criterion, 210f, 323f, 336
revisionary act, 40, 43f, 137-48,
    190-92, 212-52, 273ff, 369,
    373ff; revisability differential,
    252-58
rhythm of education, 150f, 154
Riazanov, D., 142
Rickert, H., 291
Ricoeur, P., 294n, 329-33, 340-
    43, 393n

righting the research imbalance,
    145, 324f
Rivaud, A., 166f
Robbe-Grillet, A., 187
Rodis-Lewis, G., 106
Rohault, J., 114, 168
romanticism, 12f, 84, 88, 144,
    150, 231, 322
Rosenzweig, F., 171
Ross, G. R. T., 104f
Rotenstreich, N., 170, 176n
Rousseau, J.-J., 91f, 123, 125,
    128
Royce, J., 93, 262n, 280n, 336,
    402n, 416
Ruge, A., 172n
Russell, B., 11, 42, 223, 316, 319
Ryle, G., 6, 9ff, 16n, 34

Saint-Simon C.-H. de R., 231
Sakhalin Island, 404f
Sarraute, N., 187
Sartre, J.-P., 9, 238f, 244, 259n
Schäfer, L., 281f
Schelling, F. W., 25n, 86n, 88,
    94f, 149, 171, 175; basic
    thought, 140; interpreting pres-
    ent, 215-21, 360
Schlanger, J., 220
Schlick, M., 4n
schools of philosophy, 54f, 167f
Schopenhauer, A., 4n, 90f, 93,
    187f, 223, 233; revalued, 236-
    42; World as Will, 90, 239,
    241
Schulz, W., 216f
Schumann, R., 237-38
scientific thought, 105, 112ff,
    116f, 167-69, 179f, 254-57,
    272-83, 292f, 311f, 337-39
Scotus, John Duns, 165
Seeberger, W., 147
Sellars, R. W., 257
Sellars, W., 56n, 100n, 258-61,
    329-33, 335-40, 342f
seminar experience, 201-03, 267-
    344, 369, 389f
semiosis, 360-77, 380
Shakespeare, W., 270-381

Shaw, G. B., 187
sign-source complexus, 362-77, 394
Simmons, E. J., 404n
Simon, Richard, 114
Sirven, J., 132
skepticism, 61, 73, 82, 113, 118f, 122, 158n, 159, 167n, 168, 181, 193-95, 222f, 240, 246-48
Smith, Adam, 152
Smith, J. E., 262n, 274n
Smith, N. K., 105, 151f
Socrates, 49, 246, 251
Spink, J. S., 168
Spinoza, B., 5, 22, 24, 39, 70, 95, 102f, 114, 158, 187f, 191f, 211, 230, 318n; and Leibniz, 162-65, 396; *Ethics*, 78f, 107, 192; *Healing of Understanding*, 83, 107; translations, 107f
stella hians, 156, 158n, 387
Stirner, M., 172n, 175
Stoicism, 39
Strauss, D. F., 172n
Strauss, R., 79
Stravinsky, I., 415
Strawson, P. F., 16f, 324-27, 335
structuring, 71-94
style, 65-68, 72-94, 251, 397n. *See also* art factor
Suarez, F., 64, 165
sur-teleology, 407f
Suvorin, A. S., 404
Swammerdam, J., 117
Swenson, D., 244
Sydenham, T., 116f
systemic thought, 59, 71, 78, 82, 115, 126-48, 176n, 192, 241f, 251, 328-30, 384-86. *See also* genesis and system

Tannery, P., 104ff
Tchaikovsky, P. I., 415
teleology, 190, 192, 203-10, 266, 288f, 292ff, 303, 308f, 342f, 345-417
textual imperative, 130f
Thayer, H. S., 22n, 256

thematization, 163-84, 258-66, 325ff, 335f, 413
Thomasius, J., 165, 396
Tillich, P., 216, 225
Toland, J., 86n
Tolstoy, L., 167f
Tonelli, G., 128f, 225, 277n
tradition and theory, 8ff, 13n, 14-22, 33, 147n, 210f, 250, 283n, 287ff, 319-21, 348-59, 395-98, 403f, 413
transcendental question, 289ff, 300f, 312f, 315-17, 326f, 384
translation, *see* editing and translating
truth search, 352, 357ff, 394-95, 411-17
Tucker, R., 148
Turbayne, C., 254, 256

unit ideas, 13f
university education, 23f, 73, 75f, 107, 119f, 253f, 267-72, 379, 389-90, 408f
unovert sources, 29, 99. *See also* latency in sources
utilitas et amplitudo humana, 414

Valery, P., 187
Vaux, Clotilde de, 129
Veitch, J., 104
Verdi, G., 415
Viano, C. A., 112
Verstehen, 35-38, 372
Vico, J. B., 26, 91, 120f, 371n, 414
Vienna Circle, 19ff
Vischer, F. T., 172n
vision of life, 398-403. *See also* world views
Vleeschauwer, H.-J. de, 153
Volkmann-Schluck, K.-H., 216f
Voltaire, 87
Vuillemin, J., 281f

Wagner, R., 237f, 415
Wahl, J., 244
Watson, J., 53n
Watson, R. A., 167f